WITHDRAWN

Isabel Rules

Isabel Rules

Constructing Queenship,
Wielding Power

Barbara F. Weissberger

University of Minnesota Press
Minneapolis • London

The University of Minnesota Press gratefully acknowledges financial assistance for the publication of this book provided by the Program for Cultural Cooperation between Spain's Ministry of Education and Culture and United States Universities.

A previous version of chapter 1 was published as "Male Sexual Anxieties in *Carajicomedia:* A Response to Female Sovereignty," in *Poetry at Court in Trastamaran Spain: From the "Cancionero de Baena" to the "Cancionero General,"* edited by E. Michael Gerli and Julian Weiss, Medieval and Renaissance Texts and Studies 181 (Tempe, Ariz.: Medieval and Renaissance Texts and Studies, 1998), 221–34; copyright Arizona Board of Regents for Arizona State University. A previous version of chapter 3 was published as "'¡A tierra, puto!' Alfonso de Palencia's Discourse of Effeminacy," in *Queer Iberia: Sexualities, Cultures, and Crossings from the Middle Ages to the Renaissance,* edited by Josiah Blackmore and Gregory S. Hutcheson (Durham, N.C.: Duke University Press, 1999), 291–324; copyright 1999 Duke University Press; all rights reserved; used with permission of the publisher.

Copyright 2004 by the Regents of the University of Minnesota

All rights reserved. No part of this publication may be reproduced, stored in a retrieval system, or transmitted, in any form or by any means, electronic, mechanical, photocopying, recording, or otherwise, without the prior written permission of the publisher.

Published by the University of Minnesota Press
111 Third Avenue South, Suite 290
Minneapolis, MN 55401-2520
http://www.upress.umn.edu

Library of Congress Cataloging-in-Publication Data
Weissberger, Barbara F.
   Isabel rules : constructing queenship, wielding power / Barbara F. Weissberger.
      p.   cm.
   Includes bibliographical references and index.
   ISBN 0-8166-4164-1 (hc : alk. paper) — ISBN 0-8166-4165-X (pb : alk. paper)
   1. Spanish literature—To 1500—History and criticism. 2. Isabella I, Queen of Spain, 1451–1504—In literature. 3. Women in literature. 4. Sex role in literature. I. Title.
PQ6060 .W45   2003
860.9'351—dc22
                                                      2003015328

Printed in the United States of America on acid-free paper

The University of Minnesota is an equal-opportunity educator and employer.

12 11 10 09 08 07 06 05 04   10 9 8 7 6 5 4 3 2 1

For David Samuel and Michael Lawrence,
who make everything worthwhile.

Contents

Acknowledgments ix

Introduction: Gender and Sovereignty in the Age of Isabel xi

ONE
Anxious Masculinity 1

TWO
Fashioning Isabel's Sovereignty 28

THREE
The Discourse of Effeminacy in Isabelline Historiography 69

FOUR
The Neo-Gothic Theory and the Queen's Body 96

FIVE
Luis de Lucena and the Rules of the Game 134

SIX
The Mad Queen 162

Conclusion: Isabel in the Twentieth Century 187

Notes 207

Works Cited 279

Index 311

Acknowledgments

This book has been with me for almost a decade, through thick and thin. The seeds of the project were planted long before that, however, at Harvard University, where I was privileged to study with Stephen Gilman. He first made fifteenth-century Spain come alive for me in all its tragicomic complexity.

The task I set myself in this project, a gendered remapping of the cultural territory of Isabelline Spain, has proven to be much more ambitious than originally envisioned. I might have given up long ago if it had not been for the constant encouragement and the incisive critiques of Ronald Surtz. For his knowledge, generosity, and abiding friendship, I am profoundly grateful. I have benefited from the contributions of many other scholars and friends. E. Michael Gerli, Julian Weiss, Gregory Hutcheson, and Josiah Blackmore made many helpful comments on early versions of chapters 1 and 3. Dayle Seidenspinner-Núñez and Gregory Hutcheson reviewed the manuscript for the University of Minnesota Press with extraordinary care. Their thoughtful suggestions greatly improved the style and coherence of the book. Rosa Motta-Bischof translated the Latin texts in chapter 5, and Richard White helped clarify classical allusions in chapter 1. Any errors or infelicities remaining in the book are entirely my own.

My thanks to Richard Morrison, humanities editor at the University of Minnesota Press, for his help in bringing this project to fruition. Without Nelsy Echávez-Solano, who prepared the manuscript with extraordinary skill, diligence, and patience, it would never have seen the light of day.

I benefited greatly from a sabbatical leave granted me by Old Dominion University and, more recently, from a publication subsidy awarded by the Program for Cultural Cooperation between Spain and the United States.

Finally, I express my gratitude to all those friends who cheered me on, especially Anita Fellman and Joanne Jenkins, and to my father, Sydney Franklin, who always asked how it was going. Dad, it's finally finished.

INTRODUCTION

Gender and Sovereignty in the Age of Isabel

In March 2002, the Episcopal Conference of Spain announced its intention to reopen the case for the beatification of Isabel I, known to history as Isabella the Catholic. Although the process had been initiated by the Archbishop of Valladolid in 1958, under the regime of Francisco Franco, it took until 1972 to assemble the thirty volumes of supporting documentation. In that year Vicente Rodríguez Valencia, the official postulator of the Queen's case, published a slim volume summarizing the evidence of her saintliness. *Artículos del postulador: sobre la fama de santidad, vida y virtudes de la sierva de Dios, Isabel I, Reina de Castilla* (Articles of the postulator: On the fame of sanctity, life, and virtues of Isabel I, Queen of Castile, servant of God) lists and illustrates the qualities of obedience, humility, prudence, and religious zeal that made Isabel "magnificently submissive" [una sumisa grandiosa] (17, quoting Ramón Menéndez Pidal). In 1991, at the request of the Vatican's Council for Christian Unity, Pope John Paul II halted the beatification process.[1] The Spanish bishops hope that the Vatican will now finally recognize Isabel's "Christian virtues to a heroic degree" [virtudes cristianas en heroico grado] in time for the quincentenary of her death in 2004.[2] The ultimate goal of the Spanish church is canonization, a distinction earned by only one other Spanish woman, the Doctor of the Church Teresa of Ávila.

The trope of "Saint Isabel," the archetypally Catholic Queen, has retained its cultural currency in Spain for more than half a millennium. It is largely responsible for the continuing elusiveness of this powerful monarch. But hagiography is only one of the threads used to fashion the veil that obscures our view of Isabel's personal and political life; it is tightly interwoven with strands of chauvinism, xenophobia, misogyny, and homophobia.

The infanta who would grow up to become the first queen regnant of a European nation-state was born on April 22, 1451, in the isolated Castilian town of Madrigal de las Altas Torres. Isabel was the only daughter of Juan II (1406–54) and his second wife, Isabel of Portugal.[3] At her birth, Isabel was second in line for the throne of Castile, after her half brother Enrique, son of Juan II and María of Aragon. Enrique was at the time married to Juana of Portugal, but at twenty-six years of age he remained childless. Isabel barely knew her father. He died when she was three and was succeeded by Enrique IV (1454–74). By that time, Isabel had a new brother, Alfonso (b. 1453), who, because he was male, superseded her in the line of succession.

Isabel's early relationship with her mother was no doubt affected by the latter's depression—by some accounts so deep that it verged on insanity—that began upon her husband's death. When Alfonso was born, the dowager queen Isabel moved her household to the neighboring town of Arévalo, where Isabel would remain until 1461. Enrique's ongoing problems with a dissident league of grandees and clerics began to escalate that year, leading him to call Isabel and Alfonso to court, where he could keep a closer watch over them. That year also marked the first of many of the king's efforts to make advantageous political alliances for himself by marrying Isabel to various Spanish aristocrats and European kings.

The open revolt that Enrique had long feared and tried to avert finally happened in 1464, when the dissidents accused Enrique's daughter and sole heir Juana I of Castile (b. 1462) of being illegitimate, deposed the king in effigy, and proclaimed the twelve-year-old Alfonso as legitimate successor to the throne of Castile. That plan had to be modified when Alfonso died suddenly in 1468. The nobles immediately transferred their allegiance to Isabel, and she became, at the age of seventeen, a serious contender for the crown of Castile, in opposition to its rightful heir, Juana.

In 1469, defying prohibition, Isabel chose as her husband Fernando, son of King Juan II of Aragon. When Enrique died in 1474, Isabel seized the throne. Fernando's accession to the crown of Aragon five years later united the two most powerful kingdoms of the Iberian Peninsula. The path to that union was by no means easy. It required a five-year war of succession against Juana's supporters, a series of drastic political, economic, and judicial measures designed to strengthen and centralize monarchic authority, and reversal of the long-standing devolution of power onto the aristocracy.

A major strategy enabling Isabel and Fernando's project of transforming their two rival kingdoms into one nation-state was the formulation of Spanish identity as exclusively Christian. This national self-concept was disseminated in therapeutic terms, as a purification of the body politic, a purging of alien and contaminating agents that had resided in Spain for centuries. Those threatening aliens were primarily the Jews and Muslims, whose coexistence and conflict with Christians in Spain for almost eight centuries had shaped the cultures of both Castile and Aragon in complex ways that set it apart from other European kingdoms. Isabel and Fernando eagerly promoted the belief of many of their strife-weary subjects that the sovereigns had been providentially sent to repair Spain's broken body politic. The institution of the Holy Office of the Inquisition (1480); the sanctioning of statutes of "blood purity" [limpieza de sangre] that prevented those with tainted blood from entering service in the church or the university; the long and ultimately successful war against the last Moorish kingdom of Granada (1482–92); and the expulsion of the Jews (1492) are the best known of the "therapeutic" measures taken by Isabel and Fernando to restore Spain to health. Even Isabel's financing of Columbus's first voyage must be seen in this light, because Columbus presented his endeavor in part as an extension of the holy mission against Islam that Isabel and Fernando were so successfully carrying out on the peninsula.

Isabel died in November 1504, less than three weeks after Columbus completed his fourth and final voyage. She left three daughters, her only male heir, Prince Juan, having died at the age of nineteen in 1497. The youngest daughter was Juana, whose marriage to Philip I of Austria produced Charles I. When Charles I of Spain and its transatlantic colonies became Charles V of the Holy Roman Empire, he transformed his grandparents' legacy into Europe's first global empire.

This study of literature produced in the reign of Isabel the Catholic is profoundly regicentric, but not because it deals directly with the historical Isabel, whose life I have just sketched. My goal is not to see through the hagiographic veil that still covers Isabel; it is, rather, to examine the stuff of which it is fashioned, the various threads used to weave it in a complex process that began even before her accession to the throne—in fact, before her birth. I am not so much interested in the person of the Queen as in the shaping of the Queen's power through literary representation. I focus on the ways in which Isabel's male writing subjects constructed the public image of the Queen, sometimes with and sometimes without her approval. The historical period I deal with is roughly coterminous with Isabel's life span (1451–1504), although I concentrate on the thirty years of her rule (1474–1504), the period during which the fractious medieval kingdoms of Iberia were transformed into a powerful nation-state. For each of the male writers I discuss, many of whom had close personal and professional ties with the Queen, I have asked the following question: how does his work respond to the unprecedented challenge that a powerful female sovereign poses to the patriarchal status quo?

The answer has proven to be complex and often contradictory, as each writer responds to a perceived double "ideological dissonance" (Montrose, "Elizabethan Subject," 309): on the one hand, the cultural anomaly of female sovereignty itself, and, on the other, the contradiction between this particular sovereign's gender and her profoundly masculinist and patriarchal political program. I find that the representation of gender and sexuality in late-fifteenth-century literature, whether in nonfictional works addressed to or commissioned by Isabel, or in prose fiction and poetic works in which gender representations appear to have little relationship to the Queen, is deeply affected by the presence on the throne of an absolutist monarch who is also a woman. All of the many disparate literary and visual texts discussed here—royal chronicles, the royal coat of arms, political and lyric poetry, *specula principis,* prose romances, political and amatory satire, pornography, a chess treatise—seek to articulate and contain, express and mystify the threat to masculine subjectivity that the female monarch and her patriarchal political program represent.

Thus, the male-authored works I analyze all evince the phenomenon that Mark Breitenberg has identified as "anxious masculinity." In his study of masculine anxiety in the literature produced in the reign of another powerful queen, Elizabeth I of England, Breitenberg notes that "[m]asculine subjectivity constructed and sustained by a patriarchal culture—infused with patriarchal assumptions about power, privilege, sexual desire, the body—inevitably engenders varying degrees of anxiety in its male members" (1).

Freud's definition of anxiety as a "particular state of expecting the danger or preparing for it, even though it may be an unknown one" (Breitenberg, 5, citing Freud) is central to Breitenberg's view of Elizabethan literature. The anxiety in the mind of the sufferer is prophylactic in the sense that it "protects its subjects against fright and so against fright-neuroses. It is a condition of preparation for an anticipated threat that may be of unknown origin" (5). That is to say, in this political context the act of expressing the anxiety is therapeutic in that it serves to discursively control the threat that queenship represents to the patriarchal status quo.

The strict Freudian definition of anxiety as preceding its identifiable cause in order to minimize its effects fully applies to many of the works written by the Isabelline authors included in this study, principally Fray Martín de Córdoba, Gómez Manrique, Iñigo de Mendoza, Alfonso de Palencia, Fernando del Pulgar, Antón de Montoro, Juan de Flores, and Luis de Lucena. A good example of such anxiety is the anticipatory modeling of the young Princess Isabel as queen consort rather than queen regnant in Fray Martín de Córdoba's advice treatise *Jardín de nobles doncellas* (Garden of noble maidens), discussed in chapter 2. It is also present in those works that have come down to us without indication of authorship, perhaps for good reason, given their pornographic critique of a queen lauded for her purity. This is the case in the staging of male impotence by the author of *Carajicomedia*, examined in chapter 1. In general, however, I apply the term *masculine anxiety* more broadly than Breitenberg, namely, as any discursive strategy that expresses, articulates, and/or contains a perceived loss of masculine power and privilege. I also take into account a phenomenon that Breitenberg does not address, but that cannot be ignored in the late Middle Ages in Spain: the male writer's search to secure his gender and class superiority by projecting the threatened loss of dominance outward, onto the phantasmic cause of that loss.

Thus, the focus here is on the anxious responses of Isabel's male writing subjects to the disturbing paradox of a female monarch who does not know or keep her place as either woman or wife, and who furthermore appropriates and redirects patriarchal norms and institutions to further her own political power and goals, which may or may not coincide with those of her male subjects. It is, however, difficult to separate the threat that the absolute power of a queen represents in the late-medieval period from the threat to masculine identity posed by those other women and men who stand for excessive desire in any form, for example, prostitutes or sodomites (Breitenberg, 9), or those ethnic minorities whose difference is coded feminine: Jews, Muslims, and the hybrid or liminal *conversos,* Jews whose ancestors converted to Christianity. I shall have something to say about all of these.

I am indebted throughout my study to the work of materialist feminists, who focus on the interests at stake in the construction of social identities, and who analyze literary texts in relation to other forms of the material, such as social and economic relations of production or, more pertinently here, reproduction. Particularly useful for the study of queenship is the care materialist feminists take to emphasize not just the differences *between* women and men, but also *among* women and *among* men. They recognize that complicity and resistance both have a role to play in the construction of gender roles and identities. Finally, they work along several axes of analysis, relating gender to race, ethnicity, class, sexuality, and national identity (Newton and Rosenfelt, 1).[4]

Materialist feminism's emphasis on both the physical matter associated with female bodies and the role of those bodies as "sites for the inscriptions of ideology and power" (Wayne, *Matter of Difference,* 8) often intersects with the critical lens of new historicism.[5] Particularly useful to my analysis has been the new historicists' subtle dissection of the discourses of female royal power in early modern England as a complex dialectical phenomenon.[6] In their analyses of literature produced by, for, or about Europe's other "Isabel," Elizabeth I of England (Elizabet being the Latin for both the Catholic and the Virgin Queen), they pay close attention to the complex intersection of many kinds of discourse and discursively constructed social situations in the creation of the "Queen." The study of the construction of queenship that results from and contributes to the process of nation building in both England and Spain highlights the history of women not as a tale of unrelieved oppression, but rather as conflictive, contradictory, and transformative. It speaks to "the both-ands of experience: that different groups of women at different moments in history have been both oppressed and oppressive, submissive and subversive, victim and agent, allies and enemies, both of men and of one another" (Newton, *Starting Over,* 21).

I accordingly treat Isabel neither as victim nor as agent of the patriarchal ideology that shapes and is shaped by the literature of the last quarter of the fifteenth century in the Castile that is becoming Spain. Instead, I view her as one among many participants in a wide-reaching, complex network of intersecting discourses of sovereign power, national identity, gender, sexuality, race, and ethnicity. Together, these discourses shape the mysterious and powerful "Isabel" who has been a cornerstone of the Spanish national imaginary for more than five hundred years.[7]

In its earliest stages, the official story of Isabel and her reign was characterized by its intensely messianic tone. Writers at the beginning of her reign extolled the absolute authority and firm justice of a monarch whom they felt that God had sent in order to heal Spain's self- and other-inflicted wounds. Américo Castro, one of the first and most influential scholars to discuss the messianism of Isabelline literature, attributed it primarily to highly placed *converso* writers who fervently hoped that the new queen would strengthen their increasingly precarious position in Castilian society.[8] But neither Castro nor the scholars who followed his lead in revising the cultural prehistory of Spain's national identity considered the ways that those who exalt Isabel simultaneously express anxiety over the fact that God entrusted the restoration of the essential and essentially masculine Castilian qualities of hierarchy, order, authority, unity, religious orthodoxy, and sexual and ethnic purity to a woman.

Because *woman* in medieval gender ideology was identified with the body, the very notion that a being who was perceived as naturally libidinous, irrational, and polluted might cure the nation's sickness was almost as disturbing as those feminized external and internal enemies who were the cause of its diseased state.[9] Further complicating the masculine response to the ambiguous political culture surrounding an all-powerful queen who espouses profoundly patriarchal values is the fact that many of the male writers I discuss were in Isabel's direct employ. They were, in fact, charged by the Queen with creating the propaganda needed to legitimate her contested claim to the throne and to consolidate her power singly and in conjunction with Fernando.[10] Their preferment in the new royal administration explicitly or implicitly depended on their mystification of the anomalous condition of female sovereignty.

The complex relationship between the fantasy of unity and purity that informed the Isabelline absolutist program and the specific policies of ethnic and religious repression, exclusion, and elimination that were the means employed to fulfill that fantasy has also been the subject of intense and often heated scholarly debate since the end of the Spanish civil war.[11] A privileged locus for that debate has been the "*converso* question": the role of Christian converts from Judaism in the creation of Spanish national identity. Over the last fifty years, that debate has evolved substantially, from an initial defense or denial of Spain's cultural otherness (famously expressed in Voltaire's statement that "Africa begins at the Pyrenees") to the investigation of the complexity of Iberia's multiculturalism and the mechanisms of its thwarting in the fifteenth and sixteenth centuries. Most recently, under the influence of postmodern theory, Hispanists have begun to dispel the notion of a unitary *converso*, or, for that matter, of a unitary Christian, Jewish, or Muslim identity, and to identify the multiplicity of ethnic and cultural identities that constituted late-medieval and early-modern Iberian society.[12]

Largely omitted from these analyses of the phobic fantasy of purity that shaped Spain's emerging national identity is the insistent gendering and sexualization of that fantasy and its complex relationship to the female sovereign who promoted it. The omission is surprising for two reasons. One is the immense body of work that explores the very same phenomenon in relation to the monarch who rose to power in England fifty years after Isabel's death. Studies of the mutual construction of gender, sexuality, and female sovereignty in early modern England are at the heart of the groundbreaking contribution of the new historicists and cultural materialists who since the 1980s have significantly "rewritten the Renaissance" by paying close attention to what Louis Montrose calls the "historicity of texts" and the "textuality of history" ("Elizabethan Subject," 305).[13] Montrose, Jonathan Goldberg, Stephen Greenblatt, Carol Levin, Leah Marcus, and others have shed light on the ways that the anomalous power of a female sovereign fashioned and was fashioned by early-modern patriarchal gender roles and identities. These gendered regicentric studies have provided inspiration and guidance for my own treatment of the Isabelline period.

The critical neglect of queenship in late-fifteenth-century Spain is also surprising because of the interrogation of the myths surrounding Spain's central role in the age of exploration that arose as a result of the Columbus quincentenary. Much of the scholarly and popular writing that appeared in and around 1992 was aggressively revisionist in nature. It examined the impact of Columbus and the Spanish conquerors and colonizers who followed in his wake from the perspective of the conquered peoples that they endangered or eradicated. Even the terms in which Columbus's adventure had been told for centuries, terms such as *discovery* and *New World,* were called into question by both the academy and the popular press.[14] But this vigorous deconstructive process only minimally affected study of Columbus's patron.

Why, then, has there been no investigation into the role of gender and sexuality in the fashioning of the monarch who understood the significance of Columbus's audacious plan? I suggest that the gap is owing to the fact that feminist study of medieval Iberian culture and society is still in its infancy. It is true that, thanks to the excellent research carried out by the historians associated with such centers as the Seminario de Estudios de la Mujer at the Universidad Autónoma de Madrid since the 1980s, much light has been shed on the legal status and social position of aristocratic medieval Iberian women.[15] During the same period, Hispano-medievalists have also recuperated the work of the few female writers of the period whose names we know, especially the now-canonical triumvirate of Florencia Pinar, Leonor López de Córdoba, and Teresa de Cartagena.[16] Research on Hispano-Arabic and Hispano-Hebrew women writers has also been initiated. Nevertheless, with some notable exceptions, adequately historicized and theorized feminist studies of the vast majority of medieval literary works have yet to be written.[17] And there has been no sustained consideration of the impact of female sovereignty on Spanish literature written by men or women in the last third of the fifteenth century.[18] The neglect of the role of queenship in the fashioning of secular masculinity and femininity in the late-medieval and early-modern period has impeded our full understanding of the foundations of Spain's nation-building process.

The quincentenary commemoration of Columbus's first voyage did produce several new biographies of his patron, carefully timed to appear in 1992. Nancy Rubin, Luis Suárez Fernández, Peggy Liss, and Tarsicio de Azcona have all made useful contributions. However, they neither use gender as a significant category of analysis nor, with the exception of Azcona, do they problematize the official story of Isabel's reign. This is in part owing to the sources they rely on to tell the story: the very chronicles that the Queen commissioned from her court historians in order to legitimize her contested accession and disseminate her power. The messianic and hagiographic construction of Isabel that pervades those chronicles makes them exceedingly unreliable sources for a narrative of the events of her life and rule. Continued reliance on these highly propagandistic works perpetuates the masculinist and misogynist gender ideology that they supported.

The best of the English-language biographies to appear in 1992 is Peggy Liss's *Isabel the Queen: Life and Times*. Liss takes passing note of the role of gender and sexuality in the fashioning of Isabelline ideology. For example, she observes that the British Library's 1985 subject catalog "exactly reversed the monarchs' true roles in listing her as 'Isabella. Queen. Consort of Ferdinand V of Spain'" (4).[19] The biographer also defends her use (adopted in this book) of the onomastic form Isabel over the more common English equivalent, Isabella, a diminutive that she deems an attempt not only to distinguish the Spanish queen from her English counterpart of the same name but also to undercut the awareness of her equal potency as a sovereign (vii). This is an important insight into the lasting effects on historiography of England's rivalry with Spain for world economic dominance in the sixteenth century. Unfortunately, Liss does not elaborate on this insight, nor does it guide her narrative, which relies heavily on "the vivid chronicles of her reign" (ibid.), the biased histories written by Alfonso de Palencia, Fernando del Pulgar, and other royal *cronistas*.

Also released in 1992, but for a Spanish-speaking readership, is the biography written by Luis Suárez Fernández, distinguished and prolific historian of fifteenth-century Spain. The title of his book, *Isabel, mujer y reina* (Isabel, woman and queen), might lead the reader to expect a treatment of the complex relationship of power and gender, but such is not the case. The redundancy of the title and the fact that it gives pride of place to the gender apposite *mujer,* reveals the author's concerted effort to reassure his readers that Isabel was a woman first and foremost and a monarch only secondarily. Although Suárez Fernández repeatedly warns against making anachronistic judgments about the queen and her actions, these salutary warnings against ahistoricism are invariably neutralized by his own nostalgia for a medieval society deemed more pious and more chaste than modern society. Isabel emerges in this nostalgic biography as a symbol of a more innocent age. For example, on the importance of religiosity to an understanding of Isabel's life, the historian has this to say: "She deserves to be understood in relation to her own values and those prevailing in her times. Nowadays we tend to espouse opposing values of materialistic hedonism, as if political, social, and economic problems and objectives were human goals and not means to serve man" (20).[20] In a similar vein, regarding her marriage to the womanizing Fernando: "We confuse, in our day, two concepts as diametrically opposed as love and passion, the first being abnegation and the second, lust. Having taken the decisive step ... Isabel chose her path and patiently constructed an entire edifice of love from wifely duty" (43).[21] Thus, "feminine" and "religious" are the two interrelated essential traits that Suárez Fernández uses to fashion an image of the Queen, "demonstrating thereby that femininity was not an obstacle to governance, in fact quite the contrary" (137).[22]

By far the most objective and rigorous of the modern biographers is Tarsicio de Azcona. His biography, based on meticulous archival research, is an invaluable reconstruction of Isabel's tumultuous life and reign, and I have relied heavily on it in my study.[23] By returning to chancery documents and other primary sources, Azcona is able to dispel many of the enduring myths about Isabel propagated by the contemporary *chronicles* [crónicas]. At the same time, Azcona's approach is highly traditional, and, like Liss, he deals with gender only in passing and expresses discomfort whenever Isabel appears to be overstepping the bounds of feminine decorum.

The fact that Isabelline literature has escaped the kind of scrutiny that Elizabethan literature has attracted ultimately testifies to the imaginative power and cultural productivity of the fictions of sovereignty that Isabel's writing subjects produced, as well as to the eager acceptance of those fictions by society at large. The fashioning of the Queen's gender and power according to the traditional medieval patriarchal norms for women of piety, chastity, and obedience, and the related praise of her as exceptional to the gender norm for women in her strong will, courage, and intelligence is remarkable for its persistence through time. In addition, it has proven to be amazingly adaptable to the changing discourse of Spanish nationhood, from the creation of Europe's world empire overseen by Isabel's grandson Charles I in the early sixteenth century, to the crafting of a fascist state by the Falangist Party in the mid-twentieth century.

As we shall see, however, the carefully and anxiously hagiographic construction of Isabel's gender and power never went uncontested. A good portion of my study is in fact devoted to texts that fashion Isabel as something less than virginal, at times, in fact, as downright whorish. "Dissing" the queen was just as lively, if not quite as common, a literary enterprise in Isabelline Spain as in Elizabethan England.[24] I argue that the carnivalesque tone of these satires does not preclude our taking them seriously. Their pornographic travesties of the voraciousness of female power express and mystify masculine anxiety over queenship every bit as much as the panegyrics of the court poets and chroniclers. The satires are simply the other side of the messianic and hagiographic coin stamped with the image of "Isabel."

Chapter 1 of my book illustrates this very point while simultaneously demarcating the chronological boundaries of my study. I compare two works situated at opposite extremes of the cultural hierarchy: the paradigmatically "high" text of medieval Spain, Juan de Mena's learned epic *Laberinto de Fortuna* (Labyrinth of Fortune) (1444), written seven years before Isabel's birth, and its obscene parody, *Carajicomedia* (Prickcomedy) (c. 1514), published ten years after her death. Mena's poem exhorts his patron (Isabel's father), King Juan II, to take up Spain's longstalled sacred mission: the Reconquest of the peninsula from the Moors. Some fifty years later, the sarcastic anonymous author of *Carajicomedia* mocks the more secular quest of the nobleman Diego Fajardo, a historical figure whose father was a hero of the final battles of the Reconquest waged by Isabel and Fernando. The aging Don Diego is preoccupied with repairing not Spain's broken body, but his own. He takes the reader not on a visionary journey through the planets, as Mena does, but on a tour of Iberia's most notorious brothels in search of a cure for his flaccid penis, a malfunctioning weapon that renders him unfit for service in the battle of the sexes.

Using very different registers, *Carajicomedia* and *Laberinto* both link male sexual dysfunction or deviance and its negative effects on social order to uncontrolled female sexuality. In *Laberinto* the problem lies with adulterous wives who threaten to confound patrilinear inheritance lines; the threat in *Carajicomedia* is the voracious prostitutes who can both cause and cure impotence. I argue that *Carajicomedia*'s pornographic humor is a reference to the reward Isabel granted the Fajardo family for loyal service to the crown: the exclusive rights to all the brothels in the newly reconquered Granada. *Carajicomedia*'s target is ultimately not, as has been argued, a simple contestation of the absolutism, repressiveness, and hypocrisy of Isabelline rule. It is also a biting indictment of

Isabel's "monstrous femininity," her unsanctioned appropriation of the virile, authoritarian role that Mena urged on her father. By fulfilling Mena's masculinist program for her father too well, Isabel, like the sexually threatening whores of the poem, transgresses gender-role boundaries and emasculates her male subjects. It is that emasculation of the warrior by the virago that *Carajicomedia* represents in order to contain.

Chapter 2 examines the construction of Isabel's sovereignty in a series of prose and verse *specula principis* dedicated to her between 1468, the year that her brother Alfonso's death made her accession to the throne likely, and 1479, when she and Fernando finally defeated the Castilian and Aragonese supporters of her rival, Juana I of Castile, and consolidated their rule over a united Castile and Aragon. I single out the little-studied advice treatise *Jardín de nobles doncellas* addressed to the then-princess Isabel by the Augustinian friar Martín de Córdoba at the precise moment she was deciding whom to marry. Traditionally considered a defense of female sovereignty, I show that the work actually seeks to contain Isabel's power, first, by expounding the traditional theological view of an essentially carnal and irrational femininity that must be controlled by fathers, husbands, and priests; and second, by fashioning her future role as a chaste, silent, and obedient queen consort rather than as a powerful queen regnant.

Similar strategies are used in the somewhat later verse treatises written by two of Isabel's most trusted advisers, the grandee Gómez Manrique and the friar Iñigo de Mendoza. These "mirrors of princes," which have been called highly formative for the young and inexperienced Queen, also discursively curtail her power by subordinating her authority to that of Fernando. The chapter ends with an analysis of an important visual text, the heraldic emblem commissioned around 1475 by Isabel and Fernando, shortly after Isabel's coronation. I treat the emblem as a "nuptial fiction" that serves the needs of both monarchs to negotiate delicate issues of shared power, territorial control, and dynastic succession.[25] In its balancing of two contradictory messages—romanticized conjugal equality on the one hand, and military domination on the other—the emblem performs a subtle manipulation of the masculinist gender ideology her advisers had worked hard to inculcate.

Chapter 3 scrutinizes the official story of Isabel's reign purveyed by the chronicles that she commissioned in the decade of the 1480s to legitimize her usurpation of the crown from its legitimate heir, her niece

Juana of Castile. I dissect the "discourse of effeminacy" composed at Isabel's behest by the royal chroniclers Alfonso de Palencia, Fernando del Pulgar, Juan de Flores, and others. The chroniclers accuse Isabel's predecessor Enrique IV of impotence and sodomy in order to discredit him as a man and as a monarch, as well as to prove the illegitimacy of his daughter Juana, Isabel's rival for the throne. But the typical rhetorical slippage of sodomitical discourse facilitates the shading of Palencia's homophobia into misogyny. In this way, Spain's ills come to be blamed on a genealogy of powerful, treacherous women with an unseemly will to power: Eve, La Cava (the temptress reputedly responsible for the fall of Visigothic Spain to the Moors), Enrique IV's adulterous wife Juana, and, more dangerously, the arrogant Isabel, who insists on ruling in her own right rather than subordinating herself to her husband. I relate Palencia's growing distrust of his patron to his rivalry with his colleague, Fernando del Pulgar, whom Isabel favored because he was more amenable to her censorship of his work. Finally, I place the anxiety of these university-trained men of letters or jurists, many of them of *converso* background, within the larger context of the role of European humanism in the construction of early-modern secular masculinity.

Chapter 4 is central to the elaboration of my thesis. In it I trace the paradoxical representation of Isabel as virgin and whore in the context of the medieval political theory of the kingdom as a *corpus mysticum*. I begin with an analysis of the role of the Virgin Mary in the construction of the Isabelline messianic myth, a myth that figured her as the virginal redeemer of Spain's tragic fall into the hands of Moors in the eighth century. Central to this discussion are the ballads dealing with Rodrigo, last king of the Visigoths, which began to circulate in Isabel's lifetime. The ballads moralize the political and military causes of the eighth-century Moorish conquest of Iberia, but they do so ambivalently. They alternatingly blame Rodrigo's lust for the beautiful maiden Cava—a lust that, according to medieval gender ideology, inevitably feminizes the male—and the treacherous seductiveness of the latter, whose name is Arabic for "whore." The fall of Spain is thereby attributed to the uncontrolled and illicit desire of a Christian Adam and a quasi-Muslim Eve. In this calque of the biblical story of Eden, the symbolic castration of Rodrigo perfectly fits his crime of causing the overthrow of the virile Christian Visigothic kingdom by effeminate Muslim invaders.

The many writers who comment on the legend of the destruction of a paradisiacal Christian Spain brought on by the infamous couple Rodrigo and Cava extol Isabel as a second Mary, sent by God to heal the wounds they inflicted on the body politic. But locating the restoration of the integrity of Hispania's virility in a woman's body generates profound ambivalence. I first examine traces of that ambivalence in eulogistic poems comparing Isabel to the Virgin Mary and in political treatises that emphasize Isabel's position at the head of the *corpus mysticum*. I then discuss the inversion of this hierarchy of upper body over lower in the pornographic poem *Pleyto del manto* (Lawsuit over the cloak), an account of a mock trial in which lawyers for the *coño* (cunt) and the *carajo* (prick) argue for the superior power of their respective clients. At the center of the pornographic debate about gender in *Pleyto del manto* is a critique of the harshness and corruption of a legal system imposed by a female sovereign, a voracious, treacherous cunt who is above the patriarchal laws of the land.

In chapter 5, as in chapter 1, I compare two seemingly very different texts published together around 1497 by Luis de Lucena, son of a respected humanist in Isabel's court. Probably while still a student at the University of Salamanca, Lucena paid for the printing of a luxurious book containing two works: *Repetición de amores* (Oration on love), a misogynistic parody of the academic exercise of the *repetitio*, and *Arte de axedrez* (Art of chess), a treatise on chess. *Arte de axedrez* is an important document for the history of chess because it is the first manual to explain the change that transformed the ancient game into the form it retains to this day: the greatly enhanced powers of the Queen, called in French "the enraged lady" [la dame enragée]. Chess historians agree that the change occurred with startling rapidity sometime in the last quarter of the fifteenth century, but they have never identified its country of origin. Taking into account the dedication of the chess manual to Isabel's son and heir, Prince Juan, I argue that Lucena intended his luxurious volume as a kind of professional portfolio in his application to join Juan's retinue. He had the seemingly disparate works bound together in order to demonstrate to Prince Juan and his mother (who closely supervised the education of her only male heir) that he understood the new "rules of the game," rules that work entirely to the Queen's advantage. At the same time, in its new printed context, the uneasy fusion of courtly love and clerical misogyny that informs the academic humor of *Repetición*, originally composed to regale Lucena's classmates in the rowdy all-male environment of Salamanca, becomes a kind of secular chess morality that articulates and contains the anxiety that Isabel induced in her would-be courtiers.

Finally, chapter 6 examines the threat of the powerful, uncontrolled woman to patriarchy in the works of Juan de Flores, a Salamancan-trained jurist like Lucena, but one who we know successfully negotiated the difficult passage from university to court. Rector of the University of Salamanca for a brief period before joining Isabel's court as chronicler, judge, and administrator, Flores has recently emerged as one of the most prolific of Isabelline writers. In his chronicle of the reign of the Catholic Monarchs and his other works, he works out in often contradictory ways the implications for patriarchy of an absolutist female monarch. His festive political allegory, *Triunfo de amor* (Triumph of love) goes even further in imagining the radical effects on society that such an inversion of the gender hierarchy might produce while withholding judgment about those effects. In the romance *La historia de Grisel y Mirabella* (Story of Grisel and Mirabella), the power of an "enraged queen" proves more damaging to the patriarchal status quo, although the grotesque punishment of the archmisogynist Torrellas by the furious Queen of Scotland at the end of the work can also be read as a carnivalesque inversion of the repressive power of the King of Scotland, who sacrifices his own daughter in order to uphold the misogynist law of the land.

Given the contemporary evidence of the popularity of romance among aristocratic women readers, including Isabel and her ladies-in-waiting, gender must be factored into the production and reception of Flores's works. The possibility that the writer of *Triunfo* and *Grisel* had in mind a largely female audience that included the Queen contextualizes his ambiguous representation of gender and sovereignty just as Lucena's primarily male audience (including Prince Juan) situates the conjoining of his misogynist treatise on the "battle of the sexes" and his treatise on the new queen-dominated game of chess. My interpretation of Flores's *Crónica incompleta* (Incomplete chronicle), *Triunfo de amor,* and *Grisel y Mirabella* takes into account the possibly contradictory effects on and responses of Spain's most powerful female reader, for whom Flores imagines societies turned upside down by the unleashed power of women.

In the Conclusion, I document the vitality of the dualistic medieval construction of Isabelline power. Immediately after his victory in the Spanish civil war (1936–39), Francisco Franco elevated the "saintly" Isabel to the status of national icon, along with the Cid and Saint Teresa of

Ávila. Isabel's piety, purity, and wifely obedience became a cornerstone of the fascist ideology of National Catholicism, which grounded the stability of the state in the strength of the patriarchal family. In an interesting cross-gendering, Franco often identified himself with the most Catholic of queens as he called for the nation to join him in a militant "Second Reconquest": to rid Spain of foreign contaminants.

Starting in the 1950s and continuing on through the 1990s, writers reacted to Franco's repressive and reactionary fashioning of the body politic through Isabel's body. Alejo Carpentier, Salman Rushdie, and, most vitriolically, Juan Goytisolo all reimagined Isabel as whore rather than virgin. I end with the work that provided the initial inspiration for this study: *El cuarto de atrás,* by Carmen Martín Gaite. In her autobiographical novel about growing up female under Franco, Martín Gaite therapeutically rejects the destructive effects of Isabelline hagiographic mythography on her own development. Unlike Goytisolo, however, she does not express her frustration at her miseducation by once again turning the virgin into a whore. She does so by breaking the spell cast by Isabel, closing the book of fascist fairy tales, and getting back to work writing her own life.

CHAPTER ONE
Anxious Masculinity

> Fortune, your downfalls I sing
> [Tus casos fallaçes, Fortuna, cantamos]
> —Juan de Mena, *Laberinto de Fortuna*

> Prick, your downfalls I sing
> [Tus casos falaces, carajo, cantamos]
> —*Carajicomedia*

In this chapter I compare two literary works usually situated at opposite extremes of the cultural hierarchy: Juan de Mena's *Laberinto de Fortuna* and the anonymous *Carajicomedia*.[1] Mena's poem is the paradigmatically "high" text of fifteenth-century Castilian literature, and as such it still occupies a hallowed space in the Spanish literary canon. Its early-sixteenth-century pornographic parody, *Carajicomedia*, is located at the "low" end of the cultural hierarchy, and has consequently been deemed beneath scholarly consideration until very recently. My analysis of gender ideology in Isabelline literature begins with the comparison of these works for three reasons. First, they demarcate the temporal scope of my study. Mena dedicated *Laberinto* to its addressee, King Juan II of Castile in 1444, seven years before the birth of the daughter who exactly thirty years later would inherit his kingdom. *Carajicomedia* was probably composed soon after Queen Isabel's death in 1504. Second, when taken together, the two works illuminate one of my main themes, the central role played by the threat of feminine gender and sexuality in the political culture of the Isabelline period.

The third reason is the most important. By approaching the gender ideology of a foundational text such as *Laberinto* from the vantage point of the noncanonical *Carajicomedia*, I deliberately invert not only chronological order, but also literary hierarchies of style and genre. Those hierarchies hypervalue works that ostensibly exemplify the qualities of "mind" that Western philosophical tradition has gendered masculine and devalue texts that more directly treat the "body" and that have been for that reason gendered feminine.[2] By overturning this scheme and privileging *Carajicomedia* in my analysis, I uncover the extent to which, in the Isabelline period, the "socially peripheral"—in this case, the prostitute—is often "symbolically central" (Babcock, 32). More generally, I model a materialist-feminist critique of Hispano-medieval literature that posits "feminine" aesthetic categories of the "low" (parody, pornography, the grotesque) and "masculine" categories of the "high" (allegory, moral treatise, chronicle) as inseparable and interdependent.

In *The Politics and Poetics of Transgression,* Peter Stallybrass and Allon White reaffirm Mikhail Bakhtin's contribution to the study of medieval European culture, namely, the conceptualization of a mutually constructing opposition of popular, carnivalesque culture that celebrates the "grotesque realist body" and official, high culture that values the "classical body." But they recognize that Bakhtin's cultural analytic has become mired in a debate among new historicists and cultural materialists over the political significance of carnival, that is, whether it truly subverts the status quo or is ultimately contained by it.[3] Stallybrass and White break the stalemate of the subversion–containment debate by treating the carnivalesque as only one instance of a generalized economy of transgression of the binary extremism that is fundamental to the entire process of cultural signification and organization in Europe since the Middle Ages (6–15). They identify four cultural spheres that are constructed within hierarchies of high and low: geographical space, the social order, psychic forms, and the human body. The main focus of their study is the body, and, in particular, the grotesque body—multiple, bulging, over- or undersized, protuberant, and incomplete, its openings and orifices emphasized, its lower regions valorized over the upper (9).

Stallybrass and White issue a caveat that holds particular relevance to my discussion. They warn against the tendency to essentialize the politics of carnival as populist resistance to the dominant, official culture.

They conceptualize the carnivalesque instead as a locus of contradiction and conflict, noting that "carnival often violently abuses and demonizes *weaker*, not stronger, social groups—women, ethnic and religious minorities, those who 'don't belong'—in a process of *displaced abjection*" (19). Both the role of the body in social classification and the concept of displaced abjection, specifically as directed at women, have been the focus of the feminist critique of Bakhtin's theory and are fundamental to the argument of this chapter.[4]

The *Cancionero de obras de burlas provocantes a risa* (Songbook of mirth-producing works of mockery) is a treasury of grotesque bodily realism, from "Billeting in Juvera" *(Aposento en Juvera)*, a poem in which an obese man provides lodging for the entire entourage of the papal legation on its important 1473 visit to Castile, to the *Pleyto del manto*, an account of a lawsuit to determine the preeminence of the cunt [coño] or the prick [carajo]. The *Cancionero de burlas* made its first appearance in print in the codicological "lower regions" of Hernando del Castillo's monumental *Cancionero general* of 1511, that is, as the final section of the book. In that first edition, the *Burlas* section contained sixty-two bawdy and scatological poems composed largely during the reign of Isabel. Starting with the second edition of 1514, frequent additions and deletions altered the shape of the section.[5] Finally, in 1519, the popular *Burlas* section was published separately, with fifty-eight previously published works and one new work, the longest by far in the collection, the anonymous *Carajicomedia*.

Despite a spate of editions in the last two decades—two of the entire collection and two more of *Carajicomedia* alone—undoubtedly in euphoric response to the lifting of Francoist censorship, the *Cancionero de burlas* remains little studied. The reason for this critical neglect can be glimpsed in a 1980s scholarly reenactment of the hundred-year-old debate on "the meaning of courtly love." It is worth taking a brief look at this debate before turning to *Carajicomedia*.

In *The Philosophy of Love in Spanish Literature*, Alexander Parker attributed the modern depreciation of Spain's medieval love lyrics not to any defective artistry of the works themselves, but rather to the pervasive and pernicious influence of materialism in modern times (2). In his *La poesía amatoria de la época de los Reyes Católicos*, Keith Whinnom countered the contention with a defense of *cancionero* poetry that validates the very aspects Parker rejected, the very material erotic double entendres that subtend the idealizing language of "courtly love."[6] Where Parker wanted to see in *cancionero* amatory verse a religious longing to unite with divine, albeit displaced onto a less worthy human beloved, Whinnom saw a lightly veiled desire for sexual favors. What is more, Whinnom's spirited defense of the obscene amphibology of the songbooks led to a more general rebuke of Hispano-medievalists: "I don't believe that we medievalists run the risk of undervaluing the idealism of the Middle Ages. On the contrary, I think it highly likely that we have overvalued it" (24).[7]

Whinnom's groundbreaking work on the sexual wordplay of the *cancioneros*, initiated more than three decades ago, has stimulated quite a few analyses of what Ian Macpherson calls the "secret language" of *cancionero* poetry.[8] Macpherson has been the most assiduous in uncovering the erotic puns structuring individual lyrics. But even his brilliant detective work shows a certain resistance to bawdiness, as in the preference for poems in which the obscenity is less directly expressed, those lyrics "designed not to offend, but to compliment the lady and to rejoice in an event of significance to both" ("Secret Language," 62). The assumption that the *cancionero* poets—almost entirely male—accurately represent women's subjectivity reinscribes the traditional estimation of this masculinist verse as "profeminist."[9] Macpherson's resistance suggests that the erotic paronomasia of *cancionero* poetry has been neglected not only out of scholarly modesty, but also because it exposes the "ungentlemanly" foundations of courtly longing, the male poets' desire to enhance their gender and social status by subtly flaunting their sexual prowess.[10]

Only recently have feminist critics begun to uncover the very material goals of the supposedly idealist literature of the medieval courts of Castile. María Eugenia Lacarra ("Feminist Analysis") has noted the way in which the court poet's idealization of his lady as exceptional upholds the ideology of masculine superiority while appearing to overturn it, a strategy that we shall see applied in courtly representations of Isabel. Julian Weiss ("Alvaro de Luna") has analyzed the central role such verse played in the male courtier's creation and affirmation of his masculine identity before his peers and superiors, a social transaction in which females function as symbolic objects of exchange. For example, the "amorous secrecy" [secreto amoroso], the vow of silence that the courtly lover takes to protect his lady's honor, has been shown to mask sexual blackmail based on the threat of defamation (Hermida Ruiz).

Carajicomedia represents the most material of the social transactions that shape and are shaped by the masculinist court culture: male dealings with prostitutes. Although its obscenity is very far from veiled, it is every bit as polysemic as the courtly love lyrics that fill most of the pages of the *Cancionero general*. Paula Findlen has demonstrated that in Renaissance Italy, pornography invariably contained elements of political critique, whether stated or implied. These elements ranged across the entire political spectrum, from conservative to contestatory. This ideological flexibility results from pornography's function as "a sensitive measure of shifting social hierarchies and the vicissitudes of intellectual and political culture in the complex network of republics and courts that composed Renaissance Italy" (53–54).[11] *Carajicomedia* functions in a similar way in Isabelline Spain.

Carajicomedia is a brilliantly caustic parody of Juan de Mena's much-admired *Laberinto de Fortuna* (Mena was King Juan II's Latin secretary, and he respectfully addressed his work, also known as *Las trescientas* (The three hundred) for its 297 stanzas, to his king in 1444). Historians agree that the year marked a nadir in the monarchy's adversarial relationship with the fractious Castilian aristocracy, a struggle that persisted for more than three decades, well into Isabel's reign.[12] Self-consciously classicizing in style and severely moralizing in tone, *Laberinto* exhorts Juan II to fulfill the primary role of the medieval king, that of warrior. It calls on the sovereign to control the unruly nobility, regulate its behavior, and redirect its energies toward the completion of Castile's age-old sacred military mission: the Reconquest, the war to recover Muslim-dominated Iberian territory. The long poem takes the form of an allegorical dream vision in which the poet-narrator and his guide Providence visit the House of Fortune where they behold a map of the cosmos containing seven astrological circles. Each of the concentric circles contains three wheels representing past, present, and future time. The first two wheels are populated by mythological and historical persons who exemplify positive and negative qualities associated with the different planets. The description of these famous and infamous men and women constitutes Mena's lesson to his king, a demonstration of the virtues necessary for the self-rule (and, by implication, rule of others) that is sorely lacking in his own time.[13]

Carajicomedia turns Mena's high-flown meditation on the unfortunate condition of the kingdom into worry over the sorry state of one man's penis. He is Diego Fajardo, a nobleman with close family ties to Queen Isabel. Fajardo's father was a hero of the final campaign of the Reconquista (1482–92), the war to recover the kingdom of Granada. Alfonso Fajardo's military exploits against the Muslims of Granada might well have merited him a place in Mena's Circle of Mars. Diego accompanied his father on several of the Granada campaigns. *Carajicomedia* recounts (through a variety of ill-defined and at times overlapping speakers, including its author, editor, and glossator, the character Luxuria, and Fajardo himself), the aging warrior's vision of various circles dedicated to Spain's most infamous brothels and the exemplary prostitutes who inhabit them.[14] The elusive goal of the aging warrior Fajardo's dream quest is a cure for the impotence that is hindering his performance in the battle of the sexes that now preoccupies him, presumably quite a few years after the fall of Granada.[15]

Carlos Varo, whose 1981 edition and study of *Carajicomedia* remains indispensable, was the first to see in the work a classic carnivalesque text.[16] He considers it at once a libertarian defense of bodily pleasure and a biting critique of Isabelline political and moral repression (49). Varo's regicentric analysis is not highly developed. It also falls into the trap, discussed earlier, of essentializing carnival as populist, thus failing to take into account the fact that its carnivalesque "radical opposition to the illegitimately powerful" (Stamm, quoted in Stallybrass and White, 19) is at the same time profoundly misogynistic. Nor does Varo address the broader concerns about the mutual construction of gender and power relations in Trastamaran absolutist ideology that the work raises much more pointedly than did its serious intertext fifty years earlier.[17]

In the analysis that follows, therefore, I shall argue more broadly that the masculine sexual anxiety that pervades *Carajicomedia* is a psychic response to a female sovereign who is threatening on two counts: first, because in her power Isabel inverts the medieval sex/gender hierarchy of male dominance and female submission, in this case viewed through the lens of sexual relations; and second, because she fulfills the mission set for her father Juan II better than he ever did. For the misogynist satirist, the Queen is entirely too effective at appropriating and imposing the masculinist, militaristic, and absolutist monarchic ideology that *Laberinto* expounded, but that in the medieval period is entirely inappropriate for a woman. I will then compare the bawdy *Carajicomedia* with its serious intertext, reading "backwards" and "upwards" in order to reveal how fundamentally Mena's authorization of absolutist male sovereignty depends on more concealed, but no less urgent, masculine sexual anxieties. In both works, as we shall see, those anxieties are raised by the danger that an uncontrollable feminine sexuality poses to a gender hierarchy grounded in a patrilineal system of marriage and inheritance. The opposite poles of this poetic hierarchy, collapsed into each other, vividly illustrate two primary tenets of feminist theory: first, that control of and traffic in women lie at the heart of social organization and political institutions (Gayle Rubin); and second, that relationships of gender and power in the family are elementary political forms (Bristol, 178). They also lay bare the gender ideology that formed Isabel and her subjects.

Carajicomedia: The Queen as Whore

Carajicomedia exhibits all the hallmarks of a classic carnivalesque text. First and foremost among these is the thoroughgoing inversion of the hierarchy of upper body over lower body. That inversion is driven home by the extreme care taken to preserve the solemn metrical regularity of the original poem's *arte mayor,* even as every high element of its content is debased. Thus, Mena's majestic first line, "To the greatly prepotent King Juan II" [Al muy prepotente Don Juan el segundo] (93; st. 1), becomes the equally impressive "To the greatly profound prick" [Al muy impotente carajo profundo] (150).[18] Because of the enormous popularity of Mena's text well into the sixteenth century, the obscene joke of this first line would not have been lost on many readers. Only after letting the metrical identification of the prepotent monarch Juan II and a flaccid penis sink in does the poet go on in the second verse to assign the member to its rightful owner, the poem's protagonist, Diego Fajardo.

The classical allusions central to Mena's lofty style are similarly travestied in the parody. In the second stanza, for example, Mena's exalted Virgilian evocation "Fortune, your downfalls I sing" [Tus casos falaçes, Fortuna, cantamos] (93; st. 2) is altered only slightly to read "Prick, your downfalls I sing" [Tus casos falaces, Carajo, cantamos] (152), the daring association of Fortune and a prick underscored by the subtle homophonous play of fallacious/phallus. Similarly, Mena's proud affirmation that the deeds of the Cid and Castile's other martial heroes are equal to those of the Romans, but are forgotten "for lack of authors" [por falta de auctores] (95; st. 4), allows the parodist to claim that Diego Fajardo's heroism "in love" [en amores] matches that of the Cid "in war" [en batallas], but that his fame is "harmed... because his deeds have been recorded by cunts" [dañada... por ser de sus obras los coños autores] (153). Given the extremely reduced number of female authors in the early-modern period in Spain, this cannot be an expression of the anxiety of the "phallus-as-pen" confronted with a kind of *écriture féminine avant la lettre*. It is, rather, a lament over the inadequacy of the penis as prick, a performance anxiety disavowed through projection onto the voracious vagina.

Generically, the *Carajicomedia* inverts the classical epic or medieval dream vision form of its original into a mock elegy with a mock epic ending, a lament for the death from old age of Diego Fajardo's virility.[19] Its pasquinade encompasses not only the formal self-exaltation of the original but also the status it acquired in the late fifteenth and sixteenth centuries as equal in moral wisdom and philosophical depth to the classics. Mena's work achieved this recognition largely through its extensive glossing by the humanists Hernán Núñez (1499; reprinted often) and Francisco Sánchez de las Brozas (1582).[20] The anonymous parodist is careful to provide his work with its own burlesque version of the famous Hernán Núñez glosses of 1499. His erudite *glosa* is a pastiche of sacrilegious Latin quotations from the "Whores of the Church Fathers" *[Putas Patrum]* (a blasphemous calque of the *Vitae Patrum* [Lives of the church fathers] [155]), biblical references in macaronic Latin (e.g., "Inter natus mulierum non surrexit maior puta vieja que María la Buyça" [163]), and citations of mock *auctores* like *Putarch* [Plutarco/Plutarch + puta/ whore] in La *Corónica de las illustrísimas Bagassas* (Chronicle of the celebrated sluts) (193).[21]

Carajicomedia also participates in the transcodings characteristic of the carnivalesque. The poet-narrator's tour of Fortune's house in *Laberinto* features the allegorical goddess's emblematic wheels of time past, present, and future; Fajardo's search for a cure for his "tired prick" [carajo cansado] boasts a similar vision of three "wheels," two round and still and one long and motile, that suddenly appear between his legs. But his visionary journey through the seven astrological circles takes place on a spatial rather than a temporal plane, specifically, Castile and Aragon. Beginning with stanza 58, "The first order of the Moon, applied to Valladolid" [La orden primera de la Luna, aplicada a Valladolid] (193), the poem functions much like a secret guide to some of the most notorious brothels of Spain, with precise street and site references, primarily to Valladolid and Valencia, but also to Burgos, Toledo, and Salamanca. The heroes and heroines of ancient Greece and Rome and contemporary Castile that Mena viewed and judged in the House of Fortune are replaced in *Carajicomedia* by a horde of Spanish prostitutes, several of whom have been identified as historical figures.[22] The awed narrator individualizes and immortalizes them through their distinctive talents, just as Mena had singled out the distinctive virtues of Penelope, Lucretia, and Artemisa. For example, he introduces us to the miracle worker Ana de Medina, "in whose cunt it is proven that frozen pricks ignite" [en cuyo coño se pruevan llegar / carajos elados, s'encienden de fuego] (180), and the generous Gracia, of whom the gloss says "her cunt advertises itself as a hospital/hostal for pricks or an inn for balls" [publica su coño ser ospital de carajos, o ostal de cojones] (178). In all, sixty-six whores are named in the poem, "such a lecherous lineage of whores" [estirpe de putas atan luxuriosa] (179) rivaling the Gothic "glorious lineage of kings" [estirpe de reyes atán gloriosa] (121; st. 43) that Mena proudly claimed for Spain.

Guiding the hapless hero Fajardo on his sex tour is a grotesque Celestinesque counterpart to Mena's beautiful young Fortuna: "an old whore, a procuress, and a witch" [una puta vieja, alcahueta, y hechicera] (155).[23] Fajardo's urgent plea to this debased *senexa* makes explicit the sexual topsy-turvy that informs the entire work: "Give me a cure, since you are the only one I dare to ask since you assuredly resurrect and rejuvenate the dead and the old. Make me stiff as the horns of the moon, engorge and enlarge the veins of my prick, let my deeds sow such disorder that it leaves a cradle in every house" (155).[24] These verses make clear that Diego Fajardo's goal—however elusive—is to bring about exactly what Mena exhorted John II to prevent: the bastardization of Castilian bloodlines and the social disorder that inevitably ensues. Mena's call to virtuous living, "and kill off the vile acts of Venus's libidinous fire" [e los viles actos del libidinoso / fuego de Venus del todo se maten] (161; st. 114), is turned upside down in Fajardo's libertine "Let's fuck so much that we become famous" [Hodamos de forma que fama tengamos] (226).

Fajardo's attitude toward his Celestinesque guide and the hundreds of whores he encounters is, however, profoundly ambivalent. At first glance, many of Fajardo's "whorish lives" [vidas putescas] seem to celebrate the female libido equally with the male. This is how we might read the story of Francisca de Saldana, for example, who marries a certain Arab named Catamaymón. When her family objects, she answers with a saucy "I'd sooner have a donkey that fills me up than a horse that throws me" [Más quiero asno que me llene que cavallo que me derrueque] (186), a bawdy take on the proverb "I'd sooner have an donkey that carries me than a horse that throws me" [Más quiero asno que me lleve que cavallo que me derrueque] (186). This Castilian zest for devouring the Arab may also be a parodic reference to the Reconquest mission that *Laberinto* enjoins Juan II to resume.[25] On a deeper level, and as a consequence of the accumulation of similar humor, the joke betrays a masculinist projection of the desired primacy of the penis and the corresponding fear of its actual inability to fill the void of the vagina. The effect of the poem's reiterated allusions to the menacing size of the whores' vaginas and their engulfing capacity makes this conclusion unavoidable: Francisca de Laguna bears the telling moniker Ass of Steel [Rabo d'Azero] (170); La Napolitana is similarly noted for her "her ass which was sunken and as wide as a drainage ditch" [rabadilla, que tenía muy hundida y tan grande como una gran canal de agua] (171). Then there is the bride who hired Isabel d'Ayala to restore her hymen, only to have her suspicious husband discover the crude stitches, "which, when he cut through them, causing the bride great pain, revealed by some divine mystery an immense ocean that so scared the poor husband that he renounced her/divorced her" (207).[26] It is telling that, in this case, what horrifies the groom is both the vastness of the vaginal territory he discovers and the realization that the territory has been previously explored, a laying bare of the anxieties of virility underlying the patriarchal conception of the wife as property.

The ideological relationship between pornography and prostitution must also be taken into account in reading *Carajicomedia* as carnival.[27] The violent relations of power and exchange central to prostitution, which give the lie to the masculinist view of the prostitute as omnivorous sexual desirer and seducer, quickly surface in Fajardo's anecdotes.[28] There is, for example, the comeuppance Mariflores gets when she insults two stable hands: "Grabbing her, the two of them put her in a stall in the Admiral's residence and summoned the whole household, and soon there were a total of twenty-five men from all ranks there, all of them well equipped; and quickly unbuttoning their hose, they began to hump her until they knocked her down and turned her cunt into a pool of semen" (194).²⁹ The story ends with the leader of the group calling in two black stableboys, at which point the panicked Mariflores runs off, to the merriment of all. It is noteworthy that the raciness of both the tale of Francisca and that of Mariflores is enhanced by racism, the attribution of extraordinary sexual prowess to the despised Muslim and black. It matters little to my analysis that, in the former tale, that prowess is placed in the service of female pleasure, while in the latter it enhances the sadistic thrill of a gang rape.

Although the multilayered misogyny of *Carajicomedia* merits fuller analysis (its complex concatenation with anticlericalism and sacrilegiousness, for example), the point I wish to make here is the poem's pervasive representation of masculine sexual anxieties, figured in the inadequacy of Fajardo's erection to deal with so many aggressively insatiable females. As he whines to his guide: "Because where there are so many whores not one of them obeys any but the wildest prick; that's why I call upon you, madam, and invoke you, for my sad prick suffers from being tame" [Pues do ay tantas putas, ninguna obedece / carajo ninguno que no sea muy loco; / para esto te llamo, señora, y invoco, / qu'el triste del mío de cuerdo padece] (165).³⁰

The old whore provides a temporary cure by taking Fajardo firmly (and literally) in hand, but it is clearly a losing battle. Before accepting his forced retirement, however, the hero summons up the strength for one more fight, a mock-epic battle between the *carajos* and the *coños* that parodies stanza by stanza *Laberinto*'s stirring account of the battle between Christians and Moors at Gibraltar led by the ill-fated Conde de Niebla. The well-armed warrior and his troops charge forward, "thrusting away, as in battle" [dando empuxones, a modo de guerra] (227). The soldiers, however, are met not with fear, but with delight: "The cunts, seeing the troops grow and seeing pricks from all over marching forward so randily, waving their banners, were delighted and marvelously excited" [Los coños, veyendo crecer los rabaños, / y viendo carajos de diversas partes / venir tan arrechos con sus estandartes, / holgaron de vello con gozos estraños] (227).

This victory of the fearsome vaginal troops brings the protagonist and the poem to a hilarious climax.³¹ It also strengthens the parallel, previously mentioned, between Fortuna and Carajo. In *Laberinto,* the Conde de Niebla's military prowess is no match for the unpredictability of the seas. He and his men drown when his boat founders in a storm:

"Fortune had determined the hour so that when his men began to climb on, the boat sank with everyone aboard" (200; st. 184).[32] In *Carajicomedia*, Fajardo's sexual demise is tied to the insatiability of the vagina: "Lust had determined the hour; the limp pricks charged again and the hungry cunts swallowed them up just like that, so that none of them sings or cries anymore" (230).[33] Fajardo's forces do not literally drown, as Niebla's did, but they are engulfed.

The array of libidinous women who populate Fajardo's senescent vision, be they compliant whores ("Madalenica... who never said no" [Madalenica... la qual nunca dio esquiva respuesta (214)]), or savvy procuresses ("But the wise hand of my guide, seeing my perplexed, limp dick, fondled it, rubbed it, stretched out its foreskin" [Mas la sabia mano de quien me guiava / viendo mi floxo carajo perplexo, / le sova, le flota le estira el pellejo (168)]), goes well beyond the "metaphysics of pleasure" [metafísica del placer] that Varo sees in the work (47). It projects onto prostitutes its fear of the unpredictable and uncontrollable feminine: "Because where there are so many whores, not one of them obeys" [Pues do ay tantas putas, ninguna obedece] (165). As we shall see, this psychosexual anxiety—the ever-present threat of the cunt to the prick— is in part a response to the absolute power of one particular female whom the poet calls "the number one whore in the universe" [la prima de todas las putas del universo] (198).

The first scholar to relate the demise of Diego Fajardo's erection to the politics of the Catholic Queen was Alfonso Canales. In 1974, by a stroke of scholarly *fortuna*, he was able to identity the protagonist of the parody. Diego was the son of Alonso Yáñez Fajardo, a hero of the wars against Granada.[34] In 1486, in recognition of his military service to the crown, Isabel and Fernando granted Alonso, who is in certain documents identified as a priest, a privilege "so that he could establish brothels in every town that had been or would be conquered" [para que pudiese establecer mancebías en todos los pueblos conquistados y que se conquistasen].[35] Soon he owned brothels throughout the former Kingdom of Granada, including a particularly lucrative establishment of one hundred prostitutes located in Málaga (74).[36] In 1492, that city initiated a protracted legal fight against the abuses of the "Fajardo the whoremonger" [putero Fajardo] and his henchmen.[37] Upon his death, Alonso bequeathed this valuable property to Diego, who had accompanied him on his military missions; it remained in the family until the beginning of the seventeenth century.

It was left to Carlos Varo to observe that of the some five dozen prostitutes who parade through *Carajicomedia* no fewer than eight are named Isabel. Each of them, furthermore, bears an epithet that associates her with the Queen, for example, Ysabel Towers/of the Towers [Ysabel de Torres] (172; the queen's birthplace was Madrigal de las Altas Torres); Ysabel the Warrior [Ysabel la Guerrera], a "court whore... who puts it to all kinds of people" [ramera cortesana... está en guerra con mil naturas de gentes] (172–73; perhaps a reference to the civil wars of 1475–79); and Ysabel de León (189; Isabel's legitimate title).[38]

On two occasions there are even more direct references to the Queen. The first is in connection with the aforementioned La Napolitana, a fat "court whore: Nowadays you see her married to one of Queen Isabel's stableboys. I knew this woman well, the entire Spanish court can testify to this. She is one of the nine worthies" (171).[39] Varo sees an authorial intent to defame Isabel in the ambiguous antecedent of "this woman" [esta muger], whose behavior is witnessed by the entire Spanish court, and the fact that after Isabel's marriage to Fernando she was properly addressed as Queen of Naples. The second reference to Isabel also applies the epithet "court whore" [ramera cortesana], this time to a certain Osorio, whose ostentatious dress supposedly occasioned the royal promulgation of sumptuary laws of 1499: "at one entertainment that took place in 1498, when the court was in Toledo, this Osorio woman was so decked out in gold and silk that Queen Isabel, asking who she was and being told that she was a court whore, got so angry that she forbade the wearing of silk in Castile" (188).[40]

Varo suggests that such references are a veiled critique of Isabel's involvement in prostitution and specifically of her generous patronage of the brothel-owning priest Fajardo. The work of Francisco Márquez Villanueva on the social context of the theme of proxenetism in *Celestina* supports this view. He observes that the Catholic Monarchs, in spite of their reputation as highly moral rulers, did not face squarely the problem of unchaste clergy and prostitution. This is because the former were a stable and conservative force historically allied with the monarchy, and the latter represented both a significant source of royal revenues and a means of rewarding loyal courtiers. Thus, between 1488 and 1492 the royal chancery ordered lower authorities to stop harassing and fining priests accused of having concubines. Simultaneously, the monarchs implemented their "progressive" policy toward prostitution by confining prostitution to brothels established by royal decree in major cities throughout the kingdom (445–46). Of this practice Márquez Villanueva writes: "The obscenity of the Catholic Monarchs' rewarding good service by granting to trusted men (even to priests) the rights to establish and exploit brothels seemed in certain thoughtful circles to be highly scandalous" (*Orígenes,* 154).[41] He includes the author of *Carajicomedia* in the company of those scandalized by such royal policies.[42]

It is interesting that Varo balks at his own conclusion, namely, that the poet really does represent the Queen as "the biggest whore in the universe...the forge of pricks...the goddess of lust, the mother of homeless balls" (198).[43] He hastens to reassure us that

> the somewhat daring accusation is not in the least justifiable historically, since, quite to the contrary, the Castilian queen was an exemplary woman and wife. The first relevant testimony that we have of this is by the official historian of the Catholic Monarchs, Hernando del Pulgar, who uses noble and forceful words: "She herself provided a grand example of a wife, since during her marriage and her reign she never kept favorites whom she might love, rather she loved only the King, and he only her." (74)[44]

Varo's appeal to Fernando del Pulgar in order to mystify the *Carajicomedia*'s defiant, and his own more timid, construction of Isabel as castrating whore is in line with the complex gender ideology promoted by Isabel's own court chroniclers. Pulgar, Alonso de Palencia, Juan de Flores, and others took pains to make their monarch's troubling gender less threatening to her subjects. One strategy they devised for this purpose was to represent the queen simultaneously as "legitimate daughter" [hija legítima], "perfect wife" [perfecta casada], and "manly woman" [mujer viril]. They placed these contradictory roles within the context of a larger campaign of sexual slander against her enemies.

As we shall see in greater detail in chapter 3, Isabel's disputed succession to the Castilian throne and the subsequent difficult consolidation of her power are intimately connected with her chroniclers' deployment of a stigmatizing "discourse of effeminacy." That propagandistic discourse took aim at her half brother Enrique IV's rumored homosexuality, his putative inability to control the sexual appetites of his wife, Juana de Portugal, and the resulting supposed illegitimacy of their daughter, snidely dubbed Juana la Beltraneja.[45] At Isabel's instigation and under her close supervision, the *cronistas* turned these innuendos into powerful ideological weapons in order to discredit the Queen's rivals and to fashion a messianic mythos that masked the dubious legitimacy of her claim to the throne, projecting the doubts upon Juana.

There was, of course, a substantial cultural impediment to Isabel's bid to restore order and authority in the royal family and, by extension, in the nation: her gender. In early-modern Europe, women's divinely ordained domestic and political subordination deemed them unfit to rule (Jordan, "Woman's Rule," 421–22). No less than Elizabeth I of England nearly one hundred years later, Isabel was, by virtue of her gender, deeply suspect as head of state. Carole Levin's study on Elizabeth discusses the intense debate about that queen's sexuality that went on throughout her reign. It was stimulated not only by her anomalous condition as female sovereign, but also by her confusing refusal to marry and produce an heir and her overt encouragement of suitors. Rumors flew among the Virgin Queen's subjects, even after her death, about her unchaste behavior and the many illegitimate children supposedly resulting from it. Court records are filled with examples of people charged for uttering "lewd words" against the queen, and many moral and political tracts, especially those authored by Catholics, contained similar charges. Two examples cited by Levin are especially relevant to this discussion: Thomas Wendon's 1589 claim that "the Queen's Majesty was an arrant whore" (83) and Cardinal William Allen's attack on "her unspeakable and incredible variety of luste . . . [with] the whole worlde deriding our effeminate dastardie, that have suffered such a creature almost thirty years together to raigne both over our bodies and soules."[46] The combined sexual vituperation and anxious masculinity in these attacks clearly echoes the nervous attack on female sovereignty in *Carajicomedia*.

Because her very claim to the throne rested on issues of legitimacy of birth, and because the subsequent union of her proprietary kingdom with Fernando's became a cornerstone of her political program, Isabel did not uphold the gender ideology that served Elizabeth I so well.[47] On the contrary, as I discuss in more detail in chapter 4, one of her most pressing tasks was the restoration, in the royal family and in the kingdom, of heteronormative and patrilineal stability. Isabel had to marry and produce an heir, preferably a male heir.

In this context, Diego Fajardo's ambivalence toward the carnivalesque heroines of *Carajicomedia*—their excess of libidinal energy cures, but also causes, his lack—is revealed as more than a criticism of the hypocrisy of the clergy and nobles who profit sexually and financially from the traffic in women, more than a critique of the Queen's complicity in it, and certainly more than a carnivalesque affirmation of libertinism. It is a continuation of a discourse of impotence that Isabel and her supporters effectively deployed against her enemies Enrique IV and Juana I of Castile. But *Carajicomedia* hurls the accusations of impotence back against one of her staunch supporters. This comic misdirection of her own discursive weapons is a sarcastic attack on the queen's perceived masculinity, manifested in her anomalous status as female sovereign and in her unauthorized assumption of the virile, authoritarian role Mena fashioned for her father in *Laberinto de Fortuna*. But to understand the broader cultural implications of *Carajicomedia*'s redeployment of the discourse of impotence we must turn back to its model, written in 1444, but first printed in 1481, two years after the political unification of Castile and Aragon.

War and Wifely Chastity in *Laberinto de Fortuna*

A preoccupation with female chastity, especially within marriage, and a corresponding denunciation of adultery pervade *Laberinto*. The poem decries all nonsanctioned, nonheterosexual activity ("licentious fire of illicit love" [fuego vicioso de illíçito amor] [158; st. 109]) as a primary cause of the prevailing sociopolitical disorder, but the transgressive behavior of wives merits the most sustained attention. The massive scholarship on *Laberinto* has elided the fact that its patriotic nationalism is largely predicated on the policing of female sexuality.[48]

It is no accident that two out of the seven circles in Fortune's wheels, the Circle of the Moon and the Circle of Venus, are dedicated to the virtue of female chastity and the perceived threats to it. To the Circle of the Moon, presided over by the goddess Diana, Mena initially assigns classical examples of wifely virtue and devotion such as Lucretia, Artemisa, and Penelope. He then turns to the contemporary scene, singling out for elaborate praise two queen consorts and a noblewoman. They are Juan II's sister, María of Castile, who was married to Alfonso V of Aragon; María of Aragon, Juan's recently deceased first wife and mother of his heir, Enrique; and the legendary Castilian noblewoman, María Coronel.

Mena's praise for María of Castile is telling. He acknowledges her success as guardian of the realm while her husband was engaged in the conquest of Naples,[49] but he reserves his real enthusiasm for the rarer female virtue that she exemplifies: sexual self-control: "There were very few queens of Greece who maintained the purity of the marriage bed while their husbands fought the Trojan War, but this one is a faultless Hesione, in truth a new Penelope" (142; st. 78).[50]

The third exemplar of chastity in the Circle of the Moon is the most complex. María Coronel was a member of an aristocratic family that supported Enrique II (1369–79) in his struggle against his half brother King Pedro I (1350–69). By murdering Pedro, Enrique II, great-grandfather of Juan II, was able to seize the throne of Castile for the Trastamaran dynasty, an illegitimate branch of the Burgundian house that had ruled Castile since the twelfth century.[51]

As the legend goes, King Pedro had María's father, husband, and brother-in-law killed. María and her sister sought refuge in a convent, from where the latter was abducted by Pedro's men. To avoid a similar fate at the hands of the king, María disfigured herself by pouring boiling oil on her face. But the version of the Coronel legend that Mena recalls is more sexually explicit, and much more gruesome: "The most chaste maiden of the cruel hands, worthy crown of the Coronel family, who fought the fires [of her lust] with fire. Oh, citizens of Rome, if you had known of her when you ruled the universe, what glory, what fame, what prose, what poetry, what a vestal temple you would have made for her!" (143; st. 79).[52]

Mena's glossator Francisco Sánchez de las Brozas explains the fire imagery in these verses as follows in his 1582 edition of *Laberinto:* "while her husband was away, she was so greatly tempted by the flesh that she decided to die in order to preserve her marital fidelity, and she thrust a fiery brand into her vagina, which caused her death" (quoted in Vasvari, *Laberinto*, 118 n. 79).[53] Although Mena seems to elide the more politicized version of the legend, his audience would have readily recalled it. The sensationalized version he uses promotes a comparison between María as martyr for chastity and the violently imposed Trastamaran dynasty, and Lucretia, mentioned earlier, whose rape and suicide led to the overthrow of the tyrannical Tarquins and the institution of the Roman Republic.[54]

Mena's glorification of María's horrible self-mutilation doubly erases the stigma of biological and political illegitimacy that troubles the Trastamaran dynasty from its founding by Enrique II. First, it projects onto the legitimate monarch Pedro I the shameful lack of sexual self-control of his father Alfonso XI, whose many bastard children included the usurper Enrique. It then displaces the uncontrolled desire of Pedro I onto the female victim of that desire, grounding political usurpation in the need to contain the threat of woman's sexual "bonfires" [fogueras]. The iconization of María Coronel as chaste martyr for the Trastamaran cause thus functions as a powerful foundational myth that masks the kingly crime against the body politic and grounds the political order in a dangerous female sexuality.

The political motivation for the extensive treatment of female chastity becomes clear in the final stanzas of the Circle of the Moon. There Mena exhorts his king to "always keep a watch on civic life, so as to safeguard chastity" [la vida política siempre zelar, / por que pudicicia se pueda guardar] (144; st. 81), and he calls for the nobility to live chastely so that "despicable pleasures do not corrupt the people, to the detriment of many lineages" [En vilipendio de muchos linages, / viles deleites non viçien la gente] (145; st. 83). Although it is true that Mena then goes on to define *castidat* as the avoidance of any vice, not just lust, the preponderance of his examples deal with female adultery.[55] In this way, Mena elaborates for medieval Castile the close connection between monogamy, patrilinear inheritance, and monarchy that historian Georges Duby describes for medieval France. The latter's grounding of *imperium*, state rule, firmly in *dominium*, family rule, has recently been established for Castile as well in studies of the institution of the *mayorazgo*, an Iberian variant of primogeniture.[56]

In fact, laws governing adultery in medieval Castile were clearly prejudiced against wives, who were considered the repository of their husbands' honor and held responsible for maintaining the purity of bloodlines.[57] Since the notion of masculine honor so expressed has a deep materialist basis—namely, the peaceful and proper transfer of property—the fourteenth-century institution of primogeniture made a wife's adultery even more of a threat. Furthermore, as Susan Aronstein has discussed for Europe as a whole, the movement toward centralization and consolidation of power within the family unit that was expressed in patrilinear descent benefited both the church and the monarchy. That change, she writes, "both obscured and strengthened the woman's role in the generation of the family; while it effectively reduced her to the mere conduit through which one male passed on his name and his inheritance to another, it also produced an increased anxiety about chastity and potential betrayal. A man could not choose his heir, by law that right fell to the oldest born within his marriage. What if his wife, sold by her family and purchased by himself, claimed the right to traffic in herself?" (119).

Laberinto de Fortuna, the most important political poem of the Trastamaran dynasty, attributes the interruption of Castile's national mission and the disorder of the state to the weakening of feudal patriarchy owing to a loss of *pudicicia*, "a necessary virtue in women" [virtud nesçesaria de ser en la fembra] (172; st. 131). Mena reiterates these anxieties in the Circle of Venus. It complements the first circle in its praise of those who "in the fire of their youth" [en el fuego de su joventud] (154; st. 100) turn vice into virtue through the sacrament of marriage. But the third circle is more concerned with chastising negative examples, those whose sexual activities are seen as responsible for the "many lineages fallen into disgrace" [muchos linages caídos en mengua] (154; st. 100): the adulterers, fornicators, committers of incest, and, especially, sodomites. Here again, the majority of examples are feminine and classical: Clytemnestra, Pasiphaë, Scylla, and Myrrha.

Mena's preoccupation with sexual transgression is not confined to the appropriate circles of Diana and Venus, but obtrudes at other moments as well. In the Circle of Apollo, for example, after extolling the prudence of ancient philosophers, prophets, and astrologers, he condemns their negative counterparts, the necromancers and witches. Figured here is the infamous Medea, but also the less well known Licinia and Publicia, Roman adulteresses executed for poisoning their husbands. Their crime prompts the following apocalyptic view of female transgression: "There were Licinia and Publicia, giving their husbands fatal brews prepared with poisonous herbs, to the detriment of their lineage; for once noble chastity, a necessary virtue in women, is lost, such violence grows, such hatred is sown that they take their husbands for enemies" (172; st. 131).[58] Mena's outrage over the transgressive sexuality of these Roman matrons then takes a bizarre turn, in what María Rosa Lida calls a grotesque misapplication of the Sermon on the Mount (290). Christ's injunction not to let one's left hand know what one's right hand is doing when giving alms becomes an admonition to husbands to apply a swift and secret remedy should they even suspect their wives of sexual misdeeds: "seek the remedy before circumstances cause you pain; grave times require grave measures; forewarned is forearmed" (173; st. 132).[59] The reader is left to guess what kind of remedy is meant.

The "comparison" [comparación] that immediately follows these ominous verses introduces a central metaphor of *Laberinto*, the association of Fortune and the unpredictability of the seas. This comparison will be developed more fully in the climactic Count of Niebla episode that so stimulated the sarcastic wit of the author of *Carajicomedia*. Here Mena uses it to underscore the fragility of husbands' control over their wives and therefore over their heirs and property. He goes so far as to advise the fainthearted against embarking on the perilous waters of matrimony altogether: "For whoever fears the sea's fury and dreads its storms, the best protection is not to venture out on it, to give up the desire to sail" (173; st. 133).[60] Those who do venture onto the sea of matrimony must be wary and, "At the first sign of a bad storm, should seek a safe harbor" [a la primera señal de fortuna / deve los puertos seguros tomar] (173; st. 133). On one level, *fortuna* in these lines is simply an Italianism for "storm"; on another it is a foreshadowing of the two most dramatic episodes of *Laberinto*, the struggles between the goddess Fortuna and two great Castilian heroes, the doomed Count of Niebla and the triumphant Alvaro de Luna.

There has been much critical debate about which of the two dominant medieval conceptions of fortune informs *Laberinto*, whether the classical view of Fortuna as an independent and capricious goddess, or the Christianized view whereby she is the beneficent servant of Providence.[61] The scholarly consensus is that although Mena's view is fluctuating and inconsistent, the negative valorization of fortune prevails in his work.[62] The concept of fortune as unpredictable and treacherous is reinforced in the most memorable episode of *Laberinto*, the drowning death of the Count of Niebla at the disastrous assault on Muslim-held Gibraltar. The brave but arrogant count is disdainful of the many omens that presage disaster for the siege he is about to undertake. He harangues his men to ignore the signs: "let Fortune know from us that we compel her; she does not compel us" [presuma de vos e de mí la Fortuna, / non que nos fuerça, mas que la forçamos] (195; st. 173). But Niebla's courage is useless against fortune; he and his men die "as Fortune had already determined" [Segund la Fortuna lo ya desponía] (195; st. 174). There is, however, one character in *Laberinto* who is more than a match for Fortuna's treacherous power, and that is Alvaro de Luna, Constable of Castile, Juan II's powerful favorite.

The rapid rise to power and later abrupt fall from favor and execution (1453) of Luna became synonymous in the fifteenth century with the unstable and ineluctable influence of fortune on the affairs of men. In fact, a strong argument has been made for *Laberinto* as pro-Luna propaganda.[63] Gregory Hutcheson closely examines the central role played by Luna in the poem, as in Castilian politics of the mid-fifteenth-century, when he became "an icon either of patriotism or unbounded ambition" ("Cracks in the Labyrinth," 44). In order to invoke him fully as an exemplum of the former, Mena devotes the seventh and final Circle of Saturn exclusively to this paragon of good government.

Hutcheson suggests that the concatenation of Luna the man and Luna the planet joins the seventh Circle of Saturn to the first Circle of the Moon, making Luna's charismatic persona metaphorically and structurally encompass the entire work. Here I want to focus on Luna's role in subduing unruly Fortuna; in this ability he surpasses the Count of Niebla and even Juan II (Hutcheson, "Cracks in the Labyrinth," 46). He alone, admires Providencia, can "break" fortune, represented as a wild horse: "He rides astride Fortune and tames her neck with tight reins" [Este cavalga sobre la Fortuna / y doma su cuello con ásperas riendas] (222; st. 235). Although Hutcheson does not explore the gender implications of the [L]unar presence in *Laberinto*, his suggestion that the constable's role goes beyond the political to approximate romance is provocative. Providence not only favors Luna, she falls in love with his virile power. Only Luna is able to conquer the two allegorical embodiments of the feminine in *Laberinto*, unruly Fortuna and more malleable Providencia, and prove his manliness in the process. In a sense, his masterful horsemanship resolves the entire debate about the nature of fortune that Mena himself cannot. Before our eyes, and those of Providence and Juan II, Luna tames the wild mare of fortune and makes her fit for mounting and breeding.

The portrayal of the unruly feminine Fortuna, her multivalent association with uncontrollable natural (stormy seas, wild horses) and social forces (the rebellious, greedy aristocracy), and her subjection by Luna, paragon of virility, champion of monarchy, illustrates the repressive gender ideology that subtends Mena's political message. His call to national unity through armed victory over enemies both external and internal is inseparable from his call to the king, in his capacity as lawmaker, to control the threat of the feminine to the status quo of power and property: "Lest the excessive clemency and too lenient laws of your reign allow the evils of new Medeas and Publicias" (174; st. 135).[64] The family being the microcosm of the state, unfaithful wives are as much a danger to it as disorderly nobles. It is a connection that had already been drawn in the thirteenth-century comprehensive legal code, *Siete partidas* (Seven sections). Commissioned by the politically ambitious Alfonso X, "the Learned," it stressed the need for the king to "love, honor, and watch over his wife" [amar, honrar y guardar a su mujer] (Part II, Title VI, Law III) and for the common people to do the same with their women: "because the king would not be protected if they did not protect their wives" [porque non podrie el rey seer guardado, si a ellas non guardasen] (Part II, Title XIV, Law II).

Obviously, the important work of ensuring compliance with a patrilineal order could never be entrusted to the very gender that threatens it. The two stanzas of the Circle of the Moon that are dedicated to Juan II's recently deceased wife, María, make it very clear that Mena finds gynecocracy simply inconceivable. María possesses so many virtues—prudence, justice, honesty—that "If her gender were transformed, as we read happened to Cenis, I believe that she would with her sense of justice make many people tame their vices" (141; st. 76).[65] The allusion to Ovid's tale of Neptune's transformation of Cenis into a man shows that for Mena the admirable María was excluded from sovereignty solely because of her gender.

Circumstances made it possible for Isabel, thirty years after the composition of *Laberinto*, to achieve what her father's adviser found inconceivable, to rule Castile in her own right. The influence of Mena's poem on Isabel's moral and political formation is a topos of Spanish literary history. *Laberinto* was much read throughout the reign of the Catholic Monarchs; four editions of the work appeared in the last two decades of the fifteenth century.[66] Menéndez y Pelayo saw Isabel's reign as the fulfillment of Mena's utopic vision: "[Mena] placed his dreams, the dreams of a poet to be sure, in the weak and pusillanimous Juan II; but even as he did so he was merely anticipating prophetically the passage of time, expecting from the father what the daughter would accomplish" (*Antología de poetas líricos,* quoted in Clarke, 9).[67] In her study of *Laberinto* as classic epic, Dorothy Clotelle Clarke romantically concurs: "Isabel la

Católica could hardly have failed to know well and from her earliest years the most important poem of her century.... She could hardly have failed to be impressed by the poet's vision of an expanded and unified Spain, a vision that may have been instrumental in moving her to the generosity and the courage necessary for the national expansion that took place under her reign" (9).

The biting humor of *Carajicomedia* is testimony to just how well Isabel internalized the gender ideology contained in *Laberinto*. But it is necessary to reiterate at this point that *Carajicomedia*'s transgression of *Laberinto* is profoundly contradictory. It simultaneously mocks the masculinist, authoritarian, repressive values that Mena urged on a weak King Juan and criticizes the dangerous appropriation of those same values by the strong Queen Isabel, both in her anomalous status as female sovereign and in her inappropriate virile self-fashioning. Isabel's sovereign power is thoroughly discredited by its association with Diego Fajardo's ambivalent relationship with the hordes of insatiable whores whom historically he controlled, but who in this phobic fantasy control him. It is fitting, then, that in *Carajicomedia,* unlike in its intertext, no virile Luna figure appears to recuperate the defeat of Niebla by subjugating his enemy, the unpredictable feminine Fortuna. The author of the parody chooses instead to end his poem with a travesty of the tragic Niebla episode discussed earlier. Here Fortuna, transformed into Luxuria, and firmly on the side of the battalion of *coños* who "satisfy their hunger with penises" [hartan su hambre con miembros agenos]; oversees the final vanquishing of Fajardo and his phallic forces examined earlier (228).[68]

But Fajardo's defeat by the phallic feminine at the end of *Carajicomedia* is mild compared to what happens to him earlier at the hands of "an old bawd, La Buyça," a travesty of Mena's Providencia. It is the Celestinesque La Buyça who handily restores Fajardo's erection. The protagonist is so excited by his cure and by his mentor's promise to restore his youthful vigor that he propositions the hag then and there. Distinctly unimpressed, La Buyça responds "in a voice that sounds like Satilario's: 'What can you do, Fajardo, with those balls as low-hanging as a censer?'" (166).[69] In the gloss to this stanza, the author states only that Santilario was "a cowboy, called Satilario because he was a great jumper" [un rústico vaquero, llamado Satilario por ser gran saltador] (166).

The character of Santilario is a burlesque version of Saint Hilarion, the profoundly ascetic fourth-century hermit whose eremitical trials often involved temptations by the devil.⁷⁰ *Carajicomedia*'s bawdy version of the hagiographic legend introduces the saint in the act of masturbation. A wandering devil happens upon the scene and decides to take advantage of the hermit's reverie to assault him and drag him off to hell. But the clever rustic foils the devil's plan, as the gloss explains:

> he leaped upon the sinful cowboy... and landing feet first on his belly, they slipped and he went sliding down until Satilario's member stuck up his ass.... When Satilario felt this, he tightened up and held on, yelling for his dogs. Seeing this, the devil... began to scream, yelling: "Satilario, let me go!" And he responded fiercely: "Never, unless my prick breaks off." And he held him like that until he came/flooded him, then he let go and the dogs were already approaching when the sore-assed devil began to flee and the dogs ran after him, until they locked him up in hell, where the wretch is mending his ass to this day, swearing that he'll never leave again. (167)⁷¹

The hilarity of this saintly act of buggery derives from Santilario's penetrative power, placed in the service of God. Varo calls it "a paean, free as nature, to the pleasure of loving ephebes, at least in the active role" [un encomio, libre como la naturaleza, al placer del amor a los efebos, al menos en su papel activo] (68). In the context of my discussion here, however, the celebration of the priapic Santilario is quite a bit more ambivalent than Varo allows. In the first place, we must keep in mind Santilario's association with the stock dramatic character of the rustic in early Castilian theater.⁷² For the aristocratic audience of the plays of Juan del Encina, Lucas Fernández, and Bartolomé Torres Naharro, the *rústico* or "pastor bobo" [dumb shepherd] was a favorite butt of jokes about his laziness, ignorance, gluttony, and lustfulness. As such he is an excellent example of the kind of displaced abjection of carnival discussed earlier. More important, however, Santilario's devil-taming erection is here assigned not to Fajardo, in a kind of senile wish-fulfilling fantasy, but to La Buyça, the disgusting hag who represents Providence. That identification is reinforced at the end of the prose gloss: "the author of this is the evil hag, who seems fiercer to folks than Santilario is to the devil" [Autora d'esto es la mala vieja, que más feroz parece a las gentes que Satilario al triste diablo] (167). The active role in this homosexual couple perversely belongs to the transsexualized whore La Buyça.

The cross-gendered and transgressive sexual role assigned to Fajardo's providential guide La Buyça renders the threatening sexual power of the prostitute more sinister by underscoring its instability (the epithet *diabólica* readily brings to mind the devil's well-known shape-shifting abilities). Like Celestina, on whom she is explicitly based, this "mother" is portrayed as sexually ambiguous; she is a phallic mother with a strap-on who both ministers to Fajardo and degrades him. Her sexual authority is thus both cause and cure of the Isabelline hero's impotence. The merging of wanton whore and sodomizing saint in the phobic figure of La Buyça completes Fajardo's abjection by implicitly casting him in one of the medieval period's most stigmatized sexual role: that of the passive partner in the sodomitical act.[73] As we shall see in chapter 3, accusations of sodomy played a major role in the sexual propaganda in Isabel's campaign to discredit her brother Enrique IV. But in *Carajicomedia*, through the hag La Buyça, those insults also end up being turned against the queen who many believed Providence had sent to repair Spain's broken body.

The same kind of sarcasm explains the editorial fiction that *Carajicomedia* is actually a translation and annotation of "a speculative work... composed by the Reverend Father Bugeo Montesino" [una especulativa obra... compuesta por el Reverendo Padre Fray Bugeo Montesino] (147). The reference would have been transparent to contemporary readers: the work is attributed to none other than the Franciscan friar Ambrosio Montesino, admired author of religious verse and one of Isabel's confessors and close advisers.[74] His travestied Christian name, Bugeo, holds clear sodomitical references, most probably the Italian "to bugger" [bugerare], but also *buxarra* and *bujarrón*.[75] The implication is clear: the pious friar is treated in much the same way by his queen as the queen's loyal servant Fajardo is treated by La Buyça/Santilario.

Carajicomedia's transcoding of Fortuna/Providencia as Luxuria/La Buyça can be placed in a cultural and political context broader than late-medieval Castile. In her provocative *Fortune Is a Woman: Gender and Politics in the Thought of Niccolò Machiavelli*, Hannah Pitkin studies Machiavelli's treatment of fortune as a powerful, mysterious, and feminine threat to masculine personal and political autonomy.[76] His *Discourses* contains the following characteristic warning: "Women have caused much destruction, have done great harm to those who govern cities, and have occasioned many divisions in them.... I say, then, that absolute princes and governors of republics are to take no small account of this matter" (3:26; quoted in Pitkin, 115). For Machiavelli, as for Mena and his parodist, women are both cause and sign of the ruler's political impotence.

We have seen how Mena urged Juan II to guard female *pudiçiçia* and, in particular, the fidelity of wives, in order to prevent political catastrophe.[77] Machiavelli's fear of and contempt for women has two quite different targets. One is the danger of seductive young women and the other is the more intentionally hostile power of older women. Older women, who are neither sexually attractive nor seductive, nevertheless represent the greater political danger. This is because they can be as ambitious as men, and because they are adept at using manipulation and deceit to block male aspirations, thereby fostering rivalry and weakening patriarchal bonds. As Pitkin notes: "It is almost as if a vengeful older woman *becomes* fortune, with superhuman power over the outcome of events in the world of men" (120).[78]

The particular threat of the older woman adds another dimension to *Carajicomedia*'s use of the prostitute La Buyça to satirize Isabelline power, because the earliest date for the poem's composition is 1499, when Isabel was almost fifty. The old whore who travesties Mena's benign Providencia traffics in herself, engages in both heterosexual and sodomitical acts with everyone from royal preachers to brave soldiers to the devil himself, and runs a brothel that is as large as Spain itself. It may be true that the satire of *Carajicomedia* is partially motivated, as Márquez Villanueva affirms, by its author's moral outrage at the obscenity of a "Catholic" Queen institutionalizing prostitution and then using it to repay her aristocratic supporters for services rendered (*Orígenes*, 152). But confronting this pornographic political text with its serious intertext shows that its satire ultimately springs from more deep-seated anxieties. The hapless whores of Málaga were, for the historical Diego Fajardo, lucrative if troublesome objects of sexual exchange. Their engulfing fictionalized counterparts in *Carajicomedia* easily dominate and humiliate the mock-heroic Fajardo. They stage "the fear of a feminine symbolic order, one where the distinctions between political economy and sexual economy, subject of exchange and object of exchange, masculinity and femininity are blurred" (Schiesari, 178).[79] In fifteenth-century Spain, that symbolic order is all the more fearsome for being imposed and maintained by the absolute power of a female sovereign. *Carajicomedia*'s caustic parody of the most important political poem of the Spanish Middle Ages vividly instantiates the misogynist relationship between sex, power, and politics that pervaded Trastamaran foundational myths.

In 1468, twenty-four years after the composition of *Laberinto*, when Isabel was seventeen, the death of her brother Alfonso raised the possibility that she would wear the crown of Castile. At that time the gender ideology expressed by Mena was urgently redirected to contain the threat of a female's sovereign power years before it became a reality (Isabel acceeded to the throne in 1474). Those containment strategies and the young queen's subtle manipulation of them to affirm her power are the subject of the next chapter.

CHAPTER TWO
Fashioning Isabel's Sovereignty

The Catholic Queen criticized Hernando del Pulgar, her chronicler, because in recounting in his History a certain deed performed by the King her husband, he didn't attribute it to both of them, because they had done it together, equally. Shortly thereafter, the Queen gave birth... and Hernando del Pulgar wrote: on such and such a day and such and such an hour, their Majesties gave birth.[1]

Culpó la Reyna Católica a Hernando del Pulgar, su cronista, de que refiriendo en su Historia cierta acción del Rey su marido, no la puso en nombre de ambos, por haberla executado igualamente entre los dos. Parió poco después la Reyna... y escribió Hernando del Pulgar: en tal día y a tal hora parieron sus Magestades.
—Francisco Asensio, *Floresta española*

Isabel was only two years old in 1453, when Constantinople's fall to the Turks stirred up fears throughout Christendom. In Iberia those fears produced a new sense of urgency about the completion of the Reconquest. But another event of that year had much more of an impact on the infanta's future: the birth of her brother Alfonso, who supplanted his older sister as second in line for the throne after their half brother Enrique. A year later Juan II died; his will provided financially for both the children of his second marriage, but it greatly favored Alfonso. Gender had everything to do with the unequal distribution: "it is clear that the son's economic situation was more favorable than the daughter's. Without going so far as to think that their father deliberately established a discriminatory situation, it confirms Isabel's inferior position" (Azcona, 18).[2] Sometime near Isabel's tenth birthday, Enrique IV, worried that his half siblings might be taken hostage by the grandees plotting against him, ordered Isabel and Alfonso taken from the shelter of their mother's household and brought to court to be watched over by Enrique and his new queen, Juana of Portugal.

What kind of education did Isabel receive as a child first in Arévalo and later in the royal court? We must assume that it was the typical education for aristocratic girls, but what subjects she was taught or what books she studied can only be a matter of conjecture.[3] We know that the infanta's schooling was overseen first by Lope de Barrientos, Bishop of Cuenca, and by Gonçalo Chacón, erstwhile chamberlain of Alvaro de Luna. No doubt the former ensured that her eduaction was firmly grounded in religious instruction. The first secular work that we can be fairly certain she read is a brief didactic treatise titled *Jardín de nobles doncellas*. Sometime between the summer of 1468 and the fall of 1469, the learned Agustinian friar Martín de Córdoba addressed the work to the adolescent Princess Isabel.[4] It is a work explicitly aimed at forming Isabel's attitudes and behaviors as future queen.

Jardín de nobles doncellas: Marriage Manual for a Princess

In the second half of 1468 Isabel was living through what are arguably the most decisive months of her life. July brought the sudden death of her beloved brother Alfonso, who, although younger, had priority in the line of succession. This unexpected event made inevitable the advent of a woman to the throne of Castile. In September, the likelihood that the woman would be Isabel increased significantly when a band of nobles rebelling against Enrique's authority apparently forced him to sign an agreement at Toros de Guisando that denied his daughter Juana's hereditary rights and named Isabel his legitimate heir. Fray Martín wrote his text with this fact firmly in mind. During those same crucial months, unbeknownst to Enrique and in violation of one of the clauses of the Toros de Guisando pact, Isabel and her advisers were negotiating her marriage to Fernando, heir to the throne of Aragon.[5] Those delicate negotiations came to fruition in January 1469 with Fernando's signing of the famous *capitulaciones matrimoniales,* a nuptial agreement drawn up by Isabel. The actual wedding ceremony took place in secrecy in October of that year.

It is clear that at such a delicate personal and political crossroads, the sheltered princess would have felt herself in need of sound counsel and would have read with urgent interest the doctrine that a respected theologian like Martín de Córdoba proffered.[6] The half dozen works of this type that appear on the inventory of her library provide corroborating evidence of her appreciation for the genre of *speculum principis* (Goldberg, *Jardín*, 45). Moreover, in the decade of the 1480s she paid for the printing of at least two such works. I shall have more to say in this chapter about one of these, a poem written by the powerful aristocrat and intimate of her court, Gómez Manrique. The other remains unidentified except by title, but its luxurious binding indicates a high level of esteem on the part of the Queen (Azcona, 311).

Many of the scholars who have studied *Jardín de nobles doncellas* have deemed it a kind of profeminist mirror of princes. One of its two modern editors, Fernando Rubio Alvarez, assigns it a more specific political goal: the defense of Isabel's right to rule in Castile against the longstanding opposition to female sovereignty (xxx). Harriet Goldberg agrees that the work is profeminist, but questions its impact in the debate because Isabel's rival for the Castilian crown was not a man. At the time *Jardín* was written, there were in fact only two female pretenders to the throne, Isabel and her niece Juana de Portugal, daughter of Enrique IV (87–88). Goldberg also calls into question the closeness to Isabel that Martín de Córdoba seems to affirm in the prologue, and, consequently, the personal impact the treatise would have had on the infanta who only six years later would become queen of Castile (36–39).

For my purposes, however, the importance of *Jardín* does not depend on proving that it was on Isabel's bedside table, nor that she had a personal relationship with its author.[7] Rather, its significance lies in what it reveals about the gender ideology dominant at the precise historical moment that Isabel began to envision her future as both queen of Castile and wife of Fernando, King of Sicily and heir to the kingdom of Aragon. That ideology would inevitably shape her attitude and that of her subjects toward her public and private roles as well as toward the power she would share as married queen.

The two main critical assumptions about *Jardín*—that it is profeminist and that its immediate goal is the defense of female sovereignty—are questionable. To begin with, regarding the profeminism of *Jardín*, we must keep in mind Valerie Wayne's warning about the work of Juan

Luis Vives and other supposedly profeminist Christian humanists. Even the most ardent medieval and Renaissance defenders of women assume women's inherent weakness and irrationality just as the misogynistic writers do. Consequently, the modern concept of feminism is inapplicable to the supporters of women in the pan-European debate. Vives's *De Institutione Foeminae Christianae* (The instruction of a Christian woman) (1523; Spanish translation 1528) is a particularly apposite example here, because it was commissioned by Isabel's daughter, Catherine of Aragon, when she was queen of England, for the instruction of her daughter. Of this very influential work Wayne writes: "Renaissance humanists did advocate education for women who were apt for learning and in a position to be tutored, but the aims in providing instruction for those women usually differed from the aims for men. Vives makes his own purposes plain in his preface: 'As for a woman hath no charge to se to but her honestie and chastyte. Wherefore whan she is enfurmed of that she is sufficiently appoynted'" (16).[8]

Rina Walthaus and Elizabeth Lehfeldt have argued that *Jardín* is a hybrid work that combines elements of a mirror of princes and of a conduct book, and that its defense of women's worth is ambivalent. Catherine Soriano considers the author's profeminism entirely superficial: "The truth is that he is not interested in claiming the rights of women in general, but rather in upholding the rights of Isabel, a very special woman, to the throne of Castile. His first step toward this end is to demonstrate that women are able to rule" (1462).[9] In her biography of Isabel, Peggy Liss goes furthest in overturning the traditional view of *Jardín* as profeminist and politically supportive of Isabel's ruling in her own right. She maintains that the treatise is in reality an extensive Augustinian essay justifying the subordination of women, as upheld in Genesis (69–70).[10]

My more extensive analysis of *Jardín* will confirm Liss's view that "even if she should become queen, the author did not expect the queen to be the one who ruled" (70). In order to ensure Isabel's submissiveness, Martín de Córdoba strives to inculcate in the princess a sense of her physical and intellectual weakness. That weakness is naturalized in two ways: by making it the *result* of the manner of Woman's creation and the *cause* of humankind's fall. Because of her inherent frailty, a woman—and especially a woman of noble birth—must submit to her husband, just as a child submits to his father and a subject to his (male) monarch.

The cleric does not avoid the issue of women's suitability for rule, about which Castilian opinion was strongly divided. On the contrary, he forcefully confronts the contemporary dispute on the matter in his preface: "Some people, My Lady, less well informed and perhaps ignorant of the natural and moral causes, and not having pored over the old chronicles, take it badly when a kingdom or other state comes under the rule of a woman. But, as I will explain below, I disagree since, from the beginning of the world to the present, we see that God always gave woman responsibility for humanity's salvation, so that life would emerge from death" (136).[11]

The reasoning is complex, conflating historical precedent and theological justification. Historically, there was no legal impediment in Castile (as there was in Aragon) to women ruling or to the transmission of the right to rule to their heirs. The custom of cognatic succession became codified as law in the thirteenth-century code *Siete Partidas* (Part II, Title XV, Law II).[12] In practice, however, female rights of succession and inheritance were always subordinated to those of the male, so that a woman could only succeed if there were no male heir, as was the case of Urraca (1109–26). A similar case was that of Berenguela, daughter of Alfonso VIII, who inherited the throne in 1217 but was pressured to yield her rights to her son, Fernando III (1217–52) (O'Callaghan, 335, 432). Of more immediate relevance to this discussion is the order of succession established in Juan II's will. It placed the younger child Alfonso ahead of his older sister Isabel in the line of succession. Azcona underscores the ideological significance of these terms: "One does not detect the slightest hesitation in putting Alfonso's male succession before Isabel's female succession, despite the fact that the princess was born first. This detail must be kept in mind in order to appreciate not only the Castilian mind-set, but also the paternal and legal provisions" (15).[13]

Theologically, Fray Martín's defense hinges on the paradox—figured in the Ave/Eva palindrome dear to medieval theological writing—that Woman functions both as cause and cure of humanity's sinfulness. She is at once the carnal and lustful being directly responsible for the fall and the spiritual, virginal vessel that makes possible humankind's redemption. Sacrilegious comparison of Isabel to the Virgin is a common feature of Isabelline literature. These lines in *Jardín* may well constitute its earliest literary usage.[14] And, as I discuss in greater detail in chapter 4, because the restorative role so enthusiastically assigned to Isabel by her writing subjects is one extreme of a binary opposition, it necessarily depends on and implies its other extreme, the original destructive role played by Eve. Surprisingly enough for a supposedly apologetic work, it becomes apparent very soon that Fray Martín is more concerned with the first term of the Eva/Ave opposition. It is the legacy of that ignoble *donzella* Eve, that is, the weakness, irrationality, and sinfulness innate in all females because of the manner of Eve's creation, that preoccupies the author as he addresses the woman who was most likely to become queen.

As a member of the Augustinian order and a respected professor of theology at the universities of Salamanca and Toulouse, Fray Martín is eager to display the relevant scholastic and exegetical knowledge, and, in particular, his familiarity with Saint Augustine's series of commentaries on the Book of Genesis. Augustine made an important contribution to the medieval theological debate on sin and salvation. He advocated male domination of women as a logical extension of the necessary triumph of the mind over the body. A fundamental aspect of the Augustinian position is the construction of woman as mindless carnality, both corruptible (by the devil) and corrupting (of Adam).[15] Fray Martín rehearses many of the most common Augustinian arguments on Eve's responsibility for the fall, most of them centered on the problem of her sexuality. These include the idea that procreation in the Garden of Eden would have occurred without lust and under the control of the will ("they could beget offspring without carnal passion, rather by that very power of the will" [bien podían engendrar fijos sin ardor de carnalidad, mas por aquel mismo imperio de voluntad] [184]); that if Adam and Eve had not sinned, all women would have remained virgins even after having intercourse ("Saint Augustine says... that she will remain whole and uncorrupted, that is to say, virginal" [Sant Agustín dize... que quedará sin corrupción de su integridad, que quiere dezir virginidad] [182]); and that after the fall, concupiscence became a permanent flaw in the human soul ("for after the fall, men and women lie together with passion, filth, and shame" [ca despues del peccado varón & muger se mezclan con ardor & suziedad & vergüença] [182]).

As Patricia Parker explains in her analysis of the biblical story of creation in Genesis, Adam and Eve's story follows a logic in which "priority in the temporal sequence has hierarchical superiority as its con-sequence or result" ("Coming Second," 179). She ties its misogynist "sequential or linear logic" to a "logic of reversal, whereby a threatening primacy is converted into second place" (229), the result of man's fear of being overcome, feminized, by a powerful, dominant, or self-sufficient woman.[16] Given the strength of Fray Martín's clerical misogyny, and the evidence of masculine anxiety that we have seen in both *Laberinto de Fortuna* and *Carajicomedia,* Parker's theory sheds useful light on *Jardín*'s preoccupation with "woman's place."

Nearly a third of *Jardín* is devoted to the specific conditions of Eve's creation, the why, how, where, and of what matter she was formed. The cleric considers such problems as the number of ribs Adam had, which of these God used to create Eve, and why the latter was formed in Paradise and Adam was not. His answers to these thorny questions invariably apply the biological-Aristotelian or theological-Augustinian conception of woman as secondary, supplementary, and therefore inferior to man, who is made in God's image. For example, in explaining why God created woman out of man, "since he could have created them at the same time, as he did with the angels, and not one from the other" [que pudiera criarlos en vno, como crió a todos los ángeles & no vno de otro], the cleric gives as one reason "because God wanted the man to be the source of all mankind just as He was the prime mover of all things" [porque Dios quiso que assí como El hera vn principio effectiuo de todas las cosas, assí el hombre fuese principio de todos los hombres] (145). Similarly, in a long disquisition on Adam's rib as woman's prime material, Fray Martín dwells on the physical and moral debility of woman. He attributes those traits to the flexibility and softness of the rib, following Saint Isidore's imaginative etymological identification of *muelle* ("soft") with *mulier:* "since the soul conforms to the constitution of the body, just as the female body is weak and soft, so is her soul malleable in its desires and will" (153).[17] He also ties her materiality to her instrumentality. Satan the hunter used her to trap his primary prey, Adam: "because God knew that the wicked and cruel hunter Satan would make of woman a snare to deceive man, he made her out of a rib, which hunters use to ensnare birds" (154).[18]

Almost all of the advice that Fray Martín offers Isabel pertains to the need to control and correct the vices to which women are naturally inclined. Although in Part II he concedes, again following Aristotle, that women possess a few good qualities, namely, *vergüença, piedad,* and *obsequiosidad* (modesty, piety, and compassion), he values these traits for their prophylactic efficacy, that is, as restraints on an innately weak feminine nature. Thus, for example, he explains that God made women modest because "if shame does not keep them from doing evil and cause them to do good, they will dash headlong into all sorts of evil like an unbridled animal and a horse without spurs, and they will flee from all virtue" (195).[19]

What is most striking, however, is that the author does not exempt his royal addressee from this misogynistic formulation, not even by employing the topos of the virile woman, which was another favorite of Isabelline writers and which other authors to be examined in this chapter utilize. Martín de Córdoba repeatedly interpellates Isabel as daughter of Eve. He deems her exceptional only in the exemplary function that is hers because of her status as a "noble lady" [grande señora], a status that will increase significantly if she accedes to the throne. Thus, for example, in warning women to restrain their natural loquacity, he writes: "And if this is true of other women, how much more so in noble ladies, whose words resound throughout their land and should therefore be few and serious" (156–57).[20]

There is one notable exception to this rule, a commentary on the verse from Ecclesiastes: "The evil done by men is better than the good done by women" [Mejor es la maldad del varón, quel bien hecho de la muger]. Seeking perhaps to soften the ferocious misogyny of the pronouncement, Martín interprets it "mysteriously and figuratively, that is, calling whoever is strong and firm in deed a man and whoever is weak and fragile, a woman."[21] He thus exhorts Isabel that "even though you are a woman by nature, you must endeavor to be a man in virtue" [avn que es henbra por naturaleza, trabaje por ser varón en virtud] (282). In this, one of the few gaps in the author's misogynistic discourse, he contradicts his own essentialist formulation of gender ("por naturaleza") and betrays an awareness of its social construction ("trabaje por ser").

Given the gender ideology evident in *Jardín,* Martín's attitude toward female sovereignty can only be deeply ambivalent. On the few occasions when he explicitly affirms Isabel's right to the crown, that ambivalence is expressed in the implied contrast he draws between the princess's legitimate hereditary claim to the throne and her natural unsuitability to rule. Two examples will serve to illustrate the cleric's equivocation. The first occurs in the prologue, when he touts the educational value of his work: "Let your lively intelligence consider and delight in these reasons and those I will discuss later, as in a garden of maidens, so that, since the natural line of succession has granted you sovereignty, the latter will not suffer for a lack of moral wisdom, and instead your proven wisdom will make you fit to rule, just as your royal, firstborn blood did" (140).[22] Something similar occurs toward the end of the treatise, when the author uses the example of Saint Cecilia to exalt chastity in women: "Saint Cecilia was more illustrious because she was a virgin than because she was the daughter of a king. Being a king's daughter is an ascribed virtue, for it comes from one's parents; being a virgin and chaste is inherent, for it is due to one's own virtue" (269–70).[23] In these two instances, one "natural" trait, the princess's royal blood, which indisputably qualifies her for rule, is canceled out by another that disqualifies her, her gender. Ironically, by shifting the measure of virtue and fitness for rule from blood to behavior, Fray Martín undermines the very foundation of Isabel's claim to the throne: her untainted Trastamaran blood.[24]

What can lead the princess out of this impasse and grant her the wisdom [sabiduría] necessary to rule? Fray Martín's message is clear: her submission to his words of wisdom and his list of exemplary, because exceptional, *doncellas*. This is the underlying meaning of the foundational myth the friar relates in the prologue to the third and culminating section of his treatise, which he hopes "moves the lady to love knowledge by the example of many maidens" [promueue la señora a amar sabiduría por exemplo de muchas donzellas] (239).

No sooner has he begun his list of wise ancient women, citing Isis, Carmentis, and Minerva, than he pauses for a "marvelous question" [quistión marauillosa]. Why is it, he asks, "given that in ancient times women invented so many crafts and arts, especially literature... that in our century women do not dedicate themselves to the liberal arts and other sciences, rather it seems that they are prohibited from doing so?" (243).[25] To explain the paradox, Fray Martín recounts Varro's tale of how the city of Athens came by its name. After the city was constructed, an olive tree appeared at one place and a fountain of water at another. When Apollo was consulted on the meaning of the apparitions, he responded that the olive tree symbolized Minerva and the water Neptune, and he directed the inhabitants of the new city to name it in honor of one or the other god. When the citizens were called to the vote—"the men as well as the women, since in those places it was customary for women to participate in public councils" (244)[26]—the men all voted for Neptune and the women for Minerva. Minerva emerged the winner because the women outnumbered the men by a narrow margin of one. The outcome displeased Neptune, who proceeded to flood the city and its surrounding lands. In order to placate the god's anger, the Athenians imposed three punishments on their women: thereafter, they would not participate in the city council, they would no longer be called Athenians, and their sons would not take their names.[27] It is owing to the first penalty in particular that women are now barred from study, as the author explains: "Since they are not to give counsel/participate in council, they do not need the education required for that activity, for councillors must be versed in moral and speculative philosophy, otherwise they would be unable to advise well" (244).[28]

This gendered foundational tale bars women from civic roles and therefore education, denies them citizenship, and eradicates matrilinearity. It is a telling choice for the section of *Jardín* that claims to want to inspire the future queen to acquire the knowledge that will make her fit to rule. The evocation of the egalitarian society that prevailed in Athens before its official foundation, and of the male minority's legitimate overthrow of that society functions as an anxious cautionary tale, a warning about the precarious nature of the gynarchy that the author knows will inevitably be instituted in Castile. It must be said that on this occasion, as frequently throughout *Jardín*, Fray Martín softens the prohibitions authorized by classical precedent. He assures the princess that the three punishments apply "to lowborn and plebeian women, but not to noble ladies like our lady, the Princess; you should therefore set aside several hours a day in which to study and listen to such things as are appropriate to the governing of the kingdom" (244).[29] But it is also true that the remaining nine chapters in the third part of *Jardín* say no more about the learning that is necessary for wise rule. They center instead on chastity and marital obedience, two of the three main pillars in the medieval construction of femininity.[30]

Given the anxiety that gynocracy evidently evokes in Fray Martín, how does he frame his justification of Isabel's succession? The answer lies in the discussion of chastity, a virtue examined in its three descending degrees: virginity, widowhood, and marriage.[31] Saint Jerome is the cleric's primary *auctoritas* on this matter: "The glory and triumph and fame of women is chastity and modesty" [La gloria & triunfo & fama de las mugeres es castidad & pudiçiçia] (286). But even as he praises chastity, he evinces the usual skepticism about women's ability to uphold this essential virtue, comparing the chaste woman to the phoenix, "for in all the world there is only one" [que en todo el mundo no se halla sino vna] (287). Here again, in the near-impossible task of restraining woman's natural concupiscence and carnality, Fray Martín holds the princess to a higher standard: "And if this is necessary for all maidens, it is much more so for princesses who expect to marry kings and princes, whose first inquiry about a future wife is whether she is modest and virtuous and appropriately ashamed" (197).[32] Isabel's role model in this difficult endeavor is the Virgin. They are alike in three ways, the author explains: because the two are *donzellas*, because they are both of royal birth, and because each "expects to be a queen" [espera de ser reina] (164). These lines reveal the hidden ideological agenda of Martín's work: to fashion Isabel not as future queen regnant, but rather as future queen consort. That is to say, no doubt aware that his addressee was preparing herself for matrimony, he preaches to her as a royal perfect wife.[33]

The same goal subtends the theory of monarchy that Fray Martín presents for the princess's edification. Derived principally from Aristotle's *Politics (Política)* and Seneca's *On Clemency (De clementia)*, his concept of royal power is firmly based on the divine right of kings and on the corporeal concept of the state. The latter includes the common medieval metaphorization of the body politic as a macrocosm of the human body, and, by extension, the association of the stability of social and political institutions with the stability of the family.[34] Already in the prologue the author cites Aristotle to the effect that "to rule is divine, to be ruled is lowly, as are the animals.... therefore, since man is made in the image and likeness of God, he is more like him than the animals are and consequently he rules over them" (138).[35] Reason is what approximates man to God and qualifies him to rule over beasts and other intellectually inferior beings: "for this reason old men naturally rule over young men and man rules over woman, and man over the animals, and in the human body the head, which is the seat of the brain, rules over the other members" (137–38).[36]

In the chapter dedicated to the virtue of *obsequiosidad*, compassion, the second of his triad of supreme feminine virtues, Fray Martín relies on Seneca's *De clementia* in order to equate his hierarchical concept of monarchy with domestic patriarchal gender roles:

the emperor... is the father of the land... for although my own father engendered me, if the king did not safeguard the land from the enemies of the faith as well as of the kingdom, and from other evildoers... they would enter our house by night or by day to rob or kill my father and all those living in the household. Because even though my father engendered me and gave me life, the king protected and preserved me in it, and for that reason he is a more constant father. (199–200)[37]

Further on he reinforces the authority of the familial/political patriarch by associating him with the divine father, claiming that "the earthly kingdom is well-ordered when it conforms to the heavenly kingdom" [el reyno dela tierra es bien ordenado, quando es conforme al reyno del cielo] (201). We cannot assume that "king" in this theocratic formulation of monarchy is a gender-inclusive term. For the Augustinian friar no less than for Juan de Mena, the paterfamilias of the sovereign state can only be male.

But what, then, is the queen's proper role? Fray Martín again draws on Seneca in order to propose one. The compassion natural to her gender, usually expressed in the maternal role, has an appropriate outlet in the public arena: "Just as we say that the king is a father, so do we say that the queen is a mother" [Pues como dezimos que el rey es padre, por esta misma razón dezimos que la reina es madre] (200). If Christ the judge is the model for the king, Mary logically provides the example the queen should follow, that of maternal protector and intercessor: "Since in the celestial kingdom Christ the king is judge and Mary the Queen is advocate, so it should be in the earthly kingdom that the king is judge and the queen, advocate. So that if the king tries to tyrannize or impose too many taxes on the kingdom, it is the queen's duty... to plead on behalf of the people" (201).[38]

The culminating image in this crucial chapter represents the queen as maternal shield: "the lady is a shield, for not only must she be as compassionate as a mother or as an advocate before the king, she must also be a shield, a buckler, and a targe, defending the weak from the power of the strong, for the world is like the sea and men are like fishes, where the big ones eat the small ones" (202).[39] The gender imagery is compellingly familiar: in the patriarchal family of the imperium the phallic sword of justice corresponds to the king in his two primary medieval functions, that of judge and warrior. The queen's uterine shield of compassion and clemency accompanies the sword acting not as its complement, but as its supplement. The essentializing sex–gender hierarchy of *Jardín* finds its clearest expression in this symbolism. How Isabel received and implemented the lessons of Fray Martín's marriage manual will be seen later on in this chapter.

Complicating the issue of gender in the consideration of Isabel's right to the crown was that of the relative claims of the direct and the collateral dynastic lines. As daughter of Castile's reigning monarch, Enrique IV, and granddaughter of Juan II, Juana of Castile represented the direct dynastic line, whereas Isabel and Alfonso, children of Juan II, belonged to the collateral line. Once Prince Alfonso's death removed the gender issue from the dispute over the crown, it was this primacy of the direct line over the collateral line (established in 1348, according to Azcona) that held sway. After Alfonso's death in 1468, when his supporters transferred their allegiance to his sister, it became necessary for them to discredit the direct line, represented by Juana. They did so by intensifying the sexual slurs against Enrique that they had begun to disseminate shortly after Juana's birth in 1462. The target of the propaganda campaign was simply shifted from father to daughter, from the cause—impotence and sexual misconduct—to the effect: illegitimacy.

At about the time Martín de Córdoba was composing his treatise, in the fall of 1468, Isabel had already won a major victory in the highly charged contest for succession: Enrique's signature on the so-called *Pacto de Toros de Guisando*. In that agreement, the king, under intense pressure from the high nobility, named Isabel his legitimate heir, granting her the legal right to the title of "First and legitimate Princess heir of said king and of said kingdoms and seignories" [Princesa primera legítima heredera del dicho Rey e de los dichos regnos e señoríos], as she in fact often referred to herself thereafter (Azcona, 145).[40] But Isabel and her advisers were aware that this victory was precarious, and that it was therefore imperative that she consolidate her claim by marrying and quickly producing an heir, preferably male, of unimpeachable legitimacy. At this juncture, then, it was not gender but dynastic continuity ensured by marital fidelity that would decide the contest for the throne of Castile. Seen in this light, the emphasis *Jardín* places on female chastity before and fidelity during marriage becomes another discursive weapon in the Castilian seignorial and clerical effort to ward off the dynastic claims of the legitimate heir Juana and consolidate those of Isabel, whom they believed would protect the enormous wealth and power they had accumulated throughout the fifteenth century.[41]

I am not proposing that Fray Martín promoted wifely submission as an intentional political strategy. But the treatise may have encouraged Isabel's adoption, as part of the discursive battle for the crown waged between 1468 and 1474, of the sexual invectives that had been hurled against Enrique and his heir by Juan Pacheco's band for more than four years. It may also be that the treatise formed part of a campaign among the princess's closest advisers in favor of Fernando's marriage suit over those of less attractive candidates such as Alfonso de Portugal or the Duke of Guyenne. The latter suitors were older, and therefore neither certain to produce the desired heir nor well equipped to defend militarily Isabel's problematic monarchic claim. Fernando, on the other hand, was young and known for his skill as a military strategist and his bravery in battle. A final point in his favor was his Trastamaran lineage (he and Isabel had the same great-grandfather, Juan I [1379–90]), especially if and when the issue of female rule should arise.[42]

The guidance offered by Gonzalo Chacón, Gutierre de Cárdenas, Alfonso de Carrillo, and others close to Isabel—advice influenced by generous donations from Fernando's father, Juan II of Aragon—undoubtedly coincided with the usual expectations for young aristocratic women of the period. The goal of aristocratic marriage in the Middle Ages was exogamic and patrilineal: to increase landholdings through strategic alliances and to produce male heirs. Fray Martín reminds Isabel of this early on, in chapter 5 of Part I.

He sets forth the three purposes for which woman was created. The first, the multiplication of the human race, is biblical in origin, but the second two respond to more immediate social realities, analogous to those expressed in *Laberinto de Fortuna*: "The other purpose was after the fall, which caused procreation to be very disordered; and the Bible established marriage as the way for a man to have sexual relations with his wife, so as to avoid fornication."[43] As we saw Mena do twenty-five years earlier, Martín here registers fifteenth-century concern about confusion of noble bloodlines and patrilineal inheritance patterns, and he advocates marriage and wifely fidelity as its solution. Even more topical is the third function of marriage singled out by the friar: "The other purpose is peaceful reconciliation, and this is especially true among kings. When it happens that great lords have disputes over the division of lands and possessions, a daughter allows them to make peace and create bonds of kinship" (173).[44]

Isabel was not exempt from these feudal requirements because she was an infanta; according to Martín de Córdoba, that status only binds her to them more tightly. One indication that Isabel did listen to Fray Martín's warnings about female insufficiency to rule is the rhetorical self-abasement of the letter of acceptance that she wrote to Fernando sometime in February 1469. It exudes the obedience and submissiveness expected of a good wife while simultaneously alluding to the political pressures she was experiencing: "I beg of you... to command me to do what you wish now, as I must do it. And the reason for this, now more than ever, you may hear from him [the messenger], because it must not be written down. By the hand that will do whatever you command. The princess" (quoted in Azcona, 165).[45]

It appears, therefore, that *Jardín* played a role in advancing Isabel's acceptance of the suitor her advisers deemed most appropriate, a man young enough to produce a legitimate, male heir, and strong enough to fight off rival claimants. *Jardín* is in this sense a useful corrective to the traditional romantic version of Isabel's selection of Ferdinand as the free and spontaneous choice of a romantic young woman, in love at first sight with the handsome king of Sicily. A typical example of the historiographical mystification of the intense political maneuvering surrounding her marriage is the remark attributed to the princess upon first setting eyes on Fernando, in January 1469: "He is the one" [Ese es]. A letter sent to King Juan II of Aragon by his agent in the Castilian marriage negotiations, contains the following reassurance: "and Your Highness should know that the Princess says that they will not make her agree to anyone other than the King of Sicily, that it is to be he and no other" (quoted in Paz y Melia, 85).[46] Equally romanticized, but evoking considerable anxiety about female power, is the chronicle account of one of Isabel's numerous parries of Enrique's attempts to marry her off to his own political advantage. The often-cited legend tells how one of her less desirable suitors, the forty-three-year-old magnate Pedro Girón, died suddenly on his way to their wedding, supposedly a divine response to the princess's fervent prayers (Valera, *Memorial*, 39). Despite these masculinist constructions of the princess as love-struck adolescent or *belle dame sans merci*, neither infatuation nor supernatural power dictated the choice of Fernando. The historical crossroads that produced *Jardín de nobles donzellas,* and which the treatise may have influenced, is closer to the one described by Azcona: "everything was planned and arranged according to an acute political opportunism" [todo se iba pensando y concertando bajo el signo de un agudo oportunismo político] (165).

At the same time, Azcona likely overstates Isabel's lack of agency in the process of finding her a king when he writes that "these men [Cárdenas and Chacón], won over by dint of rewards [from the crown of Aragon], were responsible for the marriage of Fernando to Isabel; they more than anyone else set the course of modern Spanish history" [a estos hombres [Cárdenas and Chacón], ganados a golpe de Mercedes [from the crown of Aragon], se debió el matrimonio de Fernando con Isabel, siendo ellos quienes contribuyeron más que ningún otro a enfilar la proa de la historia moderna de España] (141). I would argue instead that Isabel was neither completely a victim nor totally a free agent in a complex sociopolitical process that we shall probably never be able to reconstruct completely. In order to impose her real and symbolic sovereignty, Isabel had to position herself carefully in relation to three intersecting oppositional axes: legitimacy versus illegitimacy, masculine versus feminine power, and Castilian versus Aragonese supremacy.[47] The first conflict was partially resolved by her marriage to Fernando in 1469 and the birth the following year of their daughter Isabel, and more fully by the arrival in 1478 of a much-anticipated male heir, Juan. The latter two, however, continued to trouble the early years of her reign when it became increasingly clear to Castilians and Aragonese alike that Isabel fully intended to rule in her own right, an intention boldly expressed in her official signature: "Yo, la reina."

In March 1469, Fernando signed the famous "marriage contract" [capitulaciones matrimoniales], a document that placed serious limitations on the future king's governance powers in Castile. It prohibited him from granting *mercedes* and lordships or appointing officials in Castile without Isabel's approval, and it stipulated that he was not to take Isabel or any of their children out of the kingdom.[48] There was, however, ample room for interpretation of the exact division of labor and balance of power. For example, the use of the royal plural in the *capitulaciones* tended to obfuscate just whom was being referred to in a particular instance, whether Fernando alone or Isabel and Fernando jointly (Liss, 80). More fundamentally, the expectation of Fernando's supporters, Aragonese and Castilian alike, was that once the couple was married the male prerogatives granted by natural, statutory, and divine law would prevail. This did not turn out to be the case.

(Un)equally Yoked: Visual Representations of Isabelline Power

Isabel did not dutifully internalize the symbolics of power presented for her edification by Martín de Córdoba. In fact, her resistance to *Jardín*'s hierarchical union of phallic sword and uterine shield can be inferred as early as her coronation ceremony in Segovia on December 13, 1474, two days after Enrique IV's death. The precipitous nature of her accession and the fact that it took place in Fernando's absence was duly noted by "the Castilian faction, apparently rather large, that always defended male succession over female, and that therefore considered Fernando to be the real ruler of Castile" (Azcona, 243).[49]

Diego de Valera provides the most dramatic account of an event he surely witnessed firsthand. Valera, the ambitious son of Juan II's personal physician, held several influential posts in the courts of Juan II and later, Enrique IV. A staunch monarchist, he also maintained close ties with nobility and became a much-admired arbiter of courtly etiquette and protocol.[50] With his usual attention to detail, Valera describes how Isabel on the morning of her coronation threw off her white mourning habit and donned a dazzling gown and costly jewelry to receive the oath of fealty and process through the streets of Segovia. He also highlights the ostentatious display of power demonstrated in the procession: "and before her galloped a noble gentleman of her household named Gutierre de Cárdenas...who carried in front of her in his right hand an unsheathed sword so as to demonstrate to all how it was appropriate for her to punish and chastise wrongdoers, as queen and (natural) sovereign of these kingdoms and seignories" (4).[51]

By flaunting the masculine symbolics of the lofted sword of justice removed from its "vaginal" sheath, Isabel publicly appropriated the power that Martín de Córdoba's theory of monarchy had denied her. In doing so, furthermore, she boldly signaled a break with recent Castilian tradition, which designated as the symbol of monarchy a scepter topped by a gold orb and a cross, like the one depicted in Juan II's tomb effigy (Liss, 98). Her adoption of the sword, symbol of monarchic militant justice, signaled that the new queen was aligning herself with earlier, more "virile" times, diassociating herself from the perceived passivity and weakness, that is, the "femininity," of her immediate predecessors, Enrique IV and even her own father, Juan II. That her proclamation as proprietary queen of Castile implied Fernando's relegation to the role of consort was made clear in the Segovians' cry: "Castile, Castile, Castile, for our queen and lady, Queen Isabel, and for King Fernando, her legitimate husband!" (quoted by Azcona, 244).[52] In the epistle Isabel circulated a few days later formally announcing to her subjects Enrique's death and her accession, the phrase "your Queen and (natural) lady" [vuestra Reyna e señora natural] appears four times and is accompanied by detailed instructions on the correct form for the coronation proclamation and the oath of obedience (Azcona, 242).

The significance of Isabel's manly act of self-assertion was not lost on her new subjects. Valera relates how some witnesses criticized Isabel's gender-inappropriate use of the lawmaker's sword, "according to some laws that declare that women have no right to judge" [según algunas leyes que declaran acerca de las mugeres no aver lugar de juzgar] (4). He is quick to point out, however, that this general proscription against female judges does not apply to queens, duchesses, and other great ladies "to whom by hereditary right belong those lordships with absolute jurisdiction" [que por derecho hereditario les pertenece a sus señorías que tengan mero y misto imperio] (4). Thus, whereas Martín de Córdoba had insisted in 1468 that "nobles donzellas" like Isabel must follow the rules of feminine conduct such as modesty and obedience more closely than others because of their exemplary role, for Valera, writing around 1486, after the queen's authority was well established, those rules are deemed not to apply to "noble ladies" [grandes señoras]. Still, there is more than a little equivocation in this passage, because the author goes on to affirm that the ideal could not be met because of political exigency: "since the king was absent, and ... [any delay] in this accession might have proven harmful (since the most illustrious Queen Isabel had a rival in Lady Juana), it should have been and was in fact done, and was prudently and wisely implemented" (4).[53]

Other chronicles record in more detail the contemporary disapproval of Isabel's accession rituals, even among her supporters. I will refer to two of these, written by the rival court chroniclers Fernando del Pulgar and Alfonso de Palencia. Personally commissioned by the queen in the 1480s, these works are important components of Isabel's discursive self-fashioning, and for this reason cannot be considered objective sources. On the other hand, their pronounced pro-Isabelline bias makes their account of the disagreement surrounding the spouses' respective right to proprietary rule all the more convincing.[54]

In Fernando del Pulgar's *Crónica de los Reyes Católicos* (Chronicle of the Catholic Monarchs), one group of nobles present at the negotiations (not surprisingly, the group with allegiances to Aragon) maintains that Fernando, by virtue of being great-grandson of Juan I of Castile, was doubly qualified to sit on the throne of Castile: "both because the succession of these kingdoms belong to the King and because he is a man, their governance in all respects belongs to him, and . . . his wife the Queen should have no role in it" (255).[55] Isabel's supporters forcefully countered this argument by citing the ample precedents for female rule in Castile, from Ormisinda, daughter of Pelayo, through Catalina, wife of Enrique III.[56]

Alfonso de Palencia is more critical of Isabel than Pulgar. He reports Fernando's shock at his wife's symbolic sword-wielding: "We all know that it was granted to Kings; but I have never heard of a Queen who usurped that manly attribute" (*Crónica*, 162).[57] Palencia criticizes the grandees who influenced Isabel to resist "the yoke that her most illustrious spouse, relying on the authority of a husband, might attempt to impose on Castilian necks."[58] He rejects outright the nobles' claim that "marriage rights in no way refer to sovereignty and royal power" [los derechos del matrimonio en nada se refería al señorío y regia potestad] (165) and simultaneously interprets Isabel's adherence to that point of view as a sign of her feminine weakness ("Such reasoning changed the mind of the Queen, who is, after all is said and done, a woman" [Movieron tales razones el ánimo de la Reina, al fin mujer] [165]). He then praises the opposing view of the clerics, who maintained that "the harmony of the spouses" [la concordia de los cónyuges] should come first and that only once the marital relationship was in place should the couple decide the terms of govenance, which, in any case, "since remotest times favored men" [desde los más remotos siglos favorecían a los varones] (165). Throughout this chapter, Palencia continues to hammer away at the "arrogance and superiority" [arrogancia y prepotencia] that makes Isabel turn her back on the masculine prerogatives authorized by "written law, both divine and human" [derecho escrito, así divino como humano] (166).[59]

Despite such opposition to Isabel's rule, the *Acuerdo para la gobernación del reino* (better known as the *Concordia de Segovia*) that Isabel and Fernando signed on January 15, 1475, confirmed the unequal power relations outlined six years earlier in the marriage contract. It affirmed Isabel's sole proprietorship of the crown of Castile, and fixed the line of succession so that their daughter Isabel, and not Fernando, would inherit. As Azcona tersely comments: "Fernando was marginalized, kept in the position of king consort" [se orilló a Fernando, manteniéndose en un puesto de rey consorte] (245).[60] Thus, in the crucial liminal moments of her reign, Isabel and her supporters appear to have actively and successfully tested the limits of the gender ideology governing both marriage and sovereignty in medieval Iberia. In this sense, it is significant that Isabel continued to wield the symbolic sword in ceremonial events well into the 1480s. In 1484, she and Fernando rode in the annual Christmas Eve procession in Seville that commemorated the city's reconquest by Fernando III. They had the conqueror's age-blackened sword, cherished symbol of militant justice and militant faith, carried before them (Liss, 98).[61]

The second visual representation of Isabelline power I will discuss was more widely disseminated than the ceremonial sword. Shortly after Fernando and Isabel signed the *Concordia de Segovia,* the monarchs commissioned heraldic arms, possibly from Antonio de Nebrija, the renowned humanist and historian (Figure 1).[62] The visual field of the royal arms is composed of two devices: on the left a *yugo* or yoke and severed yoke straps, and, on the right, a bundle of downward-pointing *flechas* or arrows. The pithy motto "Tanto monta," roughly translatable as "each as important as the other," that is inscribed above completes the meaning of the two visual symbols. The whole figures the personal and political union of Isabel and Fernando as coequal and harmonious.

The monarchs were apparently eager to circulate this complex and ambiguous symbol of their shared sovereignty. Art historian Joaquín Yarza Luaces has commented on the proliferation of the heraldic emblem, either alone or accompanied by the royal *F* and *Y* initials. It appeared on coins, tapestries, seals, and printed works produced throughout Isabel and Fernando's reign.[63] The yoke and arrows are also featured as an ornamental motif on the monarchs' many residences, which respond not so much to the demands of itinerancy as to the desire to showcase their power (González-Iglesias, 68). The extraordinary success of this

Figure 1. Heraldic shield of the Catholic Monarchs. From Faustino Menéndez Pidal de Navascues, *Heráldica medieval española*, vol. 1, *La casa real de León y Castilla* (Madrid: Instituto Salazar y Castro [Centro Superior de Investigaciones Científicas], 1982), 198.

intentional propagation of symbolic power is all the more noteworthy "because heraldry is not exactly a popular art, and it is therefore virtually impossible to name a coat of arms that is widely recognized. The fact is that the monarchs expended an enormous effort into having theirs reproduced endlessly" (69–70).[64]

Both the emblem and the motto soon caught the popular imagination. The somewhat enigmatic "Tanto monta" was then expanded to the more explicit octosyllabic couplet "Tanto monta, monta tanto, Isabel como Fernando." From there it was only a short step to the highly sentimentalized interpretation of the emblem as a kind of love token exchanged between the spouses to mark their equality and mutuality. At some point, the chiastic referentiality of the initial letter of each device was noted: the "y" of *yugo* was considered a flattering allusion to Isabel (Ysabel) and the "f" of *flechas* was seen as returning the courtly compliment to Fernando (Aguado Bleye, 384)[65] (Figure 2). The romanticized view of the marriage of Isabel and Fernando that the initials and motto encapsulate has lasted for five hundred years.

I would argue that the meaning of the Catholic Monarchs' heraldic emblem is considerably more complex than the ballad-like couplet suggests. In the first place, the carefully balanced and symmetrical composition is itself a reelaboration of an earlier emblem fashioned exclusively for Fernando, Prince of Aragon, King of Sicily. It consisted of the motto "Tanto monta" together with the symbol of the yoke.[66] In that original context, the symbolism of Fernando's yoke and yoke straps was not marital but martial. They represented his much-admired gifts as a warrior and military strategist by associating them with no less grand a model than Alexander the Great through the Alexandrian legend of the Gordian knot.

The best-known version of the legend in the Renaissance was the one told by Quintus Curtius. According to that Roman historian, when Alexander visited the Phrygian capital of Gordium during his Asian campaign, he saw the famous oxcart driven into the city by Gordius, the farmer who became king. He also learned of the oracle prophesying that whoever untied the oxcart yoke's intricately knotted straps would become ruler of all Asia. Alexander eagerly accepted the challenge, but was unable to untie the knot. Undaunted, he drew his sword and cut through it, uttering the words that Quintus Curtius records: "Nihil interest quomodo soluantur" (It matters not how the problem is solved).[67] The fulfillment of this prophecy set Alexander on the path to realize his ambition of conquering Asia.

The motto "Tanto monta" that Nebrija incorporated into the heraldic emblem of his patrons is thus a shortened translation of a classical epigram applied to Fernando alone. In its new setting it retained its original

Figure 2. Illuminated page from Pedro Marcuello, *Rimado de la conquista de Granada*, edited by Estrella Ruiz-Gálvez Priego and Ana Domínguez Rodríguez (Madrid: Musée Condé-Château de Chantilly-Edilán, 1995), 2:f. 22r. Reproduced with permission from Edilán.

ideological connotations: resoluteness primarily, but also royal power, territorial expansion, and the political concept of the ends justifying the means. These meanings were entirely apposite to the medieval prince whose primary role was that of warrior, a role that Fernando fulfilled splendidly both before and during his marriage to Isabel. Furthermore, the motto's oracular associations befitted one who had been from birth the subject of messianic prophecies about a future conquest of Asia, which Juan Gil reminds us "went hand in hand with the fulfilment of one of the most ancient longings of western Christendom: the reconquest of the Holy Land and the capture of Jerusalem" (232).[68]

Needless to say, such imperialist associations could not so readily be applied to Isabel, whose gender barred her from the role of warrior prince. Nebrija's truncation of the classical motto brilliantly overcame this obstacle by bringing into play the broader and more ambiguous semantic field suggested by the common etymological association of *yugo* and *cónyuge* or spouse. The poet Iñigo de Mendoza invokes this time-honored sense of equally yoked marriage partners in his "Song Sermon" (Sermón trobado) (c. 1475) when he reminds Fernando of "when marriage joined you to the queen, uniting your persons, your royal crowns" [quando a la reina vos dio / el casamiento ayunto / juntando vuestras personas, / vuestras reales coronas] (315).[69]

On one level, Nebrija's recontextualization of the motto projected the masculine connotations of determination, cunning, and military might contained in Fernando's yoke onto Isabel. It strengthened the symbolic power that the Queen's arrows also signified but that she herself could not physically enact. On another level, it layered over that deeply masculine sense of the double-gendered symbolism of the marital yoke. But the conjoining of the two levels is, as we shall see, hardly seamless.

In an astute analysis of the emblem, Juan-Antonio González Iglesias demonstrates that Nebrija and Fernando were primarily interested in its broader, more accessible sense, that of political equality; that is, they promoted the interpretation of the Latin "Nihil interest" not as "cutting works as well as untying" [tanto monta cortar como desatar], but as "one monarch is the same as the other" [tanto monta un soberano como el otro] (67). He cites as evidence the careful placement of the motto on the shield so that visually it applies to Fernando's yoke and Isabel's arrows equally. He also points out that the motto's strict sense of military might and determination would have been accessible only to the educated minority owing to its classical allusion. This fact does not completely exclude the Alexandrian associations of Fernando's emblem; rather, they remain latent, "like a kind of pretext or justification that avoids excessive crassness in the proclamation of equality" [como una suerte de pretexto o de justificación que evitara la excesiva rudeza en la proclamación de igualdad] (67).

González-Iglesias's interpretation assigns primary responsibility for crafting the emblem to Fernando and downplays Isabel's role in its authorization. He focuses on its usefulness for Fernando, claiming that the reliance on the Alexandrian and messianic connotations served to soften the Aragonese bid for equal rule in Castile. Ironically, he does not ask what Isabelline goals were being promoted by an emblem that "married" conjugal equality to the affirmation that political ends justify violent means. But it is clear that both monarchs sought to disseminate the connubial symbolism of the emblem. If we take Isabel's real power and her problematic status as female sovereign into account, it appears just as likely that the emblem was chosen for the subtle way it simultaneously articulates and mystifies the imposition by force of *her* absolute power in the newly and precariously joined kingdoms.

One could object that the force Isabel used to wrest the throne from her rival and her supporters is already figured on the visual field of the royal shield by Isabel's own device, a bundle of arrows with their heads pointing downward, indicating readiness for use.[70] But if the military implications of the arrows seem clear, their bundling is less so, partly because no verbal text accompanies the device. González-Iglesias points out that the bundled arrows balance the yoke device not only visually but conceptually: "if the yoke suggests cutting, dissolving, untying, the arrows represent the union of the separate, a binding together" (72).[71] Montaner associates the arrows with the union of the Iberian kingdoms and believes that the device carries with it a sense of religious evangelization as the means to that end.[72] Liss observes that arrows were not only weapons of war. They also were used in the execution of justice: common criminals in Castile were traditionally executed by bow and arrow (111).

But I would argue that Isabel's bundled arrows [haz de flechas] contains its own classical subtext: the Roman fasces, the bundle of rods containing an axe with a projecting blade that was carried before Roman magistrates as a symbol of their power. The etymological link between *haz* and fasces, in this reading, parallels the connection between *yugo* and *cónyuge*. Like Fernando's unbound yoke straps, Isabel's bound arrows simultaneously articulate and dissimulate the absolutist reliance on force. In this view, what ultimately holds the two devices together under the banner of "Tanto monta" are the proverbial ties that bind—bind the Aragonese subjects to Fernando and the Castilians to Isabel, as much or more so than each of the rulers equally and irrevocably to the other. Over a century after the invention of the device, Cervantes acknowledges that such ties may chafe, when he has Don Quixote comment that marriage "is a loop of rope that once thrown around the neck becomes the Gordian knot that cannot be untied, unless it is severed by death's scythe" (*Don Quijote,* vol. 2, chap. 19).[73] This may well be yet another of the crazed knight's anachronistic allusions.

The notion of force subsumed in the royal emblem—the force that binds up the arrows or the force that severs the yoke straps—acts as a destabilizing presence in the multivalent visual/verbal field of the emblem, encoding a subtle threat to the political and kinship alliances it celebrates.[74] The contradictions make clear the discursive function of the emblem and the entire shield: to negotiate the delicate issues of female sovereignty, shared power, territorial control, and dynastic succession that came to the fore after Isabel acceded to the throne in December 1474.

We have seen how one of Isabel's subjects, Fray Martín de Córdoba promoted her adherence to the traditional role of the submissive and pious wife, which in late-medieval Castile was decidedly not that of the equal partner implied by the yoke symbol. Some years later, in her coronation ceremony, she used the symbolics of masculine sovereignty in a bold act of resistance to that kind of fashioning. Now we see it appropriated and manipulated in an act of self-fashioning, the connubial connotations of the yoke used to mask her will to power, the force and determination signified by the Alexandrian sword and Roman fasces, but that was unsanctioned in a woman.[75]

An interesting text dedicated to the Queen sometime between 1482 and 1492 suggests that her subjects understood the balancing act of the heraldic emblem. *La Poncella de Francia* (The maid of France) narrates for Isabel's edification and "consolation" the story of Joan of Arc. The comparison of Joan's manly bravery and skill when facing the English and their French allies to Isabel's when confronting her enemies is typically messianic: "And since from the beginning of your reign it was understood that the Messiah was come for the just and the Antichrist for the wicked" (91–92).[76] It is also Alexandrian: "Let them not say that Alexander accomplished a great deal when he controlled the world, for he did so in an era propitious to dominating the peoples he encountered, for he would find it harder to conquer and pacify a single city in your kingdom than it was to conquer the entire circle of the earth in that era" (91).[77]

The multilayered yoke–arrow emblem is best understood as what historian Abby Zanger calls a "nuptial fiction," a symbolic construct that seeks to consolidate political power in a period of interrogation and reformulation (3). In her study of the 1660 marriage of Louis XIV of France to another Spanish infanta, María Teresa, daughter of Felipe IV, she argues that the sexual, mortal body of the queen threatens monarchical power not only because it undermines the divine image of the sovereign, but also because it is fundamental to the fictions of dynastic continuity. As queen consort, María Teresa's role was not to rule but to procreate, but the fact that she *could* rule threatened the state by bringing in a second sovereign authority. That threat is uniquely marked in the symbolic practices and products of their marriage, such as the engravings on widely disseminated almanacs. Obviously, a queen regnant like Isabel represents a much greater threat to masculine-gendered sovereignty than a queen consort.

Like the marriage fictions surrounding the union of Louis and María Teresa, the polysemy of the Catholic Monarchs' heraldic shield similarly marks and masks the precarious nature of the union of Castile and Aragon effected by the marriage of Isabel and Fernando. Historians of early modern Spain have long acknowledged that the dynastic union of Castile and Aragon did not significantly alter the separateness of the two kingdoms. J. H. Elliott's description is particularly appropriate: "The Crown of Aragon was well protected by its traditional laws and liberties from the strong exercise of royal power, and in consequence the union represented an uneasy yoking of two very different constitutional systems" (43).[78] Nevertheless, many historians still believe in a trickle-down effect from a perceived balance of power at the top. If they do question the conjugal relations of power between the two sovereigns, they usually affirm Isabel's superiority and the limitations placed on Fernando's role in the governance of Castile, as evidenced by the twelve years of tension surrounding the viability of his claim to rule Castile that followed the death of Isabel in 1504. Recently, more attention has been refocused on the limitations on Isabel's governing role in Aragon. Emilia Salvador Esteban rejects what she calls the assumption of total reciprocity of rule. She insists that to maintain the monarchs' strict reciprocity would be an erroneous interpretation of the "tanto monta" emblem (320), and that the monarchs' power sharing needs to be understood instead as a rhetorical construct of the intense propaganda campaign initiated by Isabel herself and carried out by her court writers in order to legitimize her contested succession. One measure of the astounding success of this campaign is its largely uncritical acceptance by historians of her reign down to the present day.

The tenuousness of Isabel's sovereign rights in Aragon had everything to do with gender. Besides her inability to fulfill the role of warrior prince, there was the insurmountable constitutional obstacle of Salic law, which prohibited female succession in Aragon. As a result, Isabel's role in Aragon never surpassed those routinely granted to a queen consort (Salvador Esteban, 326). But it was not only in Aragon that Isabel's gender raised anxiety, as we have seen. From the moment that Isabel's accession to the Castilian throne became a real possibility, that is, at the death of Crown Prince Alfonso in July 1468, there was a strong current of resistance to her royal authority in Castile. Euphoric historiographical re-creations of Isabel's accession initiated during her reign greatly underestimate the discomfort that her agency as queen regnant continued to cause and the ongoing efforts to contain it. The resistance continued unabated well into her reign, although understandably in more veiled fashion. It is, for example, a visible thread running through a series of prose and verse advice treatises addressed directly or indirectly to Isabel from 1474 to 1479. These are the works to which I now turn.

The Queen's *Labor* according to Gómez Manrique and Iñigo de Mendoza

Written by high-ranking nobles and clerics, including some of her most intimate advisers, these verse treatises are clearly intended as *specula principis*. They remain understudied, even though several of Isabel's modern biographers have deemed them formative of Isabel's sense of her public role. Azcona even suggests that these advice treatises hold the answer to a puzzling question, namely, "how a woman like Isabel, in those characteristically immature years of between twenty-five and thirty years old, was able not only to actively win a war, but also to structure her kingdoms like a perfect statesman" (309).[79]

It would be presumptuous to claim that literary works alone hold the answer to such a complex question, especially because of their highly prescriptive rather than descriptive aims. But they do reveal the gender ideology that early-modern Europe's first female sovereign had to negotiate as she sought to impose and consolidate her authority in Castile, both alone and together with her husband. A careful analysis of these texts shows that even as they exalt Isabel's sovereignty as the providential solution to the social and political ills of fifteenth-century Castile, they use various discursive strategies to contain the perceived threat of that power to a patriarchal status quo that requires female subordination.

Gómez Manrique (c. 1412–90), author of *Regimiento de príncipes* (Government of princes), was a member of a leading Castilian aristocratic family and was related by marriage to another, the Mendozas. That powerful clan produced a high proportion of the fifteenth century's notable writers and was a guiding force in the seignorial revolt against Enrique.[80] After Prince Alfonso's death Manrique became one of Isabel's closest advisers, and he figured prominently in her rise to power. He was present at the fateful 1468 meeting at Toros de Guisando when Enrique declared Isabel his legitimate heir. The following year he conveyed Isabel's acceptance of Fernando's marriage proposal and was instrumental in negotiating the balance of power outlined in the *capitulaciones*. He also accompanied Fernando on his secretive trip from Aragon to Castile for the wedding. Manrique remained close by the princess's side in the years following her marriage, notably during her 1472–74 stay in Alcalá de Henares while Fernando was on one of his extended trips to Aragon (Liss, 78, 88).

The dedication of Manrique's *Regimiento de príncipes* to the "princes of the kingdoms of Castile and Aragon, monarchs of Sicily" [príncipes delos reynos de Castilla e de Aragón, reyes de Cecilia] indicates that he composed the work shortly before Isabel's accession in 1474. In the prose *prohemio* to his treatise, Manrique boasts of his own lineage, of the services that he had been called on to provide to the sovereigns and the deep love of country that makes him desire to see "its cruel wounds healed" [curadas sus crudas llagas] (166).

Given the self-promoting tone of this *captatio benevolentiae*, it is hardly surprising that the main thrust of Manrique's advice is the avoidance of bad counselors.[81] What is unexpected is the imbalance in the amount of advice given to Fernando and Isabel; the latter is addressed directly in only fourteen of the poem's seventy-nine stanzas. Manrique apologizes that he had originally intended to write two separate treatises, but lacked time and knowledge to follow through with his plan. We can only speculate whether the abandoned plan for "his" and "hers" treatises conceptualized the roles of male and female sovereigns differently. In any case, Manrique himself admits that what he has written for Isabel is somewhat perfunctory, calling it "a few necessary compliments" [algunos cunplimientos nescesarios] (168).

But the difference between the parts of Manrique's work addressed to Isabel and Fernando is not simply quantitative. His advice to the king stresses the need for careful attention to the affairs of state, whether in seeking counsel, pursuing learning, dispensing justice, or defending the faith. He strengthens this advice with classical and biblical examples of forceful and weak rulers, as when he urges Fernando to avoid such tragic models as Sardanapolis, "effeminate prince" [príncipe afeminado], whose disastrous end was caused by "feminine counsel" [consejos femeniles] (171). A devout love and strong fear of God must guide all the king's actions and decisions, for it was God who made him "the chosen one, and not to be ruled, but to rule" [entre todos escogido, / y no para ser regido, / mas solo para reynar] (176). Manrique then marshals the cardinal and theological virtues of Faith, Hope, Charity, Prudence, Justice, Temperance, and Fortitude as moral guideposts for the ruler. He singles out the virtue of fortitude [fortaleza], necessary to defend the faith, and gives the examples of Saints Stephen and Andrew, and the eleven thousand virgin martyrs ("With hearts of steadfast men they triumphed over their desires" [con vnos coraçones / de muy costantes varones / vençiendo sus voluntades] [186]).

Manrique's use of the *mujer viril* topos might seem an obvious one to apply to Isabel. But when he finally turns his attention to the queen, the advice he offers allows for no such exceptionality. In fact, Manrique's admonishments to Isabel are strikingly similar to Martín de Córdoba's in their construction of female virtue as essentially prophylactic, useful for restraining the natural female propensity toward excess and vice.

After praising the princess's beauty, for which she owes God services and sacrifices, the poet warns her against being *too* pious: "Leave the praying of the psalters and the chanting of the hours to the nuns in the convents, My Lady; subordinate your prayers so as to govern your peoples and your territories and make them lead honest lives, and chastise all evildoers" (192).[82] At first glance, these lines appear to contradict the traditional view of women as naturally inclined to piety and devout works. Martín de Córdoba repeats the conventional view in his chapter on the third of women's good qualities, their "compassion and pious service" [obsequio & deuoto seruicio] (203). Women's compassion, he explains, results in part from their greater faith in God, itself a product of their deficient reason, which makes them more credulous: "since when some mystery of the faith is related to men and women, the women believe it more readily than the men because they demand less proof of the proposition than do men" (204).[83]

Does Manrique's concern about Isabel's overdedication to this sanctioned role indicate that Isabel was already assiduously cultivating the pious demeanor and behavior that were a fundamental aspect of her public persona? And if so, to what extent is that cultivation a conscious effort to conform to the traditional social and theological construction of femininity so prominent in *Jardín de nobles doncellas?* What is apparent from contemporary iconographic and historiographical evidence is that the queen was eager to disseminate the image of herself at prayer.[84] In any case, it is clear that Manrique considers prayer better than more frivolous feminine pursuits. He advises Isabel not to neglect her prayers "in order to rest or dress up, or fix your hair" [por reposar / por vestir, nin por tocar], nor anything other than the duties of governance. Monarchs are models [padrones] and must guard against even the smallest vices: "And just as when embroidering incorrect samplers doubtlessly causes incorrect transfers, so you, My Lady, will cause double the errors if you adopt simple vices, for in the shepherdess's house, everyone plays the panpipes" (194).[85] The popular and homely analogies Manrique uses—the needlework sampler [dechado], the paradigmatic work [lavor] of the noblewoman, and the humbler work of the shepherdess—are strikingly different in tone from the "metaphors" [comparaciones] addressed to Fernando. I shall return to the significance of such domestic referents later.

The other lesson Manrique tries to teach his sovereign is also reminiscent of *Jardín* in its requirement that she must work against her nature as a woman. She must guide her subjects to follow the footsteps of the personified Lady Reason, eschewing the excesses of the pleasure-seeking, also feminine Voluntad: "Will desires pleasure; it wants vices and gaiety; turning night into day, postponing temperance. It seeks not great fame; it scorns health. Reason is a lady who loves great honors and pursues virtue" (195).[86]

Thus, although Manrique's brief mirror of princes acknowledges Isabel's right to rule, like *Jardín* it expresses anxiety about her ability to resist the typically feminine vice of excess, whether of pleasure or asceticism. The pleasure-seeking Voluntad in a sense recalls the unruly, unpredictable Fortune in Mena's *Laberinto de Fortuna* (tamed by Alvaro de Luna; here to be tamed by Isabel), while Reason is reminiscent of the wiser, virtuous Providencia.[87]

The second advice treatise I want to examine was composed by the Franciscan friar Iñigo de Mendoza. Mendoza was the product of the union of two members of the Mendoza and Cartagena families, both of which played key roles in the political and cultural life of fifteenth-century Castile. Fray Iñigo was thus related to such important writers as the Marqués de Santillana, Alonso de Cartagena, and Teresa de Cartagena, as well as to Juana de Mendoza, wife of Gómez Manrique. His masterpiece is the long *Coplas de Vita Christi* (Songs on the life of Christ) (1467–68). First composed under Enrique IV's reign, it is sternly critical of the dissoluteness of his court. When Isabel came to the throne, Mendoza remained at court as royal preacher and almoner. He was much favored by the queen, as the royal account books attest. The Queen's preferment of the cleric may well reflect his support in the negotiations over the marital balance of power discussed earlier.[88]

Dechado a la muy escelente Reina Doña Isabel, nuestra soberana señora (Model for the most excellent Queen Isabel, our sovereign lady) (early 1475?) forms part of a trilogy of political poems that Mendoza composed for the monarchs during the five-year war of succession.[89] Of the three poems, *Dechado* is the only one addressed to Isabel exclusively. Although it was written at about the same time as Manrique's *Regimiento*, it seems much less ambivalent about the queen's power.

The poem opens with the providentialist assimilation of Isabel and Mary that we have already seen in Martín de Córdoba: "Since we lost our life because of a woman, God wants to protect us and repair us by the same manner and measure that caused our fall" (281).[90] Unlike the Augustinian friar, however, Mendoza enigmatically claims that the cure for the country's sickness cannot be a simple reversal of the feminine corruption represented by Eve. Quite unexpectedly, given what we have seen up to this point, the Franciscan friar urges on the new queen not feminine chastity or compassion, but rather masculine justice. To do so he calls on the same sword imagery that Isabel had appropriated for her coronation just a few months earlier: "an exceptional sword, one so sharp that it can level the land, for the Castilian people are so proud and so poorly behaved that they will never be cured unless the sword of Justice works hard against the tyrants" (283).[91]

The queen must be diligent and firm in the assertion of her authority over her subjects, instilling both love and fear in her flock: "but with love and sorrow to cut the throats of the infected sheep so as to preserve the rest of the flock" (284).[92] At the same time, it is important for the Queen to know when to sheath her sword and show mercy to wrongdoers. Thus Mendoza from the start assigns to the queen the two roles that Martín de Córdoba had separated by gender: justice and mercy.

From the sword of justice and the accompanying shield of clemency, Mendoza moves on to two other feudal symbols. A fortified tower signifies the courage, vigor, and resoluteness that the Queen requires to rule effectively. She must maintain a serene and resolute manner at all times, never allowing herself to be affected by the "harsh howls" [alaridos desabridos] of her vassals. The tower is surrounded by several bulwarks: one to defend against "the flattering tongue" [la lengua roncera] (289) of the court favorite, and another to ward off the power of gold, a warrior so fierce that it can bring down the strongest castle.

The third symbol that Mendoza holds up to his addressee is equestrian, similar in spirit to the wild steed of Fortune that Alvaro de Luna tamed in *Laberinto*. Mendoza uses it to attack one of his favorite targets: the luxury and licentiousness of curial life.[93] He urges on the Queen the bridle and bit of reason to use "against the carnal stirrings" [contra el carnal movimiento] aroused in the ladies of the court by cosmetics, clothing, and other adornments (292). With bridle, bit, and reins, the queen must vigorously restrain her courtiers: "loose ladies and gentlemen mingling as if they were married, shamelessly embracing in the corners of the hall" (294).[94]

The final image of the poem departs from the feudal context to describe a pair of watchful eyes, presumably the queen's, that are identified with the virtue of prudence. Unclouded by rancor, the royal eyes must create order in the present by scrutinizing and learning from the past and anticipating the future consequences of her actions.

Mendoza's rousing representation of the clear-eyed Queen astride her spirited horse, firmly grasping the reins of Temperance and the sword of Justice, and protected by the tower of Fortitude appears to fashion her as prototypical manly woman, the rare exception to her inherently weak gender. If, however, we take a step back from this masculinized picture, we see that all of its images are elements in an overarching conceit that situates the queen firmly in a feminine context.

The conceit that structures Mendoza's virile allegory of sovereign power is discernible in the very title of the work, *Dechado a... la Reina Doña Isabel*. On a figurative level, of course, the term *dechado* means moral "example" or "model" in a high moral sense. On the literal level, however, it signifies something rather more modest: a pattern traced on a piece of cloth as a guide for the needleworker, that is to say, a sampler. The entry for *dechado* in Covarrubias's dictionary underscores the semantic link: "the sampler on which the needleworker produces a work, and metaphorically, whoever provides a good example for others and promotes imitation, we call a model of virtue" [el ejemplar de donde la labrandera saca alguna labor, y por traslación decimos ser dechado de virtud el que da buen exemplo a los demás y ocasión para que lo imite] (445). Although the original semantic field of *labor* was extensive, denoting any kind of physical or spiritual work, by the late Middle Ages it had narrowed to mean either agricultural or cloth work (Corominas, 3: 545).[95] Simply put, the masculine model of fearless warrior and harsh judge that Mendoza holds up to his female prince is ultimately contained by the homely feminine form it takes.

The painstaking detail with which Mendoza describes the queen's proper work as so much elegant stitchery demonstrates that the image is intentional. The poet describes the sampler minutely, specifying the color of the thread and the particular stitch to be used for each of the images. The sword's blade, for example, is to be stitched in blood-red twisted silk: "to frighten everyone" [por dar temor / a todos en general] (283). The hilt is to be worked in purple silk to indicate the "love and sorrow" [amor y tristura] (283) with which it must be wielded against wrongdoers. In this way, the author makes it clear that the sampler is his own creation, and that his moral and artistic hand guides the hand of the one who must follow his instructions if she wishes to complete the godly design. Although Isabel as ruler must set an example by adopting a masculine role and characteristics, Mendoza warns that she must do so without straying from the outline for feminine behavior drawn by Christian doctrine and patriarchal tradition. The clear eyes Mendoza depicts at the end of the poem are enjoined to follow his instructions obediently.

In *Dechado*, therefore, the "masculine" public sense of ideal sovereignty is contained within and constrained by a "feminine" private sense. The words *labor* and *labrar*, initially applied to the virile work of the sword of justice, turn out to be double-gendered. They are tied to a symbolic sexual division of labor that continually transforms the virile brandishing of the sword into more sanctioned feminine *labor*, the dainty handling of a needle. In his use of this metaphor, Mendoza draws on the medieval tradition that associates female handiwork with female virtue. It is based both on the Old Testament (Proverbs 31:10–13, 19, and 24) and the New, especially the latter's depictions of the Virgin as spinner and creator of the thread of life. An example of the former tradition in medieval Castile is the fifteenth-century conduct manual for women, *La dotrina que dieron a Sarra*, attributed to Fernán Pérez de Guzmán. The author invokes the authority of Solomon to advocate sewing and needlework as primary occupations for women: "a maiden should occupy herself with linen and wool, doing her needlework as Solomon stated about the strong woman, who is hard to find; by linen and wool you may understand all those tasks required to stock and adorn the home well" (680).[96]

In Vives's *De instutione Foeminae Christianae*, the most popular conduct book for women in Tudor England, the handling of wool and flax also operates as an agent of control, a way to occupy women's weak and wandering minds (Wayne, "Sad Sentence," 20). For Vives, sewing was allied with the reading of edifying works as "two craftes...both profitable and kepers of temperance: whiche thynge specially women ought to have in price" (quoted in ibid.).

Since Diego Clemencín at the beginning of the nineteenth century, modern historians have often remarked Isabel's fondness for "the needlework appropriate to her sex" [las labores de su sexo] (Gómez Molleda, 146).[97] Pablo Alvarez Rubiano evokes her homely approach to reform as follows: "She visited the convents without fanfare, as if out of interest or curiosity, and she brought her distaff or sewing so as to gather them [the nuns] together with the excuse of sharing her work with them, and she chatted with them unhurriedly, without the solemnity of an inquisitive interrogation, until she found out by a slip of the tongue of one sister or another what she needed to know" (97).[98] But this colorful evocation of the Queen's homely approach to reform—undocumented, to be sure—is more ambiguous than the author intends, for it implies that such sisterly needlework served not to control her own weak womanhood but rather to control that same weakness in others.[99]

Elizabeth Lehfeldt believes that Isabel's enforcement of strict claustration for nuns indicates the "centrality of sexual... purity to her campaign for political legitimacy.... Isabel had learned the lessons embodied in texts like *Jardín de nobles doncellas* all too well. Even though she had spent her tenure on the throne seeking to rise above stereotypical characterizations of women as both more dangerous and weaker than men, she expected no more of the religious women of her kingdom" (49). As in the case of the topos of her religious piety, in the related one of her domesticity that is figured in her fondness for needlework we cannot rule out Isabel's conscious complicity with the dissemination of such patriarchal prescriptions for femininity for herself as well as others, although with differing goals in each case. Suggestive in this regard is Silió Cortés's hint that the Queen's persuasion in maintaining the confinement of nuns to the convent was not limited to the gentle variety: "In cases of stubborn resistance, however, she used all the strict measures, imposing observance and ensuring strict enclosure" (78).[100]

There is yet another level of meaning involved in the figuration of the queen as "needleworker" [labradora]. In late-fifteenth- and early-sixteenth-century literary texts, vocabulary associated with the female-dominated occupations of sewing, spinning, and weaving is a rich source of sexual innuendo.[101] Verbs such as "spin, embroider, weave, and sew" [hilar, labrar, tejer, coser] often referred to sexual intercourse, and nouns like "needle, thread, spindle, and cloth, thimble, wool" [aguja, hilo, huso, tela, dedal, lana] were standard euphemisms for male and female genitalia, respectively (Macpherson, "Thread," and Macpherson and Mackay, "Textiles"). Furthermore, although spinning, weaving, and sewing were taught to women of all classes, they were also some of the few livelihoods available to poor, unmarried women. They often had to combine them with lowlier occupations, such as prostitution, in order to eke out a living. Macpherson cites *Carajicomedia* as evidence of the common linguistic slippage from *labrandera* to *prostituta,* noting that "as a way of referring to a prostitute, the word had become something more than a euphemism; it appears as a virtual synonym or even an advertisement for the profession" (Macpherson, "Thread," 193).[102] Needlework terminology in such works connotes not only skill in sexual techniques but also, more generally, the intelligence, wit, and capacity for intrigue that were survival skills for such marginalized women as Celestina and Aldonza in *Lozana andaluza* (MacKay, "Averroístas," 253).[103] All of this preceding discussion raises the possibility that the image of Isabel holding a spindle or needle expressed and contained anxiety over her phallic persona, her threatening sexuality and intelligence.[104] The image of Isabel sewing was no doubt comforting to those who had recently witnessed the proudly wielded sword at her coronation.

I turn now to the final poem of Fray Iñigo's political trilogy, ostensibly addressed to Fernando alone: *Sermón trobado que fizo Fray Iñigo de Mendoza al muy alto y muy poderoso Príncipe, Rey y Señor, el Rey Don Fernando, Rey de Castilla y de Aragón, sobre el yugo y coyundas que Su Alteza trahe por divisa* [Song sermon that Fray Iñigo de Mendoza addressed to the noble and powerful prince, king, and lord Don Fernando, king of Castile and Aragon, concerning the yoke and yoke straps that his highness has for an emblem] (c. 1475–76).[105] As its title indicates, this mirror of princes offers a detailed interpretation of the yoke and yoke straps of Fernando's heraldic device. The poet's inspiration is scriptural. He quotes a passage from the Gospel of Matthew ("For my yoke is easy, and my burden is light" [11:30]) to stress the need for monarchs to cushion power with humanity: "for the yoke used to subjugate must always rest upon gentle kindness, without a trace of disdain" (308).[106]

Mendoza's poem is divided into three sections, respectively devoted to the yoke [yugo], the yoke pads [melenas], and the yoke straps [coyundas]. All three are intended as metaphors for the feudal ties of vassalage that bind lords to their monarch. Vassals submitting to Fernando out of love need not be bound at all ("these should be governed without yoke straps, with sweetness" [sin coyundas, con dulçor / se deben de governar] [304]). A firmer stance is recommended for less compliant nobles. To deal with them, Fernando must take lance in hand and force them to honor the fealty on which the stability of the social order rests. The poem's refrain—"for your yoke is easy for some and heavy for others" [que es vuestro yugo suave / a unos, y a otros grave]—alters the sense of its biblical source, in which the yoke rests easily on the shoulders of Christ's followers. The yoke sits lightly, affirms Mendoza, only when applied to those who willingly submit to the restraint. He illustrates this point with a courtly metaphor that compares the monarch to the elegant lady who makes her lover "to suffer with pleasure what pleasure condemns" [sofrir de gana / lo que la gana condena]. This cross-gendering of Fernando as haughty courtly beloved is interesting for its gendered dissimulation of royal authoritarianism (as well as for pointing to the coercion underlying courtly love rituals). It provides further evidence that the royal emblem crafted by Nebrija that is the visual referent of Mendoza's poem also used courtly and amatory allusions to mask the expression of determination and force.

Mendoza's elaboration of the yoke symbol also draws upon the agricultural background of the Alexandrian legend of the Gordian knot. We recall that the yoke and yoke straps were attached to the ordinary oxcart driven by the farmer who became the city of Gordium's first ruler. Mendoza recalls King Gordius's humble background tilling the soil when he urges Fernando to use the symbolic yoke to subdue Castile's "never-tamed bulls" [toros nunca domados] (304), that is, the dissident nobles who supported Juana of Castile's claim to the throne and aided Alfonso de Portugal's invasion of Castile in May 1475.

A similar gender and power dissimulation operates in the metaphor of the king bee. The king bee is the only bee in the hive, says the poet, that does not possess a stinger: "As it is said of the nature of bees, that among all of them nature created only the king without a stinger, from which fact we learn that he who is at the top, the higher he rises, the more fitting it is that gentleness radiate from his countenance, without a sting" (310).[107]

Mendoza's evocation of the "castrated" ruler in this apiarian mini-exemplum furthers one pole of the antithetical construction of monarchic power as a "light yoke" for some and a "heavy yoke" for others. Medieval writers always assigned the governance of the beehive to a king bee rather than a queen. This gendering followed the practice of the ancient writers for whom the hive was an ideogram of a wisely and peacefully ruled community. To Christian writers, the hive and its male ruler were an apt symbol for the church and the pope, the monastery (in French, *abeille*) and its abbott (Charbonneau-Lassay, 325), or the monarchy and the king. Having a queen bee was as inconceivable as having a female pope. The virtue most frequently associated with the bee was not wise leadership, however, but rather chastity and virginity. By analogy, it symbolized the Virgin Mary (Dimler, 229). Fernando was not known for his chastity—quite the opposite, in fact—but Isabel was. Is this Mendoza's way of chastising Fernando's waywardness while indirectly acknowledging the real ruler of the royal hive? Fernando may have the superiority of gender, he implies, but Isabel holds the *moral* authority. The maternal, compassionate, and protective function that Martín de Córdoba considered proper to a queen appears to be bestowed upon the king here, but it is not in his "nature" to fulfill it.[108]

Mendoza develops the animal husbandry motif further in the section of the poem dealing with the *coyundas* or yoke straps. Once he has successfully yoked his unruly bulls together, including the "fiercest young bull" [novillo más fiero], the king can begin to till the soil of Castile. Thereafter, as one of the many proverbs Mendoza uses to enliven his poem warns, any lazy bull "struggles against the goad" [contra el aguijón cocea] (314). The [bee] sting of power, previously masked, here resurfaces somewhat more aggressively as an iron cattle prod.

In Mendoza's poem, Fernando's yoke is used primarily as a symbol of control and domination. It draws on the latent meaning of the yoke as it appears on the heraldic shield. But what of the shield's patent meaning, that of conjugal equality and shared power? It too surfaces occasionally when the poet addresses the king and queen jointly as the drivers of the yoked oxen that are their subjects. The following lines offer one example: "With the bulls tied to the yoke with these straps, your royal hands will plow the crags as easily as the plains, and you will level the hills and cultivate the fallow fields; on the high cliffs where the haughty continually sowed bribes, you will sow laws" (314).[109] Together, Mendoza predicts, Fernando and Isabel will till the heretofore stony Castilian soil, turning cliffs into plains and uncultivated lands into fertile fields.

Mendoza then shifts his attention back from the royal couple to Fernando alone. He urges him to "be a good plowman, a good plowshare, vigorous, and have good tools, a good plowshare, a good plow, and with your oxen well yoked" (314).[110] The *reja* or plowshare that prepares the earth for fertilization underscores Fernando's virile domination of his troublesome Castilian subjects. And, like the sword of justice in *Jardín de nobles doncellas*, the plowshare in *Sermón trobado* ultimately belongs to the king alone. But Mendoza's use of vigorous soil tilling as a metaphor for strong and effective governance carries another association with the monarchs' device and motto. The *Diccionario de la Real Academia* lists the following as a sixth meaning for *montar:* "When a horse or ass mates with a mare; to service" [Cubrir el caballo o el burro a la yegua, acaballar]. Camilo José Cela reminds us that the verb *montar* is applicable not only to other animals but to humans as well, "without forgetting that in coitus each partner can mount or be mounted" [sin olvidar que en el coito ambos pueden montar o ser montados] (*Diccionario del erotismo*, 644).[111] Mendoza associates the allegorical bulls to the farmer/ruler who tames them, puts them to good use tilling the soil of the kingdom, and also links the bulls' mating and breeding activity to the monarch's own (we recall that in 1475 the royal couple had produced a daughter but not the longed-for male heir). This additional level of meaning of *montar* is promoted by the tools the poet assigns to the king for his challenging task, the "good tools" [buen aparejo] that proverbially referred to male genitalia.[112]

Sermón trobado thus adds yet another, very material dimension to the symbolic complexity of the royal emblem. We saw that the yoke and arrows and the "Tanto monta" motto negotiated the imposition and sharing of sovereign power and territorial control. Here it also negotiates the anxieties about dynastic continuity that had gripped Castile since the reign of the putatively impotent Enrique IV, anxieties that Azcona believes created "a real psychosis" [verdadera psicosis] (329) in the kingdom. Isabel's unfeminine will to power only deepened these anxieties. Mendoza has the solution: Fernando should apply his virile mastery and Alexandrian resoluteness not just to subdue rebellious nobles, but also to put his wife in her place. That place was as queen consort, whose role was not to rule but to procreate. That Isabel may also have promoted this particularly material fiction of sovereignty accords well with other aspects of her self-fashioning that we have seen, such as domesticity and piety.[113]

There is a sixteenth-century anecdote about Isabel that delights in deconstructing the complex fiction of marriage and sovereignty that the heraldic emblem disseminated. Its humor suggests that the royal emblem's complex negotiation of shared sovereign power was not lost on the monarchs' subjects, and that they were cognizant of Isabel's role in promoting it. The anecdote appears in Francisco Asensio's sixteenth-century *Spanish Anthology (Floresta española):* "The Catholic Queen criticized Fernando del Pulgar, her chronicler, because in recounting in his History a certain deed performed by the King her husband, he didn't attribute it to both of them, because they had done it together, equally. Shortly thereafter, the Queen gave birth to Princess Juana, and Fernando del Pulgar wrote: on such and such a day and such and such an hour, Their Majesties gave birth" (1:206).[114] A variant of the tale adds the queen's reaction to her subject's cheeky historical and biological revisionism: "The Queen, amazed that he had put them together in that event, ordered him to remove it, and he didn't want to, since her Highness had ordered the pairing so often."[115]

This joke on the Queen operates on several contradictory levels. The tale marks the most feminine of all the sovereign's functions, the reproductive one, relegating Isabel to the role of queen consort, the very role that Martín de Córdoba had held up for her emulation many decades earlier. It also exposes the parity of the sovereigns for what it is, a fiction forged by the queen. Her insistence on Fernando's equal participation in the affairs of state contrasts with the evidence that she really is the one in charge. After all, Fernando is significantly absent while his spouse is busily engaged in manipulating the historical record on his behalf. At the same time, Pulgar slyly mocks the masculine anxiety about paternity and virility that characterized the Trastamaran period by feminizing Fernando's body, in effect relegating him to the role of consort that many Castilians and Aragonese had hoped Isabel would accept. By mockingly fusing the male and female progenitors, the anecdote leaves no doubt as to the legitimacy of the Catholic Monarchs' heir. It is telling that it is Princess Juana's birth that is so represented, for she was to become the last ruler of the Trastamaran line. Known to posterity as "Mad Juana" [Juana la Loca], Juana's rule was also threatening. Her alleged madness, supposedly born of grief over the death of her consort Felipe I, became the pretext first for her father Fernando, and later her grandson Carlos I, the first Hapsburg ruler of Spain, to take over the government.

Finally, the anecdote figures the queen as one of the early-modern period's favorite misogynist stereotypes, that is, as something of a nag. Pulgar's refusal to obey his queen's repeated order suggests that it is up to her male advisers to keep her arrogant power in check. The edgy relationship between the demanding Queen, feminized King, and resisting male adviser that the story humorously represents captures the complex dynamic of display and dissimulation, of celebration and denigration, that characterizes the cultural construction of Isabel's problematically shared sovereignty.

CHAPTER THREE
The Discourse of Effeminacy in Isabelline Historiography

> the Archbishop of Toledo... ascended the platform and took the crown off his head... they took off all the other royal adornments, and kicking him off the platform they yelled, "Eat dirt, faggot... Eat dirt, faggot!"
>
> el Arzobispo de Toledo... subió en el cadahalso, y quitóle la corona de la cabeza... le quitaron todos los otros ornamentos reales, y con los pies le derribaron del cadahalso en tierra y dixeron "a tierra, puto... ¡A tierra, puto!"
>
> —Diego de Valera, *Memorial de diversas hazañas*

The urgent tone of Iñigo de Mendoza's *Dechado a la muy escelente Reina Doña Isabel*, presented to the Queen just months after her coronation, reflects the fact that she was then facing the first great test of her authority: civil and peninsular war.[1] In early 1475, the oligarchic league supporting Juana I of Castile's claim to the throne had acceded to Alfonso V of Portugal's bid for the thirteen-year-old's hand in marriage. The union would serve Alfonso's ambitions to dominate the peninsula. Alfonso was also being pressured to wage war against Isabel and Fernando by Louis XI of France, who had claims on the Aragonese provinces of Cerdagne and Roussillon.[2]

Despite the threat of imminent war, in early April the new sovereigns organized a lavish tournament in Valladolid, site of their wedding ceremony six years earlier. The tournament lasted for seven days and was described by royal chronicler Juan de Flores as the most extravagant that had been seen in Castile in years. The king himself participated, riding into the jousting lists before the gaze of Isabel and her ladies-in-waiting, all opulently attired. As was customary, the jousters wore somewhere on their person (in this case apparently on their helmets) an *invención* or emblem. Fernando's was a blacksmith's anvil. The accompanying *mote* or motto, perhaps carried on a placard or sewn onto his horse's trappings, completed the meaning partially expressed by the visual clue: "Like an anvil I suffer in silence, because of the times I live in" [Como yunque sufro y callo, / por el tiempo en que me hallo].[3] The suitably portentous device is also double-gendered, like the royal coat of arms that was being invented around the same time: the anvil is at once a typically courtly reference to the Queen as a "belle dame sans merci" and an allusion to Vulcan or Mars, the god of war (Liss, 110–11).[4] But the difficult times alluded to—Alfonso and his troops invaded Castile sometime in May—worked to Fernando's advantage in the royal balance of power. Because Isabel's gender barred her from leading the military counteroffensive herself, she was forced to lift many of the restrictions on Fernando's governing authority in Castile that she had written into the *Concordia de Segovia* in January.

In July 1475, the monarchs assembled an army of almost thirty thousand troops. It included the personal armies of the loyal Castilian magnates and militiamen provided by towns. Flores's description of this "last medieval army to be organized in Castile" [último ejército medieval que se organizó en Castilla] (Azcona, 275) is virtually indistinguishable from his account of the spectacular tournament that had taken place at Valladolid a few months earlier: "and each one of the great lords and other noblemen appeared to have plundered the entire world in order to appear sumptuously attired that day, and they were so closely observed that people remarked not only who had the largest entourage, but whose entourage was the most elegantly attired, who was accompanied with the most musicians, who dressed his pages and his horses most luxuriously and most elegantly" (*Crónica*, 215–16).[5]

It is possible that Flores recorded many of the events of the civil/peninsular war very soon after their occurrence; he may even have been an eyewitness or combatant in some.[6] What is most relevant to my discussion, however, is not the degree of accuracy of the chronicle, or its construction of war as ludic spectacle; rather, it is the concern of Flores's royal employer to set the historical record of her reign straight ab initio, literally in the heat of battle.

Isabel clearly had a keen appreciation for the propagandistic value of historiographic discourse. From the moment of her accession, she set out to craft a master narrative of her reign. She replaced the court historians appointed by her predecessors Juan II and Enrique IV with her own appointees, and she greatly enhanced the prestige of the post, primarily by increasing and regularizing its salary (Kagan, "Clio," 75). Her charge to the chroniclers was twofold: first and foremost, to legitimize her contested sovereignty by negating her rival's claims, and second, to justify the institutionalization of royal absolutism.

In this chapter I discuss the highly sexualized discourse of the contemporary Isabelline historical record, and especially its preoccupation with both male and female sexual deviancy. My primary focus will be Alfonso de Palencia's *Crónica de Enrique IV* (Chronicle of Enrique IV), begun after 1477, but I shall also refer to the chronicles written by Diego de Valera, Fernando del Pulgar, and Juan de Flores.[7] The work of these court historians clearly exemplifies what Gregory Bredbeck identifies as "the simple but central principle that the articulation of order demands means of accounting for disorder, and these means frequently involve issues of sex, sexuality, and eroticism" (47).

I first identify and analyze a "discourse of effeminacy" crafted by Palencia and his contemporaries that causally connects transgressive sexuality and a disturbed sociopolitical order.[8] Its immediate goal is the stigmatization of Isabel's predecessor Enrique IV as sodomitic in order to denigrate him as a man and to discredit him as monarch and his daughter as heir to the throne. But it must also be situated within a broader political context of Trastamaran legitimation, centralization, and expanded monarchic authority.

Finally, I go beyond the regicentric analysis to discuss some of the implications of these masculine sexual and gender anxieties for the rise of humanism in Spain as in the rest of Europe. The *crónicas*, I argue, are significant texts for understanding not only the sexual politics of Isabel's reign, but also the deeply embedded patriarchal values of the humanist project cultivated by university-trained jurists and scholars that she and Fernando increasingly depended on to administer their growing bureaucracy. Those values were instrumental in shaping cultural masculinity in the formative period of Spain's national identity.

Perhaps the most powerful evidence of the effectiveness of Palencia's "discourse of effeminacy" is the uncritical transmission of the epithet "el Impotente" (The Impotent) for Enrique IV throughout more than five hundred years of Spanish historiography. William Phillips's judicious treatment of the monarch and his reign summarizes the vast and long-lasting influence that Palencia has had on Spanish historiography. Phillips supplies a partial list of the historians from the fifteenth through the twentieth centuries who have accepted more or less at face value Palencia's sexualized interpretation of politics and society in the last half of the fifteenth century. It includes, to name only the most prominent, Fernando del Pulgar, Diego de Valera, Andrés Bernáldez, Lorenzo Galíndez de Carvajal, Gonzalo Chacón, William H. Prescott, J. H. Mariéjol, R. B. Merriman, and Gregorio Marañón. This enumeration of Palencian historians could easily be extended into the present. The Columbus quincentenary recently contributed new hagiographic portrayals of Isabel as the virile restorer of order and light to a nation weakened by the dark chaos of Enrique's effeminacy. One example among the many that could be cited is the 1992 biography of Isabel by Luis Suárez Fernández, which describes Enrique as "inconstant, cyclothymic, cowardly, abundantly endowed with the goodness of the weak who give away everything" [inconstante, ciclotímico, cobarde, abundantemente dotado de la bondad de los débiles que todo lo entregan] (21).

Any discussion of the reciprocal inflection of sexual and political power relations is indebted to Michel Foucault and the queer theorists who have come after him, extending and sometimes revising his work.[9] Particularly useful for my examination of Palencia's *Crónica de Enrique IV* has been Eve Sedgwick's feminist formulation of queer theory. Sedgwick is careful to treat homosexuality as a point in the continuum of male homosocial desire that is constitutive of patriarchy and to make plain the misogyny that always underlies homophobia: "[H]omophobia directed by men against men is misogynistic and perhaps transhistorically so. By 'misogynistic' I mean not only that it is oppressive of the so-called feminine in men, but that is oppressive of women" (20). This concept helps to clarify the subtle and complex ways in which homophobia and misogyny interact in the chroniclers' stigmatization of a feminized Enrique IV, and it suggests that the anxieties produced by the behavior of Enrique and Isabel arise from a perceived instability of gender roles and identity caused by and contributing to a generalized disturbance in the social order. For, as we shall see, the wild accusations against Enrique and the more cautious ones against Isabel have as much to do with their gender role violations—on the one hand, a king's passivity and failure to control his adulterous queen, and, on the other, a queen's will to power and unseemly domination of her husband—as with any real or imagined sexual transgressions.

It would, of course, be anachronistic to identify any individual as possessing a homosexual subjectivity in the fifteenth century.[10] In the medieval and early-modern period, the homosexual was defined as a sodomite. A juridical category, sodomite designated any person, man or woman, who participated in a sexual act not having as its goal procreation within marriage, that is, any act that threatened the structures of alliance and consequently the power hierarchy and social stability maintained by those structures (Foucault, 37–38).[11] Sodomy was thus viewed as a temptation to which anyone, and especially unformed adolescents who did not yet have their appetites under control, might succumb. In his *Crónica de los Reyes Católicos,* roughly contemporaneous with Palencia's chronicle, Fernando del Pulgar blames Enrique's homosexuality on his being introduced at the age of fourteen to "unsuitable pleasures" [deleites no debidos] that he was unable to resist because of his inexperience and that became a habit of depravity (235).[12]

In practice, sexual acts stigmatized as sodomitical in the Renaissance only became visible when those who performed those acts, or even were accused of performing them, were persons who threatened the established social order: heretics, traitors, spies, and so on (Bray, 25). This "utterly confused" (Foucault, 101) and "slippery" (Bredbeck, 21) character of sodomy before the advent of modernity makes it virtually impossible to untangle the threads of race, class, gender, ethnicity, and sexuality that are tightly knotted in many Renaissance texts, including many works shaped by or promoting the profoundly exclusionary ideology of Isabelline Spain.[13]

The awareness that the sodomitical belongs to an undifferentiated catalog of otherness informs Bredbeck's analysis of the ideological uses of the "poetics of sodomy" in Renaissance satire, in which homoeroticism becomes embedded within a mythology of the unnatural, the alien, and the demonic (5). Precisely because it is fundamentally synecdochic, sodomitical discourse provides "a way to encompass and demonize a multitude of sins—everything from foreign languages to monstrous men—with a minimum of signs" (13–14). The use of sodomy to attack undifferentiated vice helps to explain the diffuseness of Palencia's stigmatization of Enrique, as well as its constant slippage into attacks on Jews, Moors, Portuguese, *conversos,* parvenus, and women.[14] In its aggressive efforts to demonize elements that threaten the integrity of orthodox social structures, discursive sodomy in fifteenth-century Castilian texts serves a proudly conservative purpose that perfectly suited the Isabelline political program. The establishment of the Inquisition under the aegis of the crown (1478) and the expulsion of the Jews (1492) are only the two most famous events of Isabel's reign that can be adduced to prove this point.[15]

Research by historians Bartolomé Benassar and Rafael Carrasco on Inquisitional attacks on "abominable sins" [pecados abominables] help situate the politics and poetics of sodomy in this period. Carrasco rigorously documents the confusion of the category of sodomy for a slightly later period: "[B]ehind the sodomite, bearer of pestilence, is the outline of the *converso*. They are joined together in the worst popular insult that could be hurled: faggot Jew!"[16] The English translation of "puto judío" as "Jewish whore" cannot fully convey its abjection because the masculinization of the term *puta* here doubly stigmatizes the Jewish male, figuring him not only as feminine whore, but also as the passive partner in the masculine sodomitic act.

In a similar vein, Arturo Firpo suggests that the marked sexualization of much political writing of the fifteenth century, for example, the obscene *Coplas del Provincial* (Songs of the provincial) (1465–74), in which the anonymous satirist hurls accusations of sodomy and Judaizing against contemporary aristocrats, is the result of two interrelated factors: first, the new preoccupation with purity of blood with its inevitable links to sexual control and heightened conjugal normativity, and second, the confusion in the noble lineages since the reign of Alfonso X (1252–84). Adding to the disorder caused by the large numbers of bastard aristocratic offspring was the advancement at court of many parvenus (148).

From the preceding, one can better understand why, in the foundational myths disseminated in the historiography of fifteenth-century Castile, the originary differences of sex/gender are inextricable from other alterities such as class and race. Just such a conflation of sodomy, social climbing, and Jewishness underlies Palencia's confident location of the introduction of sodomy in Castile in a single person: the powerful and ill-fated Alvaro de Luna, favorite of Juan II: "in whose time there originated the infamous obscene relations that spread so shamefully in later times" (2:30).[17] Although he was not of Jewish background, Luna was of illegitimate birth, Aragonese, and a staunch defender of centralized and expanded monarchic authority. Worst of all, he supported the preferment of lowborn *conversos* to administrative positions in the government. In the list of grievances against Juan II circulated by a group of dissident grandees in 1440, the *conversos* are significantly called *estrangeros* (foreigners) (Hutcheson, "Seeking Sodom," 225).[18]

The same slippery poetics of sodomy pervades Palencia's physical and psychological portrait of Isabel's predecessor in the *Crónica de Enrique IV*. The following comments on Enrique's appearance, character, behavior, and tastes are culled from the "Primera Década" (First decade), which recounts events occurring from 1440 until 1468, when Prince Alfonso's death ensured the succession of a woman to the throne of Castile. In his physical description of King Enrique, Palencia notes his "great resemblance to a monkey" [gran semejanza con el mono] (1:11), and observes that "he sniffed with delight the stench of putrefaction, and the stink of the shaved hooves of horses, and of burned leather... so that by the sense of smell one can judge the others" (1:12).[19] He strongly disapproves of Enrique's solitary nature, noting that "he avoided social relations" [huía del trato de las gentes] (1:39) and that, "enamored of the darkest parts of the forests, only in the deepest ones did he seek rest" [enamorado de lo tenebroso de las selvas, sólo en las más espesas buscó el descanso] (1:11). Palencia views these traits as damaging Enrique's marital relations with Juana (although, as we shall see, Palencia and his fellow chroniclers are distinctly ambivalent about assigning culpability for the sexual failure of the marriage). He also describes the king as "completely devoid of conjugal affection" [enteramente ajeno al conyugal afecto], and he reproves "the sudden absences, the constantly interrupted conversation, his severe scowl, and his delight in excursions to secluded places" (1:11).[20]

The monarch's sartorial tastes are also censured: "his inappropriate dress and slovenly footwear; his lugubrious-looking apparel, without the adornment of a chain or other royal or military insignia" (1:11).[21] The reproach targets something rather more serious than an unprincely lack of ostentation, because the primary role of the king in the medieval period was that of warrior. Enrique's credibility in this regard is further compromised by his fascination with Islamic culture. Thus, for example, Palencia reproaches the king for going to a siege of Granada "more to contemplate the city than to attack it" [más a contemplar la ciudad que a combatirla] (1:71), and he objects that Enrique "preferred the short stirrups used by Arab cavalry, suitable for marauding, incursions, and skirmishes, to our more noble bridle . . . [which] makes us imposing and strong on expeditions and military exercises" (1:11).[22] The king's maurophilia not only has an adverse effect on his personal habits, it also casts a shadow over his religious orthodoxy, for "even in his gait, in his food, and in his habit of reclining when eating, and in other secret and more indecent excesses, he had preferred the customs of the Moors to those of the Christian religion" (1:74).[23]

Enrique displays a similarly deplorable indifference to class and race hierarchy, demonstrated by his choice of advisers. Palencia condemns his "adding to his retinue many other followers whose names certainly did not bring to mind the luster of the ancient families, rather the most abject condition" (1:74).[24] He also blames him for constructing "a vast and magnificent building where he shut himself up with scoundrels . . . of which the most favored were a dwarf and an Ethiopian as horrible as he was stupid" (1:230).[25]

It is difficult to find a common denominator for such a variegated series of characteristics and affinities, among them introversion, sensuality, exoticism, misanthropy, cowardice, a love of nature and the hunt, passivity, egalitarianism. But that is precisely the point: Palencia creates a synecdochical chain that associates the king's multifarious stigmatized traits to his "nefarious iniquities" [nefandas iniquidades] (1:73); "all manner of licentiousness" [toda suerte de liviandades] (1:52); "disgusting vices" [vicios infames]; and "innumerable abuses whose enumeration makes me blush and embarrasses me" [innumerables abusos . . . cuya enumeración me sonroja y me apena] (1:83). Palencia's reticence reminds us that sex between men had been famous throughout the Judeo-Christian tradition precisely for having no name, for being "unspeakable" and "unmentionable," its very namelessness and enforced secrecy a form of social control (Sedgwick, 94). Sodomy's very lack of specificity, its undefined and indefinable nature, gives Palencia's discourse its rhetorical force, making the Henrician "abominable vice" infinitely expansive and highly contaminating. It easily reaches apocalyptic levels: "the seed of the universal ruin that was fast approaching" [el germen de la ruina universal que a toda prisa se venía encima] (1:73); "the corruption of all humanity" [la corrupción de la humanidad entera] (1:83); and a "general upheaval" [general trastorno] (1:83). Similarly, the sodomites with whom the king surrounds himself become nothing less than demonic: "friends of darkness... possessed of a certain fury to exterminate goodness and cause catastrophes" (1:83).[26]

Historical evidence of the king's impotence ranges from the documentary to the fanciful, but absolutely none of it is conclusive (Azcona, 20–22; O'Callaghan, 573). A few examples of the "proof" of the sovereign's impotence will illustrate its highly problematic nature. Enrique's detractors cited the failure of his first wife Blanca de Navarra to produce an heir after three and a half years of marriage, leading to the king's petitioning the pope for a divorce; the related claims that Blanca had bewitched the king, causing his temporary impotence; and the 1464 declaration in defense of Juana's legitimacy by the king's physician, Fernández de Soria, that at the age of twelve Enrique "had lost his potency" but had later recovered it. They also adduce Enrique's own supposed allusions to the illegitimacy of his daughter in 1464 when he declared his half brother Alfonso heir to the throne: "Be it known that I, in order to avoid any manner of scandal that may occur after our death regarding the succession to my kingdom" (quoted in Paz y Melia, lx), as well as the pact he was forced to sign at Toros de Guisando after Alfonso's death, in order to avert a civil war. There he named Isabel legitimate successor to the Castilian throne "in order that the kingdom does not remain without legitimate successors of the lineage of said King and said Princess" (quoted in ibid., lix), and agreed to a divorce from Juana because "it is public knowledge and manifest that the Queen Doña Juana, for a year now, has not been chaste in her person as befits the service of said King... and also said king is informed that he was not nor is he legitimately married to her" (quoted in ibid., lx).[27]

In addition, numerous anecdotes pertaining to this highly charged issue have survived. Among them are the king's deathbed refusal, despite the urging of his confessor, to clarify the questions surrounding his rightful heir; the testimony of a number of Segovian prostitutes, expert witnesses called upon during the divorce proceedings to testify as to the proper functioning of the royal member: "He had a virile member that was firm and paid its debt in potent seed just like any other male" (quoted in Sitges, 47); the joke about Enrique's penis told by one Gonzalo de Guzmán on the occasion of the king's wedding to Juana: "he said... that there were three things that he would not bend down to pick up if he saw them thrown in the street, namely, Enrique's sex organs, the Marquis's speech [a reference to Juan Pacheco's stutter], and the archbishop of Sevilla's gravity" (Palencia, 1:76);[28] the rumors that princess Juana's nose had been broken at birth to compensate for the fact that she bore no physical resemblance to Enrique, and that an attempt had been made to exchange her for a male child born on the same day in the same town (Paz y Melia, lviii–lix). Finally, there is the German doctor Hieronymus Münzer's diagnosis of the king's problem based on conversations with members of Isabel's court twenty years after Enrique's death: "[H]is member was thin and weak at the base but large at the head, so that he could not have an erection," and "his semen was thin and watery" (quoted in Liss, 47).

According to Orestes Ferrara, author of the first important modern revisionist treatment of Enrique's reign, the imputation to Enrique of "abominable iniquities" was widely disseminated. It functioned largely to support the accusation of impotence that was circulated some ten years earlier, two years after the birth of the Princess Juana in 1462. At the moment of her birth, the infanta Juana's legitimacy was unquestioned.[29] The rumor about her paternity was first circulated by the league of dissident nobles in the famous "protest letter" [carta-protesta] of September 1464.[30] It contained a litany of royal offenses accusing Enrique of consorting with Jews and Muslims, bestowing public office on persons of low birth, giving excessive power and privilege to his *privado* Beltrán de la Cueva (including the powerful mastership of the military order of Santiago that by testamentary right belonged to Prince Alfonso), even allowing him sexual access to Queen Juana. The alleged illegitimacy of Juana owing to the impotence of her father and the adulterous liaison between his favorite and his queen became the rallying cry of the Alfonsine faction, and, upon Alfonso's death, of the Isabelline faction. The accusation was presented as fact in the chronicles commissioned by Isabel, and eventually became crystallized in the long-lasting sobriquet "Beltran's bastard" [La Beltraneja], a pejorative reference to Juana's presumed fathering by her father's favorite. Despite the institutionalization of the accusations against her, Princess Juana's illegitimacy has never been proven. It was conjured up to justify "the triumph of the collateral branch over the direct branch [which] was determined by arms, not law" (Ferrara, 340).[31]

What is indisputable is the blatantly propagandistic nature of most of the contemporary historical writing about Enrique's reign and the fact that it was closely overseen by Isabel. There is ample evidence, presented by the historian Jaime Vicens Vives and others, that the Queen ordered the revision of chronicles and falsification of documents in order to legitimate a posteriori her assumption of the crown.[32] Furthermore, the chroniclers' severe moral condemnation of Enrique's reign, as well as their identification of the year 1464 (the date of the seditious "Carta-protesta") as the nadir of the Castilian monarchy, cannot be divorced from the belief, held by those same writers, that the succession of Isabel was the result of providential intervention (Tate, *Ensayos,* 288).[33]

Scholars have amply discussed the messianic tone of fifteenth-century historiography in Castile in the light of the *converso* origins of many of the chroniclers, Palencia included.[34] Isabelline messianism has not, however, been situated within the period's sex/gender system and its relationship with the hierarchical operations of power, that is to say, in terms of the sexual politics of the Middle Ages. Gender is implicit, however, in Robert Brian Tate's discussion of the "recuperative modeling" of the fifteenth-century chronicles from Rodrigo Sánchez de Arévalo on:

> the native historian seems to have awakened to a new sense of the integrity of his country and the uniqueness of its historical experience.... The Romans were presented as undermining the rough virtues of the primitive Iberians with their introduction of effeminate and sophisticated pleasures such as hot baths and wine drinking. The Visigoths, although equally colonizers, were seen as spiritual brothers of the Iberians, being praised for their virility and their great vigor, the ultimate cause of the collapse of decadent Rome. (Ibid., 293–94)[35]

The chroniclers' insistence that the virile Castilian temperament was inherited from the Iberians and the Visigoths is bolstered by proof, often fictitious, of an uninterrupted line of descent from the primitive tribes to the Castilian sovereigns.[36] In this foundational myth, Isabel embodies the fulfilment of the Castilian God-given mission—"Hispaniam restaurare et recuperare"—to restore what the Moorish invasion had destroyed: the integrity of the Castilian political body.[37]

The use of the human body as a fundamental symbolic site of social systems has been well studied by cultural materialists.[38] In the late Middle Ages and the early-modern period, this corporeal mode of representation can be observed, for example, in the concept of the king as the head of the state figured as a *corpus mysticum* or in the concept of the monarch's "two bodies," the one physical and temporal and the other divine and eternal.[39] A key event in the struggle for power between Enrique and the faction supporting Alfonso's (later Isabel's) claim to the throne is discursively inflected by such corporeal symbolics. It is the so-called Farsa de Ávila that took place on June 5, 1465.

Civil war had been brewing since the fall of the previous year, but had been held at bay by a frantic round of negotiations between Enrique and the dissident band that sought to curtail his power and enhance their own by supporting Prince Alfonso.[40] When negotiations broke down, the Alfonsine band gathered in Ávila on June 5, 1465, to depose their king in effigy. They based their act on ancient Visigothic tradition of nobiliary appointment of a king, medieval political theory regarding the right to depose a tyrant, and the popular right of acclamation (Liss, 59). Not all were in agreement with this seditious act. Fernando del Pulgar's chronicle describes the bishop of Calahorra's desperate attempt to impede the seditious act in the following terms: "It is well known, my Lords, that the entire Kingdom is considered to be a body, of which we take the King to be the head; which, if ill due to some weakness, it would seem best to administer those medicines that reason prescribes, rather than to cut off the head that nature defends... because if Kings are anointed by God on earth, we should not consider them subject to human judgment" (*Crónica*, 230).[41]

The bishop's conciliatory attitude did not prevail, and the rebels proceeded to carry out the ritual dramatically recorded (and embellished) by Diego de Valera in his *Memorial de diversas hazañas* (Memorandum about diverse deeds): "the Archbishop of Toledo Alonso Carrillo ascended the platform and took off his crown... and the Marquis of Villena, Juan Pacheco, took the royal scepter from his hand... and the Count of Benavente, Rodrigo Pimentel, and the Count of Paredes, Rodrigo Manrique, took off all the other royal adornments, and kicking him off the platform they yelled 'Eat dirt, faggot... Eat dirt, faggot!'" (33).[42] The violent attack on the symbolic sovereign body escalates in intensity, beginning with the removal of the crown, continuing with the ripping away of the phallic scepter and sword, and culminating in the violation expressed by the insult "Eat dirt, faggot!"[43] The graphic symbolism used to relate the ritual dethronement leaves no doubt that the task of "restoring" Castile that begins with this act of treason and is brought to fruition by Isabel and Fernando is conceived of in violently sexual terms. For my purposes, what is most significant about the reiterated historiographical motif of *reintegratio Hispaniae* is its conceptual linking of sociopolitical integrity and virility, that is, the linking of the political body and the (masculine) physical body. The restoration of the nation is presented as the restoration of a native virility corrupted not only by the repeated invasions of foreign, effeminate peoples—first the Romans and later, and more catastrophically, the Muslims—but also by the equally effeminate internal enemy who similarly threatens the health of the masculine body politic.

It is important to remember that Enrique is not the first of these degenerate enemies from within. His grandfather, Pedro I, whose murder in 1369 by his illegitimate half brother Enrique II led to the founding of the Trastamaran dynasty, was rumored to be a bastard fathered by a certain Pero Gil, a Jew. His name was assimilated to the term *perejil* or parsley, a euphemism for effeminacy (Hutcheson, "Sodomitic Moor," 111). In his *Compendiosa Historia Hispanica* (Compendious history of Spain) (c. 1470), Rodrigo Sánchez de Arévalo records the legend of the buffoon who addressed Pedro I as he lay mortally wounded in the tent of Bernard du Guesclin, a French ally in the civil war between Pedro and his half brother Enrique. The buffoon suggests that the king has had an unnatural friendship with him.[44] The accusation of illegitimacy and sodomy against Pedro I, legitimate king of Castile murdered by his brother Enrique II in 1369, has an important function in Arévalo's chronicle. It displaces a double anxiety over the legitimacy of the Trastamaran line founded by Enrique II: double because Enrique was both bastard and usurper. The slur reveals that the sexualization of political relationships was already a strategy used by the generation of historians writing immediately before Palencia. Sánchez de Arévalo's chronicle leaves little doubt about the fundamental role that the discourse of transgressive sexuality and gender instability played in the foundational myths of the Trastamara dynasty, myths crafted to a large extent by the fifteenth-century *cronistas*. As Gregory Hutcheson observes: "Enrique's defeat of Pedro in 1369 and the subsequent founding of the Trastamaran dynasty was a victory won as much in the realm of discourse as it was on the battlefield; it might be said, in fact, that here is where Spain discovered the power of the propaganda machine" ("Sodomitic Moor," 110).[45]

Palencia builds on this precedent to create a kind of genealogy of sodomy and illegitimacy.[46] He claims that Juan II, great-grandson of Enrique II and father of Enrique IV and Isabel, also had sodomitical propensities, "since from his most tender youth he had put himself in the hands of Alvaro de Luna, not without the suspicion of indecorous behavior and lascivious pleasures on the part of the favorite in his relationship with the King" (1:9).[47] This suggestion then casts doubt upon Enrique IV's legitimacy, just as the latter's familial abnormality—"wallowing in disgusting vices since his most tender youth" [encenegado desde su más tierna niñez en vicios infames] (1:74)—promotes the ultimate goal of fostering suspicion about his daughter Juana's legitimacy. Returning to the reign of Enrique, we can now see that the effeminacy obsessively associated with him in Palencia's *Crónica de Enrique IV* responds to an anxiety of legitimacy on the part of Isabel and her apologists very similar to that of the Trastamaran founding father, Enrique II. Although not illegitimate of birth like her great-great-grandfather, Isabel is equally a usurper.

But the sodomitical genealogy crafted by Palencia and other Isabelline chroniclers extends beyond the immediate context of the fierce struggle for the Castilian throne. It constitutes an important strategy in the ambitious political program of the new queen: nothing less than to impose on her heterogeneous and fractious subjects the patriarchal values of homogeneity, authority, and centralism that she considered essential to building a strong nation-state and imposing her authority over it. As Ferrara remarks, the monarchs "move from a victory of arms to a triumph of paper. Isabel, with her natural vigor, oversaw the account of the chroniclers in order to ensure a verdict favorable to posterity" (340). Ironically, this contemporary historian's naturalization of Isabel's vigor is in itself evidence of the propaganda program's success, since the enduring perception of the queen's vigor largely results from a concerted effort to construct her public persona as masculine. And that construction is coterminous with the construction of her half brother as "an execrable monster because he was not at all a man" [monstruo execrable, puesto que nada de hombre tenía] (Palencia, 1:74).

The rhetorical masculinization of Queen Isabel is inextricable from her hyperfeminization as the Virgin's earthly counterpart, treated briefly in the last chapter and examined more extensively in the next. Both treatments share the misogynist belief that the worthy woman can only be one who transcends the limitations of her gender. Examples of the fashioning of Isabel as *mujer varonil* are not as common as those equating her to Mary, but neither are they difficult to find. A vivid example is

Juan de Lucena's adulatory portrayal of Isabel in his *Epístola exhortatoria a las letras* (Epistle exhorting to letters), addressed to the queen's royal secretary. He evokes a vigorous, peripatetic sovereign, one who has covered the nation "pitching our camps, leading our battles, breaching our sieges; hearing our complaints; informing our moral judgment... circling her kingdoms, traveling, traveling, never stopping" (215).[48] The catalog ends with the exclamation: "Oh heart of a man dressed as a woman, epitome of queens, model for all women, and for all men a subject to write about!" (216).[49]

Isabel as virago also figures prominently in Juan de Flores's *Crónica incompleta*. Flores repeatedly extols Isabel's manliness in handling difficult affairs of state and military matters. In recounting her delicate negotiations to win over the politically fickle archbishop of Toledo, for example, he observes that "not like a woman but like a brave man she takes to heart the weight of such a grave responsibility" [no como muger, mas como esforçado varón toma bien en el alma el peso de tan grand cuydado] (208). He also praises the queen's bellicosity: "but even in matters of war no man could be so diligent and solicitous" [mas avn en cosas de la guerra ningund varon tanta soliçitud y diligençia podiera poner] (310). Most dramatically, on the occasion of the humiliating retreat of the Castilian troops from the siege of Toro, the chronicler puts in Isabel's mouth "words more befitting a courageous man than a fearful woman" [palabras de varón muy esforçado más que de muger temerosa] (238): "There I was in my palace with an angry heart, gritted teeth, and clenched fists, as if I were fighting with myself out of revenge, and if such anguish had taken hold of you, sirs, the greatest danger presented by your enemies would have been less than your own to yourselves. Being a woman, I am amazed at my anger, just as I am at your patience, being men" (241–42).[50]

In this extraordinary harangue (very likely invented by Flores), an irate but supremely self-controlled sovereign skillfully manipulates gender stereotypes in order to castigate the Castilian troops, led by the king himself. Isabel here appears fully conscious of her status as manly woman and entirely capable of using it to figure her husband and his soldiers as effeminate, that is, as cowardly, men.

The inversion of gender roles and power relations in Flores's portrayal of the Queen reveals the radical contradiction at the heart of the reciprocal gender construction of Enrique and Isabel. The virago whom Lucena, Flores, and others praise is as transgressive in the context of the gender ideology of the period as the effeminate man they repudiate so violently. The woman who rules is nothing short of monstrous, because of her inversion of the power hierarchy on which the patriarchal social institutions of the family, the church, and the state rest. Resistence to that inversion in the late-medieval and Renaissance periods has been well documented for Elizabethan England.[51] Clear evidence of the same attitude in Spain is found in a letter of 1486 written by Francisco de Rojas. The monarchs sent Rojas to Rome to petition the pope that Isabel be granted perpetual administration of the Spanish military orders, a position accruing enormous wealth and power. He reports back to Fernando in the following words: "I certify to your majesty that the most difficult of the many tasks I had to achieve in Rome was having the pope grant that it [the administration] be exclusively the queen's right. Because the pope and all the cardinals and the jurists considered it to be completely illegal and a monstrous thing that a woman should be allowed the administration of orders" (cited in Azcona, 728).[52]

The construction of female sovereignty as monstrous accounts for a singular slippage in Palencia's discourse of effeminacy, a seamless slide from the sodomitic to the misogynistic, from attacks on the weak Enrique to assaults on the powerful Isabel. It soon becomes evident that for the chronicler it is not the sodomite per se that is most threatening, but rather the larger category woman, and in particular, the unsubmissive, willful woman on top, who functions as the most basic alterity and the greatest threat to masculine identity and power.

Tate has pointed out the surprisingly overt criticism of Isabel that begins to accumulate in the pages of Palencia's *Crónica,* starting in the second and third "Decades." He suggests that it is part of Palencia's general stern disapprobation of what he considers a typically feminine "will to dominate" [prurito de dominar], a thirst for power that has no less disastrous consequences for the public sphere than male homosexuality (168). Palencia's censure of Isabel begins in his description of her precipitous self-proclamation upon the death of Enrique IV in December of 1474 (Tate, "Políticas sexuales," 170). As we saw in chapter 2, it appears to have been entirely Isabel's idea to have her chief steward lead her coronation procession through the streets of Segovia holding aloft an unsheathed sword. Palencia records the effect that this appropriation of the phallic symbol of royal authority by a female sovereign had on some of those present: "there were some well-intentioned subjects who grumbled about its unprecedented nature, for it seemed to them that it was foolishly ostentatious for a wife to display the attributes of the husband" (2:155).[53]

Palencia here levels his criticism at the gender inappropriateness of Isabel's ceremonial symbolism, but also, and more importantly, at her refusal to adopt, even for the sake of appearances, the role of queen consort. He invests this initial uxorial usurpation with dark portent, judging that "this created the seed of grave disputes to the liking of the grandees, fomenters of new disturbances, as shall be seen later" (2:155).[54] Later, Palencia attributes full agency to Isabel in a continuing subversion of marital relations of power: "The queen had long been preparing—since right after her marriage—what any prudent man would judge harmful to the future succession of these kingdoms: to diminish the influence of her husband in case, in the event of her death, some contingency occurred in the normal line of succession" (2:192).[55]

A common technique employed by Palencia to strengthen his criticism of Isabel is to ventriloquize it into Fernando. Concerning the same queenly ostentation of the sword, for example, he has the king say: "I would like you, Palencia, who have read so many histories, to tell me if there is any precedent in antiquity of a queen who had herself preceded by that symbol of the threat of punishment for her vassals" (2:162).[56] Also telling is Fernando's whining response to the tongue-lashing he receives from his wife on the occasion of the humiliating Castilian retreat from the siege of Toro, as told by Flores: "I thought that if we arrived routed you would have on your tongue words of consolation and encouragement; but seeing us arrive safe and with our honor intact, you berate us? What trouble we shall have with you from now on! But even when men are well-disposed, brave, capable, and elegant, women are difficult to please, especially you, madam, because the man who can please you is yet to be born" (245).[57]

Returning to Palencia, it is clear that the stronger and more dominating he portrays the Queen, the weaker the King appears. Her gender-role transgressions have the effect of feminizing him, making him dangerously uxorious (Tate, "Políticas sexuales," 168). Fernando's complaints about the Castilian efforts to limit his sovereign powers sound more petulant than forceful: "told the queen that in no way would he keep on suffering such grave offenses, nor the grumbling of the people, who attributed his abandonment of the role of the man to baseness. . . . He thus preferred to retire to his father's kingdom, thereby avoiding the shamefulness of the dispute" (2:167).[58] Such language ends up implicitly associating Fernando with Enrique, who "embraced the shield more eagerly than he grasped the scepter" [embrazó la adarga con más gusto que empuñó el cetro] (1:11) and whose weakly grasped scepter was, in the chroniclers' view, properly snatched away by Isabel's future supporters at the Farsa de Ávila.[59]

Palencia's gradual self-distancing from Isabel appears to have come to a climax during the preparations for the famous Cortes held in Toledo in 1480, shortly after the conclusion of the civil war. The monarchs used these Cortes as a forum for unveiling their program of governmental and social reform. In Liss's words, it was intended to "bring about a revolution in the scope and efficacy of central government, converting realm to state. It incorporated the vision of strong personal monarchy propounded at midcentury, the orthodoxy demanded by the critics of Enrique's reign, and...was invested with the same vigorous spirit of straightening up morally, spiritually, and administratively then also propelling a royal scheme of ecclesiastical reform" (182).[60]

Gender anxieties also attended this transition from the medieval to the modern. They made themselves felt in a clash that took place between Palencia and the Queen during the Cortes. The ostensible occasion for the convocation of the Cortes was the swearing of Prince Juan, born the previous year, as Isabel's legitimate heir (Liss, 181). During a debate on the future role of the prince, Palencia apparently disagreed with the queen (Tate, "Preceptos," 42). Although the details are not clear, an underlying issue seems to have been precisely Palencia's perception of abnormality in the monarchs' conjugal relations of power. In the "Fourth Decade" of his *Crónica,* Palencia makes the following querulous observation: "In every way possible the queen opposed those who resisted her will" [De todas las formas posibles se opuso la reina a cuantos ofrecían resistencia a su voluntad], and, more trenchantly, "she was considered a master of pretense and deception" [era tenida por maestra de disimulo y fingimiento] (translated by Tate, "Preceptos," 42).

The struggle of wills between sovereign and servant on this matter had a predictable outcome: the marginalization of Palencia and the promotion of his colleague Fernando del Pulgar, who was less resistant to royal censorship of his work (Tate, "Décadas," 226). Pulgar's famous letter "para la Reyna" written in 1482 provides evidence for the direct involvement of Isabel in the fashioning of the historical record that I discussed earlier. Most likely a response to the honor of Isabel's naming him official historian, Pulgar's epistle demonstrates his understanding of the messianic and sexualized theme of corruption transformed into order that his *Crónica de los Reyes Católicos* (much of which he had already redacted) highlights. The letter also affirms his willingness, should that understanding falter, to submit to "royal censorship" [censura de cámara] (Mata Carriazo, xlii): "I will come to your highness whenever you send for me and will bring what I have written so far so that you can have it examined; because for writing about times of such injustice, transformed by the grace of God in justice, of so much disobedience transformed into obedience, so much corruption into such order, I confess, madam, that a better head than mine is required" (*Letras*, ed. Domínguez Bordona, 62).[61]

Given this attitude, the flattering portrait of the queen that Pulgar paints in his *Crónica* is hardly surprising. Particularly revealing is his remark that "for the most part she did things according to her own discretion" [por la mayor parte seguía las cosas por arbitrio] (257) rather than bowing to that of her advisers. Such strong-mindedness is the same trait castigated by the marginalized Palencia, a contrast that provides insight into how the queen wished to be represented. Pulgar's praise of Isabel for keeping her own counsel also contrasts with his own reproof of Enrique for doing the same thing in the biographical sketch he includes in his *Claros varones de Castilla:* "He was a man who did most things according to his own will (6)."[62] The paradox vividly illustrates the gender ideology upheld by Isabel as it castigates a character trait of a weak, feminized king—willfulness—while simultaneously admiring (and fearing?) that same trait in a strong, masculinized queen.

In protesting his ungrateful treatment by his patron, Palencia consciously or unconsciously allies himself with Fernando as an undeserving victim of Isabelline emasculation. In this way, he paradoxically enhances his status as confidant to the king and assimilates them both to the royal genealogy of effeminacy that he had originally created to defame Enrique IV.

What, then, are we to make of the contradictory attitude of Palencia to the virile queen he has been in good measure responsible for fashioning? I suggest that the discourse of effeminacy Palencia aims at Enrique for the purpose of promoting Isabel's political legitimacy and authority also serves a more personal function. It expresses and contains the sexual and political anxiety that her anomalous power arouses in the ambitious intellectual, and, we may assume, in the equally ambitious nobles and courtiers that would have formed his readership. However, whereas Tate sees a change occurring in Palencia's attitude to his sovereign, I would argue that the negative view of her masculinity (her power and authority) is present all along, inherent in the constant rhetorical slippage—from sexuality to gender, from homophobia to misogyny—characteristic of the discourse of effeminacy.

Misogyny pervades the *Crónica de Enrique IV*. The following are but two examples: "a sex so weak and given to pleasures" [un sexo tan débil y tan propenso a los placeres] (1:82); "that passion characteristic of the sex that makes them willingly plunge into the promptings of desire, and will the destruction of everything, provided that their desire be satisfied" (1:18).[63] Such comments almost always occur at crucial political junctures, as in Palencia's account of the Portuguese invasion of Castile in 1476. The event gives him an occasion to hurl invective at the powerful Leonor de Pimentel, countess of Plasencia (Tate, "Políticas sexuales," 169). He states that the countess was accused at the time of unspecified "horrendous crimes, and remembering the fall of our first father, fatal for the entire human race, people said that in the same way, because of that woman's evil, everything would go to complete ruin" (2:194).[64] But the woman most frequently compared to Eve—"fragile woman and ancient principal instrument of the misfortune of humankind" [frágil mujer y antiguo principal instrumento de la desgracia de la humanidad] (1:132)—in the *Crónica* is Enrique IV's wife, the supposedly adulterous Juana de Portugal.

Palencia's account of the matter of Juana's adultery is curiously equivocal. On the one hand, he claims that the liaison between the queen and the king's favorite, Beltrán de la Cueva, putative father of Juana of Castile, was forced on Juana by the king: "the false simulacrum of his wedding over, he began to disclose his goal to the Queen, subjecting her to a constant seduction. In that manner he thought he would manage to rush her into seeking pleasure in illicit relations" (1:82).[65] The fact that Beltrán is alleged to either already or soon thereafter be Enrique's lover—the precise sequence of transgressions is intentionally vague—adds the suggestion of a royal menage à trois to the long list of Henrician iniquities: "the King asked him to be the principal master of his house and even, because he so willed, of his marriage bed" (1:113).⁶⁶ At the same time, however, Palencia is vitriolic in censuring the queen's loose behavior, as in the famous description of her arrival in Castile to marry Enrique, accompanied by her ladies-in-waiting:

> They had no honest occupations to recommend them.... Their continuous laughter, the constant comings and going of the go-betweens, carriers of vulgar missives, and the anxious voraciousness that afflicted them day and night... were more frequent among them than in the brothels.... they consumed most of the time in covering their bodies with cosmetics and perfumes, and did so without the least discretion; rather, they uncovered their breasts to below their bellies. (1:75)⁶⁷

Palencia's attacks on Juana also at times slip into xenophobia, as when he charges that Juana "later fomented the perfidy of the grandees so as to finally, as a native of Portugal, spread throughout this kingdom the flames that were to destroy it" (2:194).⁶⁸ By blaming Juana for the Portuguese invasion of Castile, Palencia conjures up for his readers another ambiguously stigmatized woman, La Cava, the lover of the last Visigothic King Rodrigo, who was also held responsible for the eighth-century invasion and conquest of Visigothic Spain by the Moors, viewed as a violation. Both cataclysms are thereby represented as earthly repetitions of the expulsion from Paradise ("women have always been the cause of Spain's ruin" [mujeres habían sido siempre causa de la perdición de España] [2:194]), and both women figured as descendants of Eve. This genealogy of powerful but sinful women is inseparable from the genealogy of weak and/or transgressive men (Pedro I—Alvaro de Luna—Juan II—Enrique IV) discussed earlier.⁶⁹

In view of Palencia's profound misogyny and his ambivalence toward his royal patron's power, it is perhaps not surprising that his genealogy of female sinners should incorporate Isabel herself. At times Palencia veils his critique of Isabel's unseemly behavior by attributing it to her flatterers. For example, as Fernando heads toward Seville to join Isabel after her controversial coronation ceremony, Palencia grumbles that "the machinations of the courtiers had the desired result" [las maquinaciones de los cortesanos tuvieron el resultado apetecido], that is, Isabel's resistance to Fernando's marital authority (2:165). Palencia also blames the queen's growing suspiciousness of him on "the influence of those ill-intentioned people who surrounded the Queen" [el influjo de los mal intencionados que rodeaban a la Reina] (2:163). At other times, however, he is daringly direct. When he refers to the Queen's attempts to marginalize Fernando, he complains that she, "a woman, after all" [al fin mujer], is full of "arrogance and haughtiness" [arrogancia y prepotencia] (2:165); he castigates "the vanity of the Queen ... convinced that the subordination of her husband would redound to her own glory and might" (2:168);[70] and he bitterly laments that she is in no way disposed to accept "the conditions of government that from the remotest centuries favored the male" (2:165).[71]

Palencia's growing discomfort with the virile queen whose image he helped to create suggests a growing realization that, contrary to the expectations held by many Castilians and Aragonese, Isabel and not Fernando rules in Castile. The gender-role inversion that Palencia observes in the royal couple is for him every bit as threatening as Enrique's sexual inversion. It stands for the political instability that did not in fact end with Isabel's accession, but continued to threaten the stability of the state and the career of its ambitious official historian. As it casts its net more widely, adding Isabel's abnormal masculinization to Enrique's sinful feminization, Palencia's discourse of effeminacy is transformed into an all-encompasing discourse of "inversion" or "unnaturalness."

Like the pornographic writing of *Carajicomedia* discussed in chapter 1, Palencia's discourse of effeminacy/inversion has broader cultural implications, having to do with the rise of humanism in late-medieval Castile. Decades ago, José Maravall noted the important political and cultural role of the "legists" [letrados].[72] During the reign of King Juan II (1406–54), these men of letters with advanced degrees in canon or civil law began displacing the noblemen on the royal courts and advisory councils, the growing bureaucracies of the state and the church, and later, the Inquisition. Their ascendancy paralleled the rapid expansion of monarchic power in the second half of the fifteenth century and was due in part to the perception that their loyalty would not be divided between king and kin. Thus, the percentage of *letrados* working for the crown doubled under Juan II and Enrique IV. The former had created the position of "royal chronicler" [coronista del rey] around 1450. He bestowed it on Juan de Mena, along with an extra salary or "ración" to produce an official history of his reign. The Catholic Monarchs tripled the number of *letrados* employed by the crown and church (Tate, "Historiografía,"

18). In his chronicle *Anales breves de los Reyes Católicos* (Brief annals of the Catholic Monarchs), the *letrado* Lorenzo Galíndez de Carvajal (1472–1528) recalls that Isabel and Fernando kept a book for recording the names of talented, moral men of modest background who would be worthy candidates for government and church positions (533).

The rise of the *letrados* as a kind of premodern meritocracy created a growing group consciousness based not on lineage, but rather on privileged access to the civil, secular "science" that the monarchs increasingly relied on for the administration of affairs of state (Maravall, "Hombres de saber," 346–47).[73] The *letrados*' assiduous cultivation of this working relationship can be seen in their frequent and hardly disinterested warning that the good monarch surrounds himself with and seeks counsel from "learned men" [hombres de saber] while the tyrant distances and mistreats them (Maravall, "Hombres de saber," 354). And for the many *conversos* among the *letrados*, starting with the extremely influential Alonso de Cartagena (1384–1456), dependency on the monarch held special significance. Because throughout the fifteenth century, Castilian society was becoming increasingly anti-*converso*, "[s]upporting the Castilian monarchy... usually meant supporting the only ally in power the *conversos* possessed" (Kaplan, 56).[74]

Palencia neatly fits this profile. A *letrado* who was very likely a *converso*, he spent several years in Italy, where he studied with George Trebizond and other renowned masters of the *studia humanitatis*.[75] In his thorough survey of fifteenth-century Iberian humanist writers, Jeremy Lawrance singles out Palencia for the variety and scope of his output. In addition to the Latin chronicle of Enrique IV's reign, Palencia wrote geographical and antiquarian studies of Spain, Lucianic satires and allegories in both Latin and Spanish, vernacular translations of Plutarch and Josephus, and a Latin–Spanish dictionary dedicated to Isabel ("Humanism," 230). Furthermore, Palencia's personal involvement in some of the most significant events of Enrique's and Isabel's reign—it was he, for example, who was selected to lead the secretive and dangerous mission that brought Fernando to Castile for his marriage to Isabel—makes his career a paradigmatic one for Castilian humanism.

The role of the *letrados* as conduits for the introduction of Italian humanist attitudes, methods, and texts to Spain has been of increasing interest to scholars studying the unique nature of Iberian humanism. Lawrance has attributed the overtly political motive behind much of the humanist project in Castile precisely to the close relationship that existed between sovereign and humanists. The *letrados*' placement of their learning at the service of the regalist and centralist cause of the Trastamaran dynasty produced in their humanistic writings a narrow chauvinism, a decided anti-Italian bias, and a consistent subordination of humanistic philological concerns to nationalistic ones (253–54).[76] The monarchy in turn encouraged the humanists' allegiance to the establishment by swelling the ranks of the *letrados* and increasing their financial support: Isabel allotted the handsome salary of forty thousand maravedís to the position of chronicler (Kagan, "Clio and the Crown," 74). Isabel herself has often been credited with promoting humanistic learning and writing in Castile in various ways. Scholars point, for example, to her generous patronage of important humanists such as Antonio de Nebrija, who also served as court historian (in which capacity, in 1509, he produced a rather free translation into Latin of Pulgar's *Crónica*), and of the Italians Pietro Martire d'Anghiera and Lucio Marinio.[77]

None of the excellent studies on the convergent enterprises of humanism and nation building in Castile deals with the gender issues I have raised in regard to Palencia. In order to find such a treatment, we must turn to recent feminist scholarship on northern European humanist writers of a slightly later period, for example, Barbara Correll's and Patricia Parker's analyses of Erasmian texts. Correll examines the colloquies on marriage (*Colloquia* [1496–1529]) and the education of boys (*De Civilitate Morum Pueriliem* [1530]) for their role in the discursive structuring of feminine and masculine identity in the Renaissance, finding in both texts

> a kind of psycho-political crisis of masculine identity and authority among members of a rising intellectual bourgeoisie who sought to negotiate positions of authority in a power structure still largely determined by the hereditary nobility and the institution of the Church.... The conflict between the two groups' claims to power reveals sexual anxiety in that shifting notions of subordination and superiority call attention to women as designated subordinates who... *might* threaten the uneasy dynamics of power. (241)[78]

In Erasmus's treatises, the discursively constructed Woman functions as an essential negative that can and must be overcome by civilizing labors and education (Correll, 246). Thus, for example, Erasmus counsels married women that in order to escape abuse by their husbands they must cultivate submissiveness. Correll relates this advice to the author's own personal situation as a humanist seeking to placate church authorities critical of his teachings; that is, when used by the male administrative underling or the court intellectual, the same strategy of submissiveness advocated for the married woman will ideally be rewarded with professional patronage and social mobility. At the same time, this scheme of bending before one's superiors "retains connections to notions of feminine decorum and duty, and discloses the uneasy presence of the socially constructed feminine, threatening to erupt from its place within the new cultural manhood" (257).

The case of Fernando del Pulgar, Alfonso de Palencia's fellow chronicler and rival, illustrates the instability of the position of the *letrado*, and especially of those with *converso* background. Sometime before 1479 (that is, at least a year before the conflict between Palencia and Isabel led to Pulgar's preferment at court), an anonymous letter accusing Pulgar of Judaizing and of "speaking ill of the queen" [hablar mal de la reina] apparently caused him to fall out of royal favor and to withdraw from court for several years.[79] It was during this time that he began the chronicle that he promised to submit to the Queen for her approval (Mata Carriazo, xxxvii–xliii). Pulgar's modern biographer and editor cites as an example of the writer's "slight interest in court life" [poco apego a la vida de la corte] a letter he wrote to a nephew who inquired about his state of mind during his retreat:

> believe, sir, no man lives a better life either at court or in all of Castile. But may I die serving God, for if I left it I would not return even if they granted me the dukedom of Burgundy, given the the anguish and sadness that is interwoven and caught up in it. And since you want to know how you should address me, know, sir, that they call me Fernando, and that they called me and will call me Fernando, and if they give me the Mastership of Santiago, I'll still be Fernando; because I want to adorn myself with a title and honor that no one can take from me. (xlviii–xlix)[80]

Shortly after this renunciation of the "anguish and sorrow" that plague the courtier, Pulgar was recalled to court to displace Palencia as official chronicler. He remained close to the queen thereafter, being present at several important events of the war against Granada. It was from that moment on, according to Tate, that their two chronicles began to diverge, Palencia's favoring Fernando, as we have seen, and Pulgar's privileging

Isabel. Whether or not this turn of events proves Palencia's greater integrity as a writer is debatable.[81] What it does demonstrate is Pulgar's greater discretion: there is no criticism of Isabel in his chronicle. At the same time, he participates wholeheartedly in the sexual stigmatization of Enrique: the first four chapters of his *Crónica de los Reyes Católicos*, covering the years 1440–68, repeatedly refer to Enrique's impotence, his indulgence of his "carnal appetites" [apetitos carnales], and his advancement of "young men who helped him in his appetites and delights" [moços que le ayudasen a sus apetitos y deleytes] (20).

Pulgar also appears to have been more adept at the humanist strategy that Correll calls "cultivating subordination." We can see it in his eagerness to submit his work for her final approval, because "if your highness orders that care be taken in buildings that eventually fall down and that don't speak, how much more care should you order be taken with your chronicle, which neither falls down nor is silent" (*Letras*, 62).[82] The guiding principle of both Pulgar's *Crónica* and his collection of biographies of aristocrats and prelates, *Claros varones de Castilla* (Illustrious men of Castile), is also instructive. Tate calls the principle a "politics of obedience," a belief in man's submission to the divine plan and to the temporal authority of the monarch who is the earthly instrument of that plan (Pulgar, *Claros* 60).

Perhaps the most telling illustration of Pulgar's ability to negotiate the unstable relations of power at court is his historiographical methodology. In the composition of his chronicle, Pulgar apparently relied heavily on firsthand accounts of important military and political events sent to him by nobles eager for the fame his pen could provide. His letter to the powerful Count of Tendilla acknowledges one such contribution:

> Most noble Sir: you cannot inform me of your deeds as a friend because the disproportion between our persons prohibits friendship between your lordship and me; much less do I receive them as chronicler, rather as your most devoted servant do I appreciate your having written them down for me so extensively.... To quote Sallust to your lordship is foolish; but bear with me, just as I bear these peasants who tell me of the deeds you do in Alhama. (Quoted in Mata Carriazo, xliii)[83]

This is a fine example of curial gamesmanship. Pulgar plays the count's superior lineage off against his own greater knowledge while elevating both against the ignorance of the peasantry. Combined with Pulgar's eagerness to please his queen by submitting drafts of his work for her approval, the letter illustrates for one of Spain's humanist *letrados* the same unease over shifting notions of subordination and superiority that Correll identifies as the source of gender anxieties in European humanists north of the Pyrenees.[84]

The conditions outlined here inform the anxieties over gender and sexual transgressions of kings, queens, and favorites that are expressed and contained in Isabelline historical propaganda. The political tensions between Isabel and Fernando and their respective kingdoms, the uneasy relationship between the monarchs and the aristocracy, the *letrados*' wary cultivation of subordination and obedience to royal and noble will or whim—all of these inform the sexualized discourse of Isabelline historiography. In the Castilian case, the sexual anxiety generalized among European humanists was uniquely inflected by issues of ethnicity, as suggested in these lines written by Pulgar: "We see by experience that the natural inclination of some of these men we judge to be of low birth forces them to leave the lowly trades of their fathers, to accquire knowledge and to become great jurists" (*Letras*, 71).[85]

Whether they project the threat of effeminacy as "Enrique," discursively constructed as "Woman" in his sexual inversion, effeminacy, weakness, lack of control, and passivity, or as "Isabel," constructed as "Man" in her unwomanly traits, and her arrogant usurpation of male power, the Isabelline chroniclers are urgently engaged in the fashioning of secular masculine identity, a process centered on "the horror of effeminacy which must be contained" (Correll, 258).

CHAPTER FOUR
The Neo-Gothic Theory and the Queen's Body

> Think how false, against reason and law, it would be to conclude that the kingdom is inside the king; well, it is no less incorrect to say that the cunt moves inside the prick.
>
> > Ved cuán falsa consecuencia
> > contra razón y su ley
> > seríe dezir que en el rey
> > el reino está por presencia;
> > pues no menos por potencia
> > está el coño en el carajo.
> > —*Pleyto del manto*

Sexing the Neo-Gothic Theory

To the extent that Benedict Anderson's influential definition of nation as an "imagined community" can be applied to the medieval and early-modern periods, late-fifteenth-century Spain offers a striking example of such imagining: the so-called neo-Gothic theory.[1] Neo-Gothicism [neogoticismo] affirmed an uninterrupted line of descent from the Visigothic kings who ruled the peninsula before the Moorish invasion of 711 through to the Trastamaran sovereigns who claimed the Castilian throne in 1369. From those worthy ancestors the royal dynasty founded by the illegitimate Enrique II were believed to have inherited Gothic—and masculine—characteristics of virility, sobriety, and vigor, the very traits required to complete the sacred mission of the Iberian kingdoms: the recuperation of the territorial and moral integrity of ancient Romano-Gothic Hispania through the expulsion of the Muslim conquerors.[2]

The neo-Gothic myth was first given coherent shape in the thirteenth-century chronicles of Lucas de Tuy *(Chronicon Mundi)* and Rodrigo Jiménez de Rada *(De rebus Hispaniae,* also known as *Historia Gothica).* Thereafter it lay dormant until the mid-fifteenth century, when it was revived and reinvigorated by the *letrado* Alonso de Cartagena (1384–1456) and his protégé Rodrigo Sánchez de Arévalo (1404–70) (Tate, *Ensayos,* 68). A twofold political motivation lay behind such grandiose claims. On an international scale it responded to the contemporary rivalry between the English and the Castilians, which came to a head at the Council of Basel of 1434–35. At that important meeting, Cartagena, representing King Juan II, used the theory to support Castilian expansionism into the Canary Islands and northern Africa, which, it was argued, formed part of the Visigothic province of Tingitania. On the national level, tracing the origins of the Castilian monarchy back to Hercules' defeat of the "Spanish" monster Gerion, king of Hesperia, served to legitimize the Trastamaran dynasty's usurpation of the Castilian throne and its subsequent drive toward royal absolutism.[3]

By the next generation neo-Gothic discourse had taken on the messianic tone for which Isabelline literature is well known. Tate has observed the crucial difference between Sánchez de Arévalo's presentation of Castile's political mission in the 1460s and that of the writers whom he influenced. Whereas in the middle of the fifteenth century the realization of God's plan for Castile could only be eagerly anticipated, barely two decades later such writers as Alfonso de Palencia, Fernando del Pulgar, and Diego Valera could claim to have witnessed its fulfillment (ibid., 101). But it was in the reign of Isabel that *neogoticismo,* the historico-literary myth of national identity, virility, and legitimacy, struck the most profound chord.

Since Américo Castro's groundbreaking essay "Lo hispánico y el erasmismo" (written at the end of the Spanish civil war out of a desire to understand "certain strange processes of Hispanic history" [ciertos extraños procesos de la historia hispana] [9]), the messianic dimension of Isabelline writing has often been attributed to a unique ethnic perspective. In Castro's formulation, "The imperialist longings and prophecies at the beginning of the fifteenth century were a projection of Hispano-Jewish messianism, which infiltrated itself as an important ingredient of the Hispanic spirit" [Los anhelos y vaticinios imperialistas a comienzos del siglo XV fueron proyección del mesianismo hispano-judío, que se infiltra como importante ingrediente en el ánimo hispánico] (22).[4] For Castro and his disciples, notably Stephen Gilman, the belief that Fernando and Isabel had been sent by God to solve Spain's social and political woes is an effect of a *converso* mentality shaped by the rapidly deteriorating multicultural *convivencia* or coexistence of the late fifteenth century.[5]

The notion of a monolithic *converso* mentality has recently been called into question.[6] There can be little doubt, however, that many of those belonging to the generation of politically and culturally influential *converso* writers active in the years spanning the accession of Isabel in 1474 and the institution of the Inquisition in 1478 located these longings in the Catholic Monarchs. They saw Isabel's political goals of unification, centralization, and augmented royal power as the most effective means to the deeply desired social stability that would allow different cultures and religions to live together and thrive. Their vision of a new Spain was in this crucial dimension diametrically opposed to the Trastamaran ideology of a Spain unified through the exclusion of corrupting ethnic and religious forces.

What has been almost completely elided in discussions of the role ascribed to and eagerly accepted by Isabel as part of her Gothic inheritance is its materialist component, the very corporeal imagery that grounds it. Sexing and gendering the neo-Gothic theory that was contradictorily urged upon, promoted by, and used against Isabel reveals that *neogoticismo* equates the incipient nation-state of Spain with the virile masculine body, a body that is closed and invulnerable to corrupting forces. Furthermore, this national body is defined in opposition to those feminine or feminized bodies—bodies of Muslims, Jews, *conversos,* sodomites, and prostitutes—that are viewed as open or broken and consequently both vulnerable to contamination and themselves contaminating. The disciplining, exclusion, or complete elimination of these broken bodies becomes the discursive and material means toward the desired end: the repair of the broken neo-Gothic body politic of Hispania. The discursive means by which these feminized others are relegated to what has been called the "phobic imaginary of patriarchy" and the inevitable resurfacing of these others (Harris, 223) are the subject of this chapter.

The location of the profoundly patriarchal, masculinist neo-Gothic mission in Isabel's body is a necessarily ambivalent project that stirs up as much unacknowledged anxiety as it does messianic hope. The paradox of the queen's symbolic function as ideological heir of the virile Visigoths and as anomalous female sovereign troubles traditional gender power relations that obtained in the Middle Ages, thereby threatening the patriarchal status quo. The discourse of *neogoticismo* expresses and contains masculine anxiety in a variety of ways, from the use of castration imagery in the ballad cycle that explains and laments the causes of the eighth-century "destruction" of Spain by the Moors, to the assimilation of Isabel to the pure, enclosed body of the Virgin Mary in courtly and epideictic poetry, to the pornographic travesty of the symbolics of queenly body, that is, its transformation from head to cunt of state. The masculinist, misogynist ideology that shapes Isabel's restorative mission reveals itself in an uneasy awareness of the contradictory relationship between Isabel's "two bodies," her body politic and her body natural. Behind both the messianic eulogies and the scathing satires lies the same anxious question: how can Spain's broken body be made whole again by a monarch whose own body is by its very nature also "broken"?[7]

The paradoxes of gender and sexuality that inflect the Isabelline writers' construction of Isabel's mission are further complicated by their imbrication with categories of race, ethnicity, and class.[8] Because they are envisioned as a curative purging from the ailing body politic of all those femininized others who threaten its masculine impermeability, the racist concepts and exclusionary policies promoted by Isabel and her supporters—the establishment of the Inquisition to police Christian orthodoxy; the "statutes of blood purity" [estatutos de limpieza], laws preventing those with non-Christian ancestry from holding important ecclesiastic, governmental, and academic posts; the war against the last remaining Moorish kingdom of Granada (1482–92) and subsequent forced conversion of its Muslim inhabitants; the Edict of Expulsion of all nonconverted Jews—fall in the domain of sexual and gender politics. A terrible irony surfaces in many of the messianic texts we shall examine and that is that the body of Jew, the *converso*, the Moor, the sodomite, and the prostitute who must be excluded from the virile body politic and the body of the sovereign who must exclude them are analogously constructed as feminine and broken.[9] That irony is especially strong in the cases of the *letrado* writers who early on eloquently supported Isabel's political goals but later suffered because of them: the *conversos* Hernando del Pulgar, Hernando de Talavera, and Juan de Lucena, to cite some of those closest to the Queen.

Two concepts central to medieval theories of monarchy are necessary for an understanding of the imagery of *neogoticismo*. The first is the widespread corporeal concept of the state; the second is the related notion of the king's two bodies. Both concepts inform Castilian political writing of the fifteenth century.[10] Ernst Kantorowicz has documented the evolution of the corporeal metaphor, tracing it from the Pauline concept of the Corpus Christi, the body of believers in Christ, to the idea of the church as *corpus ecclesiae mysticum*, to the political idea of the *corpus republicae mysticum*, and finally to the divine and natural bodies of the king (19, 506). In Castile, the ecclesiastical notion of the *corpus mysticum* is often conflated with an older analogy found in Aristotle's *Politica* and Seneca's *De clementia*, between the kingdom and the human body. Those *auctores* figured the king as the body's head and his subjects as its other members, all of them joined together indissolubly.[11]

José Maravall has documented the proliferation of the corporeal concept of monarchy in Iberian historical and political writers from the mid-fifteenth century on.[12] Rodrigo Sánchez de Arévalo, for example, defines the polity as follows in *Suma de la política:* "Similarly, the city or kingdom is like a mystical body harmoniously composed of certain parts and members" (302; quoted in Nieto Soria, *Fundamentos,* 228).[13] In the same author's *Vergel de príncipes* the king is deemed "head and foundation of his Republic, from whose power all members receive virtuous influences and whose deeds are necessary examples for his people" (21; quoted in Tate, *Ensayos,* 87).[14]

The concept of the *cuerpo místico* often served a deeply conservative function. It cohered with the providential view of medieval society whereby each of its basic groups—"churchmen, soldiers, peasants" [oradores, defensores, labradores]—and the individual members thereof occupied an unalterable hierarchical position assigned by God (Edwards). Diego de Valera sets forth precisely this notion in an epistle dated 1447: "for just as in the human body all the members strive to protect and defend the head, so in this mystical body that is the entire kingdom, whose head is the king, all subjects, who are his own members, must strive to guard, serve, love, and advise him" (7).[15] Occasionally, the various members of the body politic are assigned to different groups or estates, as, for example, in Enrique de Villena's affirmation that "the noblemen are the arms of the mystical and civil body, equipped, organized, if you will, to assure the defense, protection, and tranquillity of the other members" (*Los doze trabajos de Hércules;* quoted in Nieto Soria, 228–30),[16] or the following analogy in Juan de Lucena's *De vita beata:* "If in our mortal body the finger does not desire to be an eye, how much more must one of God's smallest creatures be content not to be greater than it is?" (204).[17]

Any attempt to alter the divinely ordained assemblage of metaphorical body parts could be catastrophic. As we saw in chapter 3, just such a disaster is evoked by then Bishop, later Cardinal Pedro González de Mendoza, in his attempt to impede the dethroning of Enrique IV's effigy at the fateful Farsa de Ávila: "It is well known, My Lords, that the entire Kingdom is considered to be a body, of which we take the king to be the head, which, if ill owing to some weakness, it would seem best to administer those medicines that reason prescribes, rather than to cut off the head that nature defends... because if kings are annointed by God on earth, we should not consider them subject to human judgment" (Pulgar, *Crónica de los Reyes Católicos,* ed. Rosell, 230).[18]

The corporeal concept could, and from the reign of Juan II on did increasingly, provide theoretical support for the growing personalization of royal power, so that the king's body itself, and especially his head, the seat of reason responsible for the harmonious functioning of all the other bodily parts, became a primary referent for political authority. This identification in turn was used to justify the Trastamara monarchs' steady move toward absolutism (Nieto Soria, *Fundamentos,* 93). It was in this personalized form that the concept was both useful and problematic for the Isabelline culture of sovereignty. For one thing, the feminine was not associated with the upper body, the seat of reason, but rather with the lower body, the site of passion and sinfulness. A woman as the head of the mystical body therefore challenged the parallel hierarchies of rule and gender, higher over lower, reason over desire, masculine over feminine. It was a profoundly unsettling idea, even more so because the challenge could not be directly acknowledged, much less openly resisted.

The author who most frequently invokes the kingdom as a *cuerpo místico* in the reign of the Catholic Monarchs is their close adviser on statescraft and protocol, the *converso* Diego de Valera (1412–after 1488). Azcona calls Valera a "genuine theorist of the restoration of the Gothic empire, the oriental domination having been overcome, and the divisions among the peninsular kingdoms having been healed" (311).[19] Valera invokes the metaphor three times in his *Doctrinal de príncipes*, a mirror of princes written between 1475 and 1479.[20] In his second chapter, Valera traces the concept back to the *Siete Partidas* and ties it securely to the divine right of kings: "The king should greatly fear and love God, because as much as God placed him in such a high position, so much more is he obligated to know him, and knowing him, to love him, and loving him, to fear him and serve him" (174).[21] More suggestive for my purposes, however, is a passage from the next chapter that deals with a principal concern of the author, the king's role as firm administrator of justice. This aspect of royal authority was understandably of special concern to Isabel and Fernando's counselors in the early years of their reign, which were marked by rebellion, lawlessness, foreign invasion, and civil war. According to Valera, in meting out punishment to wrongdoers, the king should take care to show compassion as if they were his own body parts:

> For the king with his kingdom is like a human body, whose head he is; and just as all the bodily members strive to defend and protect the head, so must it work to rule and govern and help the members, grieving when it becomes necessary to amputate them. For just as one amputates a damaged member so that whole body does not die, so must those subjects for whom there is no hope of correction be cut off so that the good subjects may live in peace and the incorrigible be punished. (187)[22]

The "damaged members" of the body politic whose excision Valera justifies in these lines are those noble families loyal to Juana who, with Portuguese aid, were then waging war on Isabel and Fernando. The image of a king reluctantly amputating diseased parts of his own symbolic body in order to maintain the health of the rest is an image of a strong, authoritarian, virile monarch, a judge and warrior.[23] But it inevitably produces and relies on its inverse, that is, the representation of the weak king as dismembered, rather than dismembering—or, in the more specifically sexual terms appropriate to neo-Gothic discourse of royal power, the castrated king. Such threatening corporeal images of the sovereign are inseparable from the more pacific and nurturing images of the reparation of the body politic's integrity through the reconnection of its fragmented members, the images most frequently assigned to Isabel.

The immediate historical context of such corporeal imagery is the events leading to Isabel's wresting of the throne from Enrique's legitimate heir. In many *neogoticista* texts, however, the sorry state of the body politic is traced much further back, to a traumatic foundational moment that lay more than seven hundred years in the past. That violent moment of violation and castration occurred in the year 711, when the Moors crossed the Strait of Gibraltar to invade and conquer the peninsula, penetrating the virile Hispano-Gothic realm, symbolized by the body of the iconic Rodrigo, "the last Gothic king."

The King's Broken Body: Castration Anxiety in the Rodrigo Ballads

Drawing heavily on Jiménez de Rada, Alonso de Cartagena argues in his *Anacephaleosis* for the preeminence of the Castilian royal house because of its antiquity, tracing the roots of its genealogical tree back to the Visigothic kings and beyond, to the early Iberians, then to Hercules, and before him, to Noah's sons Japhet and Tubal. By reason of that antiquity, he maintained, the Trastamaran dynasty was superior to all other European royal lines and was therefore entitled to rule over the entirety of what constituted the ancient Romano-Visigothic kingdom of Hispania. Any gap in the dynastic line represented by the death of the last Visigothic king, Rodrigo, and the subsequent Muslim domination is similarly denied. As Tate notes, Cartagena "is careful to make perfectly clear that Rodrigo, although he was the last king of the Visigoths, was not the last member of the dynasty. The same day that Rodrigo was assassinated, Pelayo succeeded him by *divine dispensation*.... the abandonment of the name Goth is of little importance compared to the maintenance of the royal line" *(Ensayos,* 69).[24] Cartagena saw the collapse of the Visigothic monarchy not as an irreparable historical break, but rather as a divine challenge to its Castilian successors, beginning with Pelayo, the legendary warrior who initiated the Reconquest.

"Spanish reintegration" [Reintegratio Hispaniae] is the objective urged on Juan II's son, Enrique IV, by Cartagena's protégé, Rodrigo Sánchez de Arévalo, in his *Compendiosa Historia Hispanica* (1470). The first history of Spain to benefit from the newly introduced printing press, Arévalo's version of the neo-Gothic theory continued to exert influence on historical and political writers through the first decades of the sixteenth century.[25] Arévalo was the first to identify the true "Spanish character," locating it in specific Gothic traits that have been frequently invoked throughout the succeeding five centuries, shaping Hispanism well into the twentieth century.[26] He extolled in contemporary Castilians the moral and temperamental legacy passed on by the Visigoths, and before them, the earlier indigenous tribes: valor, vigor, sobriety, virility, and the avoidance of the vices of civilization. Thus, in Arévalo and his Isabelline successors, the Goths, viewed by the rest of Europe as initiating a dark and uncivilized era, were considered the link between two heroic, virile peoples: they were descendants of the Iberians and progenitors of the Castilians.

Neo-Gothicism insistently identifies the body politic and the masculine heterosexual body natural. What Isabel inherited along with her Gothic blood, however, was not just the intact virile body politic of those seventh-century royal ancestors, but also the fragmented, impotent, and feminized body politic ruled, or misruled, by Enrique IV. It is to the disordered body politic defined by and defining the transgressive sexuality of a sodomitical king and adulterous queen that neo-Gothicist theorists such as Diego de Valera most often refer. But the ideological power of the transgressive couple Enrique and Juana is ultimately typological; that is, the fifteenth-century Enrique and Juana are types for an original transgressive couple whose sexual sin brought about the expulsion from the Gothic paradise: Rodrigo, last king of the Visigoths and La Cava, daughter of Count Julián.

Although fact and fantasy are inextricably joined in historical accounts of the Moorish invasion of 711, the most informed versions suggest that it grew out of a dynastic dispute over the rights of Rodrigo's immediate predecessor, King Witiza (702–10).[27] Witiza was appointed king by his father Egica (687–702) in an attempt to establish a hereditary monarchy in his own family, a move contested by Rodrigo, his father, and his supporters. But the story of the destruction of the Visigothic kingdom is most often attributed not to internecine political strife, but to the sinful behavior of King Rodrigo and a woman known as La Cava (Alacava in some versions, and later, Florinda), the daughter of the Visigothic Count Julián, governor of the North African province of Ceuta. As was customary for children of the nobility, she was sent to be raised at the Toledan court of King Rodrigo. Shortly after her arrival, Rodrigo (in some versions he is married) becomes enamored of her and initiates a courtly seduction. When his advances are rebuffed, he rapes her. The distraught young woman writes to her father, informing him of the dishonor done to the family. Count Julián takes his revenge by inviting his Muslim allies to cross the Strait of Gibraltar and overrun the peninsula. The prose urtext for the catastrophe is from *Primera crónica general de España,* composed at the behest of King Alfonso X in the thirteenth century: "It came to pass that ... King Rodrigo raped his [Julián's] daughter and lay with her, and before this it was said that he was to marry her, but he had not done so yet. Some say that it was Julián's wife that he raped, but no matter which one it was, this was the cause of the destruction of Spain and Gothic Gaul" (1:307–8).[28]

Spanish culture is not unique, of course, in its need to explain teleologically a swift and violent overthrow of its political order, but the story of Spain's destruction is remarkable for its enduring cultural productivity. The legend that constructed an Arab military conquest of a Visigothic kingdom weakened by dynastic disputes as an apocalyptic *flagellum dei* would continue to shape Spain's cultural identity for more than a millennium, from its formulation in the ninth century through the mid-twentieth century, when Francisco Franco appropriated it for his "second Reconquest."[29]

This sexualized version of the scourge-of-God theory applied to the fall of the Visigothic kingdom provided dramatic material for the *neogoticistas*. They specifically attributed the punishment visited upon Hispania to a divine response to two traumatic violations: the sexual one perpetrated by Rodrigo on Cava and the metaphorical one that avenges it when the Moors, invited by Cava's aggrieved father, cross the Strait of Gibraltar and penetrate Christian Hispania (Deyermond, "Death," 353). These intertwined acts of rape—of the virginal body of the maiden and of the virile body of Hispania—inflect the reconstitutive rhetoric of neo-Gothic political discourse addressed to and promoted by Isabel. The insistent calls for the queen to "repair," "restore," "reform," "recover," "recuperate" [reparar, restaurar, reformar, recobrar, recuperar] are contained in the overarching concept of *reconquista*, the defining domestic goal of the Catholic Monarchs and springboard of the sixteenth-century imperialist expansionism realized by their grandson, Carlos V.[30]

By the time Diego de Valera invokes the myth in his *Doctrinal de príncipes*, he need only summarize what was common cultural knowledge: "And because of the hateful and detestable sins of these two wicked kings, our Lord permitted King Rodrigo to rape La Cava, daughter of Count Julián, and in order to avenge his dishonor he brought the Moors into Spain" (184).[31] It is significant that the "detestable sins" attributed to Kings Egica and Wittiza here are analogous to the sins that the Isabelline *cronistas* ascribe to Isabel's immediate predecessor, Enrique IV; that is, they are sins of a sexual nature. In the case of the Visigothic kings, they include polygamy, enforcement of clerical marriage, and the dissolution of the Church Council and overturning of the canons that would have censured such behavior.

Valera's presentation of the events leading up to 711 is actually a conflation of two rival traditions regarding the fall, one placing responsibility on Egica and Wittiza, and another blaming their opponent Rodrigo and his father. In the latter, the one I shall focus on, Rodrigo was vilified as a usurper and traitor, a distinct problem for Isabel and the *neogoticistas*. The legend of Rodrigo and Cava becomes even more problematic, however, if we look closely at its assignment of blame for the sexual iniquities that caused the Visigoths' expulsion from their Christian paradise.

If the Moorish conquest was an episode that attracted "legendary embroidering" (Collins, 34), then surely one of the most elaborate of the designs it produced is Pedro del Corral's *Crónica del Rey don Rodrigo* or *Crónica sarracina* (c. 1430), a lengthy historical romance that devotes almost one hundred chapters to Rodrigo's rape of Cava and the revenge taken by her father Julián for that act. The dozen or so *romances viejos* and *romances juglarescos* that compose the ballad cycle of Rodrigo, where the legend of the destruction of Spain receives it most dramatic treatment and its widest and most enduring dissemination, derived largely from this "chronicle."[32] Although the ballads belong to a popular, oral tradition, they are similar to the chronicles discussed in chapter 3 in that they are retrospective, propagandistic interpretations of crucial events in Spanish history. And, like the *crónicas*, they are strongly partisan in their support of the Trastamaran triumphalist vision of a unified, purified Spain that was to be brought to glorious fruition by Isabel.[33] It is therefore significant that the Rodrigo ballad cycle probably began circulating in the second half of the fifteenth century, that is, around the time of composition of Alfonso de Cartagena's and Sánchez de Arévalo's revitalization of the neo-Gothic theory. It is likely, in fact, that Isabel, born in 1451, heard the Rodrigo ballads sung as she was growing up. But the value of the romances as complex and evolving cultural forms that shape and are shaped by sexual and gender ideology has been largely ignored.[34]

At first glance the ballads' representation of the relationship between Rodrigo and Cava and the destruction of Spain is one of simple and brutal causality. A closer look at those versions that we can reasonably assume were circulating during Isabel's reign reveals, however, that the nature of the sexual relationship between Cava and Rodrigo, as well as the personal and divine retribution that follows, are in fact highly ambiguous. I will examine two aspects of this ambiguity: the definition of the sexual act itself, and the grotesque nature of Rodrigo's penance for his lust.

The parallels between the story of Rodrigo's loss of idyllic Hispania to the Muslims and the biblical account of Adam and Eve's loss of paradise were not lost on the *neogoticistas* (Burt, and Deyermond, "Death"). In contrast to Genesis, however, where Eve's culpability is clearly marked, the blame for the expulsion from the Visigothic earthly paradise at first seems to fall squarely on male shoulders. We see this most clearly in a *juglaresco* version titled "Amores trata Rodrigo."[35] The poem describes the outcome of the king's two vain attempts to seduce his noble charge: "She had never wanted to do it even though he had ordered her to, and so the king did it by force and against her will" (2:106, vv. 29–32).[36]

Despite the bald statement of guilt contained in these verses, the ballad as a whole is a good deal more equivocal in assigning blame. The assertion of Rodrigo's crime, placed in the exact middle of the poem, is preceded by a subtle mystification of masculine rape by feminine seductiveness. Although Cava rebuffs the king, she does so "in jest" [burlando], and as "clever" [discreta] (2:105, vv. 13 and 18), displaying not "the blushing timidity of the frightened maiden, but skill at handling bold advances more suited to a courtesan" (Foster, 54). This is further underscored when Rodrigo summons La Cava to his chamber during the siesta, and she obeys, "very carelessly" [muy descuidada] (2:105, v. 23), an explicit contrast to the king's "suffering" [cuidado] (2:105, v. 2), or lovesickness. The association of Cava with the stereotypical heartless lady of courtly love is clear.

In the shorter, and presumably later, versions of the ballad, Cava's innocence is placed in even greater doubt. In the first place, the verses accusing the king of rape, although more poetically effective, are more ambiguous in tone: "The king had his way with her more by force than by consent" [Cumplió el rey su voluntad / más por fuerza que por grado] (2:83, vv. 27–28). Second, the ballad re-creates a motif taken from the *Crónica sarracina*, which presents the couple engaged in an intimate activity: As she knelt before him extracting mites from his noble hands, he was seducing her" (2:84, vv. 21–24).[37] As she kneels before him, Cava engages in an act of grooming, extracting mites out from under the skin of Rodrigo's "noble" hands, probably with the point of a knife. This curious scene strongly suggests that the relationship of Rodrigo and Cava is far from innocent and that Cava is in fact the active partner in the relationship.[38]

The strongest insinuation of Cava's complicity in, if not full responsibility for, the sin that destroyed Spain lies in the name she is given in the fifteenth-century ballads; for the beautiful Visigothic maiden paradoxically bears an Arabic name, one that is identical with the common Arabic noun for prostitute. The repetition of the term (seven times in the shorter version, compared with only two mentions of Rodrigo's name) clearly marks Cava as sexually ripe and available, the standard characterization of Arabic women in the ballads, as Louise Mirrer has shown in her interpretation of the contemporary "frontier" [fronterizo] ballads, which commented on victories and losses in the battles of the War of Granada, often very soon after the event described. Two of these quasi-journalistic ballads, "Pártese el moro Alicante" and "Romance de la morilla burlada" (*Women, Jews, and Muslims*, 17–30), justify the rape of a Muslim woman.

The "little Moorish girl" [morica] of the "Pártese el moro Alicante" is a sexual object of exchange in Christian–Moorish political negotiations. Her portrayal as sexually available, even aggressive, touches on another detail of Christian–Muslim hostility, the presumed "right" of Christians to Muslim Spain, played out in the stereotype of the Muslim woman who "invites, legitimates, and satisfies Christian desire" (ibid., 22).[39] The "little Moorish girl" [morilla] of the second ballad, deceived and raped by a Christian disguised as a Muslim who claims to have murdered a Christian, also is made to represent a Christian point of view, namely, that Muslim women are dangerous to Christians (the *morilla* is willing to harbor the supposed fugitive from Christian justice) and sexually inviting.

Although Cava is presumably a Christian, her stigmatizing Arabic name assimilates her to the equally young and not-so-innocent *morica* and *morilla* of these highly propagandistic frontier ballads. Before Rodrigo has uttered a single seductive word, therefore, the poet has impugned his victim's purity and qualified further the representation of Rodrigo's act as a rape. Not only is Cava a woman and therefore a daughter of Eve, but she is also labeled a Muslim and therefore a prostitute; she is thus triply stereotyped as impure, lascivious, and treacherous.[40] In this sense, the frontier ballads and the historical ballads of Rodrigo enact a kind of Christian symbolic revenge for the crimes perpetrated on the virile Goths by the decadent Muslims: they violently appropriate the Muslim woman's body as part of a chauvinistic call to restore Muslim territory and possessions to their rightful owners (Mirrer, *Women, Jews, and Muslims*, 270).[41]

It is also interesting that although Cava is *malvada*, what actually causes the Muslim invasion is not just that she is a willing participant and perhaps instigator of the sexual act, but that she does not keep her shameful secret to herself. Feminine lasciviousness is here linked to feminine loquacity, a common analogy in the early-modern period. Thus, immediately after declaring the cause-and-effect relationship between rape and invasion, the ballad distributes the blame among three guilty parties: "for this reason Spain was lost, because of that great sin. The evil La Cava told her father: Julián the traitor arranged for the Moors to destroy Spain, because [the king] insulted him so" (8, vv. 31–36).[42]

Not only is Rodrigo's rape of Cava made into an act of seduction on her part, but that act is ultimately presented as a crime against masculine honor rather than feminine virtue. To the fifteenth-century poet and his audience, it causes a rupture of the homosocial bond—the relationship between Rodrigo and his noble subject Julián—that must be redressed. This is the implication of a telling reflexive pronoun used in the ballad "The winds were unfavorable" [Los vientos eran contrarios]. When the allegorical character Fortuna awakens Rodrigo, asleep next to Cava in his magnificent golden tent, she foretells the imminent destruction of his villages and cities, and the transfer of the rule of his castle fortresses to "another lord" [otro señor]: "If you ask me who did it, I would gladly tell you: that Count Julián, because you dishonored him through her and she was his only child" (2, vv. 31–34).[43]

It is also important to keep in mind that Rodrigo's virility is called into question by his own lack of self-control, expressed in this specific instance by his unbridled lust.[44] As Phyllis Rackin explains, in medieval and Renaissance gender ideology, "sexual passion had not yet achieved the privileged position it now holds, especially for men. Excessive passion in either sex was condemned, but it was especially dangerous to men because it made them effeminate. Women were believed to be more lustful than men.... Despising lust as a mark of weakness and degradation, Renaissance thought gendered it feminine" ("Foreign Country," 74).[45] Rodrigo's effeminacy, ambivalently attributed to his own weakness and to Cava's seductiveness, is what invites the Muslim penetration of Spain's body politic. It is also what merits his exemplary punishment.

This brings us to what for my purposes is the central ballad of the Rodrigo cycle. "Después que el rey Rodrigo" recounts the aftermath of the Visigothic defeat and Rodrigo's penance for his sins. Menéndez Pidal provides strong evidence that the ballad was familiar to the musicians of Isabel's court; its popularity was immediate and long-lasting.[46] The poem recounts the defeated king's dazed wanderings through the mountains after the military debacle at Guadalete. He seeks out a hermit living in the wilderness and states his desire to do penance for his sins. God reveals the appropriate penance in response to the hermit's prayers: Rodrigo must lie in a tomb with a poisonous serpent and pray for forgiveness.

The ballad again recalls Genesis in its account of Rodrigo's fall, but in doing so it effects a displacement of the snake's original function (Genesis 3:1–7). From cause of sin through the temptation of Eve the poem transforms the serpent into the instrument of divine punishment.[47] Meekly following the hermit's instructions, Rodrigo lies in the tomb praying for three days before the snake finally strikes: "'God is with me,' answered good King Rodrigo. It is now eating the member that deserves it all for being the source of my great misfortune. The hermit encourages him; the good king died'" (16, vv. 106–14).[48] The poet, following Corral, makes the manner of Rodrigo's death follow the retaliative principle of law commonly accepted in the Middle Ages and exemplified in legends, painting, and sculpture.[49] On a symbolic level, however, there is much more going on in this scene than a legalistic application of the biblical "an eye for an eye and a tooth for a tooth." That is because in the ballad the snake figures the sinfulness of Rodrigo (Adam) and not Eve (Cava): "Then the Lord God said to the woman, 'What is this that you have done?' The woman said, 'The serpent beguiled me, and I ate'" (Genesis 3:13). The serpent, agent of Rodrigo's grotesque punishment, again marks the king as feminized victim of his own lust and of feminine seductiveness.[50] In his positioning in the tomb and in his passive acceptance of the serpent's bite, he is a figure for both Eve and Adam.

In his discussion of the relationship between nationhood and Hispanic philology (specifically, the latter's need to recover lost medieval texts in order to "nationalize the pre-nation"), Anthony Espósito observes that "Rodrigo's broken phallus becomes a synechdoche for the broken nation and the emasculated king" (5). This brilliant reading of the symbolic power of the ballad's inversion of the hierarchy of the upper over the lower body—its displacement of the body politic's seat of reason, the head, onto the seat of unreason, the genitals—remains incomplete, however, unless it acknowledges the slippage from the pity and terror elicited by the king's (self-)castration to the disgust produced by its effective cause, the Orientalized virgin/whore Cava. Rodrigo is, after all, twice called "the good king" [el buen rey] in the verses just quoted. Furthermore, his grisly penance succeeds in expiating his sin, and the ballad ends with the king's apotheosis: he ascends to heaven amid a miraculous tolling of bells that announces his soul's salvation.

The pathos of King Rodrigo's castration serves to mystify the act of rape that is the symbolic heart of darkness of the neo-Gothic myth. It is the castration, not the rape, that to the fifteenth-century Christian tellers, transmitters, and receptors of the ballad represents the traumatic originary wound of the sexualized body politic of Hispania. Cava's abjected body, with the bodily margins and penetrable orifices that construct her as woman and thereby "provide culture with a locus for displaced anxieties about the vulnerability of the... the body politic" (Boose, "Scolding Brides," 195), is denied repentance and redemption. In the Isabelline context, the Rodrigo ballad cycle is simultaneously a collective lament over a loss of a virile warrior society and a battle cry for the restoration of that society through the re-membering of the body politic, an urgent operation that requires the therapeutic expulsion of the treacherous, feminine/effeminate, Oriental others, the fifteenth-century Muslims (and Jews) who are Cava's symbolic descendants.

The Rodrigo ballads thus conflate in complex fashion a retrospective hatred for an enemy from without, the Moors, with a contemporary hatred for an internal enemy, represented by the sexually voracious Muslim woman, the spy who betrays her benefactor and divulges shameful secrets to the enemy. It is Cava who most reminds us that the ballads that circulated in the reign of Isabel constructed eighth-century "history" in the context of late-fifteenth-century values. As ideological constructs, the ballads shape contemporary attitudes toward the largely incorporated but still devalued Muslim population. They help incite the Christian population to avenge a centuries-old military defeat with a military victory that seems within grasp for the first time in centuries: the conquest of Granada.

Repairing Spain's Broken Body: Isabel as Virgin Mary

Isabel embraced the neo-Gothic theory as a powerful legitimizing strategy for her contested claim to the throne. She and her court writers worked diligently to fashion her as a direct descendant of the last Gothic king and sole legitimate heir to her brother Enrique. She alone, not the putative bastard Juana, possessed the integrity and piety to undo the sins of her father and brother. But if the Queen's royal blood made her heir to the vigorous and virile temperament of the Visigoths, her gender inevitably marked her as the direct descendant of the seductress Cava and the feminized Rodrigo (and, as discussed in chapter 3, of Eve and Juana de Portugal as well, at different points in the same genealogy of female sinfulness). Before she married and rose to power, there was more room for an adviser like Martín de Córdoba to try and control her agency, by advocating subordination to her future husband, for example. After she became queen and wife, and in both roles effectively resisted such subordination, such efforts are abandoned. They are replaced by the messianic discourse that scholars have traditionally interpreted as expressing unequivocal support for her political program. But a profound ambivalence about the fact that God had chosen a woman to be the restorer of the wounds inflicted on the virile body politic by feminine/effeminate others does not disappear from Isabelline messianic discourse. Indeed, the very grounding of the neo-Gothic myth in the physical and sexual body of the monarch ensures its anxious articulation.

Isabelline court writers developed various strategies to cope with God's way of working, mysteriously, through a woman. One such strategy was to emphasize Fernando's equal claim to the "Gothic heritage" [herencia goda] through his Trastamaran blood. Valera follows this line of reasoning in the *Doctrinal de príncipes* when he solemnly proclaims: "not only will you be lord of these kingdoms of Castile and Aragon, which by all rights belong to you, but you will also be monarch of all the Spanish kingdoms, and you will reform the imperial seat of the illustrious Goths from whom you descend, that for so long has been dispersed and scattered" (174).[51] If, as Azcona believes, Valera's *speculum principis* was formative for Isabel as well as Fernando, it is nonetheless true that in passages such as this one, and, I would argue, throughout the work, he appears to be designating Fernando specifically as heir to the Goths. The reason is simple: for Valera the most direct route to restore the "illustrious blood of the Goths" is to shed more blood, that is, to execute fully the primary military role of the medieval king. In the long parade of exemplary kings that structures his edifying treatise, his most effusive praise is reserved for the victorious battlers: Fernando III generously rewarded all the lords who served him in the battles against the Muslims, "of which he was always victor and never vanquished" [de que siempre fue vencedor e nunca vencido] (178); Alfonso II "had great victories against the Moors, and on one day killed sixty thousand in battle" [ovo grandes victorias contra los moros y en un dia mató en batalla sesenta mill] (185); and, more immediately, Juan II and Alfonso V of Aragon, who, although singled out for their learning, "nevertheless did not fail to exercise military deeds, strenuously and vigorously" [ni por eso los abtos bélicos dexaron de exercer, estrenua e vigorosamente] (182).

In Valera's militant value system, obviously, Isabel's gender barred her from fully claiming her Gothic inheritance. Several of his many letters addressed to the Catholic Monarchs over the course of the decade 1476–86 point to this gender incapacity. In 1479, at the end of the civil war, he states in an epistle addressed to his queen:

> It can truly be said that just as our Lord wanted our glorious Lady to be born so that from her could issue the universal Redeemer of the human race, so did he determine that you, My Lady, should be born so as to reform and restore these kingdoms and rescue them from the tyrannical government under which they have long remained ... so you, Lady, have united them [Castile and Leon] with Aragon and Sicily, and you have accomplished these great things with the help of God and the vigorous arm of our most Serene King and Lord. (*Epístolas*, 17–18)[52]

The passage is subtle in its reasoning. It maintains Isabel's superior position by designating the battling Fernando as *her* helpmate. At the same time, it maintains her dependence on Fernando for the successful completion of the enormous military task facing her.

The passage also contains an example of a more daring strategy devised by the pro-Isabelline writers in order to contain Isabel's gender association with Cava/Eve: her fashioning as earthly counterpart to the Virgin Mary. Scholars long ago observed that the comparison of the Catholic Queen to the queen of heaven is a leitmotiv of court poetry that proliferates in the early years of Isabel's reign (Lida de Malkiel, "Hipérbole"; R. O. Jones). Usually, the comparison has been considered an innocuously sacrilegious courtly love topos designed to flatter Spain's most powerful courtly lady but devoid of deeper social or political significance.[53] Some have taken this encomiastic minitradition as evidence that Isabel, like Elizabeth I of England, became the object of a cult that was at once conventional and sincere, an expression of fascination with sovereigns who "seemed sent to rescue their kingdoms from disorder and disruption" [parecían mandadas para rescatar a sus reinos del desorden y de la disrupción] (64).[54] That the Marian metaphor was both a symbolically potent strategy in this rescue mission and a technique for masking Isabel's undesirable gender has never been acknowledged, in sharp contrast to the standard view of her northern counterpart, early modern Europe's paradigmatically Virgin Queen.

Elizabethan scholars have amply demonstrated Elizabeth's use of her virginity to maintain and manipulate her unauthorized sovereign power. Her own comparison of her inviolate physical body to the inviolable body politic of the English state is but one of many techniques that she and her subjects used to allay the anxieties that her gender inevitably raised.[55] For reasons discussed earlier, Isabel could not choose to remain unmarried. The restoration of the legitimacy of the Trastamaran dynastic line threatened by the accusations of sexual perversion and gender-role transgressions against her predecessors made it absolutely essential that she produce a legitimate male heir in a timely fashion. Chastity within marriage was, on the other hand, a value that could be and was used to compare Isabel to the mother of Christ.

Valera compares Isabel to Mary in subtle, often contradictory ways. In the example quoted earlier, for example, although the point of comparison is the redemptive role that each woman is destined to play through her son, Valera makes no mention of Isabel's long-awaited male heir, the infant Prince Juan, who was almost a year old at the time the letter was penned.[56] Valera suggests that Isabel is the chosen vessel for Spain's redeemer, but figures as the Christ figure not her son Juan, but her consort Fernando. Such is the importance of the military role in the neo-Gothic theory propounded by Valera that he assimilates Isabel to Mary as bride of Christ, a common medieval portrayal of the Virgin. The prescribed subordination of the wife to the husband that was such a prominent feature of Martín de Córdoba's *Jardín de nobles doncellas* resurfaces here, as Valera qualifies the Queen's agency as Spain's redeemer even as he exalts it.[57]

Another Marian trait Valera extols in the queen is her piety. In chapter 2, I discussed the piety and humility advocated by Isabel's advisers as a way of lessening the anxiety occasioned by her power. Valera appears to be similarly engaged in a letter addressed to Fernando in 1485, at the height of the Granada campaign: "And what remains to be said, most victorious Prince, except that God is with you, and through your virtue and that of the most serene princess Isabel, our Queen and Lady, he wants to destroy and devastate the perfidious Mohammedan sect that [Isabel] fights as hard with her many alms and devout prayers and organizing the war effort as you do with lance in hand" (31).[58] Valera deems queenly piety a necessary but not sufficient contribution to the reparation of Spain's political health, figuring Isabel as a kind of pious and domestic troop-follower for the warrior prince. This division of labor accords with the prevailing gender division: "Whereas male virtue was so active that its meaning converges with 'service' and 'courage'... female virtue was conceptualized as primarily passive" (Frye, 14). Both together were created to carry out God's plan to restore by destroying: "God loves you and caused you to be born as you are, not only to restore, reform, and defend these kingdoms, but also to subjugate and destroy all the enemies of the Holy Catholic Faith" [Dios vos ama e vos ficço tales nacer, no solamente para restaurar, reformar e defender estos reinos, mas para debelar e destruir a todos los enemigos de la Sancta Fe Católica] (31).

When Isabel's writing subjects focus on the queen alone, however, it is virginity that proves the safest representation of her power. Virginity, or rather the redemptive function of virginity, is a leitmotiv of the *cancionero* panegyrics to Isabel. As John Bugge discusses in his useful history of the medieval ideal of *virginitas,* the linking of Eve and Mary was central to the "mystery of the redemptive economy" (143) that focused on the ontological significance of sexuality. In the most popular medieval view, Mary's sexual purity was the antithesis of Eve's damning sexual sin: "In consenting to be the virginal Mother of God, Mary accomplishes a kind of fulfillment of the virginal innocence of our first mother. The logical purpose of the typology of Eve and Mary is to oppose sin and redemption, contamination and purification; the antithesis retains its force through the inherent parallel based on virginity" (144).

Paradigmatic of the courtly paeans to the bodily integrity of the queen are the following verses by Pedro de Cartagena (b. 1456), grandson of Alonso de Cartagena's brother: "but I hit the mark without error [when I say] that you are a virgin, the foremost on earth and second in heaven" (Gerli, *Poesía cancioneril*, 73, vv. 66–70).[59] The wholeness of the queen's body contrasts implicitly with the dismembered body of Rodrigo and the permeable body of Cava, both responsible for the violation of the state.

The opposition between Mary and Eve that figured in the medieval palindrome Ave/Eva is explicitly drawn in the most interesting of the Isabelline elegists, and one with privileged access to the queen, the court preacher Iñigo de Mendoza. All three of the messianic political poems that he addressed to one or both of the monarchs in the period 1476–79 contain striking Marian imagery. *Dechado a la muy escelente Reina Doña Isabel* (discussed in a different context in chapter 2) clearly sets forth the theological grounding of the Isabel/Mary comparison: "Most illustrious queen adorned with royal greatness, come by grace of God to remedy our great ills; since we lost our life because of a woman, God wants to protect us and heal us by the same manner and measure that caused our fall" (282).[60] In presenting Isabel as the woman who remedies the lack occasioned "because of a woman," Mendoza represents the Queen as the antidote to the poison introduced into the world by Eve, and by analogy by Cava, Juana de Portugal, and her daughter Juana de Castilla.

The most direct target of Mendoza's critique is not, however, the destroyed reign of the feminized Rodrigo, but rather the disordered rule of the impotent Enrique. His misrule, as we saw in the last chapter, was linked to his sodomitical practices, his failure to impregnate his wife, his powerlessness to control her lust, and the Orientalism of his court, all gendered as feminine. Enrique's decadence and impotence are the object of a virulent attack in Mendoza's most ambitious work, *Coplas de Vita Christi*, published in 1482, but initially written fifteen years earlier.[61] Early in the poem, Mendoza identifies the three sins "that are wrapped up in those of high rank" [que andan enbueltos con grandes estados]: greed, lust, and pride. Mendoza's condemnation of lust, the primary sin of Enrique's family and court, is twice as long as his censure of the other two: "And of carnal vices we must unfortunately say that the natural ones are not enough, they glory in the unnatural ones: Oh, king! Since those who damage your fame with their corruption infect the air you breathe and the angels point them out to you, burn them like Sodom" (146, st. 25).⁶² In the revised, "official" version of the poem printed in Isabel's reign, the dark vision of sexual corruption reaches apocalyptic dimensions similar to those we saw in Palencia's chronicle: "Oh, Castilian nation, center of abominations! Oh, depraved world! Oh, hardened peoples! Oh, scorned temple! Oh, forgotten paradise! Oh, lost religious orders! (64).⁶³ Mendoza's catastrophic imagery of paradise lost cannot but conjure up those unworthy ancestors of Enrique and Juana, Rodrigo and Cava. The poet clearly views the excessive, unnatural desire of King Enrique in the same way he views King Rodrigo's. Whether represented as unnatural or natural, the excessive and transgressive desire of these kings is both cause and effect of feminine weakness, which in turn is responsible for the disorder and decay in the body politic.

The work in Mendoza's corpus that contains the most vivid imagery of fragmentation and repair is "Verses that declare how our Castile is repaired by the arrival of these most noble lords" *[Coplas en que se declara cómo por el advenimiento destos muy altos señores es reparada nuestra Castilla]* (1476–79). The connection between the two poles of destruction and restoration is underscored by the play between two verbal forms of *destrabar* or untie: "power is now obliged to bind up what was unbound, untied by sin" [ya el poder quedó obligado / a trabar lo destrabado / quel pecado destrabó] (324, sts. 18–19). More importantly for my purposes, Mendoza insistently contextualizes those images not in terms of biblical, but rather of "national" history: "and since reason has bestowed your rule on us, as I say, let us praise God for joining all that was scattered, all that King Rodrigo lost" (322, st. 13).⁶⁴ As he urges the monarchs to stand firm against those who contest their legitimate succession, he shifts the blame to Cava, just as the ballads do: "for it was Cava's fault and she should pay for it" [que fue la culpa de Cava / la qual debiera pagallo] (322; st. 16). Writing at the height of the civil war, Mendoza uses the overdue punishment of Cava's sin, the complicity of Rodrigo, and the treachery of Julián as an incitement to military action against Alfonso of Portugal and the Castilian supporters of Juana.

In his assimilation of Isabel to Mary, Mendoza chooses to extol the queen's virginity in terms of the physical integrity and wholeness of the queen's body rather than the suitability of that body as a vessel for the incarnation of a redeemer. In doing so, he draws on the typological linking of Eve and Mary that the church fathers developed to deal with the role of sexuality in human nature. On the face of it, this seems like a missed opportunity, given the grave problems occasioned by Enrique's lack of a male heir, a situation that Castilians fervently hoped the marriage of Isabel and Fernando would remedy. It is understandable, however, if viewed in the context of the neo-Gothic myth. Isabel's bodily integrity serves to symbolically remedy the original vulnerability of the body politic to penetration and castration by a threatening feminine other, figured as Oriental whore in the case of Cava, or as Portuguese whore in the case of Enrique's wife Juana.

There is, of course, a problem inherent in situating Isabel firmly within the neo-Gothic myth: her double-gendered, contradictory status as woman (Cava) and sovereign (Rodrigo). The difficulty is only partially resolved by representing her physical body as enclosed and contained, unthreatened and unthreatening in its purity, a body onto which the mythicized Gothic nation can be nostalgically mapped. The Christian's absolute faith in God's power to reassemble the body is extended to Isabel, underscoring the belief that God is working through her. Isabel's court writers thus put to political use the typological opposition of sin and redemption, of death and resurrection. The Queen's redemptive virginity ultimately brings her closer to God's promise "that division shall finally be overcome, that ultimately there is no scattering" (Bynum, *Fragmentation*, 294).

Two other metaphorical constructions of virginity in the Middle Ages are relevant to the trope of Isabel as Mary. The first is the fact that virginity allows the female body to transcend its "natural" state, identified with base matter, to become in effect masculine, identified with the higher attributes of mind or soul. This phenomenon is the source of the frequent medieval construction of saintly or martyred virgins as men (McNamara).[65] The closing of Isabel's body can also be related to the long-standing Christian iconographical and allegorical traditions that identified the inviolate body of Mary with a closed door *(porta clausa)* or an enclosed garden *(hortus conclusus)*.[66] Peter Stallybrass has studied the function of these images in the discursive assimilation of the integrity of Elizabeth I of England's body to the integrity of the state: "As she ushers in the rule of a golden age, she is the imperial virgin, symbolizing, at the same time as she is symbolized by, the *hortus conclusus* of the state.... But not only was Elizabeth the maker of that 'paradice' or 'gardein'; her enclosed body *was* that paradise" (130). As in the English case half a century later, the emblematic integrity of Isabel's body was set in a system of antithetical thinking central to absolutist theory, that is, its value derived from its opposite, the vulnerable, open female body.

This imagery of bodily enclosure is of a piece with the "closing" of Spain to foreign, feminizing influences that was in a sense the battle cry of the Reconquest. Mendoza accordingly sets his call for the closure of the Spanish body politic within an elaborate appeal to masculine warrior values. He uses terms such as *power, force, persistence, subjugate* [pujança, fuerça, porfía, sojuzgar] to rouse his monarchs to the action that will restore that body's health and wholeness. Thus, the power of Isabel's metaphorical virginity ultimately derives from its placement within a sexualized neo-Gothic myth that repudiates the feminine/Oriental and exalts masculine/Christian bellicosity as the key to the paradise lost by Rodrigo and Cava.[67] This is evident in Mendoza's contrast between Enrique IV, who "leaves the kingdom so damaged that no matter how well it is repaired, holes always remain" [dexa el reino tan dañado / que por bien que sea adobado / siempre quedan agujeros] and Fernando's uncle Alfonso V, "he who pursuing the fierce fears of fighting...left all fears behind" [el qual siguiendo los fieros / temores del pelear... a todos dexó que dar] (326–27).

The masculinization of Isabel promoted by the Marian monarchal encomiasts is also evident in the image of Isabel as *virgo bellatrix* in one of the phases of God's holy war against Islam, the War of Granada (1482–92). Although, as already discussed, it was more frequently Fernando who was cast in this role, there are some writers who figure Isabel as warrior queen. A vivid example of this strategy occurs in the *Rimado de la conquista de Granada* that the Aragonese nobleman Pedro Marcuello presented to Isabel and Fernando on various occasions during the decade-long Granadan campaign. The poems that compose the luxuriously produced volume include a long exhortation to the monarchs to complete the reconquest of Granada as a prelude to the conquest of Jerusalem.[68] At various points, Marcuello ascribes military epithets to Isabel (e.g., "great warrior" [gran guerreadora], 261, v. 490; "the great defeater" [la gran batizadera], 23, v. 32). But he places the most striking military comparison in the mouths of the Muslims themselves. Aware of their imminent defeat at the hands of the bellicose queen, they place her above the Castilian epic hero who won similar victories in the eleventh century: "This Queen, although a woman, is more of a knight than the Cid. And it is suspected that these [Moors of Granada] will be the downfall of all Islam" (133, vv. 122–25).[69]

The messianic image of Isabel as virginal warrior queen is also found in *La Poncella de Francia,* the sole retelling of the story of Joan of Arc in the Spanish Middle Ages. Dedicated to Isabel, it was most likely written sometime between 1474 and 1491.[70] From the very first chapter the work emphasizes the providential nature of Joan's coming to save France from the English: "Here begins the destruction of France for whose remedy the Maid who can be said to be almost heaven-sent" [Comiença la destruición de Francia a cuyo remedio fue casi la Poncella del cielo venida] (95). Responsibility for the "destruction" that Joan reverses is assigned to the seductive beauty of the Duchess of Burgundy, as disastrous for France as "Helen for Troy and La Cava for Spain" [Elena para Troya y la Caba para España] (96). The author draws a parallel between the state of France and of Castile, between Joan's heavenly mission and Isabel's: And so that Your Highness does not find such ills [as Spain's] too serious to remedy, I could find no queen from the past who is your equal, [so] I present you with the example of that poor shepherdess known as the Maid of France [who] . . . when she came to the aid of France found it so lost and weakened that it did not seem within men's power to save it" (94).[71] Amazon-like, Joan refuses the many offers of marriage she receives and is uninterested in hearing tales of love: "in her palace they did not talk of love, but of deeds [of men] of the past and present."[72] Not surprisingly, given the role of Alexander in the marital and monarchical symbolism created by Isabel and Fernando, the Greek hero heads the list of the famous warriors whose most daring exploits Joan asks the royal chroniclers to recount for her amusement and inspiration (204–5).

Several aspects of the famous Isabelline religious reform program suggest that sacrilegious imagery was integrated into royal reform programs.[73] Elizabeth Lehfeldt has shown how nuns merited special attention in the Isabelline monastic reform campaign precisely because of their symbolic role as virginal brides of Christ. Thus, for example, the queen's insistence on strict claustration applied more to nuns than to monks. One of two papal bulls authorizing the reform specifically empowered overseers to visit convents and alter the nuns' lifestyle as they deemed necessary, a provision that enabled the imposition of claustration. A royal dispatch of 1493 can be read as a literalization of the Marian imagery of enclosure discussed earlier: the *hortus conclusus* and *porta clausa*. It instructed that the doors and windows of a convent not look onto the street, that nuns not venture outside except when absolutely necessary and always in the company of other nuns, and that the keys to the doors be strictly controlled by the abbess (García Oro, 103).[74]

Isabel's demonstrated interest in the doctrine of the Immaculate Conception of Mary is also highly suggestive. Belief in the doctrine that Mary herself was exempt from original sin and therefore lived a completely unblemished life, second in perfection only to Christ, was widespread in late-medieval and Renaissance Spain, especially among the powerful Franciscans. Lehfeldt observes that the Marian metaphors that applied to Isabel the Virgin's redemption of Eve's sins may well have been Immaculist in intent because the doctrine was often represented in that way in the fifteenth century (52).[75]

Isabel showed particular devotion to both the doctrine and the order that promoted it.[76] We know from the royal account books that she repeatedly pledged funds to the Franciscans (Meseguer Fernández, "Franciscanismo"). The Queen asked the order's most prominent member, Archbishop Francisco Ximénez de Cisneros, her confessor since 1492, to oversee the reform of the order. She also founded three chaplaincies in honor of "La Inmaculada" and assigned substantial sums to each for the yearly celebration in December of the feast of the Immaculate Conception. The largest amount, to the monastery of the Hieronymites in Guadalupe, was donated in thanksgiving for the 1476 military victory over Portugal at Toro, "Where Divine Providence chose to demonstrate the justice of my cause" [donde la su divina providencia plogo de mostrar mi justicia] (quoted in Pérez, 80).[77] On a personal level, there is the close relationship she maintained with the Franciscan friar Iñigo de Mendoza, whose Marian panegyrics were discussed earlier. He was very close to the Queen, as the poems he dedicated to her and the frequent sums of money granted him in her account books attest.[78] It is also significant that Isabel's will specified that she be buried in a Franciscan habit.[79]

Further indication of Isabel's enthusiasm for the doctrine of the Immaculate Conception is her patronage of the female order of the Conceptionists, founded by the Benedictine nun Beatriz de Silva. In the late 1470s, the Virgin Mary appeared to Silva and charged her with founding an order to serve her. The nun discussed her plans with Isabel, her confessor Hernando de Talavera, and Cardinal Mendoza (Lehfeldt, 53). The Queen ceded Silva a palace in Toledo in which to house the order, and she helped secure the pope's approval of the new monastery in 1484. Ten years later the pope placed the Conceptionist order under the rule of Saint Clare, the female branch of the Franciscan order, once again at Isabel's request (Pérez, 87).

One popular immaculist image in painting and sculpture conflated the immaculately conceived Mary with the popular medieval image of the Woman of the Apocalypse from Saint John's Book of Revelation. She was most often depicted clothed in the sun and crowned with stars, holding the Christ child in her arms, and crushing a serpent underfoot. The multivalence of the image—the heavenly queen, mother of the Redeemer, who undoes Eve's sins—resonates in obvious ways with the neo-Gothic ideology of purity. Liss comments on the appositeness of this image to Isabel, especially upon the birth of her long-awaited male heir Juan in 1478: "Isabel was then hailed as...God's instrument, the heroine whose virtue overcame the divine disfavor brought on by her predecessors, who was chosen to guide Spain out of error and from threat of destruction into light. She was the anti-Eve, even the new Eve, destined to recover Spain and restore the loss of Eden" (160).

Isabel's support of the Immaculate Conception doctrine had a political dimension. It served to bolster her political legitimacy, an important concern, especially in the early years of her reign. More generally, as Lehfeldt observes: "By subsuming her sexuality in the metaphorical power of the doctrine of the Immaculate Conception, Isabel was able to provide sanction for her womanly nature. She was married and had borne children, but neither of these things compromised her ability to rule provided that she was identified with the purity...of this doctrine. The kingdom would not be corrupted by Isabel's female nature" (53).

We have seen that the theological discourse of sin and redemption in Isabelline verse panegyrics and the neo-Gothic political discourse of loss and restoration in Isabelline chronicle, treatise, and ballad are ideologically congruent. Both emphasize the notion of the fragmentation of the physical and political body, a dismemberment that is ascribed, directly or indirectly, to an originary woman's wantonness and men too weak to control them and/or resist their temptations. The association of Isabel with Mary, Immaculate Mother of God, is not, however, without its problems.[80] A second look at the encomiastic poems analyzed earlier shows that this divinized representation of Isabel inspires other emotions besides adoration. In Pedro de Cartagena's panegyric, for example, immediately after naming her "virginal woman, first on earth, second in heaven" [muger entera / en la tierra la primera / y en el cielo la segunda], the poet abruptly shifts the relationship of queen and subject away from the maternal to the paternal: "One thing is remarkable, that often happens too late, that she causes fear and love to coexist without conflict, because this is how God is" (Gerli, *Poesía cancioneril*, 73, vv. 71–75).[81]

Cartagena's double-gendering of Isabel's divinity, the slippage from Isabel as loving Virgin Mother to stern God the Father, is also found in an elaborate courtly panegyric written by another *converso* poet, Juan Alvarez Gato. The poet places himself among a multitude of pilgrims—"Barbarians, brown-skinned people, Guineans, Turks, Armenians, Jews, Arabs, and Chaldeans" [barbaros, loros, guineos, / turcos, armenios, hebreos, / alaraues y caldeos] (126, vv. 5–8)—who come to worship the queen's beauty. The adoration he feels, however, is clouded by anxiety: "If I want to speak I do not dare; if I want to remain silent, I cannot; like a fearful son before his ill-willed Father, I am enveloped by fear of you. Just as those condemned for a crime beg for clemency, so, with great reverence, all my senses tremble in your presence" (126, vv. 24–30; 127, vv. 1–3).[82] Later, as he meditates on the manner of his queen's formation, he makes a similar comparison, implying that Isabel, like Adam, was made in God's image: "the holy right hand of God fashioned you much more like his divine Majesty than to our common, lowly form" (128, vv. 6–9).[83] A final blasphemous conceit completes the poetic assimilation of Isabel to God by pointing out their sole dissimilarity: "This sole difference did he want there to be between you and him, so as to preserve his preeminence; that he alone should be called infinite" (128, vv. 15–19).[84]

The representations of Isabel that I have been examining clearly convey much more than innocuously sacrilegious courtly flattery. Rather, they fulfill an important ideological function, namely, to manage the disturbing paradox of the monarch's power and gender.[85] They poignantly express what Louise Fradenburg calls "the fantasy of the queen's benevolence [that] specularly reassures the narcissism of those she can compel" (*Women*, 141). But, unlike the queen consorts who are Fradenburg's subject—queens whose power was in the late Middle Ages largely restricted to an intercessory capacity, more akin to the Virgin's, in fact—

Isabel wielded power in her own right, and was all the more threatening for it. Half a century before the English cult of the Virgin Queen Elizabeth, Isabelline court poets fashioned the cult of their queen as immaculately conceived virgin mother sent to heal Spain's broken body.[86]

Sex, Power, and Property in *Pleyto del manto*

Isabel's fashioning as virginal restorer of the Visigothic paradise never completely dislodges the more material construction of the monarch as Woman, that is, "easily enslaved by bodily lusts and irrational passions [and] incapable of rational self-government,... associated with the lower parts of the body" (Rackin, "Foreign Country," 76–77). In Spain as elsewhere in the medieval period, a woman sovereign remained fundamentally disruptive, a sign of a world upside down in which the lower body triumphs over the upper.[87]

Nowhere in the Isabelline period are anxieties about the female's "open, windy, and breachable body" (Bynum, *Fragmentation*, 384 n. 107) more graphically expressed than in another of the satirical poems of the *Burlas* section of the *Cancionero general*. *Pleyto del manto* first appeared in print in the second edition of the *Cancionero* (1514), but it is thought to have been written in the final years of the fifteenth century.[88] Like *Carajicomedia*, added in 1519 when the *Burlas* section was published separately, the anonymous *Pleyto del manto* has been ignored by Hispanomedievalists because of its obscenity.[89] But its pornographic parody of the corruption of judges, lawyers, and litigants centers on precisely the symbolic axis that I have been tracing in this chapter: the perceived threat to the body politic when its head is anomalous because female. The anonymous poem attempts to fix, in both senses of the word, the dangerous blurring of gender roles and identities that Isabel's sovereignty represents. And in doing so it anxiously points to the danger that absolutist power located in a woman poses to the proper functioning of patriarchal law, specifically laws affecting property rights.

Pleyto del manto opens in a *locus amoenus* where two naked lovers— a "gentleman" [gentil hombre] and an "uncovered lady" [dama descubierta]—are locked in an embrace (46, vv. 8–9). The "dama descubierta," contemporary slang for a prostitute, does not remain so for long, however.[90] Another gentleman walking in the garden happens upon the couple, and after looking closely enough to see their "balls and crack" [turmas y hendedura (46, v. 13)], he discreetly turns away, tossing his velvet cloak over them, "as if with a veil" [como por velo (46, v. 22)]. It is a scene that invites what Patricia Parker has called "a pornographic doubleness," one that simultaneously panders to the eye and averts the gaze ("Fantasies," 94). The nobleman further disavows his scopophilic impulse by generously offering the cloak to "the one who holds it inside" [quien lo tiene dentro], the "cunt" [coño] or the "prick" [carajo]. Throughout the rest of the poem the male and female protagonists are represented only metonymically: as cunt and prick.

The dramatic opening of *Pleyto* thus dramatizes the construction of masculine and feminine as hierarchized and sexualized binary opposites, a construction whose source is a struggle over property, the velvet cloak of the noble voyeur. In this way it participates in the longstanding cultural linking of sexual and material possession.[91] The conjunction of sexual politics and material property is central to the rest of the poem, which takes the form of a dramatized mock trial to settle the genital litigants' claims to the expensive cloak. On one level, then, *Pleyto del manto* is an accomplished parody of judicial procedure and argumentation that serves the satirical function common to much early modern pornographic writing, and which we have previously seen in *Carajicomedia*. In this case the critique ostensibly targets legal corruption.[92]

The lawsuit the prick brings against the cunt hinges on a semantic technicality, namely, the correct definition of the terms in which the nobleman bestowed the cloak: "I give this cloak to the one who holds it inside" [do este manto en conclusión / para quien lo tiene dentro] (28–29). The expression "to hold it in" [tenerlo dentro], like other slang expressions cultivated in erotic verse of the period, was applied equally to both male and female participants in the sex act (Alzieu, Jammes, and Lissorgues, 260 n. 4). The gender ambiguity occasions the judicial debate that follows, in which each of the lawyers argues for a different meaning of *tener,* "to have," as evidence of the superior holding power of his client.

The *coño*'s solicitor first argues his client's right to the cloak because of her superior capaciousness, that is, *tener* in the sense of "contain." The container is necessarily superior to the contained, he states, and his client's "container" is vast indeed: "Therefore this deep ocean is so vast that it must hold and drown all that comes into its power, and so I say that it is true, as everybody knows, that everything that has is had by something bigger. You may believe, Sir, that because your member is hard, it seems to possess, when in reality it is possessed" (47, vv. 17–28).[93] The length of the "extended member" [miembro estendido] is no match for the depth of the vagina, compared here, as in *Carajicomedia*, to the vastness of the ocean.

The opposing attorney then makes the Aristotelian counterargument that the *carajo*'s staying power, the power of *tener* in the sense of "maintain," with the consequent ability to thrust, makes it the superior body part.[94] "Everything that must enter and maintain itself within another must be able to enter and push in and pull out.... And whoever does not get it up cannot enjoy this power, for the power to maintain consists of the ability to push in, like a leg into a hose" (48, vv. 3–12).[95] The internal rhyme of *poder* with *meter* and *tener* associates power with maintenance of erection and the consequent ability to penetrate. The linguistic tour de force of these lines transforms the initial mischievous blurring of gender boundaries by the cloak's donor into the sanctioned Aristotelian sex and gender roles: active male and passive female. The fear of the engulfing vagina that the impotent Diego Fajardo expressed in *Carajicomedia* is here masked by the emphasis on the erect penis's penetrative force. The implied celebration of rape becomes explicit a few lines later when the lawyer for the defense concludes his rebuttal as follows: "He is inside the thing who can force his way in" [Aquel es dentro en la cosa / que entra con fuerça en ella"] (48, vv. 26–27). In this court, possession, whether of woman as object or of material goods, is causally related to the masculine power to violate. It supports Gerda Lerner's view of the causal link between rape as a legal procedure for claiming property and the establishment of the inequality between the sexes.[96]

The mock trial drags on, drawn out by multiple objections, appeals, and counterappeals. The *coño* eventually declares a *rebeldía* or complaint at what she considers the court's biased proceedings. In the ensuing appeal, the *carajo* calls on three expert witnesses to argue for the supremacy of man over woman. The testimony of Ptolomy, Dante, and the Castilian love poet Macías fails to sway the judge, however, and he makes his final ruling in favor of the *coño*. As precedent he cites the powerful men who have been trapped by women's wiles: Adam, Hercules, Solomon, and Samson. The judge then imposes a festively Draconian sentence on the *carajo:* "by this sentence I order that he be imprisoned, jailed, confiscated in the cunt, because I condemn him to pay costs; may the lawsuit, costs, and fees be consummated in the cunt, until the foam shoots out through the tip of the prick" (58, vv. 2–9).[97] The lawyer for the *carajo* is appalled. He demands a new trial presided over by the spirit of the greatest defender of men, the famous misogynist poet Pedro Torrellas. Because Torrellas is dead, however, he must be replaced by "an illegitimate son of his" [un hijo suyo encubierto] (61, v. 35) who resides in Salamanca, the poet and playwright Juan del Encina.[98]

The carnivalesque triumph of the female in *Pleyto*, like the victory of the *coño* over Fajardo's *carajo* in the eponymous *Carajicomedia*, is, however, everywhere undermined. The poet repeatedly demonizes the vagina as a dark and dangerous void: a "tomb" [luzillo], "ossary" [honsario], "hole" [hondura], "wide road and deep forest" [gran camino y espesura], and "sepulchre" [sepultura].[99] Here also, as in *Carajicomedia*, the mysterious and mortiferous depths of the female body are attacked as devourers of money as well as semen. A good example of the association occurs in the graphic description of a sexual encounter had by Macías, the iconic Castilian martyr for love: "He kept his member simple [straight] within that great tomb until it came out doubled [bent] [dentro de aquel luzillo / su miembro tuvo senzillo / hasta que salió doblado] (54, vv. 30–31). Covarrubias defines *sencillo* as "that which is simple and without duplicity or deceit; it is sometimes said of the simple and honest man who is truthful" [933].[100] At the same time, *dobla* plays off the term *doblado*, denoting both the adjective "bent" (as in the proverbial "It is better to bend than to break" [más vale doblar que quebrar]) and the noun *dobla*, a gold coin worth two *escudos* that first circulated in the reign of Juan II. And it has a third, legal meaning: "used in the supreme courts, as in appealing with fifteen hundred doubloons, which is like depositing them so that they can be divided among the judges if the appelant does not win his case" (479).[101] The joke on the *carajo* concerns its greater worth in the weakened condition in which it withdraws from the *coño* after having made its "deposit." At the same time, it associates the power of judges with that of prostitutes, both of whom pocket money illegally.

A brief but significant reappearance of Saint Hilary [Sant Ilario], the burlesque saint who played an important symbolic role in *Carajicomedia*, confirms the threat of the feminine to the masculine in *Pleyto*. In the *carajo*'s second appeal, it invokes the same holy sodomizer of the devil in order to attack the judge's bias towards the *coño*: "Even if it displeases

Saint Hilary and the cunt's lawyer, you, as loyal notary, testify for me to that effect before the cunt's prosecutor, and may the judge who effortlessly pronounced such judgments be rewarded by having her shit on his prick, since she is cutting off his balls" (61, vv. 21–29).[102] The association of Sant Ilario, saintly bugger, with the voracious *coño* here is paradoxical, because Sant Ilario's power is active rather than passive. Nevertheless, both are figured as subversive of the patriarchal law of the land and two institutions that enforce it: the church and the courts.

But *Pleyto*'s travesty goes beyond a general indictment of Spain's judicial system to take indirect aim at the country's supreme lawmaker, Isabel herself. Two passages in the poem provide the evidence for this assertion. In the first, the *carajo*'s attorney transcodes the parts involved in the "penetration versus containment" argument from the physical body onto the body politic. In a scathing parody of the theory of the *corpus mysticism*, he argues as follows: "what a false conclusion, against reason and law, it would be to say that the kingdom is present inside the king; well, it is no less incorrect to say that the cunt moves inside the prick" (48, vv. 42–49, vv. 1–5).[103] Clearly, in Aristotelian terms, if the monarch is contained in his kingdom and not the other way around, the monarch can only be male. The penetrated cannot be the penetrator; the possessed can never be the possessor.

The more compelling evidence for a political reading of *Pleyto* comes toward the end of the poem, when the judge rejects the first of the *carajo*'s two appeals. He finds that the *coño* has proven her opponent's "legal weakness" [flaqueza de derecho] (57, v. 25), and he justifies the finding with a parody of a well-known proverb: "So as not to come off inflamed [literally, "cunted"], I agree to wash my hands of the dirty proceedings, not in order not to sentence, but for having sentenced. And if some judge ill of this that they are reading, I answer that 'cunts are a law unto themselves'" (58, vv. 10–18; my emphasis).[104]

These verses travesty the popular proverb "the king is a law unto himself" [allá van leyes donde quieren reyes], itself a calque of the legal maxim "quod principi placuit legibus solutus" (princely wishes are free from the limitations of the law) used to justify royal absolutism. In fact, as Nieto Soria has shown, this dictum was increasingly invoked from the reign of Juan II on to affirm the absolute power of the Trastamaran monarchy. References to the "absolute royal power" [poderío real absoluto] of the monarch proliferate in the documents of the Isabelline period (*Fundamentos,* 121–27). Maravall finds a theological basis to this concept of monarchy in the distinction drawn between God's *potestas ordinata,* responsible for the order of the world, and his *potestas absoluta,* whereby he may alter that order at any time, following only the dictates of his will (*Estado moderno,* 1:278). Clearly, the lines in question take the judicial satire of *Pleyto* one brazen step further, to criticize the corrupting power of the female sovereign.

The judge's brazen admission of bias complements the earlier gendered comparison between the kingdom and the cunt that the latter's attorney made in order to underscore the capacity of his client. In that case, metonomy structured the unequal relationship between the male and female sex: the *coño*/kingdom is the potent whole of which the "weak nature" [flaca natura] of the *carajo*/king is only a part. Now, the *coño* is identified as the all-powerful head of state, completing the debasement of the male member/monarch. The *corpus mysticum* is inverted as the cunt usurps the place of the head of state and Isabel, whom the court poets constructed as virginal redeemer of woman's natural wantonness, is put in her place, that of the corrupted and corrupting whore who threatens patriarchal power and property.

Corroborating my reading of *Pleyto del manto* as maliciously regicentric is another poem of the *Cancionero general* composed around the same time: "Juego trovado" by the poet identified only as Pinar.[105] A brief prose prologue, perhaps the work of the compiler Hernán del Castillo, explains that the poet made the game for Queen Isabel, and that it "can be played with dice or cards, and one can win or lose" (folio 183r, quoted in Menéndez Collera, 426).[106] The courtly game of chance contains forty-six stanzas, the first six dedicated to members of the royal family, the remaining forty to individual ladies of the court. Each of the "cards" displays four symbolic elements—a tree, a bird, the initial verse of a song, and a proverb—which are to be used, Tarot fashion, to cast each player's fortune.[107] The very first card described, appropriately enough, is the Queen's: "Your Majesty, before anyone else, as you are the first among women in chastity, take the card with the palm frond as well as the phoenix, which alone was like your highness in everything, along with the song that goes like this: 'Queen most high…' and the proverb: '*The king is a law unto himself.*'" (Quoted in Menéndez Collera,

427; my emphasis).¹⁰⁸ Chastity [the palm] and absolute power: two of the attributes that Pinar praises in the Queen are the very ones the anonymous author of *Pleyto* anxiously mocks. In the third symbol, the phoenix, Pinar may express his own ambivalence about his queen and her "games." Primarily a christological symbol, the bird's uniqueness (the repeated *sola/sólo* of verses 4 and 5 in preceding quotation), solitariness, and hermaphroditic self-reproduction were often used to represent the Virgin Mary or Mary and Christ together.

We have seen how chastity functions to create a space for Isabel within *neogoticismo* and how licentiousness closes it off. But why do Pinar and the author of *Pleyto* focus on the monarch as supreme legislative authority, and specifically in the context of property law? To grasp the import of the slurs and further historicize the misogynist humor of *Pleyto* we must recall that a primary Isabelline goal, but one that had to be implemented carefully, was the restructuring of Castile's legal codes and court and penal system. The project was undertaken in large measure as a way of curtailing the power of the nobility and strengthening that of the monarchy. Isabel addressed the issue as early as the Cortes of 1476, with the institution of the Santa Hermandad, a combination of national police force and rudimentary national army (Liss, 130). The "justices of the peace" [alcaldes] of the Hermandad were supported by local taxes, were granted greater jurisdiction than local justices, and were firmly controlled by a national general assembly.

Even more radical changes were effected at the Cortes of 1480, on the heels of the monarchs' victory over Portugal. Of signal importance was the diminution of the nobility's representation on the Royal Council, the highest court in the realm, and a corresponding increase in the participation of the *letrados*, personally chosen by the monarchs. Liss summarizes the impact of the 1480 Cortes as follows: "For Castile, the ordinances of the Cortes of Toledo were in effect the constitution of an emerging nation-state that was also a near-absolute monarchy, and they were the work of royal lawyers experienced in promoting royal interests" (184). One of these royal lawyers, Alonso Díaz de Montalvo, was ordered in the same year to prepare a single compendium of Castilian law. Completed in 1484 and printed the following year, the regalist code provided a body of precedent designed to obviate having the Cortes promulgate laws and to elevate reliance on royal decree. It became the basis of juridical action in Spain for more than fifty years.¹⁰⁹

An initiative that went hand in hand with Isabel's legal reversal of the devolution of power onto the aristocracy was her reclaiming of the royal patrimony, the monies and territories that Enrique and Alfonso had dispensed as "gifts of rents" [mercedes] to the nobility in the vexed attempt to secure their loyalty. Isabel rescinded all the rewards granted by Alfonso, as well as those that the nobles were judged to have coerced from Enrique. The rescission reveals Isabel's view of Castile's recent past, specifically, the belief that the source of the civil war had been the nobility's assault on the monarchy: "the *mercedes* reform was in fact the reversal of this injustice, and, in signalling a low opinion of the validity of either Enrique's or Alfonso's reign, it buoyed the idea of Isabel's own reign as the one most validly stemming from that of her father" (Liss, 185).[110]

Like the biblical allusions of *Carajicomedia*, the legal terminology of *Pleyto* shows that it is the work of a cultured, aristocratic author, perhaps a nobleman such as García de Astorga.[111] A rubric identifies Astorga as the author of a prose epilogue to *Pleyto* that is addressed to the more powerful aristocrat Pedro de Aguilar.[112] In it Astorga boasts of his sexual prowess in a chance encounter with a "lady" at an inn, an apparent recuperation of the original author's mock humiliation of the penis. He then adds two verse stanzas of his own "in support of the sentence against the *blessed martyr prick,* so as not to conflict with such honest judges, although licit and honorable reasons could have been found for not bringing the cunt's case to trial, but rather having it obliterated and thrown out of court in accordance with the law established by ancient monarchs, of glorious memory" (64; my emphasis).[113] This may well be a reference to the traditional de facto exclusion of female sovereignty. But the most explicit reason for not believing the *coño* is more material: "because the cunt is a miser, greedy and malicious, disqualified, condemned, because its mouth stinks" (64, vv. 14–17).[114]

Astorga's own sacrilegious representation of the *carajo* as martyr for sex, an upending of the courtly topos of martyr for love (e.g., Macías) and the related portrayal of the *coño* as foul-smelling and greedy, underscores the economic component of *Pleyto*'s travesty of Isabelline messianic discourse. In this obscene contextualization of the medieval topos of greed as the root of all sins ("Radix enim omnium malorum est cupiditas" [1 Timothy 6:10]), the greed of the prostitute's cunt for money and sex encodes an aggressive assault on the hunger for power and property of the earthly counterpart to the Queen of Heaven. The uncontrollable, voracious cunt queen of *Pleyto* commits multiple crimes against the nation. She abuses the law of the land and the judicial system, greedily and unjustly seizes others' property, and humiliatingly emasculates her subjects. Whether or not García de Astorga and Pedro Aguilar were personally affected by the legal and economic changes instituted by the Queen. They belonged to the class that was most deeply implicated.

It is interesting to compare *Pleyto*'s fashioning of Isabel as greedy whore to an exemplum included in medieval Spain's most famous misogynist treatise. Written by Alfonso Martínez de Toledo in 1438, *Arcipreste de Talavera o Corbacho* was first published in a revised version in 1498. The very first *enxienplo* of Part II, which attacks "the vices, defects, and bad nature of wicked and vicious women" [los vicios, tachas e malas condiciones de las malas e viciosas mugeres] reads as follows: "A certain queen was very honest, but not without vanity, for she thought she was more virtuous than any woman, and she used to go about saying: 'What woman is so base that she would yield her body to a man for all the wealth in the world?' She repeated this so frequently and publicly that a certain nobleman swore by the True Cross that he would persuade her to yield up her body for gifts, or die in the attempt" (González Muela, 121–22).[115] In his test of the queen's virtue, the gentleman first asks if she would give herself in exchange for the gift of a diamond ring, a ruby, or a city as large as Rome. The queen insists that she would not, "Not even if he gave me the kingdom of Castile" [Nin aunque me diese un reyno de Castilla]. When asked if she would give in to a man if "he made you empress of the world so that all men and women would come to kiss your hands as their sovereign" [vos fiziese del mundo enperadora e que todos los onbres vos besasen las manos por señora], she admits that she could not resist such a temptation. The nobleman then gloats to himself: "If I had something to give her right now, I would have this wicked woman in my hands" (Martínez de Toledo, *Sermons*, 101–2) [Si yo toviese agora qué dar, la mala muger en las manos la tenía] (122).

The unnamed *caballero* of the exemplum unmasks the queen as a high-priced prostitute whom he lusts after but cannot afford. But what is most relevant to my discussion is not the high price set by the queen for her sexual favors, but rather her obvious preference for power over money. It is that desire of the queen's that her male subject cannot hope to fill, or control. Martínez de Toledo's misogynist exemplum, like *Pleyto del manto,* lays bares the intersection of the economies of desire, power, and property disrupted by Isabel's rule. Like its companion piece, *Carajicomedia, Pleyto del manto* attacks royal absolutism and corruption, but that critique is inseparable from its *ad feminam* vituperation.

CHAPTER FIVE
Luis de Lucena and the Rules of the Game

> What monarchs do, good or bad, we all try to do. If it is good, to please ourselves; and if bad, to please them. The King gambled, we were all cardsharps; the Queen studies, now we are students.
>
> Lo que los reyes hacen, bueno o malo, todos ensayamos de hacer. Si es bueno, por aplacer a nos mesmos; y si malo, por aplacer a ellos. Jugaba el Rey, éramos todos tahures; studia la Reina, somos agora estudiantes.
>
> —Juan de Lucena, *Epístola exhortatoria a las letras*

These lines, written by Isabel's royal prothonotary Juan de Lucena in the early 1480s, are frequently offered as evidence of Isabel's dedication to learning and the arts.[1] Isabel's love of learning and promotion of the arts have been a prominent theme in the modern historiographical construction of her reign.[2] This makes it all the more surprising that there exists no systematic study of the specific manifestations of that patronage, its political uses, and the ways, direct or subtle, that it shaped the work of writers and artists of the period.[3] In this chapter, I examine the youthful works of Juan de Lucena's son, Luis de Lucena. He was a student at the University of Salamanca in the 1490s, when Antonio de Nebrija could have been one of his teachers and Fernando de Rojas a classmate. Like Rojas, Alfonso de Palencia, and Fernando del Pulgar, Lucena was—or was preparing to be—a *letrado*, a member of the self-conscious class of university-trained lawyers. Lucena aspired to secure employment at court or in the burgeoning bureaucracy of the Catholic Monarchs, following in the footsteps of his father. His two youthful works, *Repetiçión de amores* and *Arte de axedrez,* were most likely written at Salamanca. At some point before 1495, when Lucena had them printed and bound together, the young author decided to use them as a kind of writing sample, evidence of the scholarly and rhetorical skills that would enhance his application for a curial position.

There is an ideological as well as a codicological and an ideological relationship between Lucena's two works. The seemingly disparate texts are both shaped by their young author's awareness of writing for the royal family, ostensibly Prince Juan, Isabel and Fernando's heir, but also the powerful mother who closely oversaw her only son's education. It is the presence of Isabel as possible patron that explains Lucena's fascination with games and gamesmanship, and especially with what I will call, for reasons that will become apparent, a "new kind of queen." This is not the traditional view of Lucena's work. Critics have associated his writings—or rather, the *Repetiçión,* because *Arte de axedrez* has been virtually ignored—with the interrelated genres of sentimental romance and the debate about women, without considering the complex historical context that produced them.[4]

The Queen and the University

The University of Salamanca, Spain's preeminent institution of learning, was an important venue for Isabel's patronage. In 1480, to mark the end of the civil war, Isabel and Fernando made a state visit to Santiago and Salamanca. The trip symbolized the importance of both religious unity and letters to the future of the nation. To honor the occasion, they placed on the university facade a Greek inscription reading "The Monarchs for the University and the University for the Monarchs" (Gilman, *Fernando de Rojas,* 305). Isabel did not neglect the pledge expressed in the inscription. Her interest in the university reforms led not only to sponsorship of Antonio de Nebrija and other professors, but also to continuing royal protection that included frequent visits, enforcement of university statutes on faculty elections and degree requirements, suppression of abuses of university *fueros* or immunities, and even resolution of student and faculty disputes (ibid.).

There was a strong political dimension to the queen's interest in the university. Its traditional prominence in legal studies served the Catholic Monarchs well in the judicial and administrative reforms begun at the

Cortes of 1476. Isabel's preferment of Salamancan-trained *letrados* was instrumental in the consolidation of her authority, as we saw in chapter 3. *Letrados* like Alfonso de Palencia and Fernando del Pulgar played an important role in crafting, under Isabel's watchful eye, the official story of the legitimacy and authority of her rule.

The printing press, introduced to the peninsula in 1478, aided this endeavor. As is well known, Isabel encouraged the new technology by passing laws exempting the fledgling presses from taxation. Her personal library of some four hundred volumes (its nucleus inherited from her father, Juan II) contained works printed in Latin, Italian, French, and Arabic (Sánchez Cantón). She commissioned the printing of both religious and secular works such as Martín de Córdoba's *Jardín de nobles donzellas*, Gómez Manrique's *Regimiento de príncipes*, and Iñigo de Mendoza's *Vita Christi*. One of the first books to come off the press was the legal compendium that Isabel had Alonso Díaz de Montalvo write, as discussed in the last chapter. It facilitated the elevation of royal decree and the reinvigoration of the royal chancery along with a corresponding diminution in the juridical power of the Cortes. The printing and distribution of the compendium to every municipality in the kingdom exemplifies Isabel's grasp of the power of print (Liss, 254).

Much of the atmosphere pervading the university in the final years of the fifteenth century must be attributed to the reformist mission of Antonio de Nebrija (1488–1530). The scholar returned from his humanist studies in Italy fired with the utopian belief that the cultivation of a pure Latin was the necessary foundation for all other reforms, not only at the university, but in the nation as a whole. He embarked on the fulfillment of this utopian agenda by publishing his first scholarly work, the epochal comparative grammar *Introductiones latinae* (Salamanca, 1480). The messianic language Nebrija uses in the prologue to the Spanish–Latin vocabulary he dedicated to Isabel in 1495 is telling. He presents his goal as nothing less than to "demolish barbarism, for so long and so widely spread throughout all parts of Spain" [desbaratar la barbaria, por todas partes de España tan ancha y luengamente derramada] (quoted in González-Llubera, xxiii). Nebrija compares himself to the apostles Peter and Paul, who, in order to establish the church, chose not obscure villages but the centers of learning in Athens, Antioch, and Rome: "I began in no other place than the University of Salamanca, which, like a fortress taken in battle, [if it surrendered to me] I had no doubt that the other Spanish towns would soon submit to me" (ibid.).[5] Nebrija's attitude perfectly aligned with a major aim of Isabelline royal policy: to make the newly unified kingdom the intellectual leader of Europe (Gilman, *Fernando de Rojas*, 305). Here again, the instrumental role of the printing press, which scholars believe Nebrija introduced into Salamanca (González-Llubera, xxiii) must be acknowledged.

Isabel's patronage of Salamanca was also personally motivated. Her concern for the proper education of her children, and especially of Crown Prince Juan, is well known. The treatise *Diálogo sobre la educación del Príncipe Don Juan*, composed by the royal courtier Alonso Ortiz, tells us that Isabel herself designed and supervised Juan's education at court, with the guidance of Cardinal Mendoza. The education of the prince combined the training in arms proper of a medieval warrior prince with instruction in Latin, Christian theology, and moral and natural philosophy. The queen engaged Salamancan-based humanists, among them the Italians Lucio Marineo and Pietro Martire, to tutor the prince and other sons of the nobility.

Isabel's own interest in learning Latin is also relevant to issues of patronage. The epigraph to this chapter records one of the contemporary references to her attempt to master the language as an adult. Another is contained in Fernando del Pulgar's description of his employer in *Crónica de los Reyes Católicos:* "She was a very smart and clever woman ... and of such excellent wit that, along with the many and arduous matters of state she had in governing the Kingdoms, she dedicated herself to the task of learning Latin letters; and she managed to learn so much in one year that she could understand any Latin speech or document" (256–57).[6] Isabel's extensive personal library contained at least eight Latin textbooks and Prince Juan's Latin copybooks (Sánchez Cantón, 37). Most famously, the queen is supposed to have been tutored in Latin by the exceptional Beatriz Galindo, dubbed "la Latina." But, as with all adulation heaped on Isabel by both contemporary and modern historians of her reign, the praise for her abilities in Latin may have more to do with flattery than with any real level of proficiency she may have attained.[7]

Prince Juan's ties to Salamanca were deepened in 1497, when he was assigned political jurisdiction over it on the occasion of his marriage to

Margaret of Austria. In September 1497, Prince Juan made a state visit to his new patrimony.[8] In a letter recounting the event, Pietro Martire pays homage to his former student's dedication to learning: "These solemnities in honor of the Prince were arranged with the greatest care and lavishness, because this city is the literary fountain of all Spain, and it hoped that the future king—himself a lover and cultivator of letters—would grant it favor and protection beyond all other cities" (*Epistolario*, 9:344–45; quoted in Gilman, *Fernando de Rojas*, 308).

Salamanca had been for more than fifty years a laboratory for literary experimentation.[9] Among the students who might have welcomed Juan on that auspicious occasion were Luis de Lucena and Fernando de Rojas, who may have just begun working on his elaboration of the *Comedia de Calisto y Melibea* (Gilman, *Fernando de Rojas*, 270). Others in that impressive generation were poet and dramatist Juan del Encina, the musician and playwright Lucas Fernández, and the future conquistador of Mexico, Hernán Cortés (ibid., 272). For young writers, the reforms instituted by Nebrija and sponsored by Isabel were formative. As Gilman explains, "Renascent interest on accurate and elegant use of a literary language brought with it—in Salamanca as in the rest of Europe—awareness of the creative possibilities of the spoken language. The improvement of Latin was a prerequisite for the outburst of student literature which . . . occurred at the end of the century" (306).

Although training in Latin and the techniques of oral exposition and argumentation were integral components of the Salamancan curriculum, there was a considerable gap between the university regulations promoting the use of Latin and their implementation. In 1503, the Greek scholar Arias Barbosa bemoaned the universal violation among professors as well as students of the rule that Latin be spoken at all times (quoted in ibid., 287 n. 41). The disparity between rule and observance must be understood as part of a general pattern of student resistance to the adult ordering of all aspects of their lives. Salamancan student life was particularly turbulent in the years in question. A few months before his visit to Salamanca, Prince Juan was already attending to problems of student misconduct in his new jurisdiction. In a letter dated April 22, 1497, he instructs the civil authorities to help the schoolmaster to "punish and chastise" [punir y castigar] rebellious students. His attention was again drawn to the university in 1504, specifically to deal with daily disturbances caused by armed students (ibid., 286 and n. 38).

Resistance to the pedagogical rigors of Salamanca took more creative forms as well, in the abundant student burlesques of academic exercises and rituals. Most famous among the latter was the "fiesta del Obispillo," when, in classic carnival fashion, students dressed as priests and parodied religious rituals (ibid., 296 and n. 60). Aurora Egido has studied another form of student burlesque, the *gallo,* a form of *vejamen* or insulting speech delivered at an elaborate degree-granting ceremony. Other types of festive parascholarly literature produced at Salamanca are Goliardic poems, *disparates,*[10] and the mock *disputatio* or *repetitio.*

The oral *disputatio* had been the cornerstone of university training in the scholastic method since the thirteenth century. It required analysis of discipline-relevant problems or *quaestio* and the presentation of scientific solutions that took into account the opinion of the *auctores,* empirical observation, and the dictates of reason.[11] This oral explication of a legal or philosophical text was required of advanced-degree candidates at Salamanca from at least 1422 on. Doctoral candidates not only had to present and explicate the relevant *textum* but also had to respond to opposing views proffered by fellow students. At the professorial level, the *repetitio* was initially formulated as a kind of complementary lesson dictated by a junior professor, but it eventually became the responsibility of the full professor and evolved into a solemn occasion at which student attendance was required.[12]

Toward the end of the fifteenth century, as the use of Latin declined at the university, so did the practice of delivering the *repetitio.* Nevertheless, there were those who continued to champion it as an "optimum genre for the scientific advancement of each of its colleges" [género óptimo para el progreso científico de cada una de sus facultades] (Cátedra, *Amor y pedagogía,* 129). The faculty's awareness of the vocational dimension of the Salamancan curriculum can be detected in the wording of the 1538 university statutes requiring periodic *repetitiones* and dissertations by the faculty and advanced students: "because the greatest help to professional competence is the discussion and oral exercise of the students" (Esperabé Arteaga, 1:200; quoted in Gilman, *Fernando de Rojas,* 312). Nebrija took pride in fulfilling this academic duty. His fondness for the virtuoso displays of erudition and argumentative technique shows in the fact that he had some of his *repetitiones* printed, from the *Repetitio de mensuris,* which lists alphabetically all classical denominations along with their geometric or mathematical equivalents, to the autobiographical and polemical *De hispanorum quirundum corruptis litterarum vocibus* (Cátedra, *Amor y pedagogía*, 130–31).

Love, Misogyny, and Male Bonding in *Repetiçión de amores*

Lucena's *Repetiçión de amores* pokes fun both at the form and the content of a standard *repetitio*. It is only in the last decade that the festive nature of the work has been recognized; traditionally, it was classified as either an antifeminist tract or a sentimental romance.[13] In his study of the influence of the university curriculum on the development of prose fiction genres in the fifteenth century, Pedro Cátedra convincingly demonstrates the connection between Lucena's burlesque work and the serious treatises of amatory doctrine that were products of the avid cultivation of Aristotelian natural philosophy at the university. Lucena's work is particularly indebted to the work of the prolific and highly respected professor Alfonso Fernández de Madrigal, known as "el Tostado." His theoretical and exegetical treatises, such as *Breviloquio de amor y amiçiçia* (after 1432), explain the nature and power of love as a passion that man shares with other animals: "And when someone has this fire [of love] within him, nature generally inclines him toward it [reproduction]" [Et quando alguno este fuego dentro de sí tien, la naturaleza a esto lo entiende inclinar] (*Del Tostado*, 72). Love's irrationality and power, the scholar insists, has the potential for destructiveness, a potential that must be controlled through the exercise of the will and the love of God.[14]

Aristotelian amatory doctrine had an impact that went beyond the academic setting. It shaped the beginnings of prose romance—specifically, Juan Rodríguez del Padrón's *Siervo libre de amor* and Pedro de Portugal's *Sátira de felice e infelice vida* (Cátedra, *Amor y pedagogía*, 154).[15] Rojas's *Celestina* is the most powerful dramatization of the desolation that desire and passion cause. Also influential was a certain tendency toward the parodic in the Salamancan treatment of natural philosophy, as exemplified by the sly irony of the anonymous *De cómo al ome es necesario amar*.[16] The subversion of the Aristotelian deepens, furthermore, when "that characteristic element of the intellectual milieu of the waning of the Middle Ages ... is decanted and distilled in different wineskins and different environments" (*Amor y pedagogía*, 12).[17] I return in this chapter and the next to one such different environment—namely, the Isabelline court—that Cátedra considers instrumental in the subversion and fictionalization of Aristotle's philosophy of love.

Lucena's festive academic exercise enlists inversions of various kinds. The most obvious of these on a formal level is the use of the vernacular rather than Latin throughout the body of the work.[18] Also, whereas a ranking professor would preside over the delivery of a serious student *repetitio*, Lucena names as his *presidente* "the god Cupid, in whose name I begin by relating the service I gave my beloved" [al dios Cupido, en cuyo nombre comienzo por servicio de mi amiga] (44). Another target is the meticulously organized and solidly authorized argumentation of the scholastic treatise. Lucena's reference to the prescribed *ordo legendi*— "your graces will see that the order of my discourse does not differ from that used in scientific discourses" [sabrán vuestras mercedes quel orden de mi repetiçión no diffiere del que en las scientíficas letras se usa] (44)—is decidedly tongue-in-cheek. *Repetiçión de amores,* in fact, presents not a well-ordered argument but rather a patchwork of contradictory passages borrowed more or less verbatim from other treatises and romances on love and fortune.[19]

In its discursive ordering, Lucena's work seems to most closely approximate a legal *repetitio,* although it continually disrupts or disregards the prescribed rigid order of argumentation (Cátedra, *Amor y pedagogía,* 130ff.). This includes the *lemma* or *textum* or legal text to be discussed; the *casus positio* or specific case that supports the law; the *notabilia* or juridical points contained in the law that are useful for argumentation; the dialectical *quaestiones* and *oppositiones*; and the *similia* or authoritative texts that facilitate their solution. A few examples of the upending of the prescribed order will suffice to illustrate Lucena's technique. Lucena states that his *textum* "came from the book of Torrellas's thought, and is most properly termed loose, for not being incorporated into legal writ" (44).[20] This "loose" or unincorporated juridic text is the notorious misogynist poem *Maldezir de mugeres* (Defamation of women) by Pedro Torrellas, the urtext of Spain's contribution to the European debate about women.

Torrellas's poem begins with the famous lines "He who loving well pursues ladies destroys himself" [Quien bien amando prosigue Donas, a ssí mesmo destruye] (44) and was written during Juan II's reign (pre-1435). It generated dozens of rebuttals and endorsements well into the sixteenth century. By the time Lucena wrote his *Repetiçión*, Torrellas had become a cultural icon, making an appearance in several works of fiction and poetry. The most startling dramatization of this prototypical woman hater occurs in Juan de Flores's romance *Grisel y Mirabella*, which I discuss in the next chapter.[21]

Lucena's promised explication of his *textum* never materializes; after quoting the first stanza, he launches into an ironic *casus positio* that purports to illustrate the "law" of Torrellas. Copied from Aeneas Silvius's *Historia de duobus amantibus* (1444), it is an erotic autobiographical and epistolary interpolation that narrates his courtship of a "lovely lady" [linda dama] who finally rejects him despite the best efforts of a go-between. Cátedra believes that this segment is a subversion of romance themes like those contained in the best-selling *Cárcel de Amor* (1492). The brief but vivid "case" of the scorned lover is followed by the latter's tirade against the omnipotence of Love: "how he wounds lovers and even those not in love, forcing them to love" [cómo el llaga a los enamorados y aun a los no enamorados, forzándolos a amar] (68). This segment, a verbatim borrowing from the anonymous *Tratado de como al hombre es necesario amar* (Treatise on how man must love), is followed by a detailed description of Cupid copied from *Sátira de felice e infelice vida* (Satire on the happy and the unhappy life). After following this meandering line of reasoning, the *repetidor* return to his *textum*, Torrellas's poem, "so as not to stray from the order that those who discourse follow" [por no apartarme del orden que llevan los que repiten] (68).

Also noteworthy for its irony is the conclusion to *Repetiçión*, a *quaestio disputata* on "that quality for which you [ladies] most esteem men" [aquello por lo qual todas más estymays a los hombres] (86–87), that is, a debate on the relative seductive power of military prowess and scholarly attainment. For this argument Lucena draws on two popular medieval debates: the debate between the cleric and the knight and the arms versus letters polemic. He displays his rhetorical virtuosity by presenting first four syllogisms pro the scholar and then four contra. The finding in favor of the soldier is clearly a joke, however, because the arguments presented in favor of arms are all based on a false premise—the contention that arms are a good dependent on fortune. Lucena later contradicts his own statement when he maintains that "military discipline is included among the riches of the spirit, in the same way as the sciences" [la militar disciplina se contiene entre los bienes del ánimo, asimesmo como las scientias] (402). Most comically, the debate subverts Lucena's efforts made throughout the *repetitio* to establish, even flaunt, his own credibility as a scholar.

For my purposes, however, the most interesting of the many festive inversions in *Repetiçión* is Lucena's address of his dissertation to "pleclaríssimas" and "honestíssimas señoras" (40–41). Applying the requisite humility topos, the author states that any attempt to praise such excellent ladies is impossible: "not only does it instill fear in me to attempt to do it, but it would even frighten the greatest orator anywhere" [no solamente a mí, pero aun al mayor orador que se hallase, pensarlo hazer pondría miedo] (41). As Aurora Egido has explained, such elocutionary cross-gendering, a common feature of the related academic form of the *gallo*, can by no means be taken literally. This is because women were excluded from the university and therefore from the learning so ostentatiously displayed and burlesqued in the *repetitio*. They simply would not have been present at the ceremonies where such recitations were delivered. On the contrary, such introductions "reveal an obvious joke on the audience, cross-dressing the professors, rector, . . . and students as damsels, to the delight and mockery of all" (Egido, 627).[22] In other words, Lucena is engaging in a kind of friendly hazing of his classmates by calling them women. But is the laughter produced by this kind of verbal hazing—calling Lucena's classmates and teachers a bunch of women—just good, clean fun?

I would argue that Lucena's mock *repetitio* plays a role in the university's formation of masculine secular identity in the privileged young men who attended Salamanca. It points to a complex interaction of male rivalry and male bonding that pervaded the university environment. As regards the rivalry, I have already noted Salamanca's tumultuousness, its bitter quarrels among faculty members and their student supporters (Nebrija's fight with Lucio Marineo over their competing Latin textbooks is one of the best known), frequent elections, and disputes among the various colleges. The pedagogical emphasis on disputation and debate within the classroom and a rowdyism that often erupted into violence outside it added to the conflictive environment.[23]

At the same time, the similar academic tasks, language, and goals of the students were clearly a source of solidarity. Walter Ong has shown how the study of Latin served as a puberty rite that separated boys from their mother tongue and initiated them into the close-knit, elitist, and masculine society of the university (249–50). The mandated use of Latin, even if often violated, created a discursive fellowship. Discussing this phenomenon in Baldassarre Castiglione's *Il cortegiano*, written some twenty years after *Repetición,* Valerie Finucci identifies "that sense of bonding that flourishes in a homogeneous, privileged group speaking the same language, enjoying the same socio-political background" ("Jokes," 56). Although the students at Salamanca were not as homogeneous a group as Castiglione's courtiers—Rojas and Lucena were both from *converso* families—the description is generally applicable. The homogeneity of language and of gender at Salamanca, and the common goal of a career in the growing state administration, together forged the homosocial bonding necessary to the formation of masculine identity. Defining and defeating (in this case, through humor) the threat of the desirous and irrational feminine was, in this sense, an integral part of the curriculum.

The use of the vernacular and the cross-gendering of the audience in student burlesque is an anxious marker of the exclusion of the feminine from the sources of the learned discourse that played an increasingly important role in the formation of masculine identity and social status among the ambitious *letrado* class. The opening words of the *repetidor* of "Gallo Benito" are even more explicit in this regard than Lucena's: "Having ascended to the lectern, these oh so beautiful ladies ordered that the speech for today be delivered in their common Castilian language; for although it is true that many of their ladyships acknowledge that they have the time and ability to learn Latin, still and all, there are some who are of such a young and tender age that they have had no time for such an exercise" (Egido, 627).[24] As Finucci explains: "Since subjectivity is formed through language, access to the economy of discourse allows man to fashion himself actively; lack of access to the same, on the other hand, dooms woman to a passive, blatantly marginal position" ("Jokes," 53).

Certainly, the use of the vernacular instead of Latin in such student works is on one level subversive of the official culture of the university, as carnival always is, at least potentially. For example, the feminization of an audience that would have included professors as well as students is not without aggression. Likewise, the speaker's own self-feminization through the use of the vernacular in an environment that devalued it may mark a rebellious or nostalgic step backward into the prepubescent, maternal, vernacular space of the home. But the fact that the exercises were tolerated by the authorities suggests their value to the institution as an escape valve for student dissatisfactions and restiveness and as a means of reinscribing the patriarchal goals of the educational system.[25]

The insistent misogyny of Lucena's "lesson" supports this view. Gilman's concept of the role of Aristotelianism in *Celestina* is useful here, up to a point. *Celestina* is a profoundly rational work, he argues, partly because it is grounded in Aristotle's view of nature as a complex chain of cause and effect. Natural philosophy provides the training in reason necessary to an understanding of this complex process. The lessons learned from natural philosophy come into play as Rojas "peeks with dispassionate intelligence and sardonic irony inside the irrationality of human lives, and . . . records in the greatest detail the inexorable logic of their doom" (*Fernando de Rojas,* 339). Gilman rightly compares this aspect of *Celestina* to the work of Lucena, written at the same time, for a similar audience, and dealing with the same subject matter, namely, the irrational and destructive power of desire.

Both Rojas and Lucena locate that ineluctable and destructive desire in woman. The list of *auctores* invoked by Sempronio in his famous misogynist tirade in act 1 of *Celestina* and those cited by Lucena coincide in many cases, and both of their lessons are grounded in Aristotelian misogyny.[26] The authority of "el Filósofo" shows in Lucena's choice of *textum*, the *Maldezir de mujeres,* which includes the well-known Aristotelian declaration of female insufficiency: "Woman is an animal that is called an imperfect man, she is conceived in the absence of good, natural heat" [Muger es un animal / que se dize hombre imperfecto / procreado en el defecto / del buen calor natural] (Pérez Priego, 139). Lucena does not specifically comment on these verses because, as previously noted, he never gets beyond the first stanza in his *explication de texte*: "Just so is woman an imperfect man, as Aristotle says in *De animalibus,* and is unto man as sensuality to reason. Whence, just as it is unnatural for sensuality, which naturally obeys reason, to rule over it, so is it unnatural for woman to have the power to rule" (*Repetiçión,* 83–84).[27] We have seen a similar censure of women's unnatural will to power before, for example, in Palencia's chronicle. How it relates to Isabel on this occasion will be seen in what follows.

One problem for Lucena is, that in the game of love—that is, the courtly code that shapes the romances of Diego de San Pedro and Juan de Flores, and which was no doubt familiar to Lucena—the beloved does in theory *señorear*. This is precisely the point of the first stanza of Torrellas's poem, quoted approvingly by Lucena: "He who loving well pursues ladies destroys himself, for women pursue those who flee from them and flee from those who pursue them; they do not love for being loved, nor do they reward services; rather, they are all ungrateful, they distribute their rewards ruled only by obstinacy" (44).[28]

To illustrate women's perversity and capriciousness in the bestowal of their favors, Lucena launches into the embedded miniromance, the pseudoautobiographical account of his courtship of the "lovely lady," in whose service he claims to have composed his work. Like its source, Piccolomini's *Historia de duobus amantibus,* the narrative includes an epistolary exchange and a mendacious go-between, and it ends in the suitor's rejection by his lady. Her dismissal triggers a long tirade against Cupid, basically a catalog of mythological and biblical examples of men destroyed by love, interlaced with the sayings of authorities on the subject: Alexander: "It is not fitting that he who defeated men be defeated by women" [No conviene al que venció los honbres que le vençan las mugeres]; Seneca: "Rarely does God grant that men both love and be wise" [Pocas vezes otorga Dios al hombre que ame y que sea sabio] (53); Saint Isidore: "Love is so foolish, that it makes the men in whom it establishes itself into fools" [El amor ansí es nescio, ca a los honbres en quien asienta haze ser nescios] (57). And although Lucena affirms several times that it is love, not women, that undoes men, both his phrasing of the proviso—"And you think that women by themselves could deceive Aristotle and Virgil? Don't believe it; rather, love deceived them" (52)[29]—and the long section on the evils of women serve to undermine the theoretical separation between love and women.

Cátedra plays down the significance of Lucena's misogyny. For him, insofar as *Repetiçión* has a serious message, it is to be found in the initial and final sections on virtue. It is true that Lucena extols virtue as the only possession that is not subject to the mutability of Fortune: "Oh, worthy, therefore excellent virtue, which alone restores men to a tranquil and secure state and make them lordly and strong, rich and free, and gives them unchanging and eternal pleasures, and which accompanies them night and day, in the plaza, in solitude, in pleasure and danger..." (42).[30] He proclaims virtue to be the source of fame and glory: "Wherefore, after inevitable death has removed the operations of virtue from the earth, separating the soul from the body, glory and fame restore a life free from contingency and subjection to death" (44).[31]

For Cátedra, the concept of *libertas,* derived from self-control and virtue, and crucial to humanistic discussions of the dignity of man, ties in to the basic argument of the *Repetiçión*, "which is not, of course, the misogynist broadside, brought in only as a theoretical remedy that allows every impassioned man to achieve liberation, but rather the analysis of the individual in his ethical dimension" (139).[32] He thus rejects any connection between the freedom from subjection to contingency and death that, according to Lucena, is the goal and reward of the virtuous man and the identification of woman with those ills. But Lucena himself makes an explicit connection between the two toward the end of the work, when he resumes his discussion of virtue, focusing on the role of free will in achieving it: "Of what do the orators persuade us, what do the philosophers prove, what do the theologians demonstrate except the freedom of the will, through which virtue is esteemed, counsel is celebrated, cities are ruled?... It being in our power to choose between virtue and vice, man should not blame anyone but himself when he shuns virtue, embracing vice, not wishing to govern himself by reason, which is ruled by prudence and universal justice, the foundation of all other virtues" (69).[33]

What follows, however, is this reminder of the importance of maintaining self-control in order to remain virtuous an admission of the vulnerability of virtue to "the [natural] desire of man to lie with a pretty woman" [el desseo (natural) del ayuntamiento del honbre y linda muger] (72). The examination of lovesickness in turn leads to yet another misogynist tirade, this time cobbled together from Juvenal's *Sixth Satire*, Boccaccio's *De casibus illustrium virorum*, and the letters of Saint Jerome. These fifteen pages, more than a quarter of the work, constitute a sample case of medieval misogyny: attacks on female lust, deceitfulness, vanity, and mutability, on the use of cosmetics and lavish clothes, on the woes caused by wives, on male disgust at the aging female body. The final message is clear: "Thus, since the love we are discussing is useless, harsh, and bitter, and causes man to be always ill, strive to put it aside, thinking always about the defects of such women... and you will be free and in control of yourself, which is the greatest good that you can have in this world" (86).[34]

The misogyny of the environment that produced *Repetiçión de amores* is hardly theoretical. The fact that Lucena makes virtuous freedom coterminous with freedom from women, and that he delivers his "lesson" to an all-male audience in Spain's most prestigious university, the primary training ground for the men of reason who would administer the affairs of the new nation, makes it impossible to take his misogyny as anything other than central, at least in the context of its original *oral* presentation. But a very different picture of Lucena's misogynist humor emerges if we consider the form he gave it when he prepared it for publication with a very special dedicatee in mind.

From University to Court: Playing with a New Kind of Queen

Although the date of composition for *Repetiçión de amores* has not been determined, we do know its terminus ante quem: October 4, 1497, the date of Prince Juan's untimely death in Salamanca, a few weeks after his celebrated entry into his new domain.[35] This is because Lucena chose to publish his burlesque *repetitio* on love and women bound together with another work that is explicitly dedicated to the prince, who would have been about Lucena's age at the time. The luxurious volume annexes to *Repetiçión* a seemingly unrelated work, *Arte de axedrez*. Critics have unanimously deemed the two works to be totally unrelated. Jacob Ornstein, first modern editor of Lucena's work simply omitted the chess manual.[36] Its most recent editor, Pérez de Arriaga, remarks on the "strange marriage" [extraño maridaje] of the two works (26). But, as Miguel Cereceda has pointed out, their shared space was apparently not considered to be merely coincidental because subsequent editions continued to publish the treatises together.

Pérez de Arriaga describes *Arte de axedrez* as a "letter of introduction to Prince Juan, heir to the Crown, in order to obtain the coveted privilege of belonging to the select group of gentlemen who were admitted to his service," and offers the work's dedication to support his claim.[37] Certainly, Prince Juan's recent marriage to Margaret of Austria meant that he would be expanding his household, raising Lucena's and other aspiring *letrados*' hopes of securing a position in his entourage. The elaborate and expensive nature of Lucena's bound volume, with its many woodcuts illustrating the 150 chess problems analyzed in *Axedrez,* the prefatory material to the entire book, the dedication of *Axedrez,* and the "peroración" by the humanist Bachiller Villoslada intercalated between *Repetiçión* and *Axedrez* are all evidence that Lucena planned the conjoined texts as a gift to the prince. But the editor considers that *Repetiçión,* which precedes *Axedrez* in the volume, was written with an entirely different purpose: "so as to gain the favor of an unnamed, more or less illustrious young woman" [para ganar los favores de una moza anónima más o menos ilustre] (20). This conflation of the author and his fictional narrator-protagonist is completely unauthorized by the text.

Lucena must have been aware that the cultural importance of *Arte de axedrez* far exceeded that of his parodic *repetitio*. The treatise is both the earliest printed work on chess analysis and the first to record a major change in the game that took place quite suddenly during the last quarter of the fifteenth century. In what follows, I extend Pérez de Arriaga's view that Lucena (perhaps recently graduated from Salamanca) presented the elegant book to Prince Juan as a kind of professional dossier in support of a bid for a position in his household. I argue that Lucena not only meant for his two works to be read together, but that, on the occasion of their printing, he saw the *Repetiçión* in a new light. In its new positioning, the youthful burlesque becomes a kind of chess morality, a didactic allegorization of the game of a kind popular in the Middle Ages. And that morality, as we shall see, relates centrally to Isabel's presence on the throne, from where she kept a watchful eye on her only male heir. The two ludic works taken together articulate a young *letrado*'s anxieties about the inversion of the gender hierarchy that Isabel's sovereignty effected and, more immediately, about the practical effects the unmasterable queen might have on his own career prospects.

We know that chess was a favorite pastime of the young noblemen raised at court. A poem on manners by Pedro de Gracia Dei that describes the typical training given young nobles at court mentions the game alongside more serious pursuits: "reading, writing, playing instruments, singing, dancing and swimming, wrestling, fencing, archery and crossbow, writing and declaming Latin, playing chess and ball well" (70; quoted in Pérez de Arriaga, 28).[38] Gracia Dei's mention of *llatinar* reminds us of the careful attention paid to Juan's classical training by his mother, for which purpose she employed distinguished Salamancan professors. The fact that she kept in her library Juan's Latin copybooks is an indication of the importance she placed on the acquisition of Latin in preparing her son to rule. As for chess, Juan may have learned the game from his father Fernando, whom Fernando del Pulgar deemed overly devoted to the pastime: "he liked to play all games, ball and chess and he spent more time at this than he should have" [Placíale jugar todos los juegos, de pelota e ajedrez e tablas, y en esto gastaba algún tiempo más de lo que debía] (*Crónica*, 230). More direct reference to the games played by the prince is found in a description of his living quarters written by the prince's chamberlain. Gonzalo Fernández de Oviedo singles out an area apparently reserved for playing chess: "And a little table with its bench and a high-backed chair, and one or two nicely painted footstools or benches. A chess table with its pieces and boards" (*Libro de la Cámara Real del Príncipe Don Juan*, 55; quoted in Pérez de Arriaga, 35).[39]

In the dedication to *Axedrez*, Lucena reminds the prince of their shared Salamancan connection and of his own family's tradition of loyal service to the crown: "[written] by Lucena, son of the most learned Doctor and Reverend Prothonotary Johan Remírez de Lucena, Ambassador and member of our majesties' Royal Council, while studying at the most renowned University of the very noble city of Salamanca" (*Arte de axedrez*, 75).[40] The author goes on to simultaneously flatter the prince and display his own erudition by peppering his praise with references to Roman heroes and the writers who recorded their deeds. If Livy, Orosius, Herodotus, and Virgil were now living, he insists, they would have used their eloquence and style to praise Juan's great deeds, "leaving aside the deeds of the Romans, the Egyptian kings, the twelve Caesars, Troy, and the Assyrians" (ibid., 75–76).[41] The reference to Juan's excellence in the primary role of the medieval prince, that of warrior, is a particularly apt one in an introduction to a treatise on chess, originally a game of military strategy especially favored by kings.[42] Thus, in the dedication, Lucena appeals to the serious side of Juan's education, while acknowledging the importance of recreation in princely formation. In so doing, he joins a distinguished Iberian tradition that began with another landmark in the game's history, Alfonso X's thirteenth-century *Juegos de axedrez, dados y tablas*.

I would argue that Lucena is well aware of his place in this tradition, that the lavish format and design of his book attests not only to the eminence of its dedicatee and the ambitions of its author, but also to the latter's pride in the significance of his treatise. It is in these terms that Bachiller Villoslada praises his friend's work in a "peroration... in praise of and to the glory of he who dictated this work" [peroración... en lohor y gloria del que la presente obra dictó] that serves as a discursive bridge that ties together *Repetiçión* and *Axedrez*. He calls the game "that game that is better called imitation or elegance of breeding and warfare that is figured by chess" [aquel juego que mejor se llama ymitación o desemboltura de crianza, y de milicia figurado por el axedrez] (94).

The significance of Lucena's *Arte de axedrez* goes far beyond its recreational value, however. The work is not only the first printed book on chess playing; it is also the earliest documentation of a radical alteration in the rules of the game. The change took place quite suddenly in the last quarter of the fifteenth century, transforming the way chess had been played for five hundred years. It is central to my argument that this revolutionary change centers dramatically on the only female piece on the chessboard, the Queen.

Chess historians differ in their determination of the date or country of origin of the "new chess." The erudite H. J. R. Murray believed that the new moves were invented in Italy, and he cites as evidence Lucena's prefatory statement that he acquired knowledge of the game on travels to Rome and France. More recent authorities believe the moves originated in either Spain or southern France. Richard Eales, for example, states that "it is hard to ignore the fact that almost all the reliable early evidence is linked with Spain or Portugal" (76). There was, in fact, in a general acknowledgment in the late Middle Ages of Spaniards' expertise at chess, their skill at the game considered an indication of a high level of civility. In book 2 of Castiglione's *Il Cortegiano* (The book of the courtier), the nobleman Federico Fregoso touts the benefits of chess as a pastime, calling it "a refined and ingenious recreation" (1140). Interestingly, especially in light of Pulgar's comment on Fernando's excessive dedication to the game, Don Federico also advises against devoting too much time to the pastime, lest it detract from more serious pursuits. Gaspar Pallavicino responds by praising the Spaniards for their seemingly effortless skill at the game: "there are to be found many Spaniards who excel at chess and at a number of other games, and yet do not study them too exhaustively or neglect other things," to which Federico replies, "You may take it for granted ... that they put in a great deal of study, but they conceal it" (140).

Chess scholars also disagree as to when exactly the new rules came into being. There is, however, unanimity in that they replaced the old game with remarkable swiftness. By 1510, the medieval game was obsolete in Spain, Italy, and probably France. By 1550, there is no evidence for its existence anywhere in Europe besides parts of Germany, Scandinavia, and Iceland (Eales, 76). Eales expresses the prevailing scholarly puzzlement over the rapidity with which modern chess replaced the

Islamic form that had prevailed throughout the preceding millennium as follows: "The transition from medieval to modern was a complex and gradual process, in almost every area of life. Few historians or readers of history now expect to find specific events which tipped the scales from one age to the next.... So it is ironic that the game of chess experienced the only major change in its internal structure in over a thousand years of documented history through a single and dramatic shift in its rules of play at just about this time, the late fifteenth century" (71).

The drastic shift in rules centers dramatically on the Queen. In the old game, identified by Lucena as "old-style chess" [axedrez al viejo], the Queen was far weaker than the Rook or Knight and only slightly stronger than the Bishop (Murray, 776). In the new game, the Queen combines the moves of Rook and Bishop, to become by far the strongest piece on the board. This shift caused a radical alteration in the method and tempo of play. As Murray explains,

> the initial stage in the Muslim or mediaeval game, which lasted until the superior forces came into contact, practically ceased to exist; the new Queen and Bishop could exert pressure upon the opponent's forces in the first half-dozen moves, and could even, under certain circumstances, effect mate in the same period. The player no longer could reckon upon time to develop his forces in his own way; he was compelled to have regard to his opponent's play from the very first.... Moreover, the possibility of converting the comparatively weak Pawn into a Queen of immense strength ... [meant] it was no longer possible to regard the Pawns as useful only to clear a road by their sacrifice for the superior pieces. Thus the whole course of the game was quickened by the introduction of more powerful forces. (777)

It is important to note that whereas medieval players had been experimenting with extended moves for the Pawn and the Bishop since the thirteenth century, no known medieval precedent for the new Queen exists. The impression that the change in the Queen's power made on European chess players and theorists is best seen in the names they gave the new game in France and Italy: "chess of the mad lady" [eschés de la dame enragée] and "mad chess" [scacchi alla rabiosa] (Eales, 72). Lucena calls it simply "chess of the lady" [axedrez de la dama].[43] Chess authorities have proposed a variety of reasons for the sudden and drastic shift in the power of the Queen. These range from the "impact of the Renaissance" and the "urge toward individual independence," to the invention of the printing press and the geographical discoveries of Columbus, to the creation of the idealized courtly lady by the Provençal troubadours (Cereceda, 24), to strong female role models such as Joan of Arc or Catherine Sforza (Eales, 76–77; Murray, 778–79).

It is perhaps a measure of the marginalization of Iberia in modern cultural history that no one has related the transformation of the Queen's power in chess sometime between 1475 and 1496 with the unprecedented strengthening of royal authority simultaneously being effected by a historical queen who was decidedly a queen regnant and not a queen consort. Richard Eales, for example, states confidently that "It is certainly striking that the dominant piece in the new chess should be the queen, the only one with a female name, but no conceivable change in fifteenth-century history can explain it" (77).

It seems likely that the tastes and patronage of a queen who significantly shaped literature, art, and architecture in the final quarter of the fifteenth century also affected the recreational arts. Certainly, Isabel is a far more likely candidate for this distinction than the historically remote Joan of Arc (1412?–31) or the geographically displaced Catherine Sforza (1463–1509) proposed by Eales. Although there is no proof that Isabel's real and symbolic power caused the transformation in the game itself, we can say that at the very least the recording of that dramatic change was a result of the impression that the absolutist power of this "new kind of queen" made on one aspiring *letrado*.

A properly contextualized reading of *Repetiçión de amores* in its printed form must take into account more than chess's value as mental training and recreation for nobility and royalty. Equally, if not more, important are the literary uses made of the game in the Middle Ages and the Renaissance. Not surprisingly, given that mastery of the game was a sign of aristocratic status, chess is a common motif in medieval romance and poetry, where it is often enlisted as a test of the hero's martial prowess, thus retaining some of its original function as a game of war strategy. Chess also plays a role in the courtship rituals central to courtly romance. In *Huon of Bordeaux* (c. 1200), for example, the wandering hero must pass a test of chess played with the king's beautiful daughter. If he wins the game, he will receive her hand in marriage; if he loses, he loses his head as well. The princess proves herself a better player, but, in the end, distracted by the beauty of the knight, loses the match (Golombek, 88). Similarly, in *Floire and Blanchefleur* the hero gains access to his imprisoned beloved by means of a chess game.

Chaucer's *Book of the Duchess* (1369) makes a rather different amatory use of chess. The narrator compares the death of Blanche to the loss of the Queen (Fers) in a game played with Fortune:

> With hir false draughtes divers
> She stal on me, and took my fers [queen].
> And whan I saw my fers aweye,
> Alas! I couthe no lenger pleye....
> Therwith Fortune seyde, "chek here!"
> And "mate!" in mid pointe of the chekkere....
> But god wolde I had ones or twyes
> Y-koud and knowe the Ieupardyes
> That coude The Grek Pithagores!
> I shul have pleyd the bet at ches,
> And kept my fers the bet therby. (Vv. 652–69; quoted in Murray, 751)

Fifty years after the publication of *Arte de axedrez*, the thwarted suitor in the Earl of Surrey's "To the Ladie That Scorned Her Lover" (1557) threatens retaliation on the chessboard:

> For yf by chance I winne
> Your person in the feeld:
> To late then come you in
> Your self to me to yeld.
> For I will vse my power
> As captain full of might,
> And such I will devour,
> As vse to shew me spight. (Quoted in ibid., 779)

Surrey's depiction of an intense match between a nobleman and noblewoman joins other evidence that men and women often played chess against each other. Numerous fifteenth-century paintings and manuscript illuminations depict such games.[44]

The genre known as the chess morality was more ambitious in its allegorical deployment of the game. A typical example is the fourteenth-century *Les eschez amoureux*, which represents the relationship of two lovers as a match in which each of the pieces is assigned a courtly emblem and quality. For example, the Lady plays her Bautes and the Lover counters with his Regars; when she plays her Souvenir, he replies with Desirs, and so on.[45] A similar text, closer to Lucena in both time and space, is the Catalan poem "Scachs d'amour" by Mossen Fenollar. The poem uses a game played by the two gentlemen Narciso Vinoles and Francesco de

Castellví to represent the steps in the courtship of Venus by Mars. Like the *Les eschez amoureux,* the Catalan poem assigns human qualities to the various chess pieces. Thus, Venus plays with such pieces as honor, beauty, modesty, disdain, and Mars uses reason, will, desire, and favors (Murray, 781).

Some of the most popular chess moralities were explicitly didactic. These took two basic forms, one secular and the other religious. The secular morality used the game as the basis for an allegory about the different feudal estates and their prescribed functions. The religious morality created an allegory of the soul's spiritual journey out of the moves of the chess pieces on the board (Reiss, 343). An example of the former is the so-called *Innocent Morality* of the early thirteenth century.[46] Considered the earliest of the genre, the work is an excellent example of the conservative and misogynist nature of such works, as the following paraphrase indicates: "The King's move and powers of capture are in all directions, because the King's will is the law. The Queen's move is aslant only, because women are so greedy that they will take nothing except by rapine and injustice.... The Pawns are poor men. Their move is straight, except when they take anything: so also the poor man does well so long as he keeps from ambition" (quoted in Murray, 530). It is noteworthy that while the King and the Pawn are represented in terms of the power (or lack thereof) owing to their station, the Queen's allegorization focuses on her inherent moral failings.

Clerics also availed themselves of the game's rich symbolic potential in treatises and sermons that portray God playing a match with the devil, that refer to death as life's final checkmate, or that compare the equalizing power of the grave with that of the bag that holds all of the chess pieces at game's end (ibid., 529–36). A cleric probably composed the late-fifteenth-century *Le Jeu des eschés de la Dame, moralisé,* in which the allegorical chess player is a woman. Like medieval courtesy books addressed specifically to women, *Eschés de la Dame* participates in the cultural construction of femininity as chaste and pious. The author recounts a game between the noble dedicatee and Lucifer, pointing out the temptations the lady encounters and the defenses that religion affords her. Thus, for example, when Lucifer leads with a pawn called Love of Self, the Lady makes her first move with Love of God (Eales, 75). The lady easily wins the match, after which all the pieces are tumbled together in the bag, their various ranks equalized, as in death (ibid., 558).[47]

The various medieval literary uses of chess provide the proper context for understanding Lucena's *Repetiçión de amores* as a containment strategy for the power of the new kind of Queen whose symbolic presence pervades *Axedrez*. At the same time, as an introduction to the new rules of the game set forth in *Arte de axedrez, Repetiçión* is properly read as an implicit chess morality not unlike the thirteenth-century *Innocent Morality* or the contemporary *Jeu des eschés de la Dame*, that is, an allegory of love as a courtly game, but one that is unusually dangerous to male players because of the unprecedented power it grants to the object of desire, Woman.

Lucena himself provides strong evidence for this interpretation in the prefatory Latin verses to the entire volume, verses that use the metaphor of chess as war to tie the subject of the two works together.

The thirty-six verses addressed to the "happy and candid reader" are divided into two almost equal parts. Both sections speak metaphorically of the weapons and wounds of war and of man's vulnerability to them. In the first half, the warrior is none other than the "protagonist" of *Repetiçión*, the all-powerful god of love. Reading his work, says Lucena, the reader will learn why no one is safe from Cupid's winged weapons:

> Where you will come to know the flaming weapons, the diverse desires of winged Cupid: why the soft hand holds armed spears; why a quiver hangs from each shoulder; why, as he flies through the heavens, he exhausts the gods and wounds many men; why the Satyrs, Dryads, and the two-horned Fauns cannot flee the bloody weapons of this angry god. Here also in few words you will learn why no one escapes his wounds unscathed. (38)[48]

In the second half of the poem, the author calls the reader's attention to the "other subject" [altera materia] of his work, the wounds inflicted on the battlefield of chess: "There you will see hands armed for fierce battle. Lines of soldiers painted in different colors will rush forth: hence a red piece rushing in to strike, from over there one of a different color striking back."[49] Cupid's counterpart in this war is the Queen, who wields an epic-sized weapon: "From this side jumps a horse; over there the queen, holding a beam-like spear, drives off the men with furious war" [Hinc saltat sonipes, illinc regina trabali / Cuspide deturbat Marte furente viros]. The author concludes by touting the value of his work for instructing readers on how to win, presumably at chess, although his words could equally apply to love: "Here we teach ambushes, stratagems, and skills. Which piece will be able to win for you?" [Hic nos insidias, fraudes, artesque docemus / Quis victor poterit calculus esse tuus].

Thus, despite critical unanimity that the two works published by Lucena are unrelated, the author clearly takes pains to relate them. It is significant that to do so he uses not the vernacular appropriate to the burlesque, but the Latin of the serious *repetitiones* that the burlesque mocks. This is not to invalidate the ludic nature of *Repetiçión* and more obviously of *Axedrez*, but to take its humor seriously. As an application for a position at court, ostensibly in the service of Prince Juan, Lucena's book is a means of displaying the young *letrado*'s qualifications, his rhetorical skills and philosophical knowledge. But it simultaneously articulates anxiety that a successful application may depend not on actual credentials or even connections at court, but rather on the irrational whims of an all-powerful woman. Behind the primary dedicatee, the young prince whose connections with Salamanca provide a common ground with the author—they know the same professors, have studied the same texts in the same language, and have played the same games—there looms the shadow of the prince's unmasterable mother. By pairing *Repetiçión de amores* and *Arte de axedrez*, Lucena expresses his awareness that the "rules of the game" for masculine advancement have changed. In Italy during the sixteenth century, as Valerie Finucci has noted, political events "worked...to reinforce the power of the ruler... and to submit the courtier more and more to the policing eye of the prince" (Finucci, "Brother," 95). The same holds true for events of the last quarter of the fifteenth century in Castile. But in Castile the autocratic gaze belongs to a woman, so that the prince who is to ensure the social order resides in the body that is incapable of rational thought and moral action, and which is therefore inherently a source of disorder.

The reading of *Repetiçión* as a chess morality sheds new light on what Cátedra considers its most serious thread: the discussion of human virtue that is woven through the introduction, the commentary on the Torrellas text, and the conclusion. In each of these passages, the concept of virtue is deeply and anxiously gendered. In the *exordio*, Lucena defines virtue for women in terms of sexual purity and marital fidelity and for men in terms of noble deeds. He also genders his terms when he discourses on the importance of free will in the discussion of the famous Torrellas verses, but here he contradicts himself in a revealing way. While criticizing man's "effeminate" habit of blaming the stars or predestination for the harm that befalls him from pursuing women, he then indulges in a similar projection: "Oh, foolish and false judgment, oh, effeminate softness and dark blindness of understanding that prefers to attribute its weakness to another rather than loathe the sensual pleasures, seeing that from the very beginning woman both wounds and destroys!" (68).[50]

It is, however, the curious "conclusion to the text" that most clearly reveals the ambitious young author's ambivalence about the career path he has chosen. In it he revisits the medieval courtly debate on who is a better lover, the cleric or the knight.[51] The mini-*disputatio* abruptly broadens its scope to take up the humanist topos of the relative merits of arms and letters. Here again Lucena contradicts himself, this time intentionally. Taking as a given his female addressees' preference for soldiers, he goes on to give yet more virtuoso proof of his scholastic skills by first supporting that choice, and then rejecting it. He concludes the debate in favor of the soldier, feigning reluctance: "although I am obligated to the lawyers, although my father the prothonotary is one of them, I will not fail to declare the truth, defending arms as superior to letters" (88).[52]

When placed in the context of its original venue of presentation, the "scientific" finding in favor of arms at the end of *Repetiçión* constitutes yet another joke, this one on Lucena himself as much as on his fellow students and perhaps on his own father, the royal prothonotary Juan de Lucena. In the context of its printed presentation copy, on the other hand, the entire debate bears the marks of an anxious self-fashioning. For one, it reflects the real contemporary competition of the *letrados*, both "intermurally," that is, between that rising middle class and the noble, warrior class, and "intramurally," among the *letrados* themselves, as seen in the conflict between the two Isabelline royal chroniclers Alfonso de Palencia and Fernando del Pulgar discussed in chapter 3. In this sense, Lucena's debate, despite its final declaration that "in order to be famous and honored, it is more productive for men to dedicate themselves to the republic and to perform famous deeds" [de más fruto es a los hombres, para que sean esclarescidos y honrrados, darse a la república y hazer cosas famosas] (89), indicates the extent to which increased royal authority in Castile was transforming the court more into a place for "competitive bureaucrats to serve in the administration of the state than into a community where individual merit was rewarded proportionately by a benign prince" (Finucci, "Brother," 94). Even as the aspiring courtier nervously acknowledges the competition he faces in achieving his career goals, he masks the rivalry by effectively arguing the supremacy of *both* scholars and warriors. It is also possible to see this paradoxical conclusion as a response to Juan's education in both military and scholarly matters. Similarly, the confident final discussion of "what women want" counterbalances the earlier pseudoautobiographical "evidence," the inept conduct and negative outcome of his own courtship. Shoring up his credentials for the battle/game he is undertaking is the reminder that service to Isabel is a Lucena family tradition, a point to which I shall return.

All of this deepens the significance of the centerpiece of *Repetiçión*, the narrator-protagonist's misogynist tirade, triggered diegetically by his unjust rejection by the "muy noble señora." In *Arte de axedrez*, Lucena relies on his own experience ("I intend to describe all the best games that I have seen players play in Rome and throughout Italy and France and Spain and that I myself have been able to learn" [80])[53] to teach his readers—Prince Juan, first and foremost, but also other wealthy consumers of the new print culture—the difference between the old game and the new so that they can better manipulate a "dame enragée": "you will learn the difference between the game we now play, which is called chess of the lady, and the old game that was formerly played" (79).[54] In *Repetiçión de amores*, he uses a fictional experience and the wisdom of "el Filósofo" Torrellas as a complementary lesson in avoiding the evils that Cupid causes through the agency of woman. The pernicious effects of woman are wide-ranging. They include feminization, as in the case of Hercules, who "set aside his arrows and bow, took off his armor, commanded to do so by Iole, his beloved, obeying Cupid's power to do so... allowed himself to be treated like a maiden... with the same hand that up to then had wielded the battle ax, he wielded the spindle, spinning" (5);[55] loss of status, exemplified by Phoebus, who, "his divinity transformed, became a shepherd of Admetus of Thessaly, desiring the beautiful maiden Alceste.... He suffered himself then to take care of cows and, setting aside the lyre proper to him, he called the bulls with rustic flutes" (55);[56] sickness ("And those who are inflamed with passion... if they wish to be healed, should diligently do what the doctor orders" [72]).[57] Even death can result, as in the following local example: "it happened not long ago in Toledo that a woman killed her husband in bed" [no ha muchos días acaesció de hecho en Toledo matar una muger a su marido en la cama] (80). To avoid these dangers, one must exercise free will and dwell on the vileness of women, for example, the painted woman who is a "a polished temple built on a sewer, or a frying pan with butter for frying up fools" [templo polido hedificado sobre albañal, o sartén con manteca para frehir necios] (81).

Repetiçión presents other strategies for the containment of the threatening object of desire. In the introductory discussion of virtue, for example, Lucena states the importance of "purity, chastity, and cleanliness for women and for men" [puridad, castidad, y limpieza así de las mugeres como de los hombres] (41). Despite the mention of the need for chastity in both sexes, the discussion that ensues focuses almost exclusively on chaste women. Lucena cites the Romans' veneration of the vestal virgins and parades classical examples of women who died to preserve their virginity (Minerva, Cassandra, Lucrecia, Hippo) or those who "were happy with just one man" [con un solo varón fueron contentas] (Penelope, Dido). He borrows liberally from the Bible, especially the epistles of Paul (1 Corinthians 7; Romans 7), to support marriage as the only viable alternative to virginity in the struggle against carnal temptation, a discussion that concludes with the Pauline dictum: "it is better to marry than to burn" [mejor es casarse que quemarse] (68). It must be noted, however, that Lucena contradicts himself here as well, because he later inserts a lengthy paraphrase of Juvenal's Sixth Satire and of Saint Jerome's letter "Valerius Rufino ne ducat uxorem" on the woes of marriage—curious, to say the least, in a book presented to a newly married prince.

In her analysis of similar misogynistic outbursts in Old French romance, Roberta Krueger proposes going beyond noting their internal contradictions (such as those noted earlier in Lucena's treatment of marriage) and their surface strategy of displacing the origins of such hatred onto impersonal, time-honored authorities. She proposes that we instead consider such attacks as marking a dialogue about gender roles within a specific context.[58] The two complementary hypotheses of this dialogic reading are, first, that antifeminism flags its speaker's anxiety about the imposition of gender order, and second, that arguments against women and in favor of their subordination *inscribe* the persistent insubordination of at least some historical women and *invite* women's resistance (104–11). Krueger's hypotheses hold special relevance to my reading of *Repetiçión de amores/Arte de axedrez* within the specific context of Isabel's gender insubordination.

I conclude with a simple but strategically placed phrase in *Axedrez* that offers additional evidence for my regicentric interpretation. It occurs at the very beginning of the work, in the "Primera regla," as Lucena makes a point from his own experience: "Likewise, when it [the pawn] reaches the row of the opponent's king, it becomes a queen and gives check, without moving and not only as queen, but if your graces desire to play the way I do, the pawn on becoming a queen, can, for the first move it makes, take and give check as a queen and as a knight, *because we owe so much to women*" (*Axedrez*, 79; my emphasis).[59] Pérez de Arriaga remarks the incongruity between this courtly topos and the misogyny of *Repetiçión*, but in my view the contradiction supports the notion that *Axedrez* was addressed as much to royal mother as to princely son.

First of all, the comment is strategically placed. It occurs in the explanation of the queened pawn's very first move, which grants the already powerful queen even more strength. It signals Lucena's awareness of a specific female readership? Cátedra has posited a strong link between the university at Salamanca and the Isabelline court in the diffusion of the genre of parodic amatory treatises: "*Repetiçión de amores*, without being uprooted from its academic context, is reminiscent of the courtly and feminine world of Diego de San Pedro's *Sermón de amores*" (133).[60] His connection between academy and court suggests that the worthy women of *Arte de axedrez* and the "most illustrious ladies" [preclaríssimas señoras] of *Repetiçión de amores* are identifiable with the historical "ladies-in-waiting of our Lady the Queen" [damas de la Reina nuestra señora] (87) to whom San Pedro addresses his first romance, *Tractado de Arnalte y Lucenda* (Book of Arnalte and Lucenda) (1491). The problematics of such reader reception forms the background for my discussion in the next chapter of the romances of Juan de Flores. Although there is no documentary proof that Lucena negotiated the move from university to court, we know that Flores did so very successfully, essentially by making himself indispensable to Isabel. His mastery of the new rules of the game does not preclude some ambivilance toward his employer. As we shall see, the anxiety caused by the unmasterability of the royal master continues to surface in a variety of ways throughout his corpus.

CHAPTER SIX

The Mad Queen

The conjoined effects of royal patronage and technological innovation on the literary flowering of the Isabelline epoch are very much in evidence in the so-called sentimental romance.[1] Of the twenty works listed in Keith Whinnom's canon-forming bibliography of the genre, fully one-half were produced during the final fifteen years of Isabel's reign; four of these are among print culture's first international best-sellers.[2] The case of Diego de San Pedro is illustrative. He authored two widely read romances: *Tractado de amores de Arnalte y Lucenda* and *Cárcel de Amor*. Scholars have traditionally considered *Arnalte* a youthful work, that is, similar to Lucena's *Repetiçión de amor*. It was written around 1481 but published ten years later; *Cárcel de Amor* was composed around 1488 and appeared in print much more quickly, in 1492. Both works went through numerous Spanish editions, and *Arnalte y Lucenda* was translated into French, English, and Italian.[3]

San Pedro actively sought royal recognition for his literary efforts. Both of his romances are dedicated, directly or indirectly, to Isabel's ladies-in-waiting and *Arnalte y Lucenda* contains outright flattery of Isabel. Early in the romance, the lovesick protagonist Arnalte asks the Auctor, his new Castilian friend and intermediary, about Arnalte's acquaintance, King Fernando. He pointedly asks whether the king "had a companion worthy of him" [conpañía ygual que le pertenesciese tenía] (43). The fictionalized author responds with a lengthy verse panegyric whose sacrilegious imagery parallels that we have seen in lyric poetry addressed to Isabel early in her reign. The admiring Auctor reports that the Queen "is loved and feared by everyone" [de todos en general / es amada y es temida] (45), and goes on to exclaim: "she is a yoke for the strong, she is life to our death, she is light to our shadows.... She is such that she should not even exist as a human being, but God created her in order to teach us who He is, since He created her" (46).[4] Isabel was evidently pleased; she owned a copy of the book.

The marked stylistic difference between San Pedro's two romances provides a different kind of evidence that Isabel's court was very much on the author's mind when he wrote. In the preface to *Cárcel de Amor*, the author uses the humility topos to ingratiate himself to just such a readership: "In truth, so far as the present work is concerned, I am the less to blame in that I embarked upon it more because of my duty of obedience than because of my desire to write; for it was your lordship who told me that I should compose some work in the style of a discourse which I sent to the Lady Marina Manuel, since that style seemed to her less poor than that which I employed in another romance of mine which she had seen" (*Prison*, 3) (85–86).[5] Ivy Corfis, editor of San Pedro's works, believes that the changes to which the author refers, such as the use of a wider variety of discursive modes, indicate his desire to please his courtly audience: "This was no easy task since the literary norms were rapidly changing during the last decades of the fifteenth century as more and more Latin and Greek texts were made available and became widely studied" (*Arnalte y Lucenda*, 3).[6]

The implied and inscribed aristocratic women readers of the sentimental romances and other literature *de amore* such as *Repetiçión de amores* do not, however, give us much information about the reception of these works by actual female readers. To what extent did noblewomen resist the masculinist courtly ideology that such works helped to produce and to maintain through either the idealization or the denigration of women? To what extent were they complicit in this process? Roberta Krueger's analysis of French verse romance of the twelfth and thirteenth centuries provides a subtle answer to these difficult questions. Krueger affirms that romance played an essentially conservative role in transmitting patriarchal ideology and class privilege. At the same time, she reminds us that modern studies on gender and reading problematize the notion that there is an innately feminine way of reading or any static category of "female reader."[7] Nevertheless, Krueger is able to find traces of a putative female reader's identification with and interpretation of romance that differs significantly from the dominant masculine one represented by the male author or narrator. Her conclusion is that "[t]he romance genre as well as inviting identification with patriarchal ideology also records and fosters critical resistance.... The implied female public and the inscribed women readers... are the fictional traces of voices in a dialogue whose words are lost" (xiv).[8]

What happens, however, if the female reader who resists the cultural construction of femininity in romance and other courtly texts is the most powerful woman in Spain? And what if her political agenda rests on the same patriarchal ideology that such works promote? One answer can be found in the works of Juan de Flores, a writer who successfully negotiated the complicated passage from the male-dominated university to the female-dominated court and whose close working relationship with Isabel has been established.

In previous studies, I have discussed the undercurrent of carnivalesque topsy-turvy in the Spanish romances written during Isabel's reign as an expression of some female readers' resistence to a courtly ideology that deprived women of subjectivity through idealization (Politics of "*Cárcel*," "Resisting Readers"). In doing so, I argued against the prevailing view of these romances as tragic representations of the conflictive demands of aristocratic love and honor and the dual assumptions that medieval courtly texts are univocal expressions of a rigid code in which women are always passive objects of male idealization/domination, and that male readings are universally valid. Even those scholars who concede that the works contain comic elements interpret them solely from the perspective of a male reader. Keith Whinnom's judgment on San Pedro's sometimes ludicrously comic *Arnalte* is typical: "in the contexts in which they are first presented, these subjects are not at all funny. Besides, it is clear that the French and Italian translators... outdid themselves in sympathizing with Arnalte and condemning Lucenda" (58).[9]

Crónica incompleta de los Reyes Católicos: The Queen and King at War

Of the many examples of festive misrule contained in Juan de Flores's varied corpus one of the most striking is the popular topos of "woman on top," the assumption by women of roles or forms of behavior traditionally assigned to men.[10] But as in the case of *Carajicomedia* and *Pleyto del manto*, carnivalesque topsy-turvy in Flores's work is not inherently or equally liberating for all. In fact, the laughter produced by his festive "uncrownings" is often more than a little nervous. And that nervous laughter, I shall argue, marks the site of the patronage and reception of an unpredictable, unmasterable virago queen.

Remarkable archival and textual research by Joseph Gwara and Carmen Parrilla has greatly expanded our knowledge of the biography and corpus of Juan de Flores. Flores is now known to have cultivated not only the romance genre (*Grimalte y Gradissa* and *Grisel y Mirabella*), but also chronicle (*Crónica de los Reyes Católicos,* known as *Crónica incompleta*), amatory epistle (two letters exchanged by Tristan and Isolde), political allegory *(Triunfo de amor),* and perhaps an epithalamium *(Coronación de Señora Gracisla).*[11] It also is likely that Flores wrote most of his works during the decade of the 1470s, some twenty years earlier than previously thought.[12]

As for his identity, it now appears that Flores was born in Salamanca of middle-class origins.[13] During the decade beginning in 1465, he performed military service as a knight of the Duke of Alba. As Gwara notes, in this capacity Flores would have supported Isabel's armed struggle for the throne, a service that Isabel often rewarded with a court post. Parrilla's archival research has shown that Flores in fact held several positions of trust in the court starting in the mid-1470s and continuing through the 1480s. These included "royal administrator" [corregidor], "investigating magistrate" [pesquisidor], "royal scribe" [escribano de cámara], "member of the royal household" [contino], and "member of the royal council" [consejero real]. On May 20, 1476, Isabel and Fernando appointed him to the prestigious post of royal chronicler, the first person to be so honored in their reign (Bermejo Cabrero, "Orígenes," 408–9). Two years later he was elected rector of the University of Salamanca, but he filled the administrative post for only eight months, perhaps because he was called back to court.[14] While maintaining this hectic pace of activity, roughly between 1475 and 1485, he also wrote the three works that will concern me here: *Triunfo de amor* (1475–76), *Crónica incompleta* (c. 1480), and *Grisel y Mirabella* (c. 1475).

Flores has thus emerged as both a prolific and versatile writer and a loyal supporter and trusted servant of Fernando and Isabel in the difficult early phase of their reign. In his various capacities as high-level adviser, administrator, and official chronicler he would have been given access to private correspondence and other sensitive documents and enjoyed a close working relationship with the monarchs, especially Isabel (Parrilla, *Grimalte*, xiv). It is thus appropriate to place his literary representations of sovereignty in the context of this privileged relationship with the Queen. Although I will focus on the portrayal of Isabel herself in *Crónica incompleta* and of the fictional Queen of Scotland in *Grisel y Mirabella*, I will also comment on *Triunfo de amor*, more ambiguous work whose royal protagonist is a man. All three offer admiring yet anxious portraits of the queen as she was perceived by French chess writers on the new chess, that is, as a "dame enragée." This discussion of the gender role-reversal in Flores complicates my earlier interpretation of this carnivalesque motif as a marker of a female readership's critique of the passive role assigned women in courtly ideology.[15] It focuses instead on the ambivalence and anxiety latent in the author's representation of virile queens.

Crónica incompleta (c. 1480), so titled because it breaks off abruptly in 1477, narrates events of the first two years of the Catholic Monarchs' rule.[16] A unique aspect of the work is its glorification of women's strength and abilities in times of crisis (Gwara, "Identity," 121). A good example is the praise the author lavishes on Isabel's favorite lady-in-waiting, the intrepid Beatriz de Bobadilla, for her management of her husband's affairs during his severe illness.[17] It must be noted, however, that he uses the exceptionality topos to praise Bobadilla, calling her a "courageous man" [esforçado varón] (208). But Flores reserves his highest praise for Isabel herself. Julio Puyol Alonso explains in the introduction to his 1934 edition of the chronicle, betraying his own bias to the contrary: "although he does not stint his fulsome praises for Fernando...his warmest praises and panegyrics are for the queen, and he attributes to her exclusively, in clear error or obvious injustice, the initiative or completion of several important affairs of state" (18).[18]

The chronicler devotes considerable space to one Isabelline initiative that we have examined at some length: the negotiations of January 1475 that culminated in the *Concordia de Segovia*. On that occasion, as discussed in chapter 2, Isabel kept the upper hand, insisting on her proprietary right to Castile, against the expectations of her husband, most of his Aragonese subjects, and many Castilians. Flores leaves no doubt as to where his loyalty lies: "The king...believed that after their marriage the queen...would concede to him the free reign in governance that kings have had in Castile, which precludes queens having anything to do with the affairs of the Kingdom. But since she knew herself to be a woman better equipped for such governance than any other... (145).[19] The preferential treatment Flores gives Isabel in his chronicle is reinforced by the fact that in its final chapters Fernando disappears entirely from the scene and the chronicler attributes to Isabel alone the jointly executed sieges of rebel fortresses that turned the tide of the war of succession.[20] For example, in his description of the crucial battle of Toro in the fall of 1476, Flores places the Queen squarely at the center of the action, a position that other chroniclers reserve for the King: "and the queen herself... provided and ordered all the necessary provisions herself, and I don't know of any soldier who was more diligent in war than she was" (Puyol Alonso, 319).[21]

I have previously discussed (chapter 3) the reprimand that Flores has Isabel deliver to Fernando and his troops upon their retreat from the strategic stronghold of Toro. The absence of this curious harangue from all other historiographical sources makes it probable that it is Flores's own invention. Furious but self-controlled, Isabel's tongue-lashing skillfully manipulates gender stereotypes in order to castigate the cowardice of Fernando and his men. She repeatedly invokes the stereotypical construction of woman as weak only to deny it. Thus, for example, she projects herself into battle, insisting that "with more courage I would venture it, preferring to risk uncertain danger than certain shame; because I, although a weak woman, would sooner test whether fortune were my friend or enemy, than flee from her, making of her an untested enemy" (240).[22] And she demonstrates a manly knowledge of military history when she condescendingly reminds Fernando of the inferiority of brains to brawn when it comes to waging war: "Hannibal never would have passed over the cold Alps nor won the great battle of Canas *[sic]* if his heart had heeded the cowardly counsel of his head, for the rules of philosophy are one thing and the rules of the sword another" (240)[23] and "War requires the advice of the brave more than of the learned" [La guerra más quiere consejo de osados que de letrados] (241).

Gwara cites this extraordinary speech to support his argument that in Flores's entire corpus, fictional as well as historical, is unusual for its "self-conscious attempt to flatter the female audience of the work" ("Identity," 121). Unlike the more or less contemporary *Crónicas* of Alfonso de Palencia and Hernando del Pulgar, Flores's *Crónica incompleta* lacks either triumphalism or a messianic vision of the future: "The auguries of the chronicler are always for worse times to come, those that came after the accession to the throne, precisely the subject of the chronicle: the hereditary dispute" (Parrilla, *Grimalte y Gradisa*, xxi–xxii)."[24] Moreover, Flores's preferential treatment of events in which he or his acquaintances participated (one of them being the abortive siege of Toro that occasioned Isabel's anger), his exaggeration of his patron the Duke of Alba's actions, and his praise of the contributions of royal administrators and reminders of the monarchs' promises to reward such servants all indicate that his account is more than a little self-interested (Gwara, "Identity," 122, 208–17). It appears that Flores wrote *Crónica incompleta* more or less in the heat of the battles of 1475–76 that it highlights, and that he was motivated by a desire to please his new employers, to further their cause so as to further his own (ibid., 216–17).

Crónica incompleta demonstrates concern for strengthening the formulation and administration of royal justice. Most of Título 14 is devoted to the strict and swift application of justice that began soon after Isabel's accession. Flores singles out the important contribution of *corregidores* like himself to the rapid restoration of peace in the land: "in every city they meted out justice [or executions?] unlike that of the previous king; and since the magistrates the king and queen sent to each city or region were so carefully chosen for both bravery and fairness ... they were so feared that no local magistrate, no matter how noble he was, would act as tyrannical or greedy as in the past" (141).[25] At the same time, he relates the fear that the draconian laws instilled, even among the innocent: "not a day passed without great punishments, so that even the innocent who had come to court were afraid" (141).[26] There was opposition in the royal council to such draconian measures, but "at that time the king and queen did not want justice to be at all weak nor to pardon any crime even if it meant sacrificing persons and kingdoms, believing it better to suffer for being virtuous, than to deserve punishment themselves" (142).[27]

Flores's stirring portrayal of the Queen as manly woman and his praise for her firm administration of justice are not, however, unproblematic. In the first place, they follow the typical pattern of ascribing to her extraordinary virtues that set her apart from her gender. Second, the manly virtues that Flores praises in Isabel—reason, physical stamina, courage, and bellicosity—are motivated by the topsy-turvy world of civil war that he recounts. The very abnormality of the situation requires the Queen to take on attitudes and behaviors normally denied women. Ultimately, however, it is Isabel's mission to reverse the disorder caused by treacherous aristocrats or weak husbands. Once she does so, the political and gender status quo can be reinstated.

It is useful to compare Isabel's harangue at Toro to the similar speech delivered by Laurencia in act 3 of Lope de Vega's *Fuenteovejuna* (1612–14). The play is set in 1476, the exact historical moment covered by *Crónica incompleta,* and we know that Lope relied heavily on fifteenth- and sixteenth-century chronicles to fashion his historical plays. The theme of *Fuenteovejuna,* based on a historical incident in the civil war, is the abuse of power, and Lope uses Isabel's struggle for the Castilian throne as a backdrop. The play's villain is the nobleman Fernán Gómez, a knight commander in the military order of Calatrava and a member of the powerful Guzmán clan who supported the claims of Isabel's rival, Juana. A tightly interwoven dual plot underscores Fernán Gómez's villainy. The broader political plot—Gómez's manipulation of his superior, the adolescent Master of Calatrava, into laying siege to Ciudad Real, a town loyal to the monarchs—frames the chaste love story of Laurencia and Frondoso, two inhabitants of the eponymous village that is part of Gómez's fiefdom.

Fernán Gómez is a sexual predator who seduces and rapes the peasant women of Fuenteovejuna with impunity. The fathers and husbands of the victims are too afraid to resist the tyrant. In the climactic scene of act 3, a disheveled Laurencia storms on stage, having barely escaped rape by Guzmán. She passionately indicts the men of her village, including her alderman father, for tolerating the nobleman's crimes. The men's failure to perform their masculine gender role of protecting their women is a "profound crisis of masculinity [that] requires Laurencia's masculinization to serve as a catalyst for them to become 'real men' again. The men's silent acquiescence to the women's, and therefore their own, dishonor, compels Laurencia's improper speech, in which she accuses them of no longer being men, but 'spinners, faggots, effeminate, cowards' [hilanderas, maricones, / amujerados, cobardes]" (Yarbro-Bejarano, 125). In the face of male cowardice, women have no choice but to arm themselves, bringing back "that age of the Amazons / eternal astonishment of the world" [aquel siglo de amazonas, / eterno espanto del orbe] (ibid.). The shock effect of Laurencia's bellicosity has an immediate "regendering" effect on the village men, and they rise up and kill the abusive knight commander.

The speech Lope assigns Laurencia at this moment of communal crisis holds obvious parallels to the speech Flores gives Isabel after the disaster at Toro. Although the regendering of the Castilian troops takes considerably more time—the capture of Toro, the turning point of the war of succession, was not accomplished until a year later—the queenly outrage has an effect, as Flores observes: "And people always are more eager to serve women, when women wage war, and because they feel ashamed of this, they confront danger and hardship more willingly" (315).[28]

In *Crónica incompleta*, then, a middle-class *letrado* pressed into military service masculinizes his female sovereign, presenting her as a would-be warrior and virago who vents her displeasure with her husband's military caution by casting him and his soldiers in the effeminized role of petulant courtly lovers and, most ironically, of bookish jurists. Like Lope's portrayal of Laurencia, Flores's image of his new employer in the midst of her struggle for power is not unequivocally profeminist. But bearing in mind the close watch that Isabel kept on the production of the official record of her reign, we must assume that this ambivalent portrayal of the queen as virago met with at least her tacit approval.

The necessary but elusive balance of punishment and mercy in monarchic justice is a recurring theme throughout Flores's corpus. And, as in Martín de Córdoba's *Jardín de nobles doncellas*, these two aspects of justice are often gendered. The king, as the one who applies the letter of the law, wields the sword; the queen, who protects her subjects from the law's harshness by beseeching the king's mercy on their behalf, holds the shield. As we saw in chapter 2, however, although Martín de Córdoba's *speculum principis* was intent on forming a queen consort, the reality turned out to be quite different.

An interest in the instability of traditional gender roles and its effects on the institutionalization and preservation of monarchic absolutism pervades Flores's corpus. Almost all of his works reveal a preoccupation with certain "new laws" [nuevas leyes] that in one way or another invert the dominant gender relations of power within the courtly paradigm, allowing women to become agents, empowering them either to pursue or reject a relationship. But whereas in *Crónica incompleta* the inversion of gender roles and the conceptualization of royal justice are separate themes, in the romance *Grisel y Mirabella* and in the political allegory *Triunfo de amor,* which may have been written at about the same time as the chronicle, they are explicitly linked.[29]

Triunfo de amor: Political Negotiation and Gender Revolt

The political allegory *Triunfo del amor* serves as a thematic bridge between Flores's chronicle and his romances, and it contains the most extensive treatment of the theme of "new laws."[30] Already in the preface the metafictional narrator, "Johan de Flores," establishes a link between the allegorical world of "Persia" and the "real" world he inhabits with his dedicatees, later identified as the "ladies of Spain" [damas d'España]. In true courtly fashion he querulously reminds his female readers of the many courtly services he has performed at their request, including that of a roving reporter constantly searching out news from around the world. It was in this capacity as global *trotero* that he learned what he is about to recount: "Many stories are told of how the dead lovers rebelled against the God of Love. But what is most certain is to consider how things are nowadays: servants betraying their masters, from whom they receive great favors, and following the confusion of the era, they take every baseness for gentility" (75).[31] The protagonist of *Triunfo de amor* is the very same Cupid who plays such a prominent role in Lucena's *Repetiçión*. But, Flores is not as concerned as Lucena with the devastating omnipotence of the monarch of love. His interest lies rather in the precariousness of that power.

A brief sample of the repeated inversions and reversals in the plot of *Triunfo de amor* will serve to demonstrate its pervasive topsy-turvy. Cupid's supreme authority is contested by a band of aggrieved dead lovers. Medea, as the leader of the revolt, uses her necromantic powers to resurrect the dead lovers and restore them to their youthful vigor. The rebel forces then defeat Cupid and condemn him to death. When he is allowed to choose his method of execution, he decides to withdraw all love from the world so as to immolate himself "in the live flames of love, which suits me" [en bibas llamas de amor, (lo cual) me conviene] (112). Chaos ensues: friends become enemies, parents hate their children, and in general "everything is so broken ... that we seem to be changing the law and condition of the world, and everyone is turned against reason and nature" (116).[32] But the God of Love finally triumphs over his enemies, aided by an army of "living lovers" [amantes vivos] whose Spanish contingent includes the Duke of Alba, Flores's patron. The defeated king of Persia and the other kings and great lords who fight under him cede their territory to Amor, because "works of nature have a creator and a purpose who is God, whom they obey; and because in heaven there is one lord and not many, it is a perfect creation. And this our world, because there are so many lords who govern and rule, was facing ruin, or expected to perish; and now, ruled by one, we can expect its current ills to be fully remedied" (157–58).[33]

Having defeated his enemies and affirmed the value of absolute monarchy, Cupid sets about to prove himself a merciful ruler. He pardons the rebel forces and grants them a number of years of happiness to compensate for those they spent suffering for his sake; "since mercy is always the greater part of virtue in the gods than justice, I do not want your errors to cause me to change the rules that guide my virtuous conduct" (156).[34] Here the theme of legal and social contingency makes its initial appearance in the text. Cupid's "mercy" and power are so great that he transforms shepherds into courtiers, old men into young, and children into adults, so that all of his subjects may better enjoy the fruits of love.

The modern editor of *Triunfo de amor*, Antonio Gargano, treats the work as a political allegory. For him, Flores intends Cupid's recovery of absolute control over all of his subjects to reassure his aristocratic readers, who were alarmed by the radical social and political changes taking place in the last quarter of the fifteenth century. He maintains that Flores formulates the fictional plane of his romance on the basis of stable literary codes (mythological, allegorical, courtly, etc.) so as to compensate for the instability represented on the realistic plane (54). But Gargano completely overlooks the bizarre carnivalesque ending of *Triunfo de amor*, which completely undermines the theory that the author's goal is to soothe aristocratic malaise.

The paradise of love instituted by Cupid does not last. Soon his male supporters ask to be rewarded for services they rendered their ruler in the recent rebellion. What they request is a reversal of the traditional roles of courtship: "that from that day forth and forever women court men" (163).[35] Cupid recognizes the gravity of a request that is "very much against the old custom" [muy fuera de la vieja costumbre] and calls for a debate to resolve the issue. The men base their argument on the divine origin of kingship: "our sovereign Jupiter, creating us in his image, supremely favored us with power over all creatures and especially over women. And just as his commandment ordered, the same is decreed in the world by law: that nothing is born that does not obey us out of love or fear. And only in the case of love are they the mistresses and we their very obedient servants" (163–64).[36] Cupid must adhere to the higher law of God/Jupiter and correct the current gender inequity. They insist "that you repeal and restore to the rule of reason the evil custom that works to our harm and detriment" (164).[37]

Cupid's female subjects, who are evidently no less well versed in sexual politics than the men, counter with the argument that the dominance supposedly accorded them by courtly ideology is spurious. All of their suffering notwithstanding, male suitors enjoy fundamental privileges denied to females. Men, not women, are the ones who have freedom of choice, action, and expression: "they choose the one among us who most pleases them, and without shame or fear, without remorse, they ask to be rewarded for their services. And we, so as not to set aside that shame that restrains us, suffer a thousand deaths in silence, and desiring our beloved more than life, we act most disdainfully, and out of our mouths come words that we do not intend" (165).[38] In these lines the women insist that their presumed superiority in courtship actually is produced by and reproduces a patriarchal social order that denies women freedom of speech and action. They even isolate a central mechanism of that social control: "shame" [vergüença]. Sexual shame constrains women from voicing and acting on their true desire; the idealization of courtly love only mystifies the oppressive social force of the modesty or shame. Cupid's female subjects reject the unprecented law the monarch plans to impose, unless the role-reversal includes the burden of shame: "Since they desire our privileges so much, let us bestow them with the burden of our troubles" [Y pues tanto dessean nuestro bienes, con la carga de nuestros trabajos geles damos] (166).

Cupid's response to his female subjects upholds his characterization as a just and beneficent ruler. He ratifies the men's proposal, but he also accepts the women's amendment, and even expresses compassion for their plight: "your life must be very difficult, having my pleasures within reach and disdaining them with your words or weeping over your wishes.... And since freedom is the greatest good I know of in this world, and you are so lacking in it, what greater favor do you wish to receive from me than that I release your wishes from such a narrow prison?" (168–69).[39] Combining legal and religious terminology, Cupid then lifts the burden of shame from his female subjects: "So consider yourselves absolved from blame and punishment, as if you were newly born right now; and I take upon my shoulders the error of your shame and the blame for this sin" (171).[40] In these remarkable lines, the merciful monarch uses the sacrilegious language of courtly love to effect a gendered salvation. He allows the women to be reborn by taking onto himself the burden of the shame that originated in Eve's sin. In a blasphemous *imitatio Christi*, he replaces the "Old Testament" law of female subordination upheld by his male supporters with a "New Testament" absolution of female sinfulness.

The measured exchange between the God of Love and his female subjects stands in sharp contrast with the unruliness unleashed when the new gender law goes into effect. In this vivid example of the festive topos of women on top, the *damas* take to the new ordinance "as if that had always been their custom" [como si siempre aquello tuvieran de costumbre] (172). They parade through the streets all day boldly gazing at the men who peek out from behind closed windows, and in the evening they visit their favorites in their palaces, where "their faces laughing, each one starts to deliver amorous discourses and mottoes" [los rostros llenos de risa, cada una se pone en razones y motes] (173). Some less attractive men signal their availability for love with meaningful glances, but are ignored; others who give in to their suitors too quickly lock themselves in their rooms to bewail the loss of their virginity (174). The narrator places particular emphasis on the literary skill displayed by the newly empowered ladies, who, "after having benefited from hearing our amorous discourses, recited new ones, which they had secretly memorized, and which we could not grasp, because we did not know, as they did, what should be said that would be most appropriate to make them to fall in love. So that they benefited from our public knowledge and their secret one" (173).[41] Once given the word, the women prove themselves more adept than the men at manipulating it. They go even further, proving that the language of love invented by men is inadequate to its task: only women know the exact words that will win their hearts. Women thus are revealed to have a secret language of love that is more effective than the public male-dominated discourse of courtly love.[42] When the women add masculine "public knowledge" to their "new amorous discourses," they wield such power that "there was no man who could defend or save himself from them" [no avía hombre que se les pudiese defender ni amparar] (174).

Carmen Parrilla comes close to appreciating the precise political implications of *Triunfo de amor*'s festive ending. She considers Amor's reluctant restoration of the "ley de razón" (i.e., male dominance over women) to be an ironic recognition of the limits of monarchic legislative power. She concludes that *Triunfo de amor* is a kind of subversive chronicle, in which the treatment of love is articulated within an ideological structure concerned with revealing the nature and functioning of monarchy (124). For Parrilla, the imaginary world created by Flores is a *contrafactum* of the Virgilian theme of "Omnia vincit Amor" that deflates the power of Love by making him subject to human demands ("*Derrota*," 124). Like Gargano, however, she minimizes the impact of the ending and views Flores's elaboration of the woman-on-top motif as a minor alteration in the cultural code otherwise affirmed in the text: "In the sentence he imposes on the women the God of Love diminishes the importance of the problem they pose by considering it situational and banal: a usage, a custom" (123).[43]

On the contrary, it is precisely the narrator's comparison of courtship patterns to fashion that is most subversive. The fashion analogy exposes the constructed and mutable nature of gender roles that the language and "rules" of courtly love mask. Under the new law, Amor explains, shame will become "like sleeves when they are out of fashion.... Just like that ... the women who wish to enjoy the new ordinance, are empowered to do so; and those who wish to maintain the old situation, with the same challenge faced by those who wear clothes that are out of fashion, may do so" (169–70).[44] It is true, of course, that Amor uses this argument primarily to convince the women to accede to the men's request that the "law of Jupiter" (i.e., "nothing is born that does not obey us, out of love or fear" [164]) be applied to courtship as to all other social activities. But he argues that the change will be beneficial to women in that it will bring about not greater subjection but freedom from shame.

Two things are noteworthy in Cupid's explication of the "new ordinance" [nueva ordenança]. The first is the acknowledgment that shame is not in fact an inherent gender trait resulting from the legacy of Eve, but rather a social custom, subject to changing times and taste. The second is the reassurance that, in any case, the new law will not be coercive, forcing women to discard shame, but will allow them freedom of choice, along with freedom of action and expression. Cupid again travesties the sacrilegious language of courtly adulation when he admonishes his female subjects not to oppose the new law, whose consequences the men fail to grasp: "So it is that I know of no reason why you should complain about this; rather, be glad, and say to me in the name of all men: 'Forgive them, Lord, for they know not what they do'" (170).[45]

In exposing the truth that courtly ideology mystifies, namely, the social constructedness of all gender relations and the way the idealization of women naturalizes the sexual shame that subjugates them, Cupid shows himself empathetic to women's plight in patriarchy. At the same time, he is constrained by his contractual obligations to the aristocratic male subjects whose armed support restored him to the throne. His response to the men's request seriously endangers the newly regained peace: "The issue was argued and defended by both sides; and caused so much discord that the court many times was on the verge of destruction, with everyone in danger of taking up arms against some men that favored the women's side. But the God of Love, seeing his subjects so perplexed and not finding a way of making them agree, was forced to please the men, because he was so indebted to them, and with the best arguments he could think of, he ruled against the ladies" (167).[46]

The utopian world created by monarchic decree at the end of *Triunfo de amor*, in which men unwittingly and Cupid knowingly grant women freedom and agency, is not a comic afterthought but a central element in Flores's exploration of monarchic power. Given Flores's insistence on relating the disorder of Persia to that of Castile, it is licit to go even further, to speculate that the God of Love, obligated to men for his authority, and empathetic to women's subordination but unable to satisfy both, is a screen for Isabel and a covert commentary on the delicate negotiations required of a female sovereign in a patriarchal society.

Read in the way I have suggested, the seriocomic *Triunfo de amor* emerges as a kind of festive allegorized version of the *Crónica incompleta*'s official treatment of the Catholic Monarchs at war. I am not suggesting a one-on-one correspondence, say, between the God of Love and Isabel, or even Fernando. But Cupid's desire to pacify and unify his subjects after a political rebellion that has devastating effects on social relations, while also ensuring that justice is served, cannot but remind us of Flores's depiction of Isabel and Fernando during and after the war of succession. Also remarkable is *Triunfo de amor*'s inclusion of a mini-debate about gender roles that allows women to speak for themselves instead of the usual format in such debate texts (at least in Iberia), whereby men argue both for and against women. Women's full participation within the debate and, more significantly, their subversion of the insincerity, falseness, and destructive effects of such debates play a major role in Flores's popular romance *Grisel y Mirabella*, as we shall see.

The inversions and subversions of *Triunfo de amor* do not, however, qualify Flores as a champion of women. His narrator "Juan de Flores" betrays clear signs of ambivalence about the profeminine utopia that he is relating to the "Castilian ladies" [damas castellanas]. On several occasions he consciously or unconsciously affirms his solidarity with the male point of view by slipping from third- to first-person narration, for example, when he explains how the new law allows women to go out in search of love "out on those rugged mountains full of thorns, where we used to walk" [por aquellas ásperas sierras llenas de abrojos, por donde nosotros caminar solíamos] (171–72). And in one passage that recounts how the newly empowered women pressure their beloveds to grant them favors, the sacrilegious language makes the traditional identification between women's seductive wiles and Satan's: "He so sorely tempted them that neither praying, nor supplicating, nor beseeching God to save them did them any good; rather, the women, like the devil who keeps the closest watch on their souls, made them renounce the habit of such a strict religious order" (174).[47]

The Mad Queen of *Grisel y Mirabella*

It is precisely Flores's preoccupation with gender relations of power that has caused his romances to be treated as documents in the Iberian debate about women, initiated by Pedro Torrellas's mid-century misogynist diatribe, *Maldezir de mugeres*.[48] The traditional view is that particularly in *Grisel y Mirabella* Flores weighs in heavily on the pro-feminine side of the debate. If in the allegorical *Triunfo de amor* Flores expresses veiled reservations about the effects of the "new law" of female sovereignty, the fictional queen who dominates the ending of *Grisel y Mirabella* seems to express more overtly his anxieties about the effects of female power on the very foundations of the patriarchal social order.

Grisel y Mirabella is set in what would have been to its readers the fairy-tale land of "Scotland" [Escocia]. It tells the tragic tale of Princess

Mirabella and her lover Grisel whose secret romance is betrayed to the king, Mirabella's father. Acting in the name of impartial justice, but betraying a perverse bias against his own daughter, the king brings the lovers to trial to determine which of them is more culpable in the affair. The lawyers engaged to try the case are the archmisogynist Torrellas and the Trojan heroine Breçayda, often invoked as the archetypal fickle female in the Middle Ages. The confrontation between the misogynist Torrellas and the profeminine Breçayda gives ample opportunity for Flores to display his mastery of both sides of the debate about women. In the end, although both lawyers are equally eloquent, the all-male jury finds for Torrellas and against Mirabella. At this point the romance shifts it focus to the harsh "Law of Scotland" [Ley de Escocia] that decrees that "the one who was the greater cause and instigator of the other's loving deserved death, and the one who was less responsible, exile" (58).[49] The tragic end rapidly ensues: before Mirabella can be executed, Grisel jumps to his death and Mirabella then throws herself into her father's lion pit, where she is devoured.

Most critics agree that responsibility for the tragedy lies with the King of Scotland. For Marina Brownlee, *Grisel* "examines the relationship between natural law and judicial law as they pertain to the discursive authority of their guarantor—the king" (191). She believes that his transgression of natural law is motivated by incestuous desire that leads him to lock up his only daughter and heir, thereby preventing her from marrying. These actions in turn undermine the narrator's characterization of the sovereign as "a friend of all virtues, and principally in being just; and he was as just as justice herself" (54).[50] Patricia Grieve, on the other hand, exculpates the Scottish king for the increasing chain of violence and disorder that prevails in *Grisel*, attributing the chaos to the overwhelming power of feminine desire. As the object of desire, it is woman who "inspires a chaotic momentum of violence which whirls out of the characters' control—if it is a force which can ever be subject to control" (*Desire*, 68). Flores critiques the masculine belief, symbolized by the king, that the just application of the law can control the devastation caused by desire.

No critic has made an explicit connection between the fictional politics of *Grisel y Mirabella* and the actual political context in which it was composed. Among the very few who attempt such a contextualization is Jorge Checa, who sees in the romance symptoms of crisis in the conception of monarchy: "the authority of the Monarch no longer originates in the military and knightly virtues of the past, but rather in the fetishistic cult of legal ordinances, the only basis of his identity" (377).[51] Checa's brief essay is suggestive, although he contends that the imbalance between social norms and reality, between legal code and individual desires, is unintentional on the author's part, and only generally applicable to late-fifteenth-century Spain (381 n. 22). Lilian von der Walde points out the king's lack of mercy, his masculinist bias, and his egotism (*Amor e ilegalidad*, 171–94), finding in the romance a kind of pessimism typical of the waning of the Middle Ages. The corrupt kingdom of Escocia is for her an expresion of Flores's lack of faith in human beings that relates, consciously or unconsciously, to the sociopolitical circumstances of late-fifteenth-century Spain (177).

What we now know about Flores's life, and especially his close ties with Isabel, compels a more historicized reading of his romances. Flores's varied administrative and judicial responsibilities directly involved him in the final stages of the transformation of the Castilian monarchy from a contractual to an absolutist institution. As official chronicler, he was charged with legitimizing those changes, as well as the power of the female sovereign responsible for bringing them about. As a writer of romances whose readership included Isabel and her ladies-in-waiting, he had more, although by no means total, freedom to question them.

The most recent editors of *Grisel*, Pablo Alcázar López and Jose González Núñez, are more willing to take the risk of a historicized interpretation of Flores's romance. To the question of whether *Grisel* is a "political novel" [novela política] they assert unequivocally that the Flores "is inclined to . . . favor the absolutist monarchy of the Catholic Monarchs" [se decanta . . . por la monarquía autoritaria de los Reyes Católicos] (43).[52] He presents a monarch who conforms to Renaissance political theory in the importance he accords justice and his reliance on a council of jurists. This may be true, but the picture becomes clouded if instead of focusing on Mirabella's father the king, we consider the role of her mother, the wily and vengeful Queen of Escocia.

All of the scholars just mentioned have helped to resituate consideration of the degree of pro- or antifeminism in Flores's work within the context of its complex consideration of monarchic power. Most conclude that Flores's work is so fraught with ambiguity and contradiction on this matter that it cannot be deemed either misogynist nor misandrist. I would argue that the impossibility of placing Flores on either side of the debate shows that his interest lies precisely in the instability of the patriarchal gender hierarchy and of the masculine dominance it attempts to enforce. In *Grisel,* as to a lesser degree in his other texts, the precarious gender hierarchy operates as a fundamental instance of the ever-changing dynamics of power. As such, it can—and in the fictional world of Escocia does—undermine patriarchal power within the parallel private and public spheres, that of "the father who is as king in the family and the king who is as father in the state" (Barker, 31). Flores's treatment of this issue is particularly powerful in *Grisel* because in it the two spheres converge in a king who is himself a father.[53] The "Law of Scotland" that the king applies so strictly to his own daughter is emblematic of the laws that impose and uphold royal power, but Flores's goal in *Grisel* is to question not only the justice of the laws imposing and upholding royal power, but also their efficacy in maintaining the gender hierarchy that undergirds all social and political institutions.

In the Queen of Scotland, on the other hand, Flores creates what amounts to a fictional counterpart of the new chess's queen, the "dame enragée." The enraged figure who dominates the final pages of *Grisel y Mirabella* is a calculating, fearless, and violent queen who turns her back on her husband's domestic and public authority in order to enact a bloody personal revenge on her and her daughter's enemy. What triggers the final catastrophe is the king's rejection of his wife's plea that he be merciful in his application of the "Ley de Escocia" to their only daughter. On the face of it, the Auctor does not openly condemn the king for his adherence to the letter of the law. In fact, he appears to empathize with his moral dilemma, although he does point to a more sinister motivation: "But the King was thinking of nothing but how to kill Mirabella, although he loved her dearly; but justice was stronger than love" (80).[54] In pleading for the king to show mercy to their daughter, the Queen fills the traditional role of the queen consort, the very one that Martín de Córdoba advocated for the princess Isabel in *Jardín de nobles donzellas.* She acts as a shield to protect her daughter from her husband's bloody sword, the biased law of the land. Breçayda, "champion of women" and lawyer for Mirabella, sarcastically criticizes the bias when the negative verdict is rendered: "Thus consider, excellent and most illustrious Queen and noble ladies, under whose laws we live, which require the one who is compelled to die and the one who compels to live; and they are right, for they are judges, and parties, and lawyers in the same lawsuit, and certainly he would be simpleminded who found himself guilty; and for this reason no injustice has been done to us, since their absolute power allows them to find against us" (78).[55]

The Queen's opposition to her husband's unnatural prejudice against his own daughter, like Isabel's frustration at being prevented from riding into battle, or the effeminate cowardice of Fernando and his troops, uses a domestic disturbance to attack the inequities of the traditional gender hierarchy, for it has already been made clear that the entire judicial procedure set in motion by the princess's crime and rigidly upheld by the king is biased against women.

But the noblewomen of Scotland do not remain passive in the face of the gender bias of the legal process. Instead, they take the law into their own hands and conspire to overthrow the repressive male authority of fathers, kings, and judges in a grotesque inversion of the highly ritualized trial and conviction of Mirabella. The Queen, her ladies-in-waiting, and Breçaida find their opportunity for revenge when Torrellas falls in love with his erstwhile opponent Breçaida. The abrupt transformation of the archetypal woman hater Torrellas into an abject courtly lover clearly and comically subverts his authority in the preceding judicial debate with Breçaida. Given the major contribution of the historical Torrellas to the fifteenth-century feminist debate that is vividly reflected here, his about-face also undermines the entire tradition of clerical misogyny whose standard he bears. And his reversal exposes the underlying similarity of the two presumably opposed ideologies of misogyny and courtly love.

The similarity is underscored in two ways. First, the women's skill at reading between the lines of Torrellas's written declaration of love and service to Breçaida allows them to understand that his goal is base. Second, their command of the rhetoric of courtly love allows them to compose an equally insincere reply: "a witty letter... granting him in it more than he begged of her; so that the deception would make it possible for the women to kill him" (88).[56] In other words, they are not deceived by Torrellas's courtly clichés but continue to regard him as the enemy of women. The accuracy of their assessment of Torrellas's ignoble intentions is subsequently confirmed for the reader when Torrellas brags to his male friends of his imminent seduction of Brazaida: "And look, he was so malicious that he could not keep his evil secret... and praising himself and belittling her, who was going to be harder to get than he thought" (91).[57]

The importance of skill at reading and writing in any attempt to counter misogyny is evident in this passage. Just as in *Triunfo de amor*, the ability of noblewomen to compose courtly *razones* makes it possible for them to right the wrongs done by the masculinist "old law" [vieja ley]. In *Triunfo de amor*, however, the women seek to throw off the inhibiting social stricture of *vergüenza* in order to freely express and act on their desire. The goal of the women in *Grisel* is more destructive. They invite Torrellas to an assignation in the queen's chamber, where they proceed to strip him, bind his hands and feet, tie him to a stake, and torture him to death. In the narrator's description of their creative sadism—"Each one thought up a new way to torture him; and there were some who, with burning tongs, and others with nails and teeth, furiously tore him apart" (93)[58]—there is a sinister echo of the literary creativity the ladies in *Triunfo de amor* used to seduce their loved ones, those "[new] amorous discourses that they had secretly memorized" (173).

Grieve has interpreted this grotesque literalization of Torrellas's wish "to die for love" as the climax of the destructive power of love unleashed at the beginning of the romance by Mirabella's beauty. In her view, it represents a complete breakdown of social laws, family ties, and love relationships (*Desire*, 57). The majority of critics of *Grisel* agree with her interpretation of the ending as tragic, almost apocalyptic. I have argued elsewhere for a more comic interpretation of the ending's portrayal of unruly women seizing control and wreaking havoc on the misogynistic society that has victimized them. Certainly, the majority of the elements of Torrellas's torture-murder are classically carnivalesque: the physical and verbal abuse the women heap on their victim; their own downward transformation into predators and their assimilation to the hungry royal lions that had devoured Mirabella just as they destroy Torrellas; the sexual overtones of the punishment, which includes binding him naked to a stake, and attacking him with hot tongs; the references to food and feasting, including a startling allusion to cannibalism when the women sit down to a fine feast in full view of their moribund victim.[59] Also typical of Carnival is the scene's parodic religious character—the blasphemous allusions to the Last Supper in the "bitter dinner" [amarga cena] prepared for Torrellas and the reliquaries the women fashion from his remains: "after they had left no flesh on his bones, these were burned; each one preserved some of the ashes in a box as a reliquary of their enemy; and there were some who wore it around their necks like a jewel, so that remembering more easily their revenge, they could take more pleasure in it" (93).[60] More generally, the frenzied savagery of the ending functions as a festive release from the cold rationality of the male-dominated trial and sentence.

Although a case can be made for such a comic and feminist reading, especially from the perspective of Flores's inscribed female audience—a point to which I shall return—Lillian von der Walde's discussion of the negative symbolism of the ending is a useful reminder of the blurred boundary between the celebration and the condemnation of female power. In her discussion of *Grisel*'s bizarre ending, von der Walde first situates the scene within a medieval tradition of female revenge on male detractors. She cites the examples of Jean de Meun, Matheolus, and Alan Chartier, where, far from celebrating a just comeuppance to misogynists, the reversal confirms the antifeminine view of women's inherent evil, will to power, vindictiveness, even murderousness ("Episodio," 20).[61] There may also be parallels between the brutal actions of the Queen and her ladies in *Grisel* and various motifs from folklore and classical mythology, such as the wild hunt and the savage murder of Orpheus and of Pentheus at the hands of the Maenads, as well as associations with the Satanic rituals imputed to witches. All of these asociations make the "passion" of Torrellas a cathartic expression of the unconscious masculine fear of being dominated or devoured by women (ibid., 27–28).

From the regicentric perspective of this study, however, the fears exorcised in the frenzied topsy-turvy of *Grisel*'s ending must be read as stemming from a more specific source. The ending in this context is a fantasy of the dangers of a female monarch who will not and cannot be controlled by her husband, by the *vergüença* that restrains women's voice and agency, or by patriarchal laws and courts that punish any infractions to female subjection to male control. The bizarre final scene is ambiguous not because it occludes Flores's real views vis-à-vis the debate on women, but rather because he was acutely aware of a real queen who might read it.

It is significant that both *Triunfo de amor* and *Grisel y Mirabella* feature inscribed female readers. "Juan de Flores" dedicates *Grisel* to his beloved [amiga], claiming to have acted as a mere scribe in recording "the record of your cause" [la comunicación de vuestra causa] (53). But what exactly is the "cause" that the narrator serves? A similar vagueness characterizes the dedication of *Triunfo de amor* to "women in love" [las enamoradas dueñas]. In *Triunfo de amor*, however, there are indications in the introductory *carta* and the envoi that the narrator has a more specific reception in mind. The narrator remarks in the introduction that as one of "the lesser servants in the household of the monarchs" [los menores siervos en casa de los reyes] he does not expect a reward for his amatory/literary service, because "Loves and bishoprics have more to do with luck than service" [amores y obispados más son de ventura que de servicios] (74–75). The statement recalls the kind of self-serving comments Gwara has detected in *Crónica incompleta*. In the envoi the narrator takes the opportunity to warn his noble destinatees of the imminent arrival of Cupid's "letter of amorous excommunication" [paulina de amar] (a sacrilegious reference to Saint Paul's epistles), which has been delayed because Spanish ladies are known to be "more difficult to tame than other women, and more recalcitrant and disdainful to obey the harshness of this petition" (176).[62] Echoing the earlier consolation that Cupid offered to the women of Persia, the narrator explains that although the Spanish ladies may be fearful of the new law, most of them will be pleased with the salvation that this "God and Messiah" [Dios y Mexía] has granted them. He tells them "that because of Eve's sin the holiest women in love among you were in the hell and limbo of shame; therefore raise your hands up to this God, who has delivered you from such great captivity and restored you to the freedom of the free" (176).[63]

Louise Haywood has found the association of male dominance with a negative evaluation of equality, law, and justice to be a feature of many of the late-medieval Spanish romances.[64] She considers the "new laws" so often mentioned by Flores as code for the breakdown of the "old laws of love as expounded by a courtly code and presented in the *cancioneros* that are unworkable in contemporary bourgeois society" (19). But clearly, the society that Flores knows and imagines cannot be called bourgeois, nor, for that matter, does he present a single instance of the archetypal courtly love relationship modeled on feudal bonds of service and reward. I argue that what Flores's interest in unsettling "new laws" marks is an anxious awareness of the subordination of women by the old laws of patriarchy, the constructedness of all gender roles and relations, and their consequent instability and mutability. This awareness accounts for the frequency with which strong and willful women seize power and manipulate an unsettled state of affairs for their own purposes, whether it be to wage war and punish rebels *(Crónica)*, to reject a suitor *(Grimalte y Gradissa)*, to aggressively pursue a beloved *(Triunfo de amor)*, or to take revenge on an enemy *(Grisel)*. And in three out of these four works the coincidence of feminine agency and gender instability has the power to undermine the patriarchal sex/gender system that monarchic absolutism is predicated on and perpetuates. Flores's corpus is less concerned with female desire than with female power, not the illusory power granted by men to women in courtly ideology, whereby the latter remain objectified, but the real and absolute power wielded by a female sovereign whose lack of *vergüença* to speak and act is an irresistible force for the institution of a new kind of law.

As for the vexed question of Flores's pro- or antifeminism, it depends on how the unsettling endings of *Triunfo de amor* and *Grisel* were read. Because both works are dedicated to aristocratic women readers, Roberta Krueger's focus on the problem of the woman reader in and of medieval romance is applicable. Krueger warns that the marked presence of women in romance—whether as "implied" readers, that is, as an explicit external audience within the extradiegetic frame, or as "inscribed" readers, characters within the fiction who read—does not prove either that individual female patrons or readers exerted a formative influence on the composition or that the genre promoted women's interests (3). She identifies Benoit de Sainte-Maure's *Roman de Troie* (1155–60) as the beginning of the woman reader as problem and shows that its flattering dedication to no less powerful a female reader and literary patron than Eleanor of Aquitaine is highly ambiguous because it undermines female authority as much as it acknowledges a powerful female patron.[65] For example, the author places his flattering dedication to the "riche dame" at the moment of Briseida's (Breçayda) betrayal of Troilus and frames it with two passages that discourse on the fickleness of women. At the same time, his apology to his dedicatee for these misogynistic lines suggests an awareness that she might not agree with his representation of female desire in the character of Briseida and raises the general question of how women might respond to stories told about them by men (4). The ambiguities of *Roman de Troie* and the other romances analyzed by Krueger lead her to conclude that despite the fact that romance played an essentially conservative role in the transmission of patriarchal ideology, "the problematic figure of the woman reader in the frame or within the narrative is often the catalyst for a resistant, critical interpretation of courtly ideology" (xiv).

If we apply this nuanced view of gender and interpretation in romance to Flores's implied readers (the Queen and her ladies) and his inscribed readers (the resistant, rebellious readers of courtly "law" in the endings of *Triunfo de amor* and *Grisel*), we find a similar ambiguity at work. On the one hand, Flores appears to authorize their interpretation as female fantasies, as Nancy Miller defines that term in relation to women-authored texts: "a fantasy of power that would revise the social grammar in which women are never defined as subjects; a fantasy of power that disdains a sexual exchange in which women can participate only as objects of circulation" (348). On the other hand, it allows them to be seen as male phobic fantasies of female will to dominate, dangerously enabled by the power of an enraged queen to destroy the social order maintained by the law.

If Luis de Lucena's *Repetiçión de amores* records his anxieties about the difficulty of "winning the queen," and securing a position at a female-dominated court, Flores's works show that having attained such a position does not eliminate the disquiet. The difficulty of coping with a new kind of monarch, one who has the capacity to invert the traditional gender hierarchy and at the same time restore patriarchal values to Castile, often by harshly punishing her enemies, is an ever-present theme in the works he wrote while in Isabel's employ.

CONCLUSION

Isabel in the Twentieth Century

"Do you know what the answer to your question is? Yes, I believe in the Devil and in giant Saint Christopher and in blessed Barbara— in all mysterious beings, in a word. But not in Queen Isabella."
"I'm glad," he says. "You're beginning to lose your way again."

—¿Sabe lo que le digo? Que sí creo en el diablo y en San Cristóbal gigante y en Santa Bárbara bendita, en todos los seres misteriosos, vamos. En Isabel la Católica, no.
—Me alegro—dice—, está usted volviendo a perder el camino.
—Carmen Martín Gaite, *El cuarto de atrás*

This study has analyzed two interrelated strategies adopted by fifteenth-century writers in order to negotiate the anxieties raised by the tension between Isabel's gender and her patriarchal power. One strategy is found in texts that form part of Isabelline "official"culture, most of them composed by aristocratic or clerical authors and either addressed to, commissioned by, or otherwise supported by the queen. They represent her as pious, virginal, wifely, maternal, and compassionate and attempt in direct or subtle ways to contain her within the roles and behavior prescribed for women in the late-medieval and early-modern periods. The second strategy inheres in carnivalesque works, most of them understandably anonymous, but no doubt composed by men of a background similar to that of the authors of the serious works. They are preoccupied with the identification of woman and body, a grotesque, broken body whose openness and uncontrollability is threatening to a social order founded on the superiority and dominance of mind, always gendered masculine. My reading of Isabelline literature resists the representation of feminine subjectivity as "a more or less obliging prop for the enactment of man's fantasies" (Irigaray, 25). But it is also resistant to traditional critical methodology. I have argued that in order to attain a more complete understanding of the complex and contradictory gender ideology of the literature produced in the second half of the fifteenth century in Spain, it is necessary to oppose the traditional critical tendency to consider these two strategies as separate and unequal in their cultural significance. Beginning with my initial confrontation of *Laberinto de Fortuna*, the paradigmatically high text of the fifteenth century with *Carajicomedia*, its anonymous obscene parody of the early sixteenth century, my analysis posits that the official and unofficial stories of Isabel's power and reign are inseparable from each other, that they are in fact mutually constructing. That is, the official image of Isabel as Virgin Mother feeds the unofficial representation of Isabel as devouring whore, and vice versa. They are two cultural manifestations of the same anxious, at times phobic, masculine response to her absolute and anomalous sovereign power.

These two responses to female sovereignty, the high and the low, are used to construct and affirm masculine identity in opposition to the feminine, whether that feminine is located in the female body of Isabel herself or in males whose bodies are "outed" as broken and therefore feminized. This is the case of the sodomitic saint Santilario discussed in chapter 1 or the *puto* king Enrique IV examined in chapter 3. I have also examined the imbrication of these exclusionary discursive practices in the forging of a European, Christian, masculine identity for the emerging nation of Spain, for example, in chapter 4's discussion of the discursive construction of Spain/Isabel as *corpus mysticum*, a body politic purged of contaminating ethnic and racial Others, a symbolic re-membering of the intact body of Visigothic Spain violated by the Moors in 711.

Both responses to Isabelline power have stood the test of time. Disturbing proof of the enduring vitality of the hagiographic fashioning of Isabel is her appropriation in the 1930s by the Spanish Falangist Party as an icon of the fascist "Second Reconquest" of Spain. In the regime of Francisco Franco (1939–75) "Saint Isabel," together with Saint Teresa of Ávila, became an instrument of National Catholic ideology, which grounded the stability and strength of the state in the patriarchal family.

In order to preserve the sanctity and purity of the family, the church and the Falange produced copious amounts of propaganda aimed at molding women into domestic "angels of the hearth" (Grothe, 514). Falangist propaganda promoting domesticity and feminine self-abnegation succeeded in reversing the real political and social gains Spanish women made during the Second Republic (1931–36), among them the right to divorce, to vote, and to hold public office. Confined to the home and pressured by natalist policies and Catholic teachings about the subjection of wives to husbands, women were urged to contribute to the rebuilding of a nation destroyed by the pernicious "modern" values of liberals, Jews, and Communists.

Interestingly, it was the Falange's women's auxiliary, the Sección Femenina, that was most successful at inculcating these Isabelline values in young unmarried Spanish women. Images of the Catholic Queen pervade the rhetoric of the Sección Femenina. Exalted as the archetypal Spanish woman, Isabel became the paramount feminine icon of Francoist reactionary and recuperative propaganda.[1] One of several magazines published by the Sección Femenina to dispense housekeeping and sentimental advice to Spanish girls and young women was titled simply *Y*, the first letter of Isabel's name in its original spelling. The "Ysabel" it held up as role model to its female readers was decidedly bourgeois: devoutly Catholic, yes, but also cheerful, domestic, thrifty, self-sacrificing, and maternal.

On more than one state occasion, General Franco himself promoted Isabel as a role model for Spanish womanhood. Perhaps the earliest instance occurred on May 30, 1939, during the first national demonstration in honor of Franco and the victorious Nationalist army. The celebration was organized by the Sección Femenina and was held at the Castillo de la Mota in Medina del Campo, where Isabel spent the last months of her life. The site inspired Franco to deliver the following eulogy:

> You may take the life of Queen Isabel of Spain as a case study. She also knew turbulent and materialistic times. She too was negligently raised among corruption and vice. Nonetheless, she was able to maintain her faith and the purity of her virtues. This is the example that you Spanish women of today must set. These women who in these gloomy places, which are more like stepmothers than mothers, have known how to preserve the purity of their religious and patriotic feelings.

Your work did not end at the front, with your aid to the liberated towns, with your work in the rivers, the freezing waters, washing our soldiers' clothes. You still have more to do. There remains the reconquest of the home. There remains the instilling of the moral character exemplified by the Queen who died behind these walls. (*Palabras del caudillo* [Words of the caudillo], 112–13)[2]

By the time a young woman came of age, she had already been well socialized by the National Catholic agenda for a dozen years, since the fascist construction of womanhood began in the gender-segregated primary school system. A primary school textbook assigned to children in the 1940s and 1950s is *España nuestra*. (Our Spain). This social studies text is noteworthy for being authored by Ernesto Giménez Caballero, a founding member of the Falange and the "most explicit and talented literary exponent of fascism" (Labanyi, 377).[3] A central character in Giménez Caballero's book is the paragon of piety, domesticity, and submissiveness, Isabel la Católica.

Giménez Caballero's lessons in Spanish history and geography are presented "wrapped in the lyric rapture" [envueltos en los arrebatos líricos] that Isabel often inspired in Falangist writers (Rodríguez-Puértolas, *Literatura fascista* 1:690). The queen makes her initial appearance as a possible answer to a geography riddle: "Riddle, riddle, who can guess which woman Spain resembles?" [Adivina, adivinanza, / a qué mujer / tiene España semejanza?] (Giménez Caballero, 21). Isabel is a good guess, the author suggests, and he illustrates that answer with a line drawing of Isabel's profile superimposed on a map of Spain (Figure 3) "as she appears to our Falangist eyes, which are obsessed with unity and tradition" [como la ven nuestros ojos falangistas, obsesionados de unidad y tradición] (21). The sketch of the crowned head of Isabel, as the head of state who first unified and purified Spain, links the Francoist concept of nationhood to that of the late-fifteenth- and early-sixteenth century on several symbolic levels: the Queen's profile faces westward, following the route that Columbus took; her crown serves to ward off possible interlopers from north of the Pyrenees; her serious countenance roughly covers the territory of Portugal.

The correct answer to Giménez Caballero's puzzle is less obvious, however, and reveals another, more hidden, connection, one that lies closer to the young reader's heart. The author instructs the child to open the family album, take out a picture of his mother, and paste it over a map

Figure 3. "España como la Reina Isabel" (Spain as Queen Isabel). From Ernesto Giménez Caballero, *España nuestra: El libro de las juventudes españolas* (Madrid: Ediciones de la Vicesecretaría de Educación Popular, 1943), 21.

of Spain that he has colored red (the color of blood spilled for the Caudillo) and yellow (the color of the Spanish soil where the Nationalists triumphed) (22). The child is directed to wear the homemade insignia "as if it were a sacred medal" [como si fuese una medalla sagrada] (23), that is, pinned inside the school uniform, underneath the Falangist emblem of five arrows and yoke that is sewn on the outside of the shirt pocket: "Everyone should see the proud insignia of the Falange.... But no one should see the medal showing Spain and your mother; it is to be worn on the inside, next to your skin; you alone should know that it's there" (23).[4] The triumphalist geography lesson culminates in the following injunction to defend the mother country:

> And you, Spanish boy, if anyone mocks or insults the name of God, or of Spain, or of your mother in your presence, don't hesitate! With your fists, with your teeth and your feet, attack him. And if you don't, you are a coward! You will no longer be allowed to wear that paper medal over your heart, nor the arrows on your shirt. And you, Spanish girl: if anyone mocks or insults the name of God, or of your mother, or of Spain in your presence, don't be ashamed to cry! Cry with sorrow, bitter, infinite, silent. (23)[5]

The gender stereotyping of the young readers of *España nuestra*—boys must respond aggressively and girls must weep and keep silent whenever "the motherland" [la madre patria] is insulted—is an important component of patriarchal ideologies in general and of fascism in particular. More immediately relevant to my study, however, is the conflation of nationalism, militarism, and motherhood with the idealized figure of Isabel, and the inscription of the values she represents on the very body of the child (the fascist badge worn next to the skin). Giménez Caballero fashions the Catholic Queen as the archetypal mother of the essential Spain whose values of religion, militarism, unity, authority, family, and National Catholicism must be revived if Spain is to carry forward its age-old mission. His textbook is a clear redeployment of the misogynist, racist fantasy that was so politically productive in the second half of the fifteenth century.

Giménez Caballero ends *España nuestra* with a particularly vivid version of that fantasy, appropriately cast as a fairy tale:

> Spain was a princess, the daughter of a very powerful king and of a very beautiful, sweet, and good queen. Spain would also be powerful when she inherited the throne. Although she was already, like her mother, good, gentle, and extremely beautiful. Everyone adored her.... But one day her mother the queen died. And shortly thereafter the king remarried a very bad and very envious woman.... This stepmother couldn't bear the beauty and power of the princess... finally, one day, through trickery, the stepmother achieved her envious goal, giving Spain a magic fruit that, as soon as it was eaten, plunged the princess into a deep, long, and seemingly fatal sleep: a spell. From which she could only be awakened by a Leader on a white horse who touched her on the forehead with his golden sword. (233)[6]

The anachronistic fashioning of Franco as a knight in shining armor is reinforced by medieval motifs in the regime's visual propaganda (Figure 4). In one mural, the Caudillo, dressed in full medieval battle armor and holding a massive phallic sword, is flanked by armed Nationalist soldiers. Above Franco the figure of Spain's patron saint Santiago charges into battle, a probable reference to the legend of the saint's miraculous intervention in the ninth-century battle of Clavijo against the Moors that was led by King Ramiro I of Asturias. A priest kneeling at the bottom right in prayer—whether to Santiago or to Franco is unclear—

Figure 4. *Alegoría de Francisco Franco* (Allegory of Francisco Franco). Mural painting by D. Reque Meruvia from the Archivo General Militar de Madrid, Calle Mártires de Alcalá 9, 28015 Madrid, Spain. Reproduced with permission from Archivo General Militar.

and a church bell tower visible in the upper left emphasize the religious goals of the regime. Surrounded by a heavenly nimbus, Franco here appears as a dashing medieval warrior prince, heaven-sent to destroy modern Spain's godless enemies and to revive the poisoned body politic of the sleeping beauty Spain/Isabel. He is simultaneously related to King Ramiro of Asturias, to Santiago, its patron saint, and to its saintly warrior queen Isabel, who brought the original Reconquest to a glorious conclusion.[7]

According to Francoist triumphalist imagery, the providential role of Spain under Franco's leadership is to be the world's "spiritual guide"

Figure 5. "Cruzada: España orientadora espiritual del mundo" (Crusade: Spain, spiritual guide of the world). Poster from Franco era.

("orientadora espiritual" on the globe-spanning motto in Figure 5). By leading the so-called Second Reconquest, he becomes both Isabel's successor and her savior, a contradictory self-gendering that draws on the similarly complex medieval fashioning of Isabel.[8]

It is not surprising that the dialectical construction of Isabel as virgin and whore continues to this day, nor perhaps that the balance between praising and dissing has shifted significantly toward the latter. As they did in the last quarter of the fifteenth century, in the second half of the twentieth century writers in Spain, Latin America, and elsewhere "dethroned" the official "Isabel." As a kind of epilogue to my study, I will examine four of these writers, three of whom are male: Alejo Carpentier from Cuba, the Spaniard Juan Goytisolo, who lives in France and Algeria, and Salman Rushdie, an Indian living in exile in England. Their bawdy portrayals of Isabel echo (although they are all, except for Goytisolo, doubtless unaware of the fact) the medieval fashioning of Isabel not as the head of the body politic, but rather as its cunt, not as virgin, but as whore.⁹

El arpa y la sombra (The harp and the shadow), published in 1979, is Alejo Carpentier's last novel. Carpentier stated that the work was inspired by a radio broadcast he had prepared in 1937 based on Paul Claudel's laudatory verse drama of 1929, *Le livre de Cristophe Colomb* (The book of Christopher Columbus): "I felt irritated by the hagiographic intent of a text that attributed superhuman values to the Discoverer of America. Later I ran across an incredible book by Leon Bloy, where the great Catholic writer urged nothing less than the canonization of the person he compared, straightforwardly, to Moses and Saint Peter" (back cover).¹⁰

Two plots intertwine in *El arpa y la sombra*. The protagonist of the frame story is Pope Pius IX, who is faced with a beatification cause submitted in favor of Columbus. The pope must base his decision for or against beatification on a dossier similar to the one compiled for Isabel under Franco in that it has been assembled from works written in different eras, including Columbus's own reconstructed journal, *Diario del primer viaje*. The protagonist of the embedded narration is Columbus himself, as he lies on his deathbed awaiting the Franciscan friar who will hear his final confession.

Isabel features prominently in the explorer's reminiscences. He recalls that she wore the pants in the royal family—"I found the Aragonese King to be silly, weak, and without character, dominated by his condescending wife" (*Harp*, 62) (83)¹¹—and that she was arrogant and condescending to Columbus in their first interview. By their second interview, in the military camp of Santa Fe during the final siege of Granada, her attitude toward him and his audacious plan had changed dramatically. That night sovereign and sailor began a sexual affair and the latter gave new meaning to one of his professional rules of conduct: "I had never liked doing business with women, except in bed, and it was clear that at this court it was the woman who was on top and gave the orders" (*Harp*, 62) (84).¹² From then on, Columbus insists, "there has been only one woman for me in the world, the world that still waited *for me* to be fulfilled" (*Harp*, 67) (91).¹³

It is significant that Columbus's praise of his royal lover partakes of the imagery common to early-modern discourses of exploration and colonization that relate the dangerous "discovery" of new lands and their treasures to the equally perilous—and equally exciting—"opening up" of the secrets of the mysterious female body (Parker, "Fantasies"). Carpentier thereby conflates the exploration and conquest of Isabel's body with the exploration and conquest of the Indies. Columbus underscores the connection in the pet name he uses with his royal inamorata: "Columba." On one level the endearment reinscribes the ambiguous gender identity we have seen the Queen's panegyrists assign to her. At the same time, it operates as a sign of the feminization that Columbus must endure in order to secure his goal, a marker of the anxiety caused by his dependence on this powerful and capricious woman to make his dream come true. Months go by during which, "In the nights of our intimacy, *Columba*... promised me three caravels, ten caravels, fifty caravels, a hundred caravels, all the caravels I wanted; but at daybreak, the caravels evaporated, and... so I began to ask myself whether my destiny was to end up being just another one of the many men in love with the Queen" (my emphasis) (*Harp*, 67–68) (102).[14]

Critics have uncovered another layer of significance in the Columbus/Isabel affair imagined by Carpentier. Roberto González Echevarría has pointed out the autobiographical element in *El arpa y la sombra*, that Columbus's dying ruminations function as Carpentier's meditation on his own career: "Carpentier, whose most obsessive preoccupation was with the origin or beginning of Latin American literary discourse... transfigures himself into Columbus, the first narrator in Latin American literary history. The origin, then, is a pack of lies, and the inaugural figure a lecher who has gone to bed with none other than Queen Isabella of Castile" (289). Through his self-identification with Columbus's imagined confession and failed beatification trial, Carpentier half-humorously calls himself to account for his own prevarications in the writing of Latin American fictions (290). In his final work, according to González Echevarría, Carpentier achieves the precarious harmony inherent in the truest of confessions, "the one that avers that all confessions are false, that being is the telling of false tales about being" (291).

What González Echevarría does not say is that to the extent that Columbus in *El arpa y la sombra* is Carpentier's alter ego, the Italian explorer's erotic entanglement with Isabel expresses the Cuban writer's own anxious dependence on an all-powerful and assertively sexual feminine source for his ongoing "invention" of America. If being is the telling of false tales about being, not the least of those false tales has to do with masculine self-sufficiency and preeminence, because, like all fantasies of identity, this one depends on its excluded other, in this case, the feminine.

The idea of Isabel as lubricious and capricious has captured the imagination of another contemporary writer concerned with deconstructing myths of nationhood. Salman Rushdie's brief tale "Christopher and Columbus and Queen Isabella of Spain Consummate Their Relationship (Santa Fe, A.D. 1492)" first appeared in the collection *East/West*, published in 1994. The date suggests that the debates surrounding the Columbus quincentenary may have inspired the story. "Christopher Columbus and Queen Isabella" is included in the "West" section of the volume, along with two tales that reimagine fictional works. The first of these retells *Hamlet* from the decentered point of view of Yorick; the second imagines the auctioning of the ruby red slippers worn by Dorothy in *The Wizard of Oz*. The implication is clear: the "historical" Columbus and Isabel are fictional constructs just as much as the creations of Shakespeare and Frank Baum (or Hollywood).

Rushdie's description of the long, frustrating months that Columbus spent seeking an audience with the Queen is very much like Carpentier's, but perhaps because it uses third-person point of view rather than first, its portrait of Columbus is even less flattering than Carpentier's. Rushdie weaves into his tale a kind of chorus composed of Isabel's advisers, men easily identifiable with some of the writers discussed in my study, Gómez Manrique or Iñigo de Mendoza, for example. They criticize the foreigner's gaudy dress, his drunkenness, and his increasingly pathetic pleas for "consummation." At the same time, the behavior of the "tyrant" Isabel toward her humble suppliant resembles that of the high-handed whores of *Carajicomedia*, as she alternately invites the explorer to fondle her breasts and banishes him to the pigsty. "Toying with Columbus pleases the Queen," the narrator explains (109). The frustrated suppliant himself laments that "[t]he search for money and patronage . . . is not so different from the quest for love" (112).

In his iconoclastic portrayal of Isabel, Rushdie expresses the same anxious awareness of the inseparability of the private and the public, of sexual politics and the politics of nation and empire formation, as Carpentier. The following passage illustrates the anxiety:

The sexual appetites of the male decline; those of the female continue, with the advancing years, to grow. Isabella is Columbus's last hope. He is running out of possible patrons, sales talk, flirtatiousness, hair, steam. Time drags by.

Isabella gallops around, winning battles, expelling Moors from their strongholds, her appetites expanding by the week. The more of the land she swallows, the more warriors she engulfs, the hungrier she gets. Columbus, aware of a slow shrivelling inside him, scolds himself.... What chance does he have here? Some days she makes him clean latrines. On other days he is on body-washing duty, and after a battle the bodies are not clean. Soldiers going to war wear man-sized diapers under their armour because the fear of death will open the bowels, will do it every time. Columbus was not cut out for this sort of work. He tells himself to leave Isabella, once and for all. (111–12)

The evocation of Isabel's lust and fickleness, of the depiction of the Admiral of the Seas cleaning latrines, and of the warriors of the Reconquest defecating in their armor are important elements in Rushdie's travesty of the Isabelline myth. Central to his revisioning of this crucial moment in world history is the uncontrollability and unpredictability of the woman on top on whom the discovery of the "New" World depends. The pigsty, the latrine, and the diapers in Rushdie's tale mark and mock the anxiety of all the Queen's men, those whose lives and fortunes depend on a monarch who is, first and foremost, a woman, and therefore, like all women, capricious, voracious, lubricious, and unrestrained. They are the material signs of the fear of the monstrous feminine that threatens masculine private and public dominance.

As had to happen in order for history to be written, Columbus gets his wish for consummation, a symbolic marriage to Isabel (whose real husband the narrator has already declared "an absolute zero: a blank" [110]). The Queen abruptly calls Columbus back to court after he has wandered away in despair, and she imparts her decision to accept his suit. The narrator explains that the decision was the result of a vision the Queen had while staring into a blood-filled fountain in the Moorish palace of Alhambra shortly after her reconquest of Granada. Recognizing that Spain is now completely hers, to do with as she pleases, she realizes that "she will never, never, NEVER! be satisfied by the possession of the Known. Only the Unknown, perhaps even the Unknowable, can satisfy her" (116). Columbus, in Rushdie's view, wins the right to sail off into the unknown because of the insatiable thirst for power, the overweening ambition of a woman who refuses to respect boundaries.

Although the goal of Carpentier's and Rushdie's festive rewriting of the official story of Isabel and Columbus is obviously to interrogate the myths surrounding Spain's early-modern hegemony, their deconstruction of the Queen's "official story" registers anxieties of masculinity not unrelated to those provoked in her panegyrists and detractors from the fifteenth century on. On these grounds—the threat of the feminine to masculine identity and power—the postmodern and the premodern converge.

The most fiercely iconoclastic portrayal of "Isabel" in modern literature is without a doubt that created by Juan Goytisolo (1931–) in his 1970 novel *Reivindicación del conde don Julián* (Count Julian).[15] The narrator-protagonist of the work is a Spanish exile in Morocco who fantasizes a second Moorish invasion that would destroy Franco's Spain and the historical, religious, and sexual myths that sustain it. As the title of Goytisolo's work indicates, the ballad cycle of King Rodrigo and the "destruction" of Spain is one of the most prominent of the numerous intertexts satirized throughout the novel. In this biting travesty of official historical and philosophical discourse, Goytisolo takes on the national myths propagated by the Generation of '98, Francoist propagandists, modern historians Ramón Menéndez Pidal and Claudio Sánchez Albornoz, among many others. Like a latter-day Count Julian, the narrator gazes at the coastline of Spain from his home in Tangier, the place from which Tariq launched his eighth-century invasion of Visigothic Spain, and imagines his revenge on the repressive society that formed, or rather deformed, him intellectually, psychologically, and sexually. The very first words of the novel take us deep into the bitter expatriate's alienation from his native land: "Harsh homeland, the falsest, the most miserable imaginable, I shall never return to you" (*Julian*, 3) [tierra ingrata, entre todas espuria y mezquina, jamás volveré a ti] (83).

Goytisolo's belief in the connection between sexual and intellectual freedom of expression is central to his violent deconstruction of official Spain in *Don Julián*. In a 1971 interview he commented that "Spain is a living example of the fact that to repress sex is the equivalent of repressing intelligence and repressing intelligence is the equivalent of repressing sex. If the peninsula has not had a French Revolution, nor stable democratic governments, neither has it had a Laclos or a Baudelaire and much less a Sade" (quoted in Levine, *Juan Goytisolo,* 47).[16] The greater sexual freedom permitted in Islamic society, particularly as regards male homosexuality, is, in the narrator's view, responsible for "the infantile preference for Romans and Visigoths and the morbid phobia against Jews and Muslims" [el favoritismo infantil por romanos y visigodos y la fobia morbosa contra hebreos y musulmanes] (Goytisolo, "Supervivencias," 146) that marks the historiographical record of Spain from the Middle Ages on. It is that phobic reaction of Christian Spain to its Islamic and Jewish elements that motivates Goytisolo's vindication of the "traitor" Don Julián.

The fluid nature of many of the characters in *Don Julián* is the formal counterpart to Goytisolo's thematic undoing of the damage inflicted by the repressive social, moral, and religious values that undergird Spain's patriarchal, homophobic national identity. Created in opposition to the rigid hierarchization of categories of gender, sexuality, and race that characterize "the official, imposed verisimilitude" [lo verosímil oficial impuesto] (quoted in Levine, *Juan Goytisolo* 26, n. 33), many of Goytisolo's characters metamorphose freely throughout the novel, changing age, gender, and ethnicity. One of these protean characters is Isabel la Católica.

Isabel first appears as the mother of Don Alvaro Peranzules, also known as Seneca, the archetypical Castilian, "a purebred Spaniard whose Iberian lineage goes back many generations" (*Julian*, 93) [carpetovetónico por los cuatro costados de su linaje] (183).[17] The narrator describes Isabel as beautiful, sad-eyed, and elegant: "thoroughly self-disciplined, possessed of an intense spiritual life, she bore up under the rude shocks that life inflicted upon her with a serenity and strength of character that we might be tempted to describe as stoic were it not for the fact that they are perhaps more accurately described as typically Spanish" (*Julian*, 94) (184).[18] Later in the novel, the dignified and melancholy mother of Alvaro is transformed into his blonde and nun-like daughter. Observed by the narrator, she unzips her habit to reveal black silk pajamas and then performs a seductive striptease dance to the music of the Rolling Stones: "revealing the incomparable perfection of her soft, shapely limbs: long legs, but not spindly ones: open like a compass, firm and round, her thighs converging on the half-glimpsed treasure, like two peremptory traffic signs: one-way traffic, an arbitrary law that Hispanos obey like a flock of sheep and only the traitor dares to disregard!" (*Julián*, 138–39) (234).[19]

The metamorphosis of Isabel continues as she merges with the image of a sensual mulatta dancer in a James Bond movie seen earlier by the narrator. This titillating passage culminates in a tour of one of Spain's most unique and awe-inspiring sites, "an unforgettable, instructive excursion down into the depths, the folds, and the secret hiding places of the Theological Bastion: a tour of the interior of the sanctum sanctorum that ... you used to refer to as the Remote, Fantastic, Sacred Grotto from Whose Bourne No Traveler Has Ever Returned" (*Julian*, 140) (235–36).[20] In other words, a tour of Isabel's reproductive organs. This stylistic tour de force assimilates the difficult penetration of Isabel's virginal dark cave to Aeneas's epic journey to the underworld: "you will throw a honeycomb in the famished, greedy, triple mouth of Cerberus and take advantage of his sudden drowsiness to steal past him into the Fallopian tubes" (*Julián*, 143) [239]).[21]

Goytisolo's fantasy of revenge is without a doubt the most corrosively negative among the modern deconstructions of the hagiographic myth of Isabel. A contemporary recasting of the pornographic *Carajicomedia*, it is boldly direct in calling Isabel a whore. In this way, the author rejects the myth of "Saint Isabel" created during Isabel's reign and reaffirmed during the Francoist regime and affirms his solidarity with the victims of her vision of a Spanish nation: "If I feel any sense of solidarity, it is never with the image of the nation that emerges in the reign of the Catholic Monarchs, rather with its victims: Jews, Muslims, new Christians, Lutherans, Encyclopedists, liberals, anarchists, Marxists" (quoted in Lee Six, 79).[22]

It must be said, however, that the admiration for Islamic society expressed throughout *Don Julián* and the author's condemnation of Isabel for her part in eliminating Muslim culture from Spain are problematic. In fact, the displaced abjection onto women that we saw operate in the carnivalesque world of *Carajicomedia* is very much in evidence in *Reivindicación de Don Julián*. First, by stripping the virgin (or having her strip) in order to reveal the whore, Goytisolo merely inverts the terms in the misogynist binary that fashions "Isabel." Second, his anachronistic maurophile fantasy of invading Spain together with the fantasy of invading Isabel's vagina reinscribes the anxious masculinist identification of woman and (unexplored, unconquered) land. Finally, the sexual and intellectual freedom Goytisolo ascribes to Muslim society ignores the profound lack of freedom that many Muslim women and gay men suffer.[23]

Precisely because Goytisolo's obscene vindication of the Christian traitor Count Julián does not eliminate the damaging effects of misogyny from Spain's cultural legacy, its attack on the destructive effects of homophobia cannot succeed fully. Both cultural constructs, the charges of treason against Don Julián for occasioning Spain's violation by the despised other and the celebration of Isabel for prosecuting Julián's crime, will remain productive and destructive until the Orientalized Cava is vindicated as well.

The last modern work that deconstructs the saintly image of Isabel that I will discuss is also the most recent, and the only one known to have been written by a woman.[24] It is *El cuarto de atrás* (The backroom), Carmen Martín Gaite's (1925–2001) autobiographical novel about growing up female during the Franco dictatorship. Published in 1978, the novel exposes the fascist appropriation of Isabel's gender and sexuality for purposes of denying women their rights. The backroom of the novel's title is both literal and metaphorical. The literal backroom is the one located off of the back hall of the apartment in Salamanca where the narrator "C." grew up (her birthdate, December 8, 1925, the same as the author's, is an important temporal marker in the novel). The narrator relates how she used the backroom as a playroom, a refuge from adult rules and supervision. In that large room smelling of eraser and paste, she felt free, free to read, sing at the top of her lungs, jump on the old sofa, stain the rug with ink, and play with the toys stored in the old chestnut sideboard. These freedoms came to an abrupt end when she turned eleven in 1936, also the start of the civil war, an event that she sees as marking "a sort of dividing line, separating childhood and adulthood" (*Back Room*, 187) [una línea divisoria ... entre la infancia y el crecimiento] (187–88). The disagreeable mingling of the smells of erasers and glue with those of the hoarded sausages and stewed partridges that displaced her toys in the old sideboard marks the end of the narrator's preschool freedom and the beginning of forty years of Francoist repression.

On another level, the backroom references the "attic of one's brain" (*Back Room*, 85) [desván del cerebro] (91), the storehouse of painful memories of three years of civil war and thirty-six years of dictatorship that the protagonist has repressed. As mentioned earlier, the considerable rights and freedoms won by Spanish women under the Second Republic (1931–36) were quickly revoked by Franco. Feminism in Falangist ideology was constituted as a clear threat to the *patria* (Grothe, 529) and to the masculine dominance in which it was grounded.[25] That threat had to be countered by "the sacrificial nature of fascism, its cult of pain, abnegation, and submission, its exploitation of religious and maternal feelings [which] tied in perfectly with the characteristics of the feminine stereotype that remains valid to this day" (Gallego Méndez, 13).[26] No cloud of doubt or complaint must be allowed to cast a shadow over the cheerful and industrious housewifery urgently required in order to recover Spain's national identity, damaged by Jews, intellectuals, and Communists.

Commenting on her early education, Carmen Martín Gaite's protagonist places the deficient, propagandistic curriculum of the public schools (which could well have included Giménez Caballero's *España nuestra*) alongside more violent means used to control the population and stifle resistence: "I could tell him that... we lived surrounded by ignorance and repression. I could tell him about those textbooks with all sorts of things missing that kept us from getting a decent education, about the friends of my parents put to death by a firing squad or driven into exile" (*Back Room*, 64) (69).[27]

C. also recalls with bitterness her time spent in the Servicio Social program, one of Franco's primary agents for socializing young women into the National Catholic ideology of separate spheres and "true Catholic womanhood" (Morcillo Gómez, 51). Instituted by government decree in 1937 and overseen by the Sección Femenina, the program was obligatory for all unmarried Spanish women between the ages of seventeen and thirty. It consisted of one year of ideological indoctrination and community service. The first six months of the program were spent in learning domestic skills such as sewing and child care, and the last six were designed to put those skills to use in community service, often imparting health, hygiene, and child-care education to rural families. Proof of completion of Servicio Social was necessary in order to obtain a passport, a professional degree, a civil service post, and to be allowed to compete for university posts or hold public office (Gallego Méndez, 64). Martín Gaite's protagonist attributes her own difficulties in accepting a scholarship to study in Portugal to this governmental program: "A girl couldn't leave the country without having completed her Social Service, or at the very least having given a good indication, during the course of her studies at the university, that she had the makings of a good future wife and mother, a worthy descendent of Queen Isabella" (*Back Room*, 36) (42).[28]

No cloud of doubt or complaint must be allowed to cast a shadow over the cheerful and industrious housewifery and motherhood that was required to recover Spain's national integrity, damaged by Jews, Communists, and intellectuals. The fifty-year-old narrator of *El cuarto de atrás* vividly recalls the kind of indoctrination into piety, domesticity, wifeliness, and patriotism that she received as a child:

> Happiness was a reward for having done one's duty and was the diametrical opposite of doubt.... Queen Isabella never gave herself a moment's respite, never doubted. Proud of her legacy, we would learn to make the sign of the cross on our children's foreheads, to air a room, to make use of every last scrap of cardboard and meat, to remove stains, to knit mufflers and wash window curtains, to smile at our husband when he came home in a bad mood, to tell him that *tanto monta monta tanto Isabel como Fernando*, [Isabel and Fernando are equal partners], that that domestic economy helps to safeguard the national economy and that garlic is excellent for the bronchial tubes. We would learn to apply a bandage, to decorate a kitchen so that it looked cute as anything, to keep our skin from chapping and cracking and to ready with our own hands the layette for the baby destined to come into the world to be proud of the Catholic Queen, defend her from calumny, and engender children who in turn would extol her, till the end of time. (*Back Room*, 89–90) (96)[29]

Even as a child, however, Martín Gaite's narrator harbored doubts about the saintly image of Isabel that surrounded her. Gazing at the stern visage reproduced on the pages of *Y*, one of Sección Femenina's magazines for girls and young women, she found it difficult to believe the stories of the queen's unwavering cheerfulness. Similarly, she doubted the messianism and triumphalism of Isabel's official story as presented in her schoolbooks, "where each step, journey, or decision of the queen appeared to bear the mark of a superior and inevitable destiny" (*Back Room*, 98) (104).[30]

Symbolic of the persistence of this resistance to Falangist propaganda is the engraving of a topsy-turvy world that C. has hung on her wall. Its forty-eight drawings depict absurd reversals of natural phenomena: fish flying through the air and lions swimming in the sea, a sheep carrying a crook and herding two shepherds, the sun and moon encrusted in the earth beneath a sky filled with buildings, a man holding a scythe and chasing after a frightened personification of Death. The print is the axiological antithesis of the Falangist images of order, unity, and hierarchy, and it symbolizes the narrator's youthful self—intelligent, imaginative, transgressive. Slowly, with the help of a mysterious visitor, part interviewer, part lover, part therapist, the narrator recuperates that repressed youthful self. Only then is she able to overcome her writer's block and to complete the fantastic novel that she has been trying to write, and that at the novel's end proves, fantastically, to be the one we are reading.

I first read *El cuarto de atrás* while working on the essay on *Carajicomedia* that became the first chapter of this book. A late-medieval example of the kind of topsy-turvy admired by Martín Gaite's narrator, *Carajicomedia* fascinated me in part because of its exclusion from the Hispano-medieval canon. It became clear to me that, like the literal dirt that the servants battled in the immaculate home of C.'s grandparents, the literary dirt of *Carajicomedia* and similar texts had been swept under the carpet for centuries. Furthermore, I saw the exclusion of such literary filth from the Hispano-medieval canon as a political act not unrelated to the masculinist exclusion of women and feminized others from the imagined community of Spain whose medieval foundations I have explored here. As I delightedly "lost my way" in the obscenity of *Carajicomedia* and later, *Pleyto del manto,* I came to understand that they represent the dirty "backroom" of the kind of official Isabelline ideology that was still flourishing five hundred years after her death.

A second realization soon followed, however, and that was that *Carajicomedia*'s festive inversion of Mena's exalted patriotic discourse is itself problematic, for even as it critiques the repressive, authoritarian, militaristic political agenda that Mena urges on Isabel's father, Juan II, it attacks even more harshly the monstrous appropriation of that agenda by his daughter and successor. If, on one level, *Carajicomedia* and similar texts of the late fifteenth century open the door and shed light on the Isabelline backroom, on another level they close it even more tightly. Nevertheless, the messy, creative child of *El cuarto de atrás* and her grown-up self, the author of fantastic fiction, descend at least partially from the dirty-minded author of *Carajicomedia,* both voicing dissenting views of the most Catholic of queens.

From a feminist perspective, Martín Gaite's subversion of the Isabelline fairy tale used to scare girls from straying from the "right" path is the most radical of the four studied in this Conclusion. It is a rewriting of the story of Hansel and Gretel that rejects both its gendered models: that of the hero Hansel, who uses his wit and pluck to find a way home, and that of his sister Gretel, who passively follows along:

> "Do you know what my answer to your question is? Yes, I believe in the Devil and in giant Saint Christopher and in blessed Barbara—in all mysterious beings, in a word. But not in Queen Isabella."
> "I'm glad," he says. "You're beginning to lose your way again."
> "What do you mean?"
> "The one you thought you found in the second part of *The Spa*,[31] the way back. Do you remember the tale of Tom Thumb *[Hansel and Gretel]*?"
> "Yes, of course, why?"
> "When he left a trail of breadcrumbs in order to find his way back, the birds ate them. He was annoyed, so the next time he left little pebbles, and by so doing he didn't get lost, or at any rate that's what Perrault believed, that he didn't lose his way, but I'm not so sure, do you follow me?" (*Back Room*, 100) (105)[32]

That uncertainty, that openness to what lies beyond the path and outside of received wisdom is perhaps a good way to end this book. Not, certainly, with the usual fairy-tale ending "and they lived happily ever after."

Notes

Introduction

1. The Council argued that "Isabel's actions flatly contradict the teachings of Vatican Council II on religious liberty" (Woodward, 67). Throughout this book, all translations into English are my own, unless otherwise indicated. I am enormously grateful to Ronald Surtz for his help in translating the texts, especially those loaded with obsure colloquialisms and puns.

2. The news appeared in the newspaper *El Mundo* on March 3, 2002 (Vidal). The newspaper *El País* revealed that only two-thirds of the eighty-one bishops on the Council voted in favor of the proposal (Bedoya). Unlike in 1958, however, in 2002 there was outspoken opposition to the beatification of Isabel. The following trenchant critique appeared on the World Wide Web page of the Asamblea de Andalucía: "No han bastado... que la muy reina Isabel, en compañía de su muy noble marido, Don Fernando, obligara mediante la fuerza bautizar (para cristianizarlos) a los musulmanes y judíos, ni que se utilizara para ello la tortura, el pillaje, o el asesinato" [It is not enough that her royal highness Isabel, together with her very noble husband, Don Fernando, forced baptism on the Muslims and Jews (in order to Christianize them), nor that in order to bring that about torture, pillage, or murder was used]. The Asamblea defines itself as "una federación de partidos políticos andaluces que busca la unidad de todos los que trabajan por un proyecto político, social, cultural y económico que respete las características propias del pueblo andaluz" [a federation of Andalusian political parties that seeks to unite everyone working on a political, social, cultural, and economic project that respects the unique characteristics of the Andalusian people] (http://asambleadeandalucia.org).

3. For the biographical sketch that follows, I have relied on Azcona and Liss.

4. Materialist-feminist criticism repudiates idealist and universalist categories of "woman" and "patriarchy." Instead, it engages the historical specificity of women's oppression by attending to the social and economic conditions that promote it (Belsey, "Afterword," 257–58). It was initially formulated by British cultural critics in the late 1970s. See, for example, the work of Catherine Belsey, Michele Barrett,

and Annette Kuhn and Ann Marie Wolpe, all heavily influenced by Marxist theory. It was adapted in the United States by critics such as Judith Newton and Deborah Rosenfelt. For a useful introduction to materialist feminism as applied to the early-modern period in England, see the volume edited by Valerie Wayne. Two applications of the method to fifteenth-century Spanish texts are Michael Gerli's discussion of the body of Melibea (protagonist of Fernando de Rojas's *Celestina* [1499]) as a "site for cultural negotiation" ("Dismembering," 372) and Michael Solomon's book on the conjunction of women and illness in the misogynistic discourse of *Arcipreste de Talavera* and Jacme Roig's *Spill*. For a similar treatment of poetry of the same period, see my "'Deceitful Sects.'"

5. For an early outline of the distinguishing features of new historicism, see Howard and Greenblatt's introduction to Greenblatt's *Power of Forms*. New historicism parallels the English critical movement of cultural materialism to some extent, but diverges from it in its more historicized approach.

6. I am particularly indebted to the work of Carol Levin, Leah S. Marcus, Phyllis Rackin, Louis Montrose, Jonathan Goldberg, and Stephen Greenblatt on Elizabeth I of England.

7. Montrose's explanation of Elizabeth I of England's complex fashioning is equally applicable to Isabel: "The historical subject, Elizabeth Tudor, was no more than a privileged agent in the production of the royal image. At a fundamental level, all Elizabethan subjects may be said to have participated in a ceaseless and casual process of producing and reproducing 'The Queen' in their daily practices. . . . But she was also rather more systematically and consciously fashioned by those Elizabethan subjects who were specifically engaged in production of the texts, icons, and performances in which the queen was variously represented to her people, to her court, to foreign powers and (of course) to Elizabeth herself ("Elizabethan Subject," 317–18).

8. The classic formulation of fifteenth-century *converso* messianism by Castro is the essay "Mesianismo, espiritualismo y actitud personal," published in *Aspectos del vivir hispánico* (1970) but written years earlier, at the end of the Spanish civil war "con miras a entender ciertos extraños procesos de la historia hispana" [with the goal of understanding certain strange processes of Hispanic history] (9).

9. See Rackin for a cogent discussion of medieval gender ideology in which "the body itself, male as well as female, tended to fall on the wrong side of the binary opposition that divided masculine from feminine gender. Woman, said Saint Jerome, is 'different from man as body is from soul'" ("Foreign Country," 75).

10. This is true of Gómez Manrique, Iñigo de Mendoza, Alfonso de Palencia, Fernando del Pulgar, and Juan de Flores.

11. Castro's polemic with Claudio Sánchez Albornoz set the tone; Maravall shifted the terms somewhat *(Estado moderno, El concepto de España)*. Most recently, the debate has had to respond to the provocative findings of historians (e.g., Freund and Ruiz; Netanyahu; Roth) concerning Spain's failed *convivencia* among Christians, Jews, and Muslims. See, for example, Gerli ("Antón de Montoro" and "Performing Nobility"), Hutcheson ("Cracks"), Kaplan, Seidenspinner-Núñez.

12. Paul Julian Smith was one of the first to apply contemporary literary theory, primarily deconstruction and feminism, to the study of the originary differences on which Hispanic culture was founded. He acknowledges the enormous contributions of Castro and his disciples but points out their tendency to slip into essentialism

(*Representing the Other*, 46–51). He also notes the scarcity of theoretically framed studies of the discursive fashioning of Spain's national identity: "While the problem of national identity is perhaps the quintessential problem in Hispanic studies (for Spanish and Latin American nationhood can never be taken for granted, is always the object of struggle) it remains the case that little of the vast Hispanic literature on the subject draws on contemporary continental theory" (1).

13. I adapt the phrase "rewritten the Renaissance" from *Rewriting the Renaissance*, an important collection of essays edited by Ferguson, Quilligan, and Vickers. The total omission of Iberia from this important volume is an indication of its continuing critical marginalization from new-historicist medieval and early-modern European studies.

14. An excellent example is Richard C. Trexler's *Sex and Conquest: Gendered Violence, Political Order, and the European Conquest of the Americas*.

15. Beginning with the two-volume *Nuevas perspectivas sobre la mujer,* published in 1982 (see entry under Gómez Mampaso), the work of the Seminario de Estudios de la Mujer of the Universidad Autónoma in Madrid has been published as the proceedings of its annual conference. Also important is the group of feminist historians associated with the Asociación Cultural Al-Mudayna of the Universidad Complutense of Madrid.

16. Alan Deyermond was instrumental in the critical recuperation of all three writers; see especially his "Spain's First Women Writers." On Teresa de Cartagena, see chapter 1 of Surtz, *Writing Women,* and Seidenspinner-Núñez, *Teresa de Cartagena.* Ayerbe-Chaux was among the first to study López de Córdoba. Mirrer's *Women* devotes a chapter to that writer and another to Florencia Pinar. On Pinar, also see Deyermond, ("The Worm and the Partridge"), Fulks, and Weissberger ("Critics").

17. For an early theoretical orientation, see Sullivan; also Lacarra, "Notes on Feminist Analysis," and volume 1 of Díaz-Diocaretz and Zavala. Influential feminist studies in Spanish include María Milagros Rivera Garretas's *Textos y espacios de mujeres (Europa, siglos IV–XV),* the two-volume *Breve historia feminista de la literatura española (en lengua castellana),* edited by Díaz-Diocaretz and Zavala (see especially volume 1, on theory), and the collective volumes *La voz del silencio,* edited by Cristina Segura Graiño. Louise Mirrer's *Women, Jews, and Muslims in the Texts of Reconquest Spain* systematically applies gender and sexuality as categories of analysis to a wide range of medieval Iberian texts from Gonzalo de Berceo to fifteenth-century ballads. The subtle feminist analysis of the visions of late-medieval female religious provided by Ronald E. Surtz in *The Guitar of God* and *Writing Women in Late Medieval and Early Modern Spain* greatly contributes to our understanding of the interrelationship of gender and spirituality in the reign of Isabel and her grandson Carlos I. Catherine Brown and Michael Solomon have advanced our understanding of the discourse of clerical misogyny in late-medieval Spain with their very different but complementary studies of Martínez de Toledo's *Arcipreste de Talavera* or *Corbacho.* Finally, the groundbreaking anthology *Queer Iberia: Sexualities, Cultures, and Crossings from the Middle Ages to the Renaissance,* edited by Josiah Blackmore and Gregory Hutcheson, includes several essays that examine the literary representation of sexual difference in fifteenth-century Iberia. Useful bibliographies of criticism on medieval women and women writers have been compiled by Deyermond ("Las autoras") and Mérida Jiménez. See also the more general "Mujeres, misóginos y feministas en la literatura española" by María Angeles Durán and M. D. Temprano.

18. Much more work has been done on Isabel II (1833–43) and the bourgeois ideology that shapes the representation of her power (see Charnon-Deutsch, chapter 3 and bibliography).

19. The affirmation of Isabel's role as queen consort to Ferdinand rather than queen regnant is a long-standing one. Baltasar Gracián's observation in *El político* regarding Fernando's reliance on Isabel is typical of this denial of Isabel's authority: "But what most helped Fernando be endowed with happiness and heroic gifts is the never sufficiently praised queen Doña Isabel, his Catholic consort, that great princess who, being a woman, surpassed the limitations of a man. The good and prudent woman causes much good, just as the imprudent one causes much ill" [Pero lo que más le ayudó a Fernando para ser príncipe consumado de felicidad y heroicas prendas es la nunca bastantemente alabada reina doña Isabel, su católica consorte, aquella gran princesa que, siendo mujer, excedió los límites de varón. Acarrea mucho bien la buena y prudente mujer, así como la imprudente mucho mal] (59).

20. "Tiene derecho a que se la entienda desde el orden de valores en ella y en su tiempo imperantes. Hoy propendemos a actitudes opuestas de hedonismo materialista como si los problemas y objetivos políticos, sociales y económicos fuesen metas y no medios para servir al hombre."

21. "Confundimos, en nuestros días, dos conceptos tan diametralmente opuestos como amor y pasión, pues el primero es entrega y la segunda concupiscencia. Una vez dado el paso decisivo... Isabel escogió su camino e hizo del deber de esposa todo un edificio de amor, pacientemente construido."

22. "demonstrando con ello que no era ningún obstáculo la femineidad para governar, sino más bien lo contrario."

23. The 1992 edition of *Isabel la Católica: Estudio crítico de su vida y su reinado* is an updating of the original, published in 1964.

24. The term *dissing* appears in the title of Julia Walker's edited volume on negative representations of Elizabeth.

25. I borrow the phrase "nuptial fiction" from Abby Zanger's study of the marriage of Louis XIV of France and María Teresa of Spain.

1. Anxious Masculinity

1. This chapter is an expanded version of a paper delivered at the conference "Poetry at Court in Trastamaran Spain: From the *Cancionero de Baena* to the *Cancionero general*," held at Georgetown University, Washington, D.C., February 11–14, 1993, later published in a volume of the same name. I am grateful to E. Michael Gerli and Julian Weiss, organizers of the conference and editors of the volume, for providing a venue where the ideas that later grew into this book could first be shared and critiqued.

2. Cf. Sheila Delany, who exposes the misogyny underlying the resistance to sexual wordplay that "constitutes a minor but significant critical stance in current medieval studies." Delany's psychoanalytic, feminist critique of monodimensional readings of medieval texts relates the critical separation of the "coarse" and "refined" registers to Freud's discussion of the affective split that accompanies and partially constitutes the civilizing process (26). It also places the aesthetic separation within the Platonic-idealist metaphysical tradition that "identifies the ontological 'one' with

maleness, goodness, form and light, while aligning the 'many' with femaleness, badness, formlessness and darkness" (29).

3. For critiques of reductive Bakhtinian readings, see chapter 6 of Gurevich and Flannigan.

4. The classic theoretical formulation of abjection is Kristeva's. Booth, Bauer and McKinstry, and Russo provide feminist critiques of various aspects of Bakhtin's theory of the carnivalesque.

5. For example, among the fifteen poems eliminated in the 1514 edition of the *Cancionero general* is *Aposento en Juvera*. In the 1519 edition it is replaced by the less topical *Pleyto del manto* (discussed in chapter 5).

6. Although Whinnom published *La poesía amatoria* in 1981, five years prior to the appearance of Parker's, he had knowledge of the latter's work.

7. "No creo que los medievalistas corramos el riesgo de infravalorar el idealismo de la Edad Media. Al contrario, me parece muy probable que lo hayamos sobrevalorado." Of course, the resistance to erotic or obscene paranomasia is not limited to critics of Spanish literature. Delany cites Derek Brewer's warning, unsurprisingly similar in tone to Parker's, against making too much of such wordplay in Chaucer: "Chaucer's puns have now been rediscovered. Now we need to beware of excess, lest we be misled by the tendency of Neo-classical literalism to disregard intention and context, combined with the modern appetite for sexual obscenity" (13).

8. See, for example, Deyermond ("Worm and the Partridge"), Fulks ("Florencia Pinar"), Rico ("Penacho de penas"), and Rodríguez Puértolas *(Poesía crítica).*

9. Classic formulations of this view can be found in Oñate and Ornstein; it persists in recent scholarship—for example Domínguez *(Love and Remembrance).* For a concise explanation of why the courtly elevation of women is not profeminist, see Blamires. Weiss ("'¿Qué demandamos?'") discusses the masculinism that suffuses the medieval Spanish debate about women. For France, cf. Burns ("Troubadour Lyric"), Kay, and Finke.

10. See also Weissberger, "Politics of *Cárcel de Amor,*" for the similar ideology of fifteenth-century prose romance, which makes frequent use of courtly lyrics and motifs.

11. See also Hunt's introduction to *The Invention of Pornography:* "In the sixteenth century... sodomites and prostitutes were already depicted as privileged observers and critics of the established order" (26).

12. See, for example, Tate *(Ensayos sobre la historiografía,* 288). See Weiss ("Political Commentary") for an interesting analysis of Mena's treatment of the historical events of 1441–44.

13. For an ethical reading of *Laberinto* and *Carajicomedia* that complements mine in highlighting the role of sexuality, see Brocato.

14. See Canales for biographical information on Fajardo. Alvaro Alonso, most recent editor of *Carajicomedia,* points out the accuracy of its references to places (especially Valencia and Valladolid) and persons (at least a half dozen of the named prostitutes appear to be historical figures).

15. See Varo (42–45) for a detailed outline of the complex structure of *Carajicomedia;* for a similar chart of *Laberinto,* see Brocato, 330–31, and Beltrán, 321–22.

16. All quotations from *Carajicomedia* are taken from the Varo edition; page references appear parenthetically in the text.

17. "Trastamaran" refers to the dynasty that rose to power in Castile with En-

rique II (1369–79), Isabel's great-great-grandfather. For a history of the Trastamaras, see Suárez Fernández *(Los Trastámara)*. Although Varo raises the possibility of contestatory intentions behind *Carajicomedia*'s *animus ludendi,* he concludes that "There is no clear evidence of any attack, even a parodic one, on civil law or on the political authorities, nor on any type of decisions taken by them" [no existe explícita evidencia de ataque, ya sea en tono paródico, a la ley civil, a las autoridades políticas ni a las decisiones de cualquier clase por ellas tomadas] (73).

18. All quotations from *Laberinto de Fortuna* are taken from the edition by Maxim Kerkhof; parenthetical references in the text are to page number first, then to stanza numbers. The exact stanza-to-stanza correspondence between *Laberinto* and *Carajicomedia* breaks down in stanza 48 of the parody.

19. There is critical disagreement over *Laberinto*'s genre; a balanced definition is that of Gericke: "a narrative poem of epic scope and theme, set in the framework of a visionary journey and crafted by a poet who drew skillfully from various sources, primarily epic (medieval as well as classic) and vision literature" (14).

20. See chapter 4 of Weiss, *Poet's Art,* for an excellent discussion of the role of commentary in the creation of an "intellectual nobility" in the late Middle Ages.

21. *Carajicomedia*'s terminus post quem is 1498, a year mentioned in the text in conjunction with one of two explicit references to Isabel (Varo, 76). The glosses suggest a later date of post-1499, the publication date of Núñez's glossed edition of *Laberinto,* and perhaps after 1505, the date of its definitive second edition, corrected by Núñez himself. All subsequent editions of *Laberinto,* more than a dozen in the sixteenth century alone, incorporate Núñez's commentary. See Canales for a different dating of *Carajicomedia* based on textual allusions to Fray Ambrosio Montesino's *Vita Christi,* published in 1502–3. The latest dating that has been proposed is 1506 (Domínguez, *Cancionero,* 27–28), based on a possible reference to the preconization as bishop of Osma of an illegitimate son of the Admiral Don Fadrique.

22. See Canales (15–19) for the geographical and historical references. There is a literary precedent: Rodrigo de Reinosa's *Coplas de las comadres* presents a similar guide and includes some of the same prostitutes.

23. The influence of *Celestina* (1499) on *Carajicomedia* extends well beyond the work's title. The character Celestina is cited twice, in the gloss to stanzas 20 and 47. In the former, one of Fajardo's guides, La Buyça, is described as follows: "for certainly in the city of Valladolid [her name] is as feared as Celestina's, although it is also true that the unfortunate Celestina became famous and this one enjoys some of her reflected glory" [que cierto es en la villa de Valladolid (su nombre es) tan temeroso de oyr como el de Celestina; mas es cierto que la desdichada de Celestina se llevó la fama, y ésta goza el provecho de tal nombre] (162). I discuss the symbolic importance of this Celestinesque hag later in this chapter.

24. Dame remedio, pues tú sola una
eres a quien pedirle me atrevo,
pues resucitas y hazes de nuevo
lo muerto, lo viejo, sin dubda ninguna.
Pon mi potencia en cuerno de luna,
las venas del miembro estiendan, engorden,
vayan mis hechos en tanta desorden,
que no dexe casa que no tenga cuna. (155)

25. I owe this suggestion to Ronald Surtz.

26. "las cuales cortando con gran dolor de la novia, luego fue por misterio de los dioses abierto un grandíssimo piélago; de lo cual el triste novio muy espantado, *relinquit eam*."

27. Susan Kappeler usefully extends the meaning of pornography to include "high" as well as "low" texts like *Carajicomedia:* "What feminist analysis identifies as the pornographic structure of representation—not the presence of a variable quality of 'sex' but the systematic objectification of women in the interest of the exclusive subjectification of men—is a common place *[sic]* of art and literature as well as of conventional pornography" (103).

28. Schiesari exposes a similar dynamic in a contemporary Italian work, a letter written by Macchiavelli to Luigi Guicciardini in 1509. See below, note 78, for a fuller discussion of this text.

29. "Pues travando d'ella los dos, la metieron en casa del Almirante... y metida en una camara cavallar, convocaron toda la familia de casa, y luego de presente se hallaron por cuenta veynte y cinco ombres de todos estados, bien apercibidos; y, prestamente desatacados, començaron a desbarrigar con ella hasta que la asolaron por tierra y le hicieron todo el coño lagunajo d'esperma."

30. Cf. Vasvari's study on erotic polysemy in the *Libro de buen Amor* (Book of good love) tale (sts. 189–97) about the miller's son who wants to take three wives ("Hijo del molinero"). Vasvari notes that its fantasy of the male sexually frustrated in his desire to satisfy an unlimited number of women has as its opposite the fantasy of male sexual impotence, displaced onto the devouring female: "Los dos temas, a veces emparejados, proveen la estructura profunda de un sinnúmero de cuentos y chistes sexuales" [The two subjects, often paired, provide the deep structure of innumerable sexual tales and jokes] (464). The connection between *Carajicomedia* and *Libro de buen amor* offers further evidence for Pedro Cátedra's contention that the Arcipreste de Hita's book was well known to Alfonso Martínez de Madrigal and other intellectuals writing on *naturalismo amoroso* at the University of Salamanca from the mid-fifteenth century on, parodies of which in turn influenced new fictional genres such as prose romance. Could the highly cultured author of *Carajicomedia* have been associated with Salamanca, like his fellow parodist Luis de Lucena (the main subject of my chapter 6), Fernando de Rojas, author of *Celestina*, and other late-fifteenth-century writers on amatory matters?

31. Cf. the battle between Carnal and Cuaresma in *Libro de buen amor* (sts. 1081–1127), where the weapons carried by Carnal's meaty forces—lances, roasting spits, and so on—have obvious phallic symbolism.

32. "Avía Fortuna dispuesto la ora, / e como los suyos comiençan a entrar, / la barca con todos se ovo anegar."

33. "avía luxuria dispuesto la ora; / los floxos carajos a entrar se tornaron, / los coños hambrientos así los tragaron, / que ninguno d'ellos ni canta ni llora." I am indebted to Julian Weiss for pointing out to me the importance of the *Carajicomedia* poet's use of the Conde de Niebla episode and of the Carajo/Fortuna parallelism. Mena develops the comparison between the "disorderliness" [desordenança] of fortune and the unpredictability of the seas in stanzas 11–12.

34. López Beltrán notes his "vertiginous ascent" at court (28). On Fajardo's military career, see Torres Fontes.

35. Cited by Canales (74) from a document in a nineteenth-century lawsuit to

recover the property for the Fajardo family. After Diego Fajardo's death, his devout widow, Leonor de Mendoza, convinced her son Luis to cede her a brothel. When she obtained papal bulls to convert the *mancebía* (brothel) into a *beaterio* (community house for lay sisters), her son objected and enlisted the help of the Mercederian Friars to oppose the plan. So great was the ensuing scandal that in 1519 (the date *Carajicomedia* first appeared in print) King Charles V intervened, ordering the "beaterio de Magdalenas Arrepentidas" placed under royal protection.

36. Márquez Villanueva notes that the royal decree granted to Fajardo ownership of brothels in Ronda, Marbella, Alhama, Granada, Baeza, Guadix, and Almuñécar, as well as Málaga (*Celestina*, 446 n. 3).

37. Galán Sánchez and López Beltrán study this litigation and later Fajardo family lawsuits over the property.

38. See Varo (79–86) for a complete description of the eight Isabels in *Carajicomedia*, which he summarizes in the following "Retrato-Robot": "Isabel I, of Leon, of Naples, of Spain ['of our nation']; of [Madrigal] of the High Towers, married to a stableboy [Fernando of Aragon]; she holds royal audiences night and day, courtesan, the first and foremost [whore] in the universe, warrior, the nadir, great tyrant, insatiable, she would like to have all of mankind's [lust] at her command, weighted down by laws, she allows royal cuts [of clothing], baptises the circumcised. The entire Spanish court is witness to this. She is the protagonist of this story" [Isabel Primera, de León, de Nápoles, de España ('de nuestra nazión'); de (Madrigal) de las Altas Torres; casada con un mozo de espuelas (don Fernando de Aragón); tiene audiencia real noche y día, cortesana, la primera de todas (las putas) del universo, guerrera, en ínfimo centro, gran tirana, insaciable, querría tener a su mando toda la humana (lujuria), cargada de leyes, deja corte de reyes, bautiza a los circuncisos. Testigo de esto toda la corte española. Es la principal de esta historia] (79–86). The list (twenty-eight prostitutes) included in Rodrigo de Reinosa's *Coplas de las comadres* (Songs of the old wives) includes four Isabels.

39. "ramera cortesana: Agora en día se muestra su persona casada con un moço de espuelas de la reyna doña Ysabel. A esta muger conocí yo muy bien. Autora es d'esto toda la corte española. Esta es una de las nueve de la fama."

40. "estando la corte en Toledo, año de mil CCCCXCVIII, en fiestas, esta Osorio sacó tan ricos atavíos de oro y sedas, que la Reyna Doña Ysabel, preguntando quién era, supo ser ramera cortesana, y con enojo mandó quitar la seda de Castilla." The famous Isabelline sumptuary laws were promulgated in 1478, 1479, and 1499 (not 1498, as *Carajicomedia* states) and were directed primarily at Jews (Domínguez, 27).

41. "La obscenidad de que unos reyes 'católicos' concedieran como recompensa por buenos servicios el derecho al estableimeinto y explotación de mancebías a personas de su confianza (a veces incluso sacerdotes) no dejaba de verse como un supremo escándalo en ciertos círculos reflexivos."

42. Nevertheless, Márquez Villanueva fails to see the work's misogyny; on the contrary, he makes the provocative suggestion that its author may have been of *converso* background because: "Inquisitorial Spain, caste-conscious and Old Christian, was always both an openly misogynist and a fornicating society.... We now know the extent to which the values of family based on paternal-filial love and respect for women in their roles as mothers and wives were marginal to the upper classes, being virtually confined to the pre-bourgeois consciousness of the *converso*" [La España inquisitorial, casticista y cristiano vieja fue siempre una sociedad abiertamente

misógina a la vez que fornicadora.... Sabemos ahora hasta qué punto los valores de vida familiar basados en amor paterno-filial y respeto hacia la mujer en su papel de madre y esposa eran marginales en las clases altas y se hallaban virtualmente confinados a la conciencia preburguesa del grupo converso] (*Orígenes*, 155). For more on this point, consult his earlier essay, "*Celestina.*" On the history of prostitution in Spain, see Rodríguez Solís. Perry's feminist treatment of early-modern Spanish policy on prostitution elucidates the many contradictions in its regulation of prostitutes as "deviant insiders." For an excellent historical study of prostitution in Málaga during the period in question, see López Beltrán. Lacarra ("Prostitución") discusses the founding by royal decree of a new public brothel in Salamanca that coincided with Fernando de Rojas's composition of *Celestina*.

43. "la prima de todas las putas del universo... la fragua de los carajos... la diosa de la luxuria, la madre de los huérfanos cojones."

44. "la acusación, no exenta de desvergonzado atrevimiento, no tiene la más remota justificación histórica, pues, al contrario, la reina castellana fue modelo como mujer y como esposa. El primer testimonio en este sentido nos lo ofrece el historiador oficial de los Reyes Católicos, Hernando del Pulgar, con nobles y enérgicas palabras: 'dio de sí un gran exemplo de casada, que durante el tiempo de su matrimonio e reinar, nunca ovo en su corte privados en quien pusiese le amar, sino ella del Rey, y el Rey della.'" Luis Montañés, editor of a 1975 luxury edition of *Carajicomedia*, is less apologetic: "es un desahogo de quien albergaba en su pecho un odio insano hacia la figura de Isabel I, Reina de España" [it is an unburdening by someone who harbored an unhealthy hatred of Isabel I, Queen of Spain] ("*Carajicomedia*" 45).

45. Beltrán de la Cueva, Juana's putative father, was one of a number of young courtiers of humble origin elevated to high office (he became Master of the military order of Santiago) by Enrique IV to serve as a buffer between him and the nobility (O'Callaghan, 572).

46. The quotation is from his 1588 *Admonition to the Nobility and People of England*, which sought support for Felipe II of Spain's proposed invasion (quoted in Levin, "Heart and Stomach," 81).

47. Marcus describes the various strategies Elizabeth used to reinforce the sense of her self as male, for example, dwelling on her virginity in order to suggest that the inviolability of the English body politic depended on the inviolability of her physical body; referring to herself as *prince* rather than *queen*; appealing to her composite nature—the frailty of her female "body natural" combined with the strength of her "body politic"; giving her famous Armada speech in martial costume ("Comic Heroines," 138–39). The effects of this complex self-fashioning on contemporary writers, and their contributions to it, have been studied extensively.

48. The sole and noteworthy exception is Brocato.

49. See Earenfight on María's (1401–58) considerable governing power during her lieutenancy.

50. Muy pocas reinas de Grecia se falla,
    que limpios oviessen guardado los lechos
    a sus maridos demientra los fechos
    de Troya non ivan en fin por batalla
    mas una si ovo, es otra sin falla,
    una nueva Penélope aquesta por suerte.

51. See O'Callaghan (419–27) for a summary of the events leading to Enrique II's overthrow of the legitimate king of Castile, Pedro I, branded "El Cruel" by his victorious opponents.

52. la muy casta dueña de manos crüeles,
digna corona de los Coroneles,
que quiso con fuego vencer sus fogueras.
¡O quírita Roma, si d'ésta supieras
quando mandavas el grand universo,
qué gloria, qué fama, qué prosa, qué verso,
qué templo vestal a la tal le fizieras!

Anthony Lo-Ré shows that there is no historical evidence that Pedro ever pursued María. The Trastamaran martyr's story was first recorded by Pedro López de Ayala in his *Crónica del rey don Pedro* (Chronicle of the king don Pedro), but Mena probably borrowed it from Diego de Valera's *Tratado en defensa de las virtuosas mujeres* (Treatise in defense of virtuous women) (pre-1453), which Valera dedicated to another of Mena's triumvirate of exemplary chaste women, Juan II's wife, María of Aragon. On Valera and other contributors to the debate about women in fifteenth-century Spain, see Weissberger ("Deceitful Sects").

53. "estando el marido ausente vínole tan grande tentación de la carne que determinó de morir por guardar la lealtad matrimonial, y metióse un tizón ardiendo por su natura, de que vino a morir."

54. For a feminist interpretation of the Lucretia legend, see Jed. Cf. Maroto Camino.

55. Stanza 84 defines *castidat* not only as the quality of "he who shields himself from the arrows of Venus, but also he who strips himself of any vice at all and who adopts a new habit of virtue" [quien contra las flechas de Venus se escuda, / mas el que de vicio qualquier se desnuda / e ha de virtudes novel vestimento (146; St 84). Most critics have taken this generalization at face value (e.g., Vasvari, *Laberinto*, 23). Mena's sixteenth-century commentator, Francisco Sánchez, "el Brocense," pointed out the similarity of Mena's chastity to Ciceronian *temperantia:* "Temperance is a firm command and control of lust and other disorderly appetites of the soul" [La templança es un mando y señorío firme y moderado contra la luxuria y otros desordenados apetitos del ánima] (quoted in Beltrán, 324).

56. On *imperium* and *dominium,* see Stallybrass ("Patriarchal") and Schochet. On the institutionalization of *mayorazgo,* see Beceiro Pita and Córdoba de la Llave. Harney's discussion of agnatic lineage and primogeniture in *Poema de mío Cid* (Poem of the Cid) is also useful, for example, for pointing out the homosocial bonding that the system fostered: "an essential tenet of agnatic ideology is that paternity defines group membership—female deference confirms the emphasis on masculinity as a principle of social action" (*Kinship and Polity,* 44). He also recalls, vis-à-vis the Cid's daughters, the specific Peninsular tradition according to which a woman of high birth was able to transmit patrilineal status to her children, in effect functioning as a surrogate male heir (45). See also Harney's *Kinship and Marriage.*

57. On the legal status of aristocratic wives in medieval Castile, see Ratcliffe, Segura Graiño ("Situación jurídica"), Mitre Fernández, and Pastor.

58. Estavan las fembras Licinia e Publicia,
dando, en oprobio de los sus linages,

a sus maridos mortales potages,
mezclados con yervas llenas de malicia;
ca desque se pierde la gran pudiçiçia,
virtud nesçesaria de ser en la fembra,
tal furia cresçe, tal odio se siembra,
que an los maridos en inimiçiçia.

Bauman connects the poisoning trials of Licinia and Publicia and the spate of similar trials from 186 B.C.E. to the 150s B.C.E. to the threat represented by the female-dominated, if not pro-feminine, Bacchanalian cult. With a membership of more than seven thousand men and women, largely from the underprivileged classes, this Roman version of the cult of Dionysus had considerable power. Livy and Cicero both blamed women for the cult's encouragement of promiscuity and other crimes such as forgery and murder, and for making young men effeminate and unfit for military service. Female members of the cult may have poisoned their husbands in order to raise funds for the cult through the forging of wills. The cult's obvious danger to the state accounts for the assiduous prosecutions and executions in the poisoning cases. The fact that the condemned women were handed over to their families or husbands for punishment implies their execution (35–40). Mena's examples, Lucinia and Publicia, were tried and executed in 154 B.C.E. along with 170 other women. Of this mass execution, Fantham notes: "Poisoning of husbands was linked in the Roman mind with adultery, and yet the scale of this operation goes beyond such an explanation... to reflect the suspect, alien nature of women, as if they were some defeated enemy mistrusted by their conquerors and rulers" (282–83). I am grateful to Richard White for bringing this material to my attention.

59. "sean remedios enante venidos / que nescesidades vos trayan dolores; / a grandes cabtelas, cabtelas mayores / más val prevenir que non ser prevenidos."

60. "Para quien teme la furia del mar / e las tempestades reçela de aquélla, / el mejor reparo es no entrar en ella, / perder la cubdiçia del buen navegar." It is tempting to consider this a pointed warning to the recently widowed king, who the following year married Isabel of Portugal—later accused of licentiousness by Isabel's chroniclers—in a union arranged by Alvaro de Luna. The exalted portrayal of Luna in *Laberinto* shows Mena's admiration and support for Luna, Constable of Castile.

61. The classic work on Fortuna in the European Middle Ages is Patch. For a more recent treatment that deals exclusively with Castilian literature, see Mendoza Negrillo.

62. Lapesa summarizes the critical consensus: "In *Laberinto* there is... an unresolved conflict: Mena tries to find a solution that satisfies his requirements as a Christian, defining himself as a providencialist... but he is unable to control the more spontaneous tendency to see men's worldly fortune as the result of capricious fate" [Hay en el *Laberinto*... una antinomia no superada: Mena trata de encontrar una solución satisfactoria para sus exigencias de cristiano, se define como providencialista... pero no logra dominar la tendencia, más espontánea, que le hace ver la suerte mundanal de los hombres como resultado de un azar caprichoso] (116). As Lida de Malkiel carefully documented (*Juan de Mena*, 22–30), *Laberinto* reflects the heated literary debate of the first half of the fifteenth century in Castile over the nature of Fortuna. It is typical in its attempt to reconcile the two opposing views of fortune in favor of the providential. Lapesa, Gericke, and Gimeno Casalduero

have all pointed out that, despite the poet's initial assertion of divine Providence's ascendancy in the affairs of men (sts. 20–25), fortune as chance comes to the fore as the work unfolds.

63. Deyermond points out that the poem was composed during a political crisis that remained unresolved in 1444, the dedication date. In that year, in a coup launched by Luna's enemies, Juan II was taken prisoner. He was freed and the plotters defeated partly through Luna's political savvy. A year later, Luna defeated his most powerful enemies, the Infantes de Aragón, at the Battle of Olmedo. Deyermond speculates that Mena's poem may have played a role in these events that temporarily strengthened the monarchy ("Structure and Style," 164). On Luna's exemplary career, see Round. See also Bermejo Cabrero ("Ideales políticos").

64. "La mucha clemençia, la ley mucho blanda / del vuestro tiempo non cause maliçias / de nuevas Medeas e nuevas Publiçias."

65. "Si fuesse trocada su umanidat, / segund que se lee de la de Ceneo, / a muchos faría, segund que yo creo, / domar los sus vicios con su justedad."

66. Although it does not appear by name in the inventory of Isabel's library, we know that she inherited her father's royal library. It is therefore more than likely that she possessed the presentation copy of the poem (Lawrance, "Lay Literacy," 93 n. 44).

67. "[Mena] puso sus sueños, sueños de poeta al fin, en el débil y pusilánime D. Juan II; pero aún en esto qué hacía sino adelantarse con fatídica voz al curso de los tiempos, esperando del padre lo que había de realizar la hija?"

68. It is entirely possible that the uppity whores of *Carajicomedia* recall the 1492 suit brought by the city of Málaga against the abuses of "the whoremonger Fajardo" (Alonso Yáñez Fajardo, Diego's father) and the men and women who rented his brothels, known as "fathers" or "mothers." As a result of the lawsuit, the city council gave the prostitutes freedom to do their laundry and take their meals wherever they wished, freeing them from the exorbitant fees imposed by the brothel landlord (López Beltrán, 67–68).

69. "en boz que parece la de Santilario: / Con luengos cojones, como un encensario, / tú, Diego Fajardo, ¿qué puedes hazer?"

70. The summary of his life (first recorded by Saint Jerome) in the *Dictionary of Christian Biography* holds interesting parallels to *Carajicomedia*'s burlesque hagiography (which the author attributes to the *Tripas patrum* [Guts of the fathers]): "His disordered fancy summoned up a thousand temptations of Satan, demons of lust and feasting, terrors of wild beasts, visions of being driven by the devil as a beast is driven by its riders" (3:54).

71. "dio un gran salto sobre el pecador vaquero...y açertándole con los pies en el ombligo, resvaláronse, y fuesse deslizando hasta que se hincó el miembro de Satilario por el culo.... Lo qual sintiendo Satilario, le apretó y tuvo firme, llamando a bozes sus perros. Lo qual viendo el diablo...començó a dar grandes voces, diziendo: 'Satilario, suelta.' El qual...con feroz boz respondía: 'Nunca si el carajo no quiebra.' Y assí le tuvo hasta remojar; y entonçes le soltó, y ya llegavan los perros cerca quando el diablo culi roto començó de fuyr, y los perros tras él, hasta le encerrar en el infierno, adonde el triste se está remedando el culo hasta oy, jurando que nunca ha de sallir fuera."

72. The raunchy rustics of the early theater also rape, but their violent sexual assaults there are heterosexual, perpetrated on a hapless shepherdess or milkmaid. See, for example, the *introito* to Torres Naharro's *Comedia Himenea* (Wedding comedy).

73. Mena includes "those tainted by the unspeakable crime" [los maculados de crimen nefando] alongside adulterers and fornicators as examples of "evil love" [amor malo] in the Circle of Venus. On sodomitical accusations against Juan II and Alvaro de Luna, see Hutcheson ("Seeking Sodom"). On sodomy in the European Middle Ages, see Boswell and Goodich.

74. Montesino is best known for his amplified translation of Ludolph of Saxony's ("el Cartujano") *Vita Christi* (Life of Christ), published in 1502–3. In his edition of *Carajicomedia*, Alvaro Alonso proposes this date as the work's terminus post quem "because it seems more likely that the burlesque was written during his lifetime rather than immediately after his death" [porque parece más probable que la obra burlesca se haya escrito durante su vida que no inmediatamente después de su fallecimiento] (11). See chapter 2 for a similarly irreverent treatment of another of Isabel's court preachers, Fray Iñigo de Mendoza.

75. See the introduction to Alonso's edition (11) for contemporary instances of the term, for example, in Rodrigo de Reinosa. Cela's *Diccionario del erotismo* derives bugger *[bujarrón]* from the Latin *bulgarus,* Bulgarian, and notes its frequent use by Quevedo. Cela suggests that the word preferentially designated the active sodomitical partner, in contrast to *puto,* but he admits that this may be too subtle a distinction (1:168). On the use of *puto* by the royal chronicler Alonso de Palencia and others to slander King Enrique IV, see my chapter 3.

76. Pitkin ties her study of "the anxious and defensive effort of men to prove their manliness" in Machiavelli's works to contemporary Hispanic culture by calling it machismo: "In my understanding, this is the meaning now attached to *machismo* in American English. It is not what the term means in Spanish, the language to which it owes its origin. To members of Hispanic culture, whether their pursuit of that ideal is nevertheless anxious and defensive, I do not presume to say" (5 n. 1). Obviously, my discussion of the medieval roots of this culturally coded psychosexual trait (the degree to which it has become a stereotype is another matter) views it as precisely that. On machismo and its application to medieval literature, see Vasvari ("Phallic Aggression").

77. It is noteworthy that in the final chapter of his *Discourses* Machiavelli cites the very same episode from Roman history that Mena uses to exemplify the female threat to the body politic: the conspiracy of Roman wives to poison their husbands. There were several waves of such poisonings; like Mena, Machiavelli seems to refer to the trials of 154 B.C.E. when 170 matrons were sentenced to death (Pitkin, 121).

78. Most of the *Discorsi sopra la prima Deca di Livio* (Discourses on the first Decade of Livy) was written in 1513, that is to say, six years before the publication of the *Cancionero de obras de burlas provocantes a risa* that contains *Carajicomedia*. Machiavelli's misogynist concept of fortune is also evident in a letter he wrote to a friend in 1509. In it he describes in a joking manner a bizarre sexual encounter with a prostitute who lives in a dark and half-buried house with another woman who lures him inside by offering to sell him a beautiful shirt. When he lights a lamp after the sexual transaction, he is horrified to discover that the woman is a loathsome old hag and proceeds to vomit all over her. Julia Schiesari has uncovered the symbolic importance of this anecdote, dismissed by most male critics as an insignificant joke, by focusing on the letter's initial reference to fortune's differential treatment of Machiavelli and his friend: "Damn it Luigi, see how much with one blow fortune gives different ends to men. Once you fucked her you felt like fucking her again, so you

want another go at her, but I, having been here several days, came across an old woman" (quoted in Schiesari, 172). Schiesari points out not only Machiavelli's misogynistic metaphorizing of fortune as the capriciousness of women, but also his use and abuse of the prostitute to negatively symbolize the commercial world as feminine (therefore the "bait-and-switch" tactic of the prostitutes): "For the economic scandal of prostitution is that the woman/commodity can sell herself; its ethical and political scandal is that anything and anybody can be bought and sold... the commercial exchange of prostitution merely makes explicit what is already the case (albeit repressed) throughout the society at large" (177).

79. There are also striking parallels between *Carajicomedia* and the contemporary Italian pornographic works Findlen analyzes. In Antonio Vignali's *A Bunch of Pricks (La Cazzaria)* (1525–26), for example, the narrator is a noble member of the Sienese humanist academia who imparts to an uninitiated young man the heterosexual and homosexual knowledge that he claims is the core of natural philosophy. Closest to *Carajicomedia* in spirit (e.g., in their anticlericalism) are the works of Pietro Aretino (1492–1556), especially the *Discussions (Ragionamenti)* (1534–36), whose protagonist, the prostitute Nanna, is not unambiguously female (Findlen, 100).

2. Fashioning Isabel's Sovereignty

1. I discuss this joke on Isabel at the end of this chapter.

2. "se ve con claridad cómo la situación económica del varón era más rediticia que la de la infanta. Sin llegar a pensar que el padre establecía una discriminación deliberada, queda corroborada la inferioridad en que permanecía Isabel."

3. Little is known about the education of noble girls in Castile at the time. Quite a bit more can be surmised regarding aristocratic boys. See, for example, Gutierre Díez de Games's *El Victorial. Crónica de Pero Niño* (The victorial: Chronicle of Pero Niño) (1448) and the treatise written about Isabel's own son, Prince Juan, by Gonzalo Fernández de Oviedo, *Libro de la Cámara Real del Príncipe Don Juan* (Book of Prince Juan's royal chamber). A crucial difference between male and female education was the study of Latin, a kind of masculine rite of passage, as Ong has observed. Evidence for this is the famous letter written by Fernando del Pulgar to Isabel sometime after she became queen. In it he praises her for undertaking the difficult task of learning Latin as an adult (*Letras*, ed. Elia, 63).

4. In the introduction to his edition, Fernando Rubio Alvarez (xxx) speculates that the work was written a few months after the death of Isabel's brother Alfonso in July 1468, and most likely after the famous pact of Toros de Guisando (see note 5). Catherine Soriano (1465) dates it somewhat later, closer to Isabel's marriage to Fernando in October 1469. She bases this dating on textual parallels between *Jardín* and a letter written by Isabel to Enrique on September 8, 1469. *Jardín* first appeared in print in 1500.

5. The *Pacto de los Toros de Guisando* (Toros de Guisando Pact) concluded another chapter in the ongoing fifteenth-century struggle between monarchy and nobility in Castile. In exchange for the nobles' demand that Enrique name Isabel his legitimate heir, thereby denying his biological daughter, Isabel agreed to respect Enrique as her lord and sovereign and to marry "whomever the aforesaid Lord and King decided and determined, according to the will of said Infanta, and in accor-

dance with and counseled by the said Archbishop, Master, and Count" [con quien el dicho señor Rey acordare e determinare, de voluntad de la dicha señora Infanta e de acuerdo e consejo de los dichos Arzobispo (Alfonso de Fonseca), e maestre (Juan Pacheco) e conde (Alvaro de Stúñiga)] (quoted in Rodríguez Valencia, 61). On October 26, 1470, that is, less than two weeks after Isabel and Fernando's secret marriage, Enrique rescinded the terms of the agreement made at Toros de Guisando (which had, in any case, not been approved by the Castilian Cortes) and reinstated Juana as heir to the throne (Soriano, 1458 n. 5). The *Pacto* can be consulted in *Memorias de don Enrique IV* (561–62). It should be noted that modern historians disagree on the authenticity of the extant document, signed on September 19, 1468. Azcona states the following: "The version commonly circulated... is not creditable, and I believe it to be a subsequent manipulation by the Isabelline faction in the propaganda campaign that both factions, the royal and the Isabelline, engaged in during the years that followed" [La versión que se suele dar corrientemente... no merece crédito y la creemos una manipulación posterior del bando isabelino en la fase de campaña publicistica a que se entregaron ambos bandos, el real y el isabelino, los años siguientes] (125; cf. Suárez Fernández, *Conquista*, 25–26). I discuss the significance of the agreement, but also the actual place, later in this chapter.

6. Born around the turn of the fifteenth century, Martín de Córdoba was, since 1420, a *lector* at the Augustinian convent of Salamanca. He was no stranger to controversy, being caught up in a monastic debate between those who believed that the monastery should serve primarily as a site of spiritual retreat and observance and those who thought it should be a teaching institution with greater ties to the community. Fray Martín's alliance with the latter group and his opposition to the reform program started by Fray Antonio de Córdoba in 1430 apparently led him to leave Castile for one or more periods of study at the University of Toulouse, where he may have earned a doctorate. The credential allowed him to assume a chair at the University of Salamanca sometime after 1461 (see Goldberg, *Jardín*, 18–28 for more complete biographical information).

7. The extent to which Isabel, first as princess and later as queen, relied on clerics to guide her through the rough seas of Castilian politics is well known. Closest of all to her, and yet not always firm in his allegiance, was the highly political Archbishop of Toledo, Alfonso Carrillo de Acuña. He was a leader of the opposition to Enrique that was ultimately responsible for Isabel's accession (Liss, 51 and passim).

8. For another critique of Vives's feminism, see Kaufman. The paradigmatic misogynist writers in medieval Castile are the Catalan poet Pere Torrellas and the cleric Alfonso Martínez de Toledo. On the debate on women in Spain, see Matulka ("Anti-Feminist Treatise"), Ornstein, Weiss ("'Qué demandamos'"), and Weissberger ("Deceitful Sects"). Consult Brown and Solomon on Martínez de Toledo and his *Arcipreste de Talavera*. Antony van Beysterveldt first made the point about the misogynism of "profeminist" works in medieval Castile. For a European perspective, see Jordan.

9. "La verdad es que no le interesa reivindicar los derechos de la mujer, en abstracto, sino reivindicar los derechos de Isabel, que es una mujer muy especial, al trono de Castilla. El primer paso es demostrar que las mujeres pueden gobernar."

10. Harriet Goldberg demonstrates that Fray Martín draws heavily on Augustine's entire corpus, not only for commentary and doctrine, but also as an encyclopedia of knowledge (*Jardín*, 76–77).

11. "Algunos, Señora, menos entendidos & por ventura no sabientes las causas naturales & morales, ni reuoluiendo las crónicas de los passados tiempos, auían a mal quando algund reino o otra pulicía viene a regimiento de mugeres. Pero yo, como abaxo diré, soy de contraria opinión, ca del comienço del mundo fasta agora vemos que Dios sienpre puso la salud en mano dela fembra, porque donde nasció la muerte, de allí se levantase la vida."

12. See Gómez Mampaso for a useful summary of female succession in medieval Iberia. Of course, it was only at the top of the political hierarchy that women had the right to participate: "From all remaining political work they were completely barred" [El resto del trabajo político les estaba totalmente vedado] (Segura Graiño, "Sabias mujeres," 22). Furthermore, female rule was often contested, abrogated, or criticized. Mirrer cites the case of Isabel's grandmother, Catalina of Lancaster (1390–1416), who was derided by her contemporaries for her attempts to exercise authority as coregent for her minor son, Juan II (84). Catalina is the only woman represented in Pérez de Guzmán's biographical compendium *Generaciones y semblanzas* (Generations and profiles) (c. 1450). Significantly, he describes her as physically masculine: "In size and bodily movements she seemed as much a man as a woman" [En el talle e meneo del cuerpo tanto parecía onbre como muger] (9).

13. "No se aprecia el más mínimo titubeo en anteponer la sucesión masculina de Alfonso a la femenina de Isabel, no obstante que la infanta hubiese nacido antes que el varón. Este detalle debe ser tenido en cuenta para apreciar no sólo la mentalidad castellana, sino también la disposición paterna y jurídica."

14. Azcona (311) dates the first appearance of this motif as 1475, in Gómez Manrique's *Regimiento de príncipes*, discussed later in this chapter. Cf. Campo, 86.

15. On the misogyny of Augustine and other patristic commentators on Genesis, see Burns (*Bodytalk*, chapter 2) and Bloch.

16. Parker's discussion is wide-ranging, spanning all of the Judeo-Christian cultural tradition, from Genesis 2 on. As she points out, that version is actually the second of two versions; in the first version, in Genesis 1, God creates woman and man simultaneously. It was frequently cited in defenses of the equality of women and men.

17. "por quanto el ánima sigue las conplesiones del cuerpo, así como la muger enel cuerpo es flaca & muelle, así enel ánima es vertible en deseos e voluntades."

18. "por que Dios sabía quel maldito y cruel caçador, Sathanás, auía de hazer armadijo conla muger para engañar al varón, fizo la muger de costilla con que suelen los caçadores armar a los páxaros."

19. "si vergüença no las refrena del mal & las promueue al bien, yrán como bestia desenfrenada & como cavallo sin espuelas en todo mal; & huyrán toda virtud."

20. "E si esto es verdad enlas otras dueñas, tanto más es verdad enlas grandes señoras, cuyas palabras suenan por todo su imperio & por ende deuen ser pocas & graues."

21. "por misterio & semejança, que digamos que aquél es varón que es fuerte & firme en sus hechos; aquél es muger que es flaco & delicado."

22. "Enestas presentes razones & enlas que porné después, como en jardín de donzellas, mire vuestro vivo entendimiento & tome deleyte, por que, pues que la sucessión natural vos da el regimiento que no fallezca por defecto de sabiduría moral; antes la vuestra aprouada sabiduría vos haga digna de regir, como vos haze digna la real & primogénita sangre."

23. "Más clara fue Santa Cecilia por que fue virgen que porque fue hija de rey. Ser hija de reina es claridad ajena, que viene de sus parientes; ser virgen & casta es claridad propia que le viene de su propia virtud." Harriet Goldberg remarks the change here from "hija de rey" to "hija de reina" and wonders whether it intentionally refers to the controversy surrounding the paternity of Isabel's rival Juana, daughter of Enrique IV and Isabel of Portugal (270, n. 4).

24. A similar ambivalence can be observed in writers attempting to justify the accession of a woman to the throne of England in the 1550s. As Judith Richards points out: "the debate about the legitimacy of female monarchs in principle was inconclusive on both sides, and the acceptability of such rulers (always given the absence of plausible male alternatives) remained an open issue." She quotes the following lines from Sir Thomas Smith's *De Republica Anglorum* (1583), very similar in tone to Martín de Córdoba's: "those whom nature hath made to keepe home and to nourish their familie and children ... except it be in such cases as the authoritie is annexed to the bloud and progenie, as the crowne, a dutchie, or an erledome for there the blood is respected, not the age nor the sexe" (103). This claim, made during the reign of a forceful queen, Elizabeth I, was historically dubious. Richards cites the example of Edward VI, who cut his unmarried half sisters Mary Tudor (granddaughter of Isabel) and Elizabeth from the succession, preferring the married Lady Jane Grey, whose exercise of sovereign power would not conflict with the general belief that a wife was by definition subordinate to her husband's authority (105–6). Richards also points out the uneasiness expressed by the frequent sixteenth-century retellings of the story of Queen Semiramis of Assyria. Although some authors praise her military skill, many seize on the unbridled lust that led to her becoming pregnant by her own son in order to caution against the danger of unmastered queens.

25. "pues que enel antiguo siglo mugeres fallaron tantas industrias & artes, especialmente las letras; ¿ ... agora, eneste nuestro siglo, las henbras no se dan al estudio de artes liberales & de otras ciencias, antes paresce como le sea deuedado?"

26. "assí varones como fembras, que estonces en aquellos lugares hera de costumbre que las hembras estuuiessen enlos públicos consejos."

27. Goldberg suggests that Fray Martín knew the Varro tale through his reading of Saint Augustine's *The City of God* and from allusions made by Saint Jerome (242 n. 3). Of the punishment Athens meted out to its female citizens, Augustine states that it "was compelled to punish the very victory of the victress, fearing the waters of Neptune more than the anger of Minerva" (616).

28. "Pues no han de entrar en consejo, no han menester ciencia para ello, ca los consejeros han de ser philósophos morales & theólogos, otra mente no podrían bien aconsejar esto."

29. "alas escuras & plebeyas hembras, mas no alas altas dueñas como es nuestra señora, la Princesa, por lo qual deue captar algunas oras del día en que estudie & oya tales cosas que sean propias al regimiento del reyno."

30. The third pillar, silence, is dealt with in the first chapter of Part I. The classic study is Kelso. See also Benson and Hull for a discussion of these traits urged on women in English advice manuals from 1475 to 1640. For similar advice in fifteenth-century Castile, directed specifically at married women, see Pérez de Guzmán's *La dotrina que dieron a Sarra* (The teaching that they gave Sarah) and the anonymous *Castigos y dotrinas que un sabio daua a sus hijas* (Chastisements and lessons that a wise man gave his daughters). Both single out obedience and chastity, but silence is

also advocated, for example, in Pérez de Guzmán's injunction against "speaking, looking, and laughing with a happy expression and a free and easy countenance" [fablar, mirar y rreyr / con alegre gesto y suelta senblança] (665). In his focus on spiritual rather than secular education, Fray Martín anticipates the work of Renaissance proponents of education for women, such as Erasmus, Thomas More, and Juan Luis Vives, whose treatises on marriage and education feminist scholars have shown to be more repressive than liberating in their emphasis on women's adherence to traditional roles within a domestic setting.

31. On the centrality of chastity in *Jardín* and in the gender debate tradition, see Walthaus. She also points out that Part III, a kind of minitreatise on exemplary women from the historical and legendary past, is similar to Alvaro de Luna's *Libro de las virtuosas e claras mugeres* (Book on virtuous and famous women) (before 1453). Cf. Goldberg, who also cites Diego de Valera's *Tratado en defenssa de virtuossas mugeres* (before 1445) as a possible source for *Jardín* (*Jardín*, 79). On Luna and Valera, see Weiss, "Power of Courtly Love" and "'¡Qué demandamos?'"

32. "E si esto es necessario a todas las donzellas, mucho más alas princesas que esperan casar con reyes & príncipes, los quales lo primero que pesquisan dela esposa es si es honesta e virtuosa & de compuesta vergüença."

33. Perhaps for this reason, both his advice and his tone are entirely similar to those of the fifteenth-century manuals for wives cited in note 30.

34. On the corporeal concept, see Le Goff ("Head or Heart?"), Kantarowicz, and Rico *(Pequeño mundo)*. I shall have more to say about the threat of having a woman as head of the body politic in chapter 4.

35. "regir es obra divinal, ser regido es obra de cosas baxas como son las criaturas.... Donde, por quanto el hombre fecho a ymagen & semejança de Dios, es más a Él semejante que las bestias, por ende, es natural mente señor dellas."

36. "por esto los viejos natural mente han de regir a los moços & el varón ala muger & los hombres alas bestias, & enel cuerpo humano la cabeça, do es la silla del seso, rige los otros miembros." Cf. the following lines of Diego de Valera's *Tratado en defenssa de virtuossas mugeres*, dedicated to a queen consort, María, first wife of Isabel's father, Juan II: "And the principal [power] that men have over women is the same one that the teacher has over the pupil, because the husband must be the master over his wife, because our Lord gave the law to man, that is to say, to Moses, and not to woman" [E la mayoría que ha el onbre sobre la muger es la que ha el maestro sobre el discípulo, porque el marido deve ser maestro sobre la muger, porque nuestro Señor al varón dio la ley e no a la muger, conviene a saber, a Muisén] (58). For a critique of the traditional view of Valera's work as profeminist, see Walthaus.

37. "el emperador... es padre de la patria... que avn que a mí me engendró mi padre, pero si el rey no guardara la tierra delos enemigos, assí de la fe como del reino, & de otros malhechores,... entraran de noche o de día a robar & matar a mi padre & a mí & a quantos éramos en casa. Pues avn que me engendró & me dio la vida, el rey me guardó e conseruó enella; e por ende es más continuado padre."

38. "Pues como enel reyno celestial el rey, Jhesu Cristo, es juez & la Virgen Reina es abogada, así ha de ser enel reyno terrenal, que el rey sea juez & la reyna abogada. Donde, puesto que el rey quiera tiranizar o echar demasiados tributos enel reyno, ala reyna pertenece... abogar por el pueblo."

39. "la señora es escudo, ca no sólo ha de ser piadosa como madre, ni como

abogada cerca del rey, mas ha de ser paués & adaraga & escudo, defendiendo los menudos de las fuerças de los mayores. Ca el mundo es como la mar & los hombres como los peces, donde los mayores comen alos menores."

40. Cf. the often-quoted "carta circular" sent by Isabel on March 1, 1471, which maintains that at Toros de Guisando Enrique had sworn before the papal legate Antonio Venier "that the queen's daughter... was not his daughter, nor did he claim her as such, and that the legitimate heir and successor to these kingdoms after his death was I" [que la fija de la reina... no era su fija, nin por tal la tenía y que la legítima heredera y sucesora en estos regnos para después de sus días era yo] (quoted in Vicens Vives, *Historia crítica*, 241). Vicens Vives calls such an assertion "pure propaganda... signed with Isabel's signature, who did not hesitate to sling mud on the honor of the royal family. For if the sad privilege of forging the legend of Enrique's impotence fell to Alfonso... the responsibility for the much more disturbing legend of the king's moral abjection must be assigned to his sister" [propaganda pura... rubricada con la firma de doña Isabel, que no se recataba de echar lodo en el honor de la familia real. Pues si a don Alfonso le cupo el triste privilegio de forjar la leyenda de la impotencia de don Enrique... a su hermana cabe atribuirle directamente la leyenda mucho más penosa de la abyección moral del monarca] (241). In chapter 3, I treat the use of this highly sexualized discourse in the official chronicles of Isabel's reign.

41. Rodríguez Valencia considers the issue of legitimate succession the preeminent concern of the Guisando agreement, as stated in the proem: "to ensure that these kingdoms do not end up without legitimate successors of said King's lineage... and that, given Isabel's age, she may, with the grace of God, marry and produce offspring" [proveer cómo estos regnos non hayan de quedar nin queden sin *legítimos subcesores del linaje del dicho señor Rey... e porque segund la edad en que ella* (Isabel) está, puede luego, mediante la gracia de Dios, *casar e aver generación*] (61; his emphasis).

42. Relevant here is the striking testimony of the royal historian Fernando del Pulgar, whose chronicle of Isabel's reign she personally commissioned in the 1480s. His work vividly evokes the indecision of a young and inexperienced princess faced with a disconcerting number of suitors and conveys the anxiety her hesitation caused among her most intimate counselors, notably the powerful noblemen Gonzalo Chacón and Gutierre de Cárdenas. Cárdenas insisted on the rightness of Fernando as spouse "because the Prince was her same age, and because he expected to inherit Aragon and the other seignories belonging to his father the King that border on the kingdoms of Castile... and because these kingdoms and seignories joined together in one, constitute the greater part of Spain" [porque era Príncipe de edad igual con la suya, e porque esperaba la subcesión de Aragón y de los otros señoríos del Rey su padre que confinan con los reynos de Castilla... e porque estos Reynos e señoríos juntos con ellos puestos en un señorío, era la mayor parte de España] (239). Of course, we must remember that Pulgar's account is a propagandistic reconstruction of the trajectory followed by Isabel when faced with the momentous problem of her marriage. The classic biography of Fernando is by Jaime Vicens Vives.

43. "La otra vtilidad fue después del pecado, por el qual la generación fue muy desordenada; & ésta ordena el matrimonio quando el marido conoce a su muger por causa de evitar fornicación."

44. "La otra vtilidad es reconciliación de paz, & esto es especial entre los reys. Acaesce que han contienda los grandes señores sobre partimiento de tierras & de lugares & con una hija hazen paz & trauan parentesco."

45. "Supplicos... a mí mandeys lo que quisierdes que haga agora, pues lo tengo de hazer. Y la razón que más que suele para ello hoy dél [her adviser Gómez Manrique, bearer of the letter], porque no es para scrivir. De la mano que fará lo que mandardes. La princesa."

46. "y tanbien sabrá Vuestra Alteza que la Señora Princesa dize que otra cosa no podrán sacar della saluo el Rey de Cecilia, y este ha de ser y nunqua otro ninguno."

47. See Liss's excellent discussion of the pressures on the princess in her chapter 4, "The Right Marriage: 1467–1469."

48. For a summary of the stipulations of the *capitulaciones*, see Vicens Vives (247–48).

49. "el sector castellano, al parecer bastante numeroso, que siempre defendió la sucesión masculina sobre la femenina, y que por tanto, pensaba en Fernando como verdadero rey de Castilla."

50. On Valera, see Gerli ("Performing Nobility"), on whom I have relied for this biographical sketch.

51. "y delante de ella iba cavalgando un gentil hombre de su casa, de noble linage, llamado Gutierre de Cárdenas [the same courtier who had advocated that she marry Fernando]... el qual llevaba delante de ella, en la mano derecha, una espada desnuda de la vayna, a demostrar a todos como a ella convenía punir e castigar los malhechores, como reyna e señora natural de estos reynos e señoríos."

52. "¡Castilla, Castilla, Castilla, por la reyna e señora nuestra, la reyna doña Isabel, e por el rey don Fernando, como su legítimo marido!"

53. "mas como el rey fuesse absente, y... la tardanza de esta sublimación pudiera ser dañosa (como la preclarísima reyna doña Isabel tuviesse competidora en doña Juana) de hecho se pudo e debió facer, e fué discreta e sabiamente puesto en obra."

54. For biographical information on Pulgar and Palencia, see chapter 3, where I discuss their work, and their attitudes toward Isabel, in some detail.

55. "ansí por pertenecer al Rey la sucesión destos Reynos, como por ser varón, le pertenecía la governación dellos en todas cosas, e que la Reyna su muger no debía entender en ella."

56. But see note 12 above for the reality of female rule.

57. "Todos sabemos que se concedió a los Reyes; pero nunca supe de Reina que hubiese usurpado este varonil atributo."

58. "el yugo que tal vez el ilustrísimo cónyuge, apoyado en la autoridad de marido, intentara imponer a las cervices castellanas."

59. For a full treatment of Palencia's misogyny, see chapter 3.

60. Azcona asserts that Fernando's reaction to the terms of the Segovian proclamation was one of suspicion toward his wife. A letter sent to Fernando's father, Juan II of Aragon, by the jurist Alfonso de la Cavallería conveys a sense of crisis. It urges King Juan to intervene between his son and daughter-in-law, "enamouring them of the union and harmony between them... and warning against and reproving discord and disagreement between them, the unseemly harm that could come from it" [enamorándolos de la unión y concordia dellos... conminando y reprobando la discordia y diferencias dentre ellos, los danyos inconvenientes que desto les

podría seguir] (quoted in Azcona, 213). Elliott summarizes the prevalent view of the imbalance of power set forth in the *Concordia* in the following terms: "The terms were humiliating, but the prize before Ferdinand seemed so great and the necessity so urgent that refusal was out of the question" (22). As Azcona points out, however, the war with Portugal that lay only three months away would require the granting of extensive powers to Fernando that effectively nullified many of the stipulations of the *Concordia*.

61. Another referent for the Isabelline sword was John the Evangelist, patron saint of both Juan II and Isabel (Lehfeldt, 38).

62. The attribution to Nebrija and its application to both monarchs goes back to José de Sigüenza's history of the Hieronymite order, first published in 1600: "and [Nebrija] made the Monarchs that very fitting, ingenious, and lofty device of the arrows, yoke straps, and yoke, with its soul TANTO MONTA that was a witty allusion to the device's body and soul" [y les hizo (Nebrija) a los dos Reyes aquella tan acertada, aguda y grave impressa de las saetas, coyundas y yugo, con el alma TANTO MONTA, que fue ingeniosa alusión en el alma y cuerpo de ella] (quoted in González-Iglesias, 59). The attribution is almost unanimously accepted by modern historians and heraldry scholars. On the interpretation of the shield, see also Aguado Bleye and Montaner.

63. A royal ordinance of 1497 decreed that the initials appear on all new silver coins (Menéndez Pidal de Navascues, 1:204).

64. "porque la heráldica no es una ciencia precisamente popular, y es casi imposible citar unas armas de alguien que sean generalmente reconocidas. Y es que los monarcas pusieron un enorme empeño en que se repitieran hasta la saciedad." Ian Macpherson offers evidence of Isabel's enthusiasm for the kind of verbal/visual puzzle that the emblem represents in his studies of the related courtly form of the *invención* ("*Invenciones y letras*"). The "invention" [invención], consisting of a visual "device" [divisa] and a verbal "motto" [mote or letra] had its origins in courtly tournaments. Typically embroidered on the jouster's raiment or affixed to his helmet or the trappings of his horse, the *invención*'s usual addressee was a noblewoman whose favor the jouster sought. Macpherson notes that the majority of the 106 works contained in the section of the *Cancionero general* titled "Inventions and Mottos of Jousters" (Invenciones y letras de justadores) are attributable to a tight-knit group of relatives, friends, and rivals associated with the Isabelline court in the 1480s and 1490s.

65. See Figure 2 for a curious version of the transposed initials in a lavish songbook presented by Pedro Marcuello to Isabel's daughter (and perhaps to Isabel herself) at the end of the fifteenth century. The miniature depicts a jouster's helm that bears a fennel plant as its *divisa*. Flanking the unusual visual symbol are the *letras* "F" and "Y." Marcuello is quick to crack the code for the reader: "The crest of this helmet has two meanings pertaining to these fortunate Monarchs. Castile calls it *ynojo*, which begins with Ysabel's letter. Aragon calls it *ffenojo*, which is Fernando's letter, and both of the letters are on the same side" (61).

Deste yelmo: la cimera
trahe dos sinifficados
destos Reyes prosperados

Llama la castilla ynojo
ques su letra de ysabel...
Llamala aragon ffenojo
ques su letra de fernando
y deste las dos de vn bando.

The placement of the devices on the shield reinforces the chiastic referentiality of the initials, because it inverts the order of the monarchs' quartered coat of arms, where Castile's arms come first. It should be noted that the courtly interpretation of the emblem continues to circulate among contemporary heraldry scholars, for example, Menéndez Pidal de Navascues, who notes that "the yoke and the bundled arrows are devices of a courtly nature, based on the first letter of the monarchs' names" [el yugo y el haz de flechas, son divisas de sentido galante, fundadas en la inicial de los nombres de ambos esposos] (1:204).

66. Cf. Juan Gil, who believes that the yoke emblem was created by an Aragonese historian and later attributed to Nebrija by revisionist Isabelline historiography (236ff.).

67. A modern Spanish translation of Curtius renders it "Poco importa la manera de cómo sean desatados" (quoted in González-Iglesias, 60 n. 5).

68. "llevaba aparejado el cumplimiento de uno de los más viejos anhelos de la Cristiandad occidental: la reconquista de la Tierra Santa y la toma de Jerusalén." The Italian humanist Lucio Marineo Sículo records the portents attending Fernando's birth in his *De rebus Hispaniae memorabilibus* (1533): "there was suddenly a great calm and the sun...shone much more brightly than usual; furthermore, a crown adorned in various colors and resembling a rainbow appeared in the sky. These signs indeed appeared to demonstrate to many of those present that the child about to be born...would become the most celebrated among men" [se hizo de repente una gran calma, y el sol...resplandeció con mucho más fulgor de lo acostumbrado; además se vio en el aire una corona adornada de diversos colores y parecida al arco iris. Estas señales de hecho parecían mostrar a muchos de los presentes que el niño que iba a nacer...habría de ser el más famoso entre los hombres] (quoted in Gil, 235 n. 15). After 1492, such messianic discourse proliferated; Christopher Columbus eagerly adopted it, for example, when he exhorted the monarchs that all of the treasures to be obtained from the Indies "be spent on the conquest of Jerusalem" [se gastase en la conquista de Hierusalem] (quoted in ibid., 234). Similarly, the conquistador Rodrigo Ponce de León predicted that Fernando would conquer not only Granada, but also Jerusalem, Rome, the Turks, and Africa as far as Ethiopia (Hillgarth, 2:371). Many of the prophetic texts about Fernando are collected in Sarasa.

69. The full title of the poem, however, expresses Mendoza's awareness that the *yugo* was originally Fernando's symbol: *Sermón trobado que fizo Fray Iñigo de Mendoza al muy alto e muy poderoso Príncipe, Rey y Señor, el Rey Don Fernando, Rey de Castilla y de Aragón, sobre el yugo y coyundas que Su Alteza trae por devisa* (Song sermon that Friar Iñigo Mendoza wrote to the noble and most powerful Prince, King and Lord, Fernando...on the yoke and yoke straps that his highness has for a derice) (299). I deal with Iñigo de Mendoza's political poems more extensively at the end of this chapter.

70. The number of arrows in the device varied, but a document of 1482 orders that candlesticks donated by the queen to the cathedral of Santiago be engraved with "las armas del Rey mi señor y mías y con mi divisa que son once flechas atadas por medio" (quoted in Menéndez Pidal de Navascues, 205).

71. "si el yugo supone cortar, resolver, desatar, las flechas representan la unión de lo disperso, la atadura."

72. Supporting this view is a treatise written around 1487 by one of the monarchs' chaplains, Antonio de Villalpando: *Razonamiento de las reales armas de los sereníssimos e muy esclaresçidos prínçipes e muy altos e muy poderosos reyes e señores, los señores don Fernando el quinto e doña Ysabel la segunda* (Discourse on the royal coat of arms of the most serene and illustrious and most noble and powerful monarchs and lords, Don Fernando V and Doña Isabel II) (c. 1487). Villalpando bases his intricate allegorical interpretation of the royal arms on Psalm 2:10 ("Listen, monarchs, and since you judge the earth, apply this" [Vos reyes, entended agora e, pues jusgáys la tierra, mirad en esto] [373]). He refers to Isabel's device in his exhortation for the monarchs to attend to "The cleansing of our Holy Catholic Faith, and to the Holy Inquisition against the heretics and apostates and to the war against the infidels of Muhammad. And the Muslims and the Jews... destroy them and frighten them away and strike them with the Queen our lady's arrows." [el alimpiamiento de nuestra Santa Fee Cathólica, e en la Santa Ynquisiçión contra los herejes e apóstatas e en la guerra contra los infieles de Mahoma. E a ellos e a los judíos... destruyrlas e aredrarlas e tyrarles con las frechas de la Reyna nuestra señora] (373–74).

73. "es un lazo que si una vez le echáis al cuello, se vuelve en el nudo gordiano, que si no le corta la guadaña de la muerte, no hay desatarle."

74. It is interesting to consider the emblem's play of meanings as it is applied to another famous "couple," Don Quixote and Sancho Panza. Don Quixote humorously refers to the motto as he contemplates using force to resolve Sancho's dilatoriness in self-administering the lashes required to disenchant Dulcinea: "If Alexander the Great cut the Gordian knot saying cutting works as well as untying, and doing so did not prevent him from becoming universal ruler of all of Asia, nothing less could happen now with the disenchantment of Dulcinea, if I whipped Sancho against his will; for if the price of the remedy is that Sancho receive the three thousand lashes, what do I care if he administers them to himself or if others do it, since the point is that he receive them, no matter where they come from?" [Si nudo gordiano cortó el Magno Alejandro, diciendo "Tanto monta cortar como desatar," y no por eso dejó de ser universal señor de toda la Asia, ni más ni menos podría suceder ahora en el desencanto de Dulcinea, si yo azotase a Sancho a pesar suyo; que si la condición deste remedio está en que Sancho reciba los tres mil azotes, ¿qué se me da a mí que se los dé él, o que se los dé otro, pues la sustancia está en que él los reciba, lleguen por do llegaren] (vol. 2: chap. 60).

75. Could it also have been intended to exert subtle pressure on Fernando to restrain his well-known womanizing, which by the time of his marriage had already produced one, and perhaps two, illegitimate children? Although Jaime Vicens Vives, Fernando's most respected modern biographer, acknowledges that "from these facts we can surmise that as a young man Fernando could not exactly be called 'the Chaste'" [de estas noticias se desprende que en el alborear de su hombría a don Fernando no se le pudo denominar, precisamente, el Casto], he hastens to turn the

character flaw into a strength, stating that "this reveals one of the most striking aspects of his psychological makeup: his boundless sensuality, given over to the admiration of beauty" [nos aproxima a una de las facetas más claras de su psicología: su desbordante sensualidad, entregada a la admiración de lo bello] (208). Cf. the letter written to Fernando by Hernando de Talavera, Isabel's confessor and close adviser, shortly after her accession, in which he urges him to be "much more constant in the love and respect due to such an excellent and worthy companion, much more constant and certain and true in every agreement and promise" [mucho más entero en el amor y acatamiento que a la exçelente y muy digna compañera es debido, mucho más constante y más çierto y verdadero en toda contrataçion y promesa] (quoted in Azcona, 261). A recurring motif in the hagiographic treatment of Isabel is her forgiveness of her husband's extramarital liaisons. See, for example, Alvarez Rubiano's conflation of her wifely and maternal forbearance: "She marvelously combined love for her husband, whose flirtations, though they saddened her deeply, she was able to overlook with royal dignity, and the maternal love she felt for her people, whom she rescued with her virtue and her example from the baseness in which they lay" [Conjugó a maravilla el amor al esposo, cuyos devaneos, que le pesaban en lo más hondo de su alma, supo disimular con regia dignidad, y el amor maternal que sentía por su pueblo, al que rescató con su virtud y con su ejemplo de la bajeza en que yacía] (45–46).

76. "E como en el principio de vuestro reinar ovieron conocimiento que era venido el Mexías para los justos y Antechristo para los malos."

77. "E no digan Alexander aver fecho mucho en señorear el mundo, según el tiempo muy aparejado a sojuzgar las gentes que falló, que por mayor caso ternía una sola ciudad en vuestros reinos pacíficamente tomar, que en aquel tiempo señorear la redondez del mundo." Alexander and Hector are repeatedly invoked in the work, showing that "The Maid...is not considered a lady, but rather a warrior and a hero" [A la Ponçella...no se la ve como a una dama, sino como a un guerrero y como a un héroe] (*La Ponchella*, 93 n. 23). I discuss the ambivalent construction of Isabel as "manly woman" in chapter 3.

78. The chapter titled "Unequal Partners" in J. H. Elliott's *Imperial Spain* is a succinct and evenhanded summary of the political effects of the marriage of Isabel and Fernando.

79. "cómo una mujer como Isabel, en ese lustro de característica inmadurez, entre los veinticinco y treinta años, pudo no sólo ganar activamente una guerra, sino estructurar sus reinos como un perfecto estadista."

80. Gómez Manrique was the nephew of two of the fifteenth century's most respected literary figures, Iñigo López de Mendoza, Marqués de Santillana, and Jorge Manrique. On Manrique, see Deyermond ("Women").

81. This is no doubt a reference to the havoc wreaked by the notorious *privados* of previous monarchs, notably Alvaro de Luna and Beltrán de la Cueva, alleged biological father of Enrique's daughter Juana. My thanks to Gregory Hutcheson for pointing this out.

82. El rezar de los salterios,
el dezir bien de las oras
dexad a las oradoras
qu'estan en los monesterios;

> vos, Señora, por regir
> vuestros pueblos e rigiones,
> por fazerlos bien vevir,
> por los malos corregir,
> posponed las oraciones.

83. "Pues quando a varones e mugeres se requenta algund misterio dela fe, más aýna lo creen las mugeres que los varones, por que menos demandan razón del propuesto que los varones."

84. For examples of paintings depicting Isabel praying, see Sánchez Cantón, *Retratos*. Lucio Marineo Sículo, the Italian humanist who was a frequent visitor at court and wrote a history of Isabel and Fernando's reign, offers the following portrait of his patron's piety: "Every day she would say the canonical hours, in addition to other devotions, and her piety was so strong that if one of the religious who were celebrating [the Mass] or singing the psalms and other things of the Church made a mistake in a word or syllable, she perceived and noticed it, and later, as teacher to student, she would rectify and correct it" [Acostumbraba cada día decir todas las horas canónicas, de más de otras devociones que tenía, y era tanta su devoción que si alguno de los que celebraban o cantaban los salmos y otras cosas de la Iglesia erraba alguna dicción o sílaba, lo sentía y notaba, y después, como maestro a discípulo, se lo enmendaba y corregía] (quoted in Ballesteros Gabrois, *Isabel la Católica*, 134). The *cronistas* often attribute military victories as much to Isabel's prayers, fasts, and masses as to Fernando's direct participation (e.g., "so that no fewer wars of religion did she wage, according to her abilities, than the very courageous king with his lance in hand" [conque no menos guerras de creer segund su meresçimiento a los enemigos façia que el valentíssimo rey con la lança en la mano] [Valera, *Memorial*, 7]; "although a woman, and consequently weak of flesh, she was endowed with talents and spiritual grace... most Catholic and devoted Christian, most faithful to God... she was constantly engaged in the holy offices" [aunque muger, y por esto de carne flaca, era alumbrada de dones y de gracia espiritual... cathólica y christianísima devota, fedelísima a Dios... ocupábase en los oficios divinos muy continuamente] [anonymous continuation of Pulgar: *Continuación*, 522]). Isabel's piety remains a favorite commonplace among modern historians, who often link it to her femininity. The classic locus is Clemencín. Among more recent examples is the following from Suárez Fernández's 1992 biography: "Feminine and religious; these are the two essential elements of her character" [Femenina y religiosa; he aquí las dos notas esenciales de su carácter] (137). A logical culmination of the construction of Isabel as pious is the case for her canonization, begun during the Franco regime. For a different view of Isabel's religiosity, namely her management of her relationship with her confessor, Hernando de Talavera, see Weissberger ("Confessional Politics").

85. > E bien como los dechados
> errados en las lauores
> son syn dubda causadores
> de los corrutos traslados,
> assi bien sereys, Señora,
> siguiendo vicios senzillos,
> de doblados causadora,

       qu'en casa de la pastora
       todos tocan caramillos.

86. Uoluntad quiere folgança,
    quiere vicios, alegrias,
    y fazer noches los dias,
    posponiendo la tenprança:
    no procura grande fama,
    menosprecia la salud;
    la razon es vna dama
    que grandes honores ama
    y corre tras la virtud.

87. My thanks to Gregory Hutcheson for pointing this out to me.

88. In the introduction to his edition of Mendoza's works, Rodríguez-Puértolas argues that Fernando disliked the friar. He cites a poem written by Cartagena, apparently at the king's request, that accuses Mendoza of plagiarism, and notes the very different tone of the condolence letters the friar sent to each of the monarchs on the occasion of the deaths of two of their children (xv).

89. Rodríguez-Puértolas gives it a terminus ad quem of May 1475, the date of the Portuguese invasion of Castile (lxvi).

90. como quando fue perdida
    nuestra vida
    por culpa de una muger,
    nos quiere Dios guarnecer
    e rehacer
    por aquel modo y medida
    que llevó nuestra caída.

91. una espada singular,
    de tal cortar
    que haga la tierra llana,
    que la gente castellana
    es tan ufana
    e tan mal acostumbrada,
    que nunca será curada
    si el espada
    de la Justicia no afana
    entre la gente tirana.

92. mas con amor y pesar
    de degollar
    la oveja inficionada
    por guarecer la manada.

Mendoza was fond of the "rustic style" [estilo pastoril], and he used it in *Coplas de Vita Christi* and perhaps in the *Coplas de Mingo Revulgo* (Songs of Mingo Revulgo) (c. 1464; attributed to him by Rodríguez-Puértolas, xii), a biting satire of the political and moral chaos of Castile under Enrique IV.

93. Cf. Mendoza's debate poem "Historia de la questión y diferencia que ay entre la Razón y la Sensualidad" (1483–84?), where sensuality is compared to "a horse in rut... requires firm handling so that it doesn't run wild" [un caballo rixoso... quiere gran tiento en la mano / para no ser desbocado] (241).

94. damas y galanes sueltos
y rebueltos
como si fuesen casados,
por rincones abraçados,
sin vergüença por la sala.

95. Cf. The *Diccionario medieval* (Alonso), which records for the fourteenth and fifteenth centuries the following meaning of *labor:* "A decoration on cloth, either woven or hand-sewn or done in some other manner on other objects" [Adorno tejido o hecho a mano, en la tela, o ejecutado de otro modo en otras cosas] (1282).

96. la dueña se deue ocupar
en lino y en lana, fazer sus labores,
segunt Salamon lo quiso ditar
de la muger fuerte, graue de fallar;
por lino y lana pueden entender
todas las lauores que son menester
para bien la casa guarrnecer y ornar.

97. Clemencín explicitly links the reform of female religious to the Queen's stitchery: "She visited them, carrying her distaff or other work as was her wont; and as much by her example as by the gentleness of her persuasion she got them involved in handiwork and the religious reform" [Iba a visitarlas, llevando su rueca u otra labor, según su costumbre; y tanto con su ejemplo, como con la suavidad de sus persuasiones las aficionaba al trabajo de manos y a la reforma] (194). According to Gómez Molleda (146), samples of Isabel's needlework are preserved in the cathedral of Granada.

98. "Visitaba, sin dar relieve a la visita, como por atención o curiosidad, los conventos de monjas, y llevaba la rueca o la costura, para reunirlas con el pretexto de asociarlas a sus labores, y conversar sin apresuramiento, ni solemnidad de interrogatorio inquisitivo, hasta enterarse por descuido de esta o de aquella hermana de lo que le importaba conocer." César Silió Cortés joins praise for Isabel's "sewing circle" approach to conventual reform to admiration for her maternal concern for the nuns: "by dint of sweetness and affability she exhorted them, like a good mother, to leave aside frivolity and to adhere strictly to enclosure and monastic rules" [en fuerza de dulzura y agrado, las exhortaba, como una buena madre, a dejar la vida frívola y a guardar severamente la clausura y las reglas monásticas] (98).

99. It is interesting to remark the use of the needlework metaphor in a work addressed to Mendoza by the poet Cartagena at Fernando's request. In "By order of the king, reproving Fray Iñigo for the verses he composed in the manner of a joust" [Por mandado del rey reprehendiendo a Fray Iñigo las coplas que hizo a manera de justa] (a reference to Mendoza's *Historia de la questión y diferencia que ay entre la Razón y Sensualidad* [Story about the difference between Reason and Sensuality]), Cartagena scolds Mendoza for plagiarizing from Juan de Mena's "Coplas contra

los pecados mortales": "also merits reproof because he did not follow the outline that we all saw traced by Juan de Mena's hand" [va tambien digno de pena / porque salio del dechado / que todos vimos labrado / de mano de Juan de Mena] (quoted in Rodríguez-Puértolas, lv). Here the feminine-coded *dechado* is cross-gendered and applied to the work of Castile's most exalted poet, its lowly domestic status thereby enhanced. Cartagena mocks Mendoza for his inability to stay within the lines of the master (Mena's) pattern, the same error Mendoza advises Isabel to avoid in *Dechado*.

100. "En los casos de resistencia contumaz empleó, sin embargo, los modos fuertes, imponiendo la observancia y asegurando la clausura efectiva."

101. *Celestina* and Francisco Delicado's *La lozana andaluza* (The lusty Andalusian woman) are particularly rich sources of this kind of double meaning. See also the poems in Alzieu, Jammes, and Lissorgues.

102. The author of *Carajicomedia* offers the following commentary on the whore Gracia: "Gracia is a prostitute, a great needleworker.... She is always in her doorway sewing, and it's a miracle if someone passes by without her looking him over.... Right now she is the lover of a tailor, and she also has some bits of ecclesiastical cloth, some of which she darns and whipstitches" [Gracia es una muger enamorada, gran labradera.... Es muger que continuo está en su puerta labrando, y por maravilla passa ninguno que ella no lo mire.... Agora es amiga de un sastre, y tiene también algunos girones eclesiásticos; a los quales, alos unos surze y sobrecose] (178).

103. In *Lozana andaluza*, for example, the Lavandera comments on Aldonza's cleverness in the following manner: "you'll turn cunts into pricks" [tú ruecas de husos harás], that is, get the better of men (quoted in Macpherson and MacKay, *Love, Religion*, 253).

104. More than a century later, the threat of feminine power still lurks beneath the surface of queenly domesticity in Lope's retrospectively celebratory *El mejor mozo de España* (The best lad in Spain) (1610–11). At the beginning of act 1, Isabel appears on stage with a distaff and spindle. She is weaving a cloth for the Holy Sepulchre in Jerusalem, a sign of her entwined domesticity and religiosity. When her courtiers' chide her overdedication to her sewing, she speaks lines that might have been taken from Vives: "Three things are seemly, the cleric praying, the gallant gentleman wielding his sword, and the chaste lady spinning" [Tres cosas parecen bien: / el religioso rezando, / el gallardo caballero / ejercitando el acero, / y la dama honesta hilando] (vv. 36–40). Later, she reluctantly gives up her feminine distaff [rueca] for the masculine sword [espada] in order to fight the forces supporting her rival Juana. Rapidly growing into the new manly role, she herself uses the spinning metaphor to warn her opponents: "For although I am a mere woman I will know how to force her to abandon such deceit, by making a staff of this distaff. And from this year's yarns that make up a few skeins, I will fashion ropes to tie the hands of the traitors who attempt to disinherit the legitimate lords, and from their bound hands I will raise the ropes to their necks, and if these ropes are not enough, my hair will do for nooses" (251–60).

Que yo sabré reducilla,
aunque soy pobre mujer,

hecha esta rueca bastón,
a que deje tanto engaño.
Y del hilado de este año
que algunas madejas son,
haré cuerdas para atar
las manos a los traidores,
que a legítimos señores
pretenden desheredar;
y de las manos atadas
se las subiré a los cuellos,
y si hay pocos, mis cabellos
les servirán de lazadas.

The sinister, Medusa-like image of the final verses transforms an insecure and sheltered princess into an Amazon queen. Lope wrote this history play in the final years of the reign of a weak king (Felipe III). It seems to express both nostalgia for and anxiety over a powerful queen at the start of her long reign. I am grateful to DeLys Ostlund for bringing this play to my attention; for further analysis, see chapter 2 of her *Re-Creation*.

105. Rodríguez-Puértolas (lxvi) dates it after the Portuguese invasion in March 1475 but before the decisive Castilian victory at Toro exactly one year later.

106. "quel yugo del sujuzgar / se debe siempre fundar / sobre blanda humanidad, / sin muestras de esquividad." The light yoke placed on the followers of Jesus contrasts with the heavy yoke that Solomon's subjects bore, for example, in 1 Kings 12:4 and 12:9–11.

107. Según de la condición
de las abejas se reza,
entre todas quantas son
solo el rey sin aguijón
crió la naturaleza,
do nos quedó la doctrina
que quien se halla en la cunbre
tanto quanto más se enpina
tanto más es cosa digna
que sin aguijón relunbre
en su rostro mansedunbre.

108. I am grateful to Ronald Surtz for alerting me to medieval bee symbolism.

109. Con estas coyundas tales
los toros al yugo atados,
las vuestras manos reales
ararán los peñascales
tan sin pena como prados,
y haréis las cuestas llanos
los heriales barbechos,
y los riscos altoçanos;
do sembraban los ufanos

continuamente cohechos,
senbraréis vos de derechos.

110. que seáis buen labrador,
buena reja, buen vigor,
y tengáis buen aparejo,
buena reja, buen arado,
bien uñidos vuestros bueyes.

111. Cela (1:85) illustrates this statement with several bawdy poems of the eighteenth century, but the connotations were no doubt present much earlier.

112. Interestingly, the poem by Francisco de Quevedo that Cela uses to illustrate the term *aparejo* also features a *labrador:* "The farmer, taking his tool out and holding it in his hand, answered her: 'Take a look and lust after it, madam whore'" [El labrador, sacando el aparejo, / la respondió, tomándolo en la mano: / Pues ver y desear, señora puta] (1:85).

113. The bawdy connotations of the agricultural imagery of *Sermón trobado* and the sewing motif in *Dechado* are in keeping with Mendoza's contemporary reputation as something of a ladies' man. Whether because of a perceived hypocrisy on his part—the fulminating moralist of *Vita Christi* also penned amatory lyrics—or because as a mendicant he was subject to the common attacks on their worldliness, or simply because of his close relationship with the queen, he earned a reputation as a bawdy wit that lasted well into the sixteenth century. He appears as the protagonist of several racy anecdotes collected in the popular *florilegia* of Melchor de Santa Cruz and others. One such collection, *Miscelánea de anécdotas y curiosos casos* (Miscellany of anecdotes and curiosities) by Alonso de Fuentes (c. 1540), contains no fewer than nine "cases" featuring Mendoza. One of them reads as follows: "The Queen ordered him to go on ahead of her in the road, saying that the dust would bother him. He answered: 'what's dust for the sheep is eyeliner for the wolf'" [Mandáuale la Reyna que passasse adelante yendo camino, diziendo que le ofendería el poluo. Respondió él: "el poluo de la oueja, alcohol es para el lobo"] (quoted in Rodríguez-Puértolas, xiii n. 14). The friar's saucy retort to the queen's courteousness places him before her, if not on the dusty path, then in courtly wit and euphemism. Like Mendoza's own *Sermón trobado,* the anecdote uses the terminology of animal husbandry, although in this case in a more explicitly suggestive way, with a titillating suggestion of predatory assault. Another tale in Fuentes's collection uses the sewing/sex act correlation to poke fun at the friar: "A lady was sewing some buttons on a doublet and Fray Iñigo himself entered and asked what she was doing; she said, 'I've been trying to sew on this button and failing, even after ten stitches.' He answered, 'So what will you give me to show you how to stick two on (together?) with a single stitch?'" [Estaua vna dama pegando vnos botones a vn jubón y entró el mismo fray Iñigo, y preguntó que qué hazía allí; dixo ella: "aquj estoy, que de diez puntadas no acabo de poner este botón." Dixo él: "pues ¿qué me daréis y mostraros e a poner dos de vna puntada?"] (quoted in Rodríguez-Puértolas, xiii).

114. "Culpó la Reyna Católica à Hernando del Pulgar, su cronista, de que refiriendo en su Historia cierta acción del Rey su marido, no la puso en nombre de ambos, por haberla executado igualmente entre los dos. Parió poco despues la Reyna à la Princesa Doña Juana; y escribió Hernando del Pulgar: en tal dia y à tal hora parieron sus Magestades."

115. "La Reina, maravillada de haberlos puesto en tal caso juntos mandábale que lo quitase, y él no lo quería hacer, pues que su Alteza se lo había mandado tantas veces."

3. The Discourse of Effeminacy in Isabelline Historiography

1. This chapter is an expanded version of an essay published in *Queer Iberia*. I am grateful to the editors of that volume for their helpful comments on the original.
2. For the historical background, I have relied on Liss, 110–16, and Azcona, 269–79.
3. Flores's entire "Título XX" is devoted to the Valladolid festivities. Of the *invenciones* he writes: "and both the pages and the grandees wore on their helmet crests the most original inventions imaginable, and the texts of their poems and mottoes were the most witty and charmingly novel, words never before seen at any festivity in Spain" [y así los pajes como ellos (los grandes) çimeras de las más nuevas inuenciones que pensar se podieron, y las letras de sus trobas y motes de las mejores graçias y más linda nouedad, palabras que jamás en España en ningunas fiestas se sacaron] (*Crónica*, 166). See Macpherson ("Invenciones") on the genre.
4. Flores emphasizes the monarchs' apparent unconcern with what lay ahead; "and in that place the king and queen showed how little they concerned themselves with the king of Portugal and his allies, in attending the festival belittling the harm they could do" [Y allí se mostró en quánto poco al rey de Portugal y a sus valedores tuuiesen...el rey y reyna en fiestas menospreçiando quanto hazerles podían] (*Crónica*, 168–69).
5. "y cada vno de los señores grandes y otros ricos ombres el mundo pareçía que auían despojado para salir tan pomposos este día, donde tanto eran mirados, que non solamente se miraua quién traya más gentes... mas quién las traya más luzidas, quién con más estrumentos, quién los pajes y cauallos de su persona supo más costosa y galanamente vestir."
6. See chapter 6 for more on Flores's service to Isabel and Fernando.
7. *Crónica de Enrique IV* is the title Antonio Paz y Melia gave to his 1904–7 translation of Palencia's original Latin *Gesta hispaniensia: ex annalibus suorum dierum collecta,* commonly known as *Décadas* for its Livy-inspired temporal organizational scheme. Although Palencia's chronicle centers on the reign of Enrique IV (1454–74), it treats events occurring between 1440 and 1477, in many of which the author personally intervened. Subsequent references to Palencia's *Crónica* are to the more accessible 1973–75 three-volume edition in Biblioteca de Autores Españoles and appear parenthetically in the text as volume and page number; references to the Spanish translation of the fourth "Decade" by José López de Toro are indicated parenthetically by page number. Robert Brian Tate and Jeremy Lawrance have now published the entire work in a Latin–Spanish edition. On Palencia's life, see Paz y Melia *(Cronista)* and Tate ("Biography").
8. I have adapted the phrase "discourse of effeminacy" from the similar "anxieties of effeminacy" that Patricia Parker has found to pervade male-authored works in sixteenth-century France ("Gender Ideology"). As used in this chapter, the term combines elements of two of the four prehomosexual categories of male sex and gender deviance identified by David Halperin in his useful "How to Do the History of Male Homosexuality." They are effeminacy, "for a long time defined as a symptom of an

excess of what we would call heterosexual as well as homosexual desire," that is, applicable to both inverts and womanizers (92), and passivity or inversion, in which men "actively desire to submit their bodies 'passively' to sexual penetration by men, and in this sense are seen as having a woman's desire, subjectivity, and gender identity" (102). I am grateful to Gregory Hutcheson for bringing Halperin's essay to my attention.

9. See especially the *Introduction* to *The History of Sexuality*. Cf. the work of Bredbeck, Bray, Jonathan Goldberg, and Eve Sedgwick, all of whom in turn are indebted to Foucault.

10. Before the late nineteenth century there simply was no consciousness of homosexuality as a definable identity or subjectivity (Foucault, 43). See Boswell for a general overview of the attitude toward and treatment of homosexuals in medieval Europe. Halperin's more nuanced "geneaology" of prehomosexual discourses, practices, categories, or patterns rejects the notion of a unitary history of homosexuality. He identifies four principal prehomosexual categories: effeminacy, pederasty or "active" sodomy, friendship or male love, and passivity or inversion.

11. It is noteworthy that there were also significant differences in the ways that sodomites were prosecuted by the Inquisition and the civil authorities, even in the same city, as Perry *(Gender and Disorder)* discusses.

12. He reiterates the point in his biographical collection *Claros varones de Castilla* (terminus post quem 1483), writing that in his youth Enrique "gave himself over to some pleasures that youth tends to require and decency should deny" [se dio a algunos deleites que la mocedad suele demandar y la onestad deve negar] (5).

13. See, for example, the analyses of *Celestina* by Paul Julian Smith *(Representing the Other)* and Gossy. Cf. Nirenberg on Aragón.

14. Unfortunately, most modern Spanish scholarship on the reign of Enrique still embraces this kind of sodomitical slippage, especially toward xenophobia. In Menéndez y Pelayo's classic study *Antología de poetas líricos castellanos*, for example, he laments that the royal marriage bed was "stained by scandalous lewdnesses... customs infected with the secret and enervating contagion of Oriental vices" [mancillado con escandalosas liviandades el tálamo regio... inficionadas... las costumbres con el secreto y enervador contagio de los vicios de Oriente] (6:2–3). Cf. the totalizing statement of Palencia's modern editor, Antonio Paz y Melia: "These ignoble habits, always present, in certain eras recrudesce, as in the fifteenth century, owing to the dealings with the Moors, which made necessary the Catholic Queen's warrant, with its terrible punishment of burning at the stake; in the seventeenth century, owing to the Italian influence, and in our days, owing to cynical and alien ideas" [Estos indignos hábitos, siempre existentes, tienen épocas de recrudecimiento, como la del siglo XV, por el trato con los moros, que hizo necesaria la Cédula de la Reina Católica, con el terrible castigo de la hoguera; en el siglo XVII, por la influencia italiana, y en nuestros días, por cínicas y extranjerizas doctrinas] (lviii–lix). Cf. Eisenberg.

15. As Paul Julian Smith reminds us, the exclusionary ideology that supports the Catholic Monarchs' project of nation building, a project in which such texts as Palencia's participate, is deeply vexed because "Spanish faith in *casticismo* is counterbalanced by an awareness of a lack of clear divisions between the three communities [Christian, Moorish, Jewish] even as late as 1500, and of their history as one of relational development" (*Representing the Other*, 47). For evidence that the awareness of difference extends well beyond 1500, see Bass on *El Abencerraje* (1565).

16. "Detrás del sodomita portador de la pestilencia se perfila la figura del converso. Juntos van en la peor injuria popular que se podía proferir: '¡Puto judío!'"

17. "en cuyo tiempo tuvieron origen en Castilla los infames tratos obscenos que tan vergonzoso incremento tomaron después."

18. Cf. Hutcheson's perceptive analysis of the poetics of sodomy in anti-Luna discourse in "Seeking Sodom."

19. "respiraba con delicia la fetidez de la corrupción, y el hedor de los cascos cortados de los caballos, el del cuero quemado... que por este sentido del olfato podía juzgarse de los demás."

20. "las repentinas ausencias, la conversación a cada paso interrumpida, su adusto ceño y su afán por las excursiones a sitios retirados."

21. "su indigno traje y más descuidado calzado; su traje de lúgubre aspecto, sin collar ni otro distintivo real o militar que le adornase." It should be noted that wearing Moorish garb was considered fashionable as far back as the thirteenth century. See Bernis for the practice in Palencia's time.

22. "prefirió, a usanza de la caballería árabe, la gineta, propia para algaradas, incursiones y escaramuzas, a la más noble brida, usada por nosotros... imponente y fuerte en las expediciones y ejercicios militares." References to Enrique's preference for Arab military tactics recur throughout the *Crónica*. I am grateful to Jeremy Lawrance for reminding me of the deeply pejorative nature of such comments.

23. "hasta en el andar, en la comida y en la manera de recostarse para comer, y en otros secretos y más torpes excesos, había preferido las costumbres todas de los moros a las de la religión cristiana."

24. "agregar a su séquito a otros muchos secuaces... cuyos nombres y apellidos no recordaban ciertamente el lustre de antiguas familias, antes bien la más abyecta condición."

25. "un vasto y magnífico edificio donde se encerraba a solas con los rufianes... de los cuales los más queridos eran un enano y un etiope tan horrible como estúpido."

26. "amigos de las tinieblas... poseídos de cierta rabia para exterminar el bien y acarrear las catástrofes."

27. Quotations from Paz y Melia: "Sepades que yo, por evitar toda materia de escándalo que podría ocurrir después de nuestros días cerca de la subcesión de dichos mis reynos"; "para que los reinos no queden sin legítimos subcesores del linaje del dicho Señor Rey é de la dicha Señora Infanta"; "es público é manifiesto que la reina doña Juana, de un año a esta parte, non ha usado limpiamente de su persona como cumple al servicio del dicho Señor Rey... e asimiscmo, el dicho Señor Rey es informado que non fue nin está legítimamente casado con ella." The veracity, even the existence, of a written pact drawn up at Guisando has been questioned by several historians, notably Vicens Vives *(Historia crítica)* and Val Valdivieso. Tate observes that whatever such a pact might have contained, Enrique's desperate attempt to avert civil war in Castile by naming Isabel his successor did not mean that he acknowledged Juana's illegitimacy, nor his intention to divorce her mother (*Claros*, 14).

28. "decía... que había tres cosas que no se bajaría a coger si las viese arrojadas en la calle, a saber: la virilidad de don Enrique, la pronunciación del Marqués y la gravedad del arzobispo de Sevilla."

29. In view of this fact, Tate affirms that the whole fraught question of her legitimacy is best viewed as a corollary of the antagonism between those nobles who

favored the classic system of "favoritism" [privanza] and those who upheld cooperation with royal authority (*Claros*, 11).

30. The league's membership changed frequently as nobles opportunistically changed sides; at the time, it was headed by Juan Pacheco, Marquis of Villena, his brother Pedro Girón, master of the military order of Calatrava, and Alfonso Carrillo, archbishop of Toledo.

31. In reality, it is difficult to separate the two accusations, often intertwined in the opposition's many letters and circulars of the tumultuous year 1464–65.

32. A good example of the former, according to Julio Puyol, is Pulgar's *Crónica de los Reyes Católicos,* commissioned by Isabel in 1482 specifically to justify her ascension to the throne. A similar case is Enríquez del Castillo's *Crónica del Rey Don Enrique el Cuarto* (Chronicle of King Enrique IV), which he rewrote to be more flattering to the Catholic Monarchs after the original manuscript was destroyed when he was arrested by the queen's supporters. See Avenoza's study of a recently discovered manuscript in the library of the University of Santiago de Compostela containing, among other texts, another version of Castillo's chronicle in which the description of Enrique is much more degrading than in the most widely known version. For examples of the falsification of documents under Isabel (including the famous Pact of Toros de Guisando), see Vicens Vives (*Historia crítica,* 209–43 and 282–87).

33. See Tate (*Ensayos,* 13–32) for an excellent overview of the issue, succinctly put in these words: "the political ascendancy of Spain is accompanied by an efflorescence of mythological history, created to serve a particular ideological purpose" [la ascensión política de España va acompañada de una eflorescencia de historia mitológica, creada para servir a un determinado propósito ideológico] (28).

34. For example, as he begins his record of the reign of the Catholic Monarchs, Palencia uses the light imagery that is a common stylistic feature of such messianism: "For this reason I begin the narration of marvelous events with the happiness of someone who, after suffering sharp pains, achieves a deserved well-being . . . like someone who . . . trembling with joy, sees light again after being lost in darkness, living in saddest gloom for a long time" [Por esto emprendo la narración de admirable sucesos con la alegría de quien, tras agudos dolores, alcanza lícito bienestar . . . como el que . . . estremecido de gozo, vuelve a ver la luz, el que extraviado en las tinieblas, permaneció largo tiempo en tristísima lobreguez] (2:159). On messianism and *conversos,* see Castro *(Aspectos)* and Cepeda Adán. In chapter 4, I discuss Isabelline messianism in a different context.

35. "el historiador nativo parece haber despertado a un sentido nuevo de la integridad de su país y de la unicidad de su experiencia histórica. . . . Se presentaba a los romanos como minando las virtudes rudas de los primitivos iberos al introducir placeres afeminados y sofisticados tales como los baños de agua caliente y el beber vino. A los visigodos, aunque igualmente colonizadores, se les mira como hermanos espirituales de los iberos, siendo alabados por su virilidad y su fuerte vigor, causa en último término del derrubamiento de la Roma decadente." Cf. Tate's later and more explicitly gendered treatment in "Políticas sexuales," discussed later in this chapter.

36. In his thirteenth-century *De rebus Hispaniae,* Archbishop Rodrigo Jiménez de Rada traced the ancestry even further back, claiming that the Iberians were descendants of Tubal, grandson of Noah. The lineage was often reiterated by later historians (Castro, *Realidad,* 3–4).

37. The restoration was deemed completed by Nebrija ("Hispania tota sibi restituta est") with the fall of Granada, the last Muslim kingdom in Spain (quoted in Tate, *Ensayos*, 296). In chapter 4, I discuss the image of Spain's broken body in relation to the ballad cycle of "La destrucción de España," which revolves around the crime and punishment of King Rodrigo, the last Visigothic king.

38. For English uses of similar corporeal symbolism, see Stallybrass and White and the essays in Burt and Archer. Many of these analyses are indebted to the work of anthropologist Mary Douglas.

39. Both Kantorowicz and Axton discuss the medieval political theory. For a more detailed treatment of the figuration, see my chapter 4.

40. The negotiations included the frantic granting of benefices and privileges by both Enrique and Prince Alfonso and Enrique's attempts to marry Isabel to various European monarchs, among them Edward IV of England and Alfonso of Portugal. See Azcona (85–101) for a balanced account of the events leading up to the outbreak of civil war.

41. "Notorio es, Señores, que todo el Reyno es habido por un cuerpo, del qual tenemos el Rey ser la cabeza; la qual si por alguna inhabilidad es enferma, parecería mejor consejo poner las melecinas que la razón quiere, que quitar la cabeza que la natura defiende... porque si los Reyes son ungidos por Dios en las tierras, no se debe creer que sean subjetos al juicio humano."

42. "el Arzobispo de Toledo Don Alonso Carrillo, subió en el cadahalso, y quitóle la corona de la cabeza... y el Marqués de Villena, Don Juan Pacheco, le quitó el cetro real de la mano... y el Conde de Benavente, Don Rodrigo Pimentel, y el Conde de Paredes, Don Rodrigo Manrique, le quitaron todos los otros ornamentos reales, y con los pies le derribaron del cadahalso en tierra y dixeron 'a tierra, puto... ¡A tierra, puto!'"

43. My thanks to David Weissberger for the suitably colloquial and injurious English translation. On the Farsa de Ávila, see Angus MacKay ("Ritual and Propaganda").

44. The anecdote most likely belongs to the oral tradition; Tate (*Ensayos*, 89) observes that it is not found in any other written source. Leonardo Funes has kindly pointed out to me the ambiguity of Tate's wording in his discussion of this sodomitical couple: the "him" in question may be either the French ally du Guesclin or the buffoon himself. I have been unable to consult Arévalo's chronicle in order to clarify the target of the slander.

45. See also Anne Cruz and Louise Mirrer's sociolinguistic analysis of anti-Pedro propaganda in the official chronicles and in the ballad cycle that developed around him *(Language of Evaluation)*.

46. Palencia's sodomitical genealogy forms part of a generalized "cult of genealogy" that permeates fourteenth- and fifteenth-century Castilian culture. Tate observes that the cult's "insistence on the Visigothic inheritance is nothing more than a facet of the political struggle between the monarchy and the nobility" (*Ensayos*, 121). For a useful gendered analysis of a similar preoccupation with genealogy in Elizabethan England, see Rackin, "Genealogical Anxiety."

47. "como quiera que... ya desde su más tierna edad se había entregado en manos de D. Alvaro de Luna, no sin sospecha de algún trato indecoroso y de lascivas complacencias por parte del Privado en su familiaridad con el Rey." See Hutcheson's nuanced discussion of Luna as a source of "queerness" in the chronicles written during the reign of Juan II ("Seeking Sodom").

48. "asentando nuestros reales, ordenando nuestras batallas; nuestros cercos pasando; oyendo nuestras querellas; nuestros juicios formando...rodando sus reinos; andando, andando, y nunca parando."

49. "¡O corazón de varón vestido de hembra, ejemplo de todas las reinas, de todas las mugeres dechado, y de todos los hombres materia de letras!"

50. "Yo en mis palaçios, con coraçón ayrado y con dientes çerrados y puños apretados, como si en la mesma vengança estouiera conmigo mesma peleando, estaua, y si tal ansia a uosotros, caualleros, tomara, el mayor peligro de vuestros enemigos fuera menor que el de vosotros mesmos. De mi saña, seyendo muger, y de vuestra paçiençia, seyendo varones, me marauillo."

51. Cf. the similar textual representations of Elizabeth I of England, and their gender slippage from *vir* to *virago* to *virtus* (Goldberg, *Sodometries*, 40 n. 14). See also Marcus ("Comic Heroines") and Jordan ("Woman's Rule").

52. "Certifico a vuestra magestad que conceder el Papa que fuese para la reina sola fue la más dificultosa cosa de acabar de quantas en Roma despaché. Porque el Papa y todos los cardenales y letrados habían por cosa contra todo derecho y por cosa monstruosa que mujer pudiera tener administración de órdenes."

53. "No faltaron algunos sujetos bien intencionados que murmurasen de lo insólito del hecho, pereciéndoles necio alarde en la mujer aquella ostentación de los atributos del marido." It should be noted that the cause-and-effect relationship of the gender-hierarchy inversion that Palencia reproves is never totally clear. See Louise Mirrer *(Women, Jews, and Muslims)* on the same blurring in the contemporary ballads. In their frequent portrayal of strong women, the ballads suggest that female power and its destabilizing consequences (adultery, murder, for example) are the result of men's inability to control them.

54. "[de] aquí surgió el germen de graves contiendas a gusto de los Grandes, fomentadores de nuevas alteraciones, como más a las claras se verá luego."

55. "La reina venía preparando desde hacía mucho tiempo—desde recién casada— lo que a juicio de cualquier hombre prudente no convenía para la futura sucesión de estos reinos: disminuir la influencia de su marido por si acaso, por muerte suya, se presentaba alguna contingencia en el curso regular de la herencia."

56. "Quisiera que...tú, Palencia, que leiste tantas historias, me dijéseis si hay en la antigüedad algún antecedente de una Reina que se haya hecho preceder de ese símbolo, amenaza de castigo para sus vasallos."

57. "Yo me creya que veniendo desbaratados, oviera en vuestra lengua palabras de consuelo y esfuerço; y veniendo sanos y honrrados ¿os quexays? ¡Grand trabajo ternemos con vos de aqui adelante! Mas siempre las mugeres, avnque los hombres sean dispuestos, esforçados hazedores y graçiosos, son de mal contentamiento, espeçialmente vos, señora, que por nasçer está quien contentar os pueda." This complaint could easily have been uttered by a character in Flores's romance *Grimalte y Gradisa*. Grimalte is the long-suffering courtly lover of the similarly ungrateful and overbearing Gradisa, who rejects him after sending him on an impossible mission. The connection between hapless courtly lover and humiliated royal consort is not fortuitous; the romance was very likely written in the 1470s, and it most certainly circulated at court. I discuss the possibility that Flores's courtly romances were written at the request of the Queen or at least with her image and readership in mind in chapter 6.

58. "dijo a la Reina que en ninguna manera seguiría sufriendo tan duras ofensas, ni las murmuraciones del pueblo, que atribuía a bajeza aquel abandono de su cuali-

dad de varón.... Prefería así retirarse al reino paterno, excusando así lo vergonçoso de tal pleito."

59. Fernando thereby extends Palencia's genealogy of kingly effeminacy discussed earlier.

60. Key to the reform program and the consolidation of monarchic power was the reorganization of the Royal Council of Castile, the most important advisory body to the monarchs and the highest court in the kingdom. The monarchs reduced the number of magnates sitting on the Council and increased representation from the petty nobility and the *letrados*, who could be counted on to support more fully royal authority. Another important outcome of the Cortes was an authoritative compendium of Castilian law that Isabel ordered her secretary, Alfonso Díaz de Montalvo (who had also served her father, Juan II), to draw up. Printed in 1485, it "proved less a collection of existing laws than a regalist code with imperial Roman origins" (Liss, 184). Cf. Azcona (418–21) on the two major Cortes called by Isabel early in her reign—the one at Madrigal in 1476 and the Cortes of 1480 in Toledo. He observes that the Cortes were not consulted about but rather informed of the administrative, legislative, and judicial changes, which always served to increase royal power (419).

61. "Yo yré a vuestra alteza segund me lo enbía a mandar e llevaré escrito fasta aquí para que lo mande examinar; porque escrevir tienpos de tanta iniusticia, convertidos por la gracia de Dios en tanta iusticia, tanta inobediencia en tanta obediencia, tanta corrubción en tanta orden, yo confieso, señora, que ha menester mejor cabeça que la mía."

62. "Era ome que las más cosas fazía por sólo su arbitrio." Julian Weiss drew this contradiction to my attention.

63. "esa pasión propia del sexo que las hace precipitarse de su grado a los impulsos del deseo, y ansiar que todo se pierda con tal que su anhelo se cumpla."

64. "horrendos crímenes, y recordando la caída de nuestro primer padre, funesta para todo el género humano, decían que del mismo modo, por la maldad de aquella mujer, todo caminaría a completa ruina." Surtz ("Fray Juan López") discusses the political accomplishments of this strong aristocratic woman and an interesting containment strategy adopted by her confessor. For the list of women whose "prurito de dominar" has disastrous consequences, see Tate ("Políticas sexuales," 168). On the threat of the adulterous queen, see McCracken.

65. "[T]erminado el vano simulacro de sus bodas, empezó a descubrir sus propósitos para con la Reina, sometiéndola a una constante seducción. Así creyó lograría precipitarla a que buscase el placer en ilegítimas relaciones."

66. "el Rey le pidió que fuese el principal señor de su casa y aún por su deseo, también en el lecho conyugal." See also Castro Lingl.

67. "Ninguna ocupación honesta las recomendaba.... Las continuas carcajadas en la conversación, el ir y venir constante de los medianeros, portadores de groseros billetes, y la ansiosa voracidad que día y noche las aquejaba, eran más frecuentes entre ellas que en los mismos burdeles.... consumían la mayor parte en cubrirse el cuerpo con afeites y perfumes, y esto sin hacer de ello el menor secreto, antes descubrían el seno hasta más allá del estómago."

68. "fomentó después la perfidia de los Grandes, para al cabo, como originaria de Portugal, propagar por este reino las llamas que habían de destruirle."

69. Se Burt. I discuss the myth of La Cava y Rodrigo extensively in chapter 4. Condemnation of Juana is pervasive in all the Isabelline chronicles. Cf. Diego de

Valera, Pulgar, Enríquez del Castillo, and especially Flores (*Crónica incompleta,* 196–99). The antidote to Juana/Eve is, of course, Isabel, redeemer of a Spain long tainted by original sin (i.e., the Moorish conquest, the invasion of the Portuguese): "for whose repair was chosen a Virgin and a most singular mother, so that the extraordinary and illustrious virtue of one woman would remedy the original sin that the corruption of another woman introduced into the world from its beginnings" [para cuya reparación fue escogida una Virgen y madre singularísima, a fin de que por la extraordinaria e insigne virtud de una mujer se remediase el pecado original que la corrupción de otra introdujo en el mundo desde sus comienzos] (1:132).

70. "la vanidad de la Reina... persuadida de que la postergación del marido redundaría en su propia gloria y poderío."

71. "las condiciones del gobierno que desde los más remotos siglos favorecían al varón."

72. The term *letrado* is used by Hispanists to refer to university-trained scholars and legists of the latter part of the fifteenth century in Castile. In considering the *letrados* humanists, I am conscious of the elements that set Iberia's "Renaissance" and "humanism" apart from the traditional conceptualization of these terms, closely linked to the particular political situation of northern Italian city-states in the fifteenth century. Nevertheless, as Nader has argued, "Agrarian, monarchical, rural Castile *did* produce a Renaissance.... Renaissance historians have ignored this" (16).

73. Palencia was well aware of his status as a servant of the crown. Tate observes that he "writes from the chancery as a *letrado* and with the consciousness of a *letrado,* insisting repeatedly on the need for a readjustment of seignorial relations with the crown" [escribe desde la cancillería como letrado y con conciencia de letrado, insistiendo repetidas veces en el necesario reajuste de las relaciones señoriales con la corona] ("Preceptos," 47–48).

74. See Di Camillo for an excellent study of Cartagena, whom he calls "the first Spanish humanist" (16).

75. Historians have considered Palencia's early years as a *familiaris* of Cartagena, who became bishop of Burgos, to be evidence of his *converso* background (Tate, "Biography," 176). See also the biographical information compiled by Paz y Melia in his *Cronista* (v–xxxv), and the condensed version appearing in the preface to his edition of Palencia's *Crónica.* On Pulgar's probable *converso* background, which may have led to his denunciation as a "Judaizer" [judaizante], see Tate ("Historiografía," 21–22) and Mata Carriazo (xxi–xxv); for Juan de Lucena's *converso* status in connection with his pre-Erasmianism, see Lapesa.

76. Cf. Nader's study of the noble Mendoza family, whose members included many of the most important writers of the late-fifteenth and early-sixteenth centuries in Spain. Nader goes so far as to contend that the *letrados,* with their theory of monarchy that placed the king at the apex of a divinely ordained and immutable hierarchy of institutions administered by anonymous bureaucrats, actually "rejected the most basic religious and historiographical assumptions of the humanists" (132).

77. I deal with issues of royal patronage and reception more extensively in chapter 6.

78. See Kelly's classic formulation of women's loss of power during the Renaissance (19–50).

79. Significantly, Pulgar's self-exile was probably provoked by a letter he wrote to Isabel, protesting the functioning of the newly established Inquisition. For the letter

"on the execution of the *conversos*" [sobre la ejecución de los conversos], and the anonymous attack on it, see Mata Carriazo (xlix–lviii).

80. "creed, señor, que en corte ni en Castilla no biue hombre mejor vida. Pero así fenezca yo siruiendo a Dios, que si della fuese ya salido no la tornase a tomar, aunque me la diesen con el ducado de Borgoña, por las angustias y tristezas que con ella están entretexidas y ençarçadas. Y pues queréis saber cómo me auéis de llamar, sabed, señor, que me llaman Fernando, y me llamauan y llamarán Fernando, y si me dan el maestrazgo de Santiago, tanbién Fernando; porque de aquel título y honra me quiero arrear que ninguno me pueda quitar."

81. Pace Tate: "All of this means the destruction of an official career, and whoever calls Palencia a propagandist should take into account his open criticism of his patron and his defense of his professional integrity" [Todo eso significa la destrucción de una carrera oficial, y cualquiera que tilde a Palencia de propagandista debe tener en cuenta la abierta crítica de su propia patrona y la defensa que ofrece de su integridad profesional] ("Políticas sexuales," 172).

82. "si vuestra alteza manda poner diligencia en los hedificios que se caen por tiempo y no fablan, quánto más le deve mandar poner en vuestra ystoria que ni cae ni calla."

83. "Muy noble Señor: como a amigo no me podeés comunicar vuestras cosas, porque la desproporción de las personas niega entre vuestra señoría e mí el grado de la amistad; ni menos las rescibo como coronista, pero como el mayor seruidor de los que tenés, os tengo en merced hauérmelas escrito por extenso.... Alegar yo a vuestra señoría el Salustio bien veo que es necedad; pero sofridla, pues sufro yo a estos labradores que me cuentan a mí las cosas que vos hacés en Alhama."

84. The *letrados*' anxieties of effeminacy may have been increased by their very dependence on the art of words. Patricia Parker's work on the construction of gender in humanism (also focused on northern Europe, specifically Erasmus and Montaigne) is applicable here. The professional involvement of the humanist with words rather than weapons made him vulnerable to contamination by the feminine-gendered excess of loquacity. Loquacity was gender-coded feminine in the early-modern period and was a central concern of the abundant conduct literature addressed to women. In his *Lingua, sive de linguae usu ac abusu* (1525), Parker observes, Erasmus decries the spread of the feminine "disease of the tongue"—a contamination of the *brevitas* associated with the manly style by the *copia* of feminine speech—to men ("On the Tongue," 448; on Montaigne, see Parker's "Gender Ideology"). This kind of cross-gendering is equally applicable to the tellingly named *letrados* and their copious chronicles.

85. "veemos por esperencia algunos ommes destos que iudgamos nacidos de baxa sangre forçarlos su natural inclinación a dexar los oficios baxos de los padres, e aprender ciencia, e ser grandes letrados."

4. The Neo-Gothic Theory and the Queen's Body

1. For Anderson, the creation of the "cultural artifacts" of nation-ness and nationalism occurs toward the end of the eighteenth century, but he acknowledges and explores the cultural roots of nationalism prior to that century (chapter 2).

2. Tate *(Ensayos)* and Maravall *(El concepto de España)* are the classic studies on the medieval concepts of Spanish prenational identity.

3. Tate considers Cartagena's *Anacephaleosis* (c. 1435), based on his Basel speech (which also circulated in a vernacular version), foundational: "one of the first explicit testimonies to the Castilian awareness of its own past and the unique/particular role that it claims for itself during the late Middle Ages" [uno de los primeros testimonios explícitos de la toma de conciencia de Castilla de su propio pasado y del papel particular que reclama para sí durante la tardía Edad Media] (*Ensayos*, 56). Cartagena's student, Rodrigo Sánchez de Arévalo, elaborates the genealogy further in his *Compendiosa Historia Hispanica* (1470). On both works, see Tate (*Ensayos*, 55–104). On Cartagena, see also Di Camillo and Kaplan.

4. Some scholars have shown, however, that Castro's racialist perspective at times became racist. See especially Kamen, Smith (*Representing*, 45–56), and Nirenberg.

5. The locus classicus is Castro's *Aspectos del vivir hispánico*; see also Gilman, "Generation."

6. See Gerli's proviso: "The image of the *converso* as an unwavering form of alternate transcendental self—the Other by whom the figure of the autonomous, unified Old Christian agent of history is defined—needs to be rethought in light of the shifting reconfigurations of the subject and hererogenous social discourses" ("Performing Nobility," 33). Cf. Smith on the dangers of reifying the *conversos* as a universal category of identity (*Representing*, 27–58). For a useful introduction to recent, more nuanced studies of the *conversos*, see Seidenspinner-Núñez ("Inflecting").

7. See Kantorowicz and Axton, respectively, on the medieval political theory dealing with the conflict between the king's and the queen's "two bodies," the one mortal and the other divine, in medieval political theory. Cf. Abby Zanger's feminist refocusing of the older analysis. She points out the paradox that the mortal body of the queen, and especially her sexuality, threatens the divine image of the sovereign but can also be a primary component of the fiction of dynastic continuity that image serves. Zanger restricts her analysis to a queen consort, the Spaniard María Teresa, daughter of Felipe IV, who married Louis XIV in 1660. I maintain that the threat and the ambivalence are much greater in the case of a queen regnant such as Isabel.

8. For the theoretical formulation of the inextricability of categories of identity in the medieval period, see Biddick and Kruger ("Racial/Religious"). One of the salutary effects of the recent reexamination of the *converso* "problem" in Spain is the reminder that in many cases race and religion were secondary factors to the struggle for economic power and social status between "Old" and "New" Christians (see, e.g., Kamen). Although not a class issue in the Marxian sense, the reality of this intergroup strife compels rethinking the emphasis on issues of race and religion traditional to the analysis of Jewish-Christian relations in early-modern Spain.

9. In no way do I mean to imply Isabel's victimization by this misogynistic formulation of the emerging Spanish nation; as we saw in the last chapter, she is often highly complicit in it.

10. See especially Maravall, *Estudios* (193–213), a reprinting of his often-cited 1956 essay "La idea de cuerpo místico en España antes de Erasmo." Nieto Soria's more recent *Fundamentos* gives a clear explanation and many examples of the concept as elaborated in Castile (90–97).

11. In chapter 2, I discussed one application of these theories in Martín de Córdoba's *Jardín de nobles donzellas*. Another of the longer poems contained in the *Cancionero de burlas* (besides *Carajicomedia*, discussed in chapter 1, and *Pleyto del*

manto, discussed later in this chapter) is in fact a carnivalesque parody of the corporeal concept. *Aposento en Juvera* critiques the billeting of the members of the papal legation of 1473 headed by Rodrigo Borgia (later to become Alexander VI, the pope who granted Isabel and Fernando the title of Catholic Monarchs), "which billeting was done in the body of a very fat man named Juvera" [el cual aposentamiento fue hecho en la persona de un ombre muy gordo llamado Juvera]. After evicting the Castilian occupants of the fat man's body (e.g., the powerful family of Alvaro de Acuña is forced to vacate "the inn of the fingernail" [la posada de la uña] [31 v. 3]), the papal delegates and their hosts are lodged in hierarchical order according to their social status, starting with the head and moving down through Juvera's various grotesque body parts (e.g., Diego de Valera is sent to the "district of the hips" [barrio de las caderas], where he is joined by thirty whores [40 v. 34]). The poet's disgust with the legation is most directly expressed in the excremental finale, when the unfortunate Juvera is administered a powerful purgative in order to flush out the unwanted foreigners (44–45). See *Burlas* (26–27 n. 2) for examples of highly critical accounts of the politically important visit of the papal legation in the Isabelline chronicles. Not surprisingly, Alfonso de Palencia is the most virulent: "The legate, with what insolent frivolity did he spread licentiousness! . . . I won't linger on everything that the cardinal failed to do or did against what was required by the dignity of his high position; his love of luxury and other unbridled passions; the bombastic pomp that he delighted in and flaunted" [El legado ¡con qué insolente liviandad empezó a extender la liçencia! . . . No me detengo en referir todo aquello que el cardenal omitió o hizo contra lo exigido por la dignidad de su elevado cargo; su afición al lujo y a otras desenfrenadas pasiones; la hinchada pompa en que se complacía y de que alardeaba] (*Crónica*, 2:79).

12. See also Tate *(Ensayos)* and Nieto Soria *(Fundamentos*, 93–98). John Edwards has demonstrated that the formulation occurs in non-*converso* as well as in *converso* writers, pace Castro.

13. "Assí la cibdad o reino, como sea de un cuerpo míxtico y proporcionado de ciertas partes y miembros."

14. "cabeça e fundamento de su Republica, de cuya virtut todos los miembros resçiben influencias virtuosas e cuyos fechos son a su pueblo necessarios enxiemplos." For other examples from fifteenth-century legal, political, and historical works, consult Nieto Soria *(Fundamentos*, 227–30).

15. "que como en el cuerpo humano todos los miembros se esfuerçen de anparar y defender la cabeça, ansi, en este cuerpo misto que es todo el reino, cuya cabeça es el rey, se deven esforçar todos sus subditos que son mienbros propios suyos, a lo guardar, servir e amar, consejar." Valera's epistles span the years 1441–86. I will return to some of his later letters, written to Isabel and Fernando.

16. "los cavalleros son braços del cuerpo místico e çevil dotados siquiera ordenados a defendimiento, guarda e reposo de los otros miembros."

17. "Si en nuestro cuerpo mortal el dedo no desea ser ojo, ¿quánto más el menor miembro de Dios será contento que ser mayor no desee?" Maravall quotes from a sermon by San Vicente Ferrer that goes to colorful extremes in describing the role of each member of the *corpus mysticum*, for example, "the ears that hear are the confessors who hear the confession of the people, the nose that smells is the devout persons who smell the virtues of Christ . . . the mouth that takes in food is the rich who have the wealth; the thighs are married people" [les orelles que hoen, són los

confessors que hoen les confession de poble; lo nas qui odore, són les persones devotes que odoren les virtuts de Jesuchrist...; la boqua que rep la vianda, són los richs qui tenen es riquees; les cuxes, son les persones de matrimoni] (*Estudios,* 206).

18. "Notorio es, Señores, que todo el Reyno es habido por un cuerpo, del qual tenemos el Rey ser la cabeza; la qual si por alguna inhabilidad es enferma, parecería mejor consejo poner las melecinas que la razón quiere, que quitar la cabeza que la natura defiende... porque si los Reyes son ungidos por Dios en las tierras, no se debe creer que sean subjetos al juicio humano."

19. "teorizante neto de la restauración del imperio gótico, superada la dominación oriental y colmada la fisura de los reinos peninsulares." On Valera's fascinating career, see Gerli, "Performing."

20. Azcona considers this one of three treatises that were formative for Isabel (the other two, Gómez Manrique's *Regimiento de príncipes* and Iñigo de Mendoza's *Dechado del regimiento de príncipes,* were discussed in chapter 2). *Doctrinal* was formally addressed to Fernando, but "his wife undoubtedly was inspired by it" [en él indudablemente bebió inspiracion su esposa] (Azcona, 311).

21. "Conviene al rey ser mucho temeroso e amador de Dios, porque tanto quanto en mayor lugar lo puso, tanto es más obligado de lo conoscer, e conosciéndolo, amarlo, e amándolo, temerlo e servirlo."

22. "Ca el rey, con su reino es como un cuerpo humano, cuya cabeça es él; e así, como todos mienbros se esfuerçan a defender e anparar la cabeça, así ella deve trabajar de regir e governar e ayudar los mienbros, dellos mucho se doliendo, quando de necesidat son de cortar. Porque, así como se corta un mienbro mortificado porque todo el cuerpo no muera, así son de cortar aquellos de quien no ay esperança de emienda, porque los buenos bivan en pas e los incorregibles sean castigados."

23. Cf. Redondo ("Mutilations") on the severing of body parts as punishment for various crimes in the early-modern period in Spain: "The good health of this body, its equilibrium, imply the head's constant surveillance of the different components and the different members of the organism that are the subjects. When one of these is tormented by illness, it is necessary... to cut off—to mutilate—the part that is not healthy" [La bonne santé de ce corps (the body politic), son équilibre impliquent la constante surveillance de la tête sur les diverses composantes et les divers membres de l'organisme qui sont les sujets. Lorsque l'un de ceux-ci est rongé par la maladie, il faut... couper—mutiler—la partie qui n'est pas saine] (197–98).

24. "se cuida de dejar perfectamente claro que Rodrigo, aún siendo el último rey de los godos, no fue el último miembro de la línea. El mismo día que Rodrigo fue asesinado, alega, Pelayo le sucedió por *dispensación divina.*... el abandono del nombre de godo es de poca importancia al lado del mantenimiento de la línea real."

25. On Sánchez de Arévalo's career and copious literary output, see Tate (*Ensayos,* 74–104).

26. Most influentially in the work of Menéndez Pidal, who identified as inherently Spanish such moral traits as austerity and chastity and proceeded to find their reflection in the apposite literary styles, for example, realism ("Carácteres"). For a discussion of one example of the effect this moralizing literary history has had on modern Hispano-medievalism, see Weissberger ("Taxonomy").

27. As historian Roger Collins demonstrates, it is virtually impossible to separate fact from fantasy in the many Arabic and Christian accounts of the conquest:

"the striking consistencies that can be found [in the sources] are symptomatic of the highly-developed nature of the legendary core by the time these materials came to be included in the extant texts" (34). According to Collins, the most reliable source for the events leading up to and immediately following the Arab conquest is the *Chronicle of 754*, which records only the defeat of Rodrigo's army by one of several Arab forces that invaded the peninsula around 710 and states that the defeat was motivated in part by the involvement of Rodrigo in a struggle for power with rivals who opposed his accession to (or usurpation of) the throne. All of the elements emphasized by the Isabelline writers—the central role of Count Julián, the rape of his daughter by Rodrigo, the treachery of Witiza's son, Bishop Oppas, the manner of Rodrigo's death—were added in much later and less reliable Christian and Arabic accounts. All of these figures (with the possible exception of Oppas) and the actions attributed to them are literary accretions, ideologically motivated on both sides. For the Arabs they serve as martial proof of the validity of Islam, for the Christians, as evidence of the sinfulness of the Hispano-Goths on which the Arabs had come to wreak divine vengeance.

28. "Auino assi que... tomol el rey Rodrigo aca la fija por fuerça, et yogol con ella; e ante desto fuera ya fablado que auie el de casar con ella, mas non casara aun. Algunos dizen que fue la muger et que ge la forço; mas pero destas dos qualquier que fuesse, desto se leuanto destroymiento de Espanna et de la Gallia Gothica."

29. The concept appears already in Jiménez de Rada; Deyermond analyzes its presence in Alfonso X's *Estoria de España* ("Death").

30. To cite only two examples: Antonio de Villalpando's exegesis of the symbolism of Isabel and Fernando's monarchic shield, discussed in chapter 2, states that the device "tanto monta" signifies the following: "a sign of blessedness, that your highnesses have gained, *redeemed,* and *repaired,* what through sad and unfortunate events of fortune some of your predecessors lost" [en bienaventurança lo que han cobrado, *redemido* y *rreparado* vuestras altezas grandes, commo lo que por tristes y desaventurados acaesçimientos de fortuna algunos predesçesores suyos perdieron] (381; my emphasis). Antonio de Nebrija proclaimed similarly, "Hispania is all restored unto itself" [Hispania tota sibi *restituta* est] (quoted in Tate, *Ensayos,* 296; my emphasis).

31. "E por los aborrescibles e detestables pecados destos dos malvados reyes, permitió nuestro Señor qu'el rey Don Rodrigo forçase la Cava, fija del conde don Julián e para vengança de su desonrra él oviese de meter moros en España."

32. For a comprehensive treatment of the Rodrigo cycle, see Lapesa et al. Modern variants of the ballads recorded in remote areas of South America and among Sephardic Jews in northern Africa are included on pp. 61–67. Little is known about Pedro de Corral. For general background on the *Crónica del Rey don Rodrig* consult the introduction to Fogelquist's edition and Alvarez-Hesse. Burshatin's "Reconquest" focuses on an episode in Rodrigo's life—his unlawful "penetration" of the Tower of Hercules in Toledo—that is related to the one I focus on. As Burshatin notes in passing: "a more frutiful discussion [of the Rodrigo legend] would concern the nature of the correspondences between the (de)structuring violations—entering the House of Hercules, ravishing La Cava" (15).

33. There is a strong connection between the ballad tradition and the institution of the Trastamaran dynasty. The earliest datable group of ballads on the peninsula arose in response to the civil war between the legitimate branch of the Burgundian

dynasty, led by King Pedro I, and the illegitimate one, headed by his brother, the ultimately victorious Enrique II: As Deyermond observes, the ballads were composed to vilify Pedro. Although there were ballads that denounced the Trastamaras, most of these did not survive, because after Enrique's victory it became dangerous to circulate ballads favorable to the losing side (*Middle Ages*, 125–26). On the ballad cycle's demonization of Pedro, see Mirrer *(Language of Evaluation)*.

34. Two notable exceptions are Cruz ("Female Figure" and "Illicit Love") and Mirrer *(Language of Evaluation)*, both of whom have analyzed the Trastamaran ideology of the "Pedro el Cruel" cycle from this perspective. Mirrer has also uncovered the politics of denigration and subjugation aimed against Muslim women in several key *fronterizo* ballads (chapter 1 of *Women, Jews, and Muslims* and "Men's Language"), a subgenre that scholars have long touted as demonstrating a high level mutual respect between Christian conquerors and Muslim conquered (see, e.g., Deyermond, *Point of View*).

35. *Juglaresco* designates those mid- to late-fifteenth-century ballads that retain the mark of the court minstrels and poets who composed them. Contrary to the *romances viejos*, they undergo relatively little development in the process of oral transmission (Smith, *Ballads*, 16). The Rodrigo ballads I discuss, *juglarescos* and *viejos* alike, are taken from volume 2 of Menéndez Pidal's *Floresta de leyendas heroicas españolas: Rodrigo, el último godo*; page and verse numbers are indicated in the text.

36. "Ella nunca hacerlo quiso, / por cuanto él le ha mandado; / y así el rey lo hizo por fuerza / con ella, y contra su grado."

37. "Ella hincada de rodillas / él la estaba enamorando / sacándole está aradores / de las sus xarifas manos." The complete poem reads as follows: "Rodrigo talks of love, "Listen, my dear Cava," he says to her, confessing his passion to the one he loves, "listen to what I'm saying. I will give you my heart and it will be at your command." Cava, since she is clever, takes it in jest; she answered very calmly with a humble expression. "I think your Highness is joking, or wants to test the waters. Don't command me to do that, my lord, or I will lose my good name." Rodrigo responds by ordering her to do what he has begged of her "for you can order whatever you will in this kingdom of Spain." As she knelt before him, extracting mites from his noble hands, he was seducing her. The king went to sleep his siesta; he called for Cava. The king had his way with her more by force than by consent, for which reason Spain was lost for that great sin. The wicked Cava told her father about it: Julián, who is the traitor, made a pact with the Moors, that they destroy Spain, as he had sworn to do" (2:83–84).

> Amores trata Rodrigo
> —"Mira, mi querida Cava,"
> a la Cava se lo dice
> descubierto ha su cuidado
> de quien anda enamorado.
> Mira agora lo que te hablo
> darte he yo mi corazón
> y estaría a tu mando."
>
> La Cava como es discreta
> en burla lo ha tomado;
> respondió muy mesurada

y el gesto bajo humillado
—"Pienso que burla tu Alteza
o quiere probar el vado.\
No me lo mandéis, señor,
que perderé gran ditado."
    Don Rodrigo le responde
que conceda lo rogado
"que de este reino de España
puedes hacer tu mandado."
    Ella hincada de rodillas
él la estaba enamorando
sacándole está aradores
de su odorífera mano.
    Fue a dormir el rey la siesta;
por la Cava había enviado.
Cumplió el rey su voluntad
más por fuerza que por grado
por lo cual se perdió España
por aquel tan gran pecado.
    La malvada de la Cava
a su padre lo ha contado:
don Julián que es el traidor
con moros se ha concertado
que destruyesen a España
por lo haber así jurado.

38. Covarrubias defines the parasite as "a little organism that breeds between the skin and the flesh, that moves and leaves a trail that is compared to a furrow, which is why they call it a ploughman" [humorcillo que se cría entre cuero y carne, que va discurriendo y dexa una señal y rastro que comparan al sulco, y por esso le llamaron arador], and he cites two lines from a *romance viejo* that indicate the method of the parasites' removal: "with the point of a javelin they will extract a mite" [Con la punta del venablo, / sacarán un arador] (137). Menéndez Pidal completely misses the erotic implications of the act, calling it "some type of manicure procedure, like polishing nails, that women normally do for men" [alguna operación de manicura, análoga a la de pulir las uñas que suelen hacer las mujeres a los hombres] (*Floresta*, x). A passage in Francisco Delicado's *La lozana andaluza* (1528) cited by Lapesa et al. in *Rodrigo* (33–34) could not be clearer. The prostitute protagonist banters with a watchman, who asks her to rid him of a mite while telling him how her business is going. Lozana complains that men are spending their money on food rather than sex of late. Examining her acquaintance, she says the following: "May your grace live for many years, you have the mange. So hand me a pin, for I want to dig out ten mites from your skin" [Viva vuestra merced munchos años, que tiene del peribón. Por eso, dadme un alfiler, que yo os quiero sacar diez aradores]. A jailer then joins in the conversation:

JAILER: Go ahead and dig them out, and I'll give you a *groso* for each one you remove.

> LOZANA: I know your grace has a fat one, because I heard your blessed whore say so, and that you really stuck it to her. Better give me silver *grosos* instead. (164)
>
> ALCAIDE: Pues sacá, que por cada uno os daré un grueso.
>
> LOZANA: Ya sé que vuestra merced lo tiene grueso, que a su puta beata lo oí, que le metíades las paredes adentro. Dámelo de argento.

39. Mirrer points out that the prosified chronicle version of the ballad makes it clear that the "morica" (the diminutive is not affectionate, but rather condescending) was raped (*Women, Jews, and Muslims*, 24). On the "borderotics" of *fronterizo* ballads and the "morilla burlada" ballad in particular, see Vasvari, *Heterotextual*.

40. Cf. Moner on the increasing castigation of Cava in literary representations of the sixteenth century: from innocent victim of Rodrigo's violence, she was transformed into "a tempting and guilty Eve, until she joined... the pantheon of deadly females responsible for mankind's misfortunes" (79). Moner cites one late ballad version in which Cava compares herself to Lucretia, whose rape also brought down a nation (79; on Lucretia and the formation of the Roman republic, see Jed).

41. Feminists have long acknowledged the use of rape as a weapon of war.

42. por lo cual se perdió España
    por aquel tan gran pecado.
    La malvada de la Cava
    a su padre lo ha contado:
    Don Julián que es traidor
    con los moros se a concertado
    que destruyessen a España
    por le aver assi injuriado.

Cava's anguish over whether to tell her father is emphasized in one of the longer versions of this ballad, which devotes twenty lines to her conversation with "una donzella, su amiga." It is the friend who convinces her to confide her secret and then to divulge it to her father (*Floresta*, 28, vv. 35–56).

43. Si me pides quién lo ha hecho,
    yo muy bien te lo diría:
    ese conde don Julián
    porque *se* la deshonraste
    y más della no tenía. (My emphasis)

Cava's status as object of exchange is even more apparent in other prose versions of the legend, for example, the one contained in the twelfth-century *Crónica silense*, where she is sent to Toledo to be married to Rodrigo. This is maintained in corrupted fashion—perhaps recalling the charges of polygamy made against Rodrigo's predecessors—in the *Crónica del Rey don Rodrigo* when the king asks her, in the presence of his wife, if she would like him to marry her and she responds, coyly or admonishingly: "Sir, my father gave me to you" [señor mi padre me dio a vos (77)].

44. Another kind of royal excess, pride, is indicted in the Tower of Hercules episode analyzed by Burshatin ("Reconquest").

45. Cf. Halperin, 92–93.

46. Menéndez Pidal cites a reference to the ballad in an anonymous song found in a manuscript collection of 1515, indicating that by the beginning of the sixteenth century the older *juglaresco* ballad had already become traditional (*Floresta,* xxv). At the beginning of the seventeenth century, Cervantes has Doña Rodríguez recite verses from the ballad (*Don Quijote,* 2:33); she is aware that they referred to Rodrigo. The ballad, devoid of its historical referents, has persisted into modern times; several versions were collected in Chile at the beginning of the twentieth century (xxvi; the modern ballads are printed in *Romancero tradicional,* 1:77). Menéndez Pidal also points out that the details of Rodrigo's penance were added to the myth around the end of the fourteenth century; prior versions of the legend had not indicated his fate after the defeat. The only earlier hint of his death was in the *Crónica de Alfonso III* of the ninth century, in which that king comes upon a sepulchre in Portugal bearing the inscription "Hic requiescit Rudericus ultimus rex gothorum" (77–78). The prominence of the tomb in the ballad versions I will discuss may stem from this early reference.

47. The ballad omits Corral's telling detail that Rodrigo himself chose the baby serpent and nurtured it until it reached a menacing size. On bodily mutilation in the Spanish penal code of the late fifteenth and sixteenth centuries, see Redondo.

48. Dios es en la ayuda mía,
—respondió el buen rey Rodrigo—;
cómeme ya por la parte
que todo lo merecía
por donde fue el principio
de la mi gran desdicha.
El ermitaño lo esfuerza;
el buen rey allí moría.

49. Lapesa, et al., *Rodrigo* (82); cf. Goldberg's reminder of similar episodes of castration as the appropriate punishment for fornication in Berceo's *Milagros de Nuestra Señora* and Alfonso X's *Cantigas de Santa María* ("Letter," 196). The lasting impact of the castration motif in the Rodrigo ballad can be felt in the two lines from the ballad that Cervantes puts in the mouth of Doña Rodríguez: "Now they are eating me, now they are eating me, in the very place where the sin was greatest" [ya me comen, ya me comen / por do más pecado avía] (*Don Quijote,* 2:33).

50. Warner cites iconographic evidence for the identification of Eve and the serpent in Christian thought, for example, Michelangelo's Sistine Chapel ceiling of 1508–12, where the serpent bears female features (50–67).

51. "no solamente seréis señor destos reinados de Castilla e Aragón, que por todos derechos vos pertenescen, mas avréis la monarchía de todas las Españas e reformaréis la silla inperial de la ínclita sangre de los Godos donde venís, que de tantos tiempos acá está esparsida e derramada."

52. "Bien se puede con verdad desir, que así como nuestro Señor quiso en este mundo nasciese la gloriosa Señora nuestra, porque della procediese el universal Redentor del linaje humano, así determinó, vos, Señora, nasciésedes para reformar e restaurar estos reinos e sacarlos de la tiránica governación en que tan luengamente han estado... así vos, Señora, los [Castilla and León] avéis ayuntado con Aragón e Secilia, e avéis acabado tan grandes cosas con el ayuda de Dios e del viguroso braço de nuestro Serenísimo Rey e Señor."

53. Francisco Márquez Villanueva, although mistaking the object of one such poem's sacrilegious adoration as Queen Juana, considers that such poetry conveys only "a partially literary, partially amorous flirtation, more the former than the latter" [galanteo entre literario y amoroso, con más de lo primero que de lo segundo] (*Investigaciones*, 232).

54. Jones rejected Lida de Malkiel's ethnic rationale for this phenomenon: that it was cultivated primarily by *converso* writers who hoped through this flattery to garner Isabel's support and protection (58 n. 6).

55. The bibliography on the uses of Marian imagery by and for Elizabeth is extensive. Berry and Hackett are good introductions; see also Heisch and Villeponteaux.

56. The reasonable dating of 1479 is suggested by Mario Penna, the editor (41).

57. Valera's enthusiasm for Fernando's martial prowess continues to color his praise for Isabel throughout the following decade. Six years later, with the war against Granada in full swing, he extols Fernando's victories in Andalusia: "Who would not be astonished to see and hear how in twenty-two days your Highness has destroyed, conquered, and subjugated a third of the kingdom of Granada, during which time you won thirty-two principal towns... each one of which reasonably should have taken a year to win?" [¿Quién no esté atónito en ver e oir en espacio de veinte e dos días, Vuestra Alteza aver debelado, vencido, e sojuzgado el tercio del reino de Granada, en que ganastes treinta e dos lugares principales, donde... en que de rasón, en cada unas dellas ganar, deviérades tardar un año?] (31).

58. "¿Pues qué diremos aun, vitoriosísimo Príncipe, sino que Dios es con vos, y en virtud vuestra e de la serenísima princesa Doña Isabel, Reina e Señora nuestra, quiere destruir e desolar la pérfida mahomética seta? La qual no menos pelea con sus muchas limosnas e devotas oraciones, e dando hórden a las cosas de la guerra, que vos, Señor, con la lança en la mano."

59. Mas carrera verdadera
que sin defecto se funda
es que soys muger entera
en la tierra la primera
y en el cielo la segunda.

60. Alta reina esclarecida,
guarnecida
de grandezas muy reales,
a remediar nuestros males
desiguales
por gracia de Dios venida,
como quando fue perdida
nuestra vida
por culpa de una muger,
nos quiere Dios guarnecer
e rehacer
por aquel modo y medida
que llevó nuestra caída.

61. Its modern editor, Rodríguez-Puértolas, places it between 1467 and 1468, about the time of Prince Alfonso's death. There are three versions extant; the official one printed in 1482 altered the plan of the original significantly (xviii–xxii).

62. Pues lo del viçio carnal
digámoslo en ora mala;
no basta lo natural,
que lo contra natural
traen en la boca por gala:
¡o rey!, los que estrañan
tu fama con su carcoma
pues que los aires te dañan
y los ángeles t'enseñan,
quémalos como a Sodoma.

63. ¡O castellana naçión,
centro de avominaciones!
... ¡O mundo todo estragado!
¡O gentes enduresçidas!
¡O templo menospreçiado!
¡O paraíso olvidado!
¡O religiones perdidas!

64. y pues razón nos ha dado
vuestro mando, según digo,
llamemos a Dios loado
por juntar lo derramado
que perdió el rey don Rodrigo.

65. See McNamara, and Ruether ("Misogynism") for examples; also Bynum, 151–79. Cf. Coletti.

66. On the extensive Marian allegorical exegetical tradition related to the *Song of Songs*, consult Matter, chapter 6.

67. Cf. Le Goff on the legacy of Saint Augustine's repudiation of the flesh as the locus of wicked desires: "the repression of sexual desire was but one form of the exaltation of the will characteristic of the new man, pagan as well as Christian. In the warrior society of the Middle Ages abstinence would be evidence of the highest prowess" (*Medieval Imagination*, 98). See also Miles.

68. Marcuello apparently presented his beautifully illuminated work one final time in 1502, to Isabel's daughter Juana. Marcuello frequently draws on the Alexandrian prophecies surrounding Fernando (discussed in chapter 2), as in the following example: "I have already told that there is a prophecy found in ancient books that Fernando would be the one who conquered Jerusalem and Granada" [Ya les dixe ay profecía / de antigos libros sacada / que Fernando se diría / aquel que conquistaría / Jherusalén y Granada] (29, vv. 94–98).

69. Esta Reyna, aunque es muger
es más quel Cit cauallero
y ay recelo que han de ser
estos los que han de perder
la morisma, dezir quiero.

My thanks to Ron Surtz for bringing these lines and Marcuello's manuscript to my attention.

70. For background on the work, consult the excellent introduction to the edition by Victoria Campo and Víctor Infantes.

71. "E por que males tan grandes a vuestra Alteza no parezcan graves de remediar, a ninguna de las passadas no fallé tan grande que con vuestra grandeza iguale, quiero dar enxemplo de aquella pobre pastora a quien llamaron la Poncella de Francia.... E tan perdido y mortificado falló el reino de Francia cuando vino a valerle, que no parecía ser en el poder de hombres darle vida."

72. "en su palacio no se platicavan amores, mas famosos fechos de los passados y presentes."

73. García Oro's is the classic work on the religious reform, one of the most often cited achievements in traditional accounts of Isabel's reign.

74. This is in keeping with prevailing European trends in monastic claustration (Lehfeldt, 46 n. 43). The reform of the Order of Saint Clare in Barcelona required that a wall be constructed in the convent's garden to separate it from neighboring houses and that black curtains be hung before the choir and locutory grilles. Similar restrictions were applied to the Conceptionist Order (46–47; see also García Oro, 239–69).

75. The doctrine of the Immaculate Conception had been articulated in the fourteenth century. It was much disputed throughout the medieval and early-modern periods, and was finally declared official dogma in the nineteenth century (Warner, chapter 16). See Stratton on the iconography of the Immaculate Conception in Spanish art from the Middle Ages on. There is some evidence that devotion to the Immaculate Conception on the peninsula began in Aragon and that Isabel's promotion of it was in some measure intended to support Fernando's role in Castile (Stratton, 8–9). Jaime Roig's poem *Libro de Conseills,* which saw five editions, offers one example (cited in Pérez, 72–73).

76. In Iberia as in the rest of Europe, Franciscan Immaculists opposed the claims of the Dominican Maculists. Meseguer Fernández points out that the Franciscans were by tradition the confessors of the Castilian royal family ("Franciscanismo," 157). See also López.

77. Chapters 11–13 of Pérez's historical survey of the Immaculate Conception in Spain deal with the reign of the Catholic Monarchs. García Oro discusses the Franciscan reform and Cisneros's leadership (173–237). See Recio on the Franciscan Immaculists.

78. See Meseguer Fernández ("Franciscanismo") for relevant excerpts from the *cuentas* kept by the Queen's treasurer, Gonzalo de Baeza, and for her Franciscanism. The account books also record payment to Ambrosio Montesino for an illuminated copy of *Las oraciones del Cartujano,* a translation of the final chapters of Ludolph of Saxony's influential *Vita Christi.* Besides being a much-favored royal preacher like Iñigo de Mendoza, Montesino was apparently the inspiration for the scandalous Fray Bugeo Montesino, ascribed author of *Carajicomedia.* Another important writer named there is the Catalan Francesc Eiximenis. Isabel owned a copy of his *Lo libre de les dones* (1396), an advice treatise for women.

79. See the curious poem, a kind of dance of death, that the Franciscan Francisco de Ávila dedicted to Cisneros in 1508, four years after Isabel's death. In it Death speaks of the many famous clerics, knights, kings, and queens that he has claimed. The last to be praised is Isabel, "more than a woman, a manly ruler" [más que muger, / varonil gouernadora] (quoted in Meseguer Fernández, "Isabel," 9).

80. That the identification of Isabel with Eve can never be fully erased is clear in the following lines by the sixteenth-century Dominican chronicler, Juan de la Cruz. Commenting on the Queen's admiration for her confessor Tomás de Torquemada (better known for his role as Inquisitor General), the cleric remarks: "and after finding the fruit of that tree beautiful and sweet to eat, she gave it to her husband, with more loyal and true love than Eve gave Adam the forbidden fruit, I mean that she persuaded the king also to accept him as his confessor, and he did so" [y hallando después el fruto de aquel árbol que era hermoso y suave para comer, dióle a su marido, con más fiel y verdadero amor que Eva a Adán la manzana vedada. Digo que persuadió al Rey que también le tomase por su confesor, y así lo hizo] (quoted in Niño Jesús, 175).

81. Una cosa es de notar
que mucho tarde contesce:
hazer que temer y amar
estén juntos sin rifar,
porqu'esto a Dios pertenesce.

82. Si quiero hablar no oso,
si quiero callar no puedo;
como hijo temeroso,
ante el padre rrençilloso,
me cubro de vuestro miedo.
Como piden la clemençia
los condenados a crimen,
ansi con gran rreverencia,
ante la vuestra presençia
todos mis sentidos tremen.

83. "la sagrada mano diestra / os hizo muy mas veçina / a su Magestad diuina / que a la forma común nuestra."

84. Esta sola diferençia
de el a uos quiso que vuiese,
por guardar su preheminençia:
que él solo por exçelençia
ynfinito se dixese.

85. On the social function of courtly love poetry in general, as artful "ways of formulating actual or wished-for social transactions," see Rosalind-Jones and Stallybrass and for Spain, Gerli, *Poesía cancioneril*, 5–10, and Weiss, "Alvaro de Luna," 175.

86. The classic works on the cult of Elizabeth are by Strong and Yates. Most Elizabethan scholarship has accepted their interpretation of the Marian representation of Elizabeth as "filling a post-Reformation gap in the psyche of the masses, who craved a symbolic virgin-mother figure" (Hackett, 7). Cultural materialists—for example, Greenblatt and Montrose—have added new dimensions to the discussion. See Hackett for a useful overview and critique of the scholarship (1–12).

87. In chapter 6, I return to the world upside-down theme in romances written with Isabel in mind.

88. For a plausible dating of *Pleyto* based on internal references to the poet Juan del Encina, famous for his 1496 *Cancionero*, see Rubio Arquez (243). *Pleyto* replaced

Aposento en Juvera in the 1514 *Cancionero general*, perhaps because the latter satirized an event that had occurred more than forty years in the past. *Pleyto*'s humor, as we shall see, was less immediately topical. On *Aposento en Juvera*, see note 11.

89. Antonio Rodríguez-Moñino, in the introduction to the supplement to his facsimile edition of the 1511 *Cancionero general* (1958), calls it "useful reading for the linguist and the historian of literary roguery, but not recommendable from an aesthetic point of view" [lectura útil para el lingüista y para el historiador de la bellaquería literaria, pero nada recomendable desde el punto de vista estético] (12). For similar condemnations of the work, see Rubio Arquez, the first scholar to devote serious attention to the obscene poem. He also summarizes its attribution to various fifteenth-century poets.

90. Alonso Hernández explains that "uncovered lady" [dama descubierta] is a pun on "covered lady" [dama encubierta] or "dama tapada," the streetwalker wrapped in a cloak. He also cites the related terms "blanket whore" [puta de manta] found in *La lozana andaluza* (1528) and "spread-blanket girl" [moza de manto tendido], later used by Góngora (29, 41). The association of both *manta* (blanket) and *manto* (cloak) with prostitution is clearly relevant to *Pleyto*. Cf. Frago García.

91. For a stimulating exploration of the links between the sexual and the monetary in English Renaissance theater, see Bruster. Also useful is Ruth Karras's discussion of the prostitute as a symbol of the distrust of money and female independence in medieval England.

92. On the increasingly litigious legal climate in late-fifteenth- and sixteenth-century Spain, consult Kagan. The venality and bias of judges was frequently targeted by Spanish moralists, starting as early as the reign of King Pedro I. See especially Pero López de Ayala's attack on the corruption of justice in his *Rimado de palacio* (especially stanzas 342–53). In the fifteenth century, many royal advisers urged their monarchs to attend to the problem. Rubio Arquez (245) cites examples in the poetry of Juan de Mena and Alfonso Alvarez de Villasandino. Especially relevant to the messianic writing that is my focus in this chapter is the prophetic text *Espejo del mundo*, written by Alonso Jaén around 1481 (258 n. 74). He calls on Fernando and Isabel to listen to "your vassal subjects who complain of the carnivorous vultures (which are the bad governors, civil and criminal justices and their advisers) who purchase positions with money so that with bribes and collusions, condemning the innocent and absolving the guilty, they can rob the people who live in your kingdoms" [vuestros súbditos vassallos que se quexan de los buytres carniceros (que son los malos governadores, justicias civiles e criminales con sus assessores) que compran los officios por dineros para con sobornaciones e composiciones, condepnando los justos e absolviendo los criminosos, poder robar las gentes que biven en vuestros regnos] (229). For an interpretation that diverges from mine, see Rubio Arquez (245–46). He argues for a moralizing interpretation of *Pleyto*, finding in it "a call to charity, to generosity among men, which does not exist even among those who arrive at carnal union" [un llamamiento a la caridad, a la generosidad entre los hombres, que no existe ni siquiera entre aquellos que llegan a unión carnal] (246). He finds the source of the message in the New Testament, specifically in Christ's teachings on the power of the law and his criticism of Talion law (Matthew 5:40): "And if any man will sue thee at the law, and take away thy coat, let him have thy cloak also." But see the proverb "to fight over the just man's cape" [reñir sobre la capa del justo] (e.g., in act xiii of *Celestina* [282]), about which Covarrubias writes:

"It is sometimes applied when men make off with another's property and divide it up among themselves" [Aplícase algunas veces a la ocasión de alzarse algunos con la hazienda agena y repartirla entre sí] (294). See Kane (14, 154, 157) for other medieval occurrences of proverbs containing the terms "cape" [capa] and "cloak" [manto] that are clearly satiric in meaning, including the suggestive "Beneath my cloak, I kill the king" [So mi manto al rrey mato (174)], that asserts the individual's right to private opinions of any kind, even regicidal ones. Ciceri suggests that the poem draws on both Spanish and French debate texts.

93. Pues este muy hondo mar
tal grandeza en sí contiene,
deve tener y anegar
cuanto a su potencia viene;
y assí digo que conviene,
por razón muy conoscida,
toda cosa que se tiene
de otra mayor ser tenida.
Y si vos pensáis, señor,
que por miembro estendido
paresce más tenedor
en la verdad ser tenido.

94. See book 1 of Aristotle's *Generation of Animals* on the question of how semen contributes to reproduction. He concludes the following: "this power [i.e., of the semen] is that which acts and makes, while that which is made and receives the form is the residue of the secretion in the female.... For, if we consider the question on general grounds, we find that, whenever one thing is made from two of which one is active and the other passive, the active agent does not exist in that which is made; and, still more generally, the same applies when one thing moves and another is moved. But the female, as female, is passive, and the male, as male, is active, and the principle of movement comes from him" (1132). See also Burns (*Bodytalk*, 89–91.)

95. Toda cosa que ha de entrar
y tenerse en otra dentro
ha de ser que pueda estar
para meter y sacar....
Y de aqueste tal poder
no goza quien no se alça,
pues consiste en el meter
el poder para tener,
como la pierna en la calça.

96. Trexler cites Lerner in support of his analysis of homosexual rape—"the punitive gendering of foreign and domestic enemies to show them as akin to women" (14)—as a primary instrument in the Spanish conquest of the Americas. Relevant also is Gravdal's stimulating discussion of the preoccupation of canon lawyers with rape in medieval France. They diverged from the older Justinian concept of rape as a crime against an individual woman, adhering instead to Gratian in considering rape an issue of men's property and honor (Solterer, 17).

97. por esta sentencia ordeno
que esté preso, encarcelado,
en el coño confiscado,
porque en costas le condeno;
y en el coño se consuma
pleito, costas y trabajo,
hasta que salte el espuma
por la punta del carajo.

98. As mentioned above, Rubio Arquez uses the reference to Encina to date *Pleyto* to around 1500. I would add that the burlesque genealogy of misogynists in these lines may play off of the Old Christian genealogies flaunted by the simpleton rustics in Juan del Encina's plays, which began appearing in print in 1495 (see, e.g., *Egloga*, 1). The possible ties to the University of Salamanca where Encina studied suggests that *Pleyto*, like Luis de Lucena's *Repetiçión de amores*, which I discuss in chapter 6, may be a student parody of a legal *disputatio*, composed at about the same time and for the same all-male audience. Its references to Aristotle and exemplary lovers of antiquity, and the joke about male intellectuals compensating with brain power for genital inadequacy, may well place the poem in the minigenre of mock treatises on love written by Salamancan faculty such as the famous "El Tostado" and students such as Lucena. They were mischievous responses to the prominent place Aristotelian natural philosophy occupied in the university curriculum. See Pedro Cátedra, *Amor y pedagogía*, for a thorough discussion of this burlesque academic genre.

99. Interestingly, the term *luzillo* is the same one used in the *Crónica del Rey don Rodrigo* for Rodrigo's tomb, where his penance by castration occurs. A curious addendum to *Pleyto*, attributed to the nobleman García de Astorga and discussed later in this chapter, emphasizes the conflation of sexual and fiscal economy in the misogyny of the poem. The finding for the *coño* is fair, Astorga ironically insists, "because it is evil and cruel it is fitting that the body should be in the tomb" [después de malo y cruel / que a de estar, según natura, / el cuerpo en la sepultura, / no la sepultura en él] (64, vv. 14–22).

100. "lo que es simple y no tiene doblez; dízese algunas vezes del hombre llano y claro que trata verdad."

101. "usado en los tribunales supremos, como apelar con las mil y quinientas doblas, que es tanto como depositarlas, para que se repartan entre los jueces si el apelante no sale con su intención."

102. Aunque pese a Sant Ilario
y al procurador del coño
vos, como fiel notario,
me lo dad por testimonio;
y al juez que sin trabajo
pronunció tales razones,
que le den por galardones
que se cague en el carajo,
pues le quita los cojones.

103. cuan falsa consecuencia
contra razón y su ley

serie dezir que en el rey
el reino está por presencia;
pues, no menos por potencia
está el coño en el carajo.

104. Por no quedar enconado *[sic]*
acuerdo de me lavar
de lo suzio processado;
no para no sentenciar,
mas por aver sentenciado.
Y si algunos juzgaran
mal de aquesto que leyeren,
respondo que "*leyes van
allí donde coños quieren.*"

105. The author is generally believed to be the brother of poet Florencia Pinar, one of the few named female poets represented in the *Cancionero general*. Menéndez Collera believes that the poem, which appeared only in the first edition of *Cancionero general*, was written between 1497 and 1498 because there is no mention of Prince Juan and Princess Mary's "card" refers to the negotiations for her marriage that took place in 1498 (428).

106. "con el qual se puede jugar como con dados o naypes, y con él se puede ganar o perder."

107. There may well have been accompanying instructions on how to play the courtly game. Cf. Fernando de la Torre's similar "Juego de unos naypes por coplas," which contains a detailed prose description of the illustration on each card (128–36).

108. Tome vuestra Magestad
primero como primera
la palma por castidad
porqu'en vos sola s'esmera;
y un fénix que sólo fue
como vuestra alteza en todo,
con la cancion d'este modo:
"reina de muy alta.c" *[sic]*
y el refrán que "*Allá van leyes,
donde las mandan los reyes.*"

109. In his previous position as secretary to Isabel's father, Juan II, Montalvo had formulated the legal justification for the king's claim of "absolute royal power" [poderío real absoluto] (Liss, 184). The strengthening of royal absolutism from the mid-fifteenth century on has been thoroughly documented by Nieto Soria. He observes at least two "qualitative leaps" in the power arrogated by the monarch; from about the time Juan II orders the execution of his erstwhile favorite Alvaro de Luna (1453), "there is a move from using the formula as a simple mechanism of derogation of a specific law or laws to using it as an argument that fully justifies the complete exemption of the king from any law, norm, or agreement" [Se pasa de utilizar esta fórmula como simple mecanismo de derogación de una ley o leyes concretas, a utilizarlo como argumento que justifica plenamente la total desvinculación del rey con respecto a cualquier ley, norma o compromiso] (*Fundamentos*, 125). It is in this

expanded sense that the phrase "poderío real absoluto" is repeated at least six times in Isabel's testament. This does not mean that the increase in royal power went uncontested, as *Pleyto del manto* attests. Maravall discusses the limitations on sovereign power in the early-modern period; one of them, the growth of private property rights, is clearly relevant to my discussion: "Inspired by the individualist and bourgeois mentality, propelled by the new economic circumstances that the development of capitalism imposed, and aided by the legal technique of the Romanists, the notion of property evolved into the free disposition of one's goods, a concept that diverges from medieval criteria" [inspirada por la mentalidad individualista y burguesa, impulsada por las nuevas circunstancias económicas que impone el desarrollo del capitalismo y servida por la técnica jurídica de los romanistas, la propiedad evoluciona en un sentido de libre disposición individual sobre los bienes, que se aparta de criterios medievales] (*Estado*, 347–56, at 349).

110. It should be noted, however, that Isabel's retrieval of the *mercedes* in no way constituted the stripping of privilege from the nobility. The grandees retained the territories that had been properly awarded by Enrique—that is, not coerced from him. More important, six years after the Cortes at Toledo, Isabel guaranteed the institution of primogeniture [mayorazgo], thereby ensuring the preservation of the nobility's holdings in perpetuity (Liss, 185).

111. Rubio Arquez argues that the poem was elaborated over an extended period by three separate authors, of whom only the last, García Astorga, is known.

112. Pedro Fernández de Córdoba, lord of Aguilar, was the father of Gonzalo Fernández de Córdoba, the military hero known as the "Gran Capitán." Astorga also wrote several poems collected in the *Cancionero de burlas*, in one of which he defends himself against charges of Judaizing and accuses his addressee, the Duke of Medinasidonia, of sodomy (162).

113. "en favor de lo sentencioso contra el *mártir bien aventurado carajo,* por no ser en discordia con tan honrados juezes; aunque bien se hallaran causas lícitas e honestas para que el dicho coño no fuera oído en juizio, antes anichilado y echado de él, según ley de derecho establecida por los reyes antepassados, de gloriosa memoria."

114. porque el coño es un avaro / condicioso [sic] y malicioso / inábil y condenado, / porque le hiede la boca.

115. "Un[a] reyna era muy honesta con ynfingimiento de vanagloria, que pensava aver más firmeza que otra. Diziendo que quál era la vil muger ha onbre su cuerpo librava por todo el aver que fuese al mundo. Tanto lo dixo públicamente de cada un día, que un cavallero votó al vero palo, sy sopiese morir en la demanda, de la provar por vía de requesta o demanda sy por dones libraría su cuerpo." Goldberg includes the anecdote in her motif-index of medieval Spanish folk narratives under the heading "Jokes concerning Prostitutes" (207).

5. Luis de Lucena and the Rules of the Game

1. Lucia Binotti's recent diplomatic edition and thoughtful study of *Epístola exhoratoria a las letras* promises to stimulate critical interest in a work that has been unjustly neglected. It effectively supersedes Paz y Melia's 1892 edition.

2. See, for example, Clemencín's "Ilustración XVI" (394–429), where he presents the often-repeated evidence for Isabel's love of learning and promotion of literature and the arts, her study of Latin, her supervision of the education of her children and

the children of her courtiers, her employment of such noted Italian humanists as Pietro Martire and Lucio Marineo for that purpose, the numerous musicians, poets, and troubadours she invited to court, her support of Spain's premier university at Salamanca, and, in general, her commitment to overcoming the aversion to intellectual pursuits of the Castilian nobility. In short: "The Queen... was able to persuade Castilians that the refinement of the mind was not at odds with the strength of the heart; and inspiring in them the desire to join the new learning with the bravery inherited from their elders, she ensured that they would pass on both qualities together to their descendants" [La Reina... supo persuadir a los castellanos que la perfección del entendimiento no estaba reñida con los alientos del corazón; e inspirándoles el deseo de hermanar la nueva cultura con la valentía heredada de sus mayores, hizo que trasmitiesen ambas calidades reunidas a sus descendientes] (401). Segura Graiño's brief essay on the cultured noblewomen surrounding the Queen at court affirms that the royal division of labor made cultural affairs, considered "domestic," Isabel's domain. She also calls into question the commonplace of the high degree of Latinity and learning that characterized the noblewomen in Isabel's circle, notably Juana de Contreras, Isabel de Vergara, and the famous Beatriz Galindo, "la Latina." She rightly observes that these cases are exceptional ("if the knowledge of Latin were frequent [among women], they would not have given her the nickname, which, furthermore, I don't believe any man ever had" [si el conocimiento del latín fuera frecuente, no le habrían dado el apodo, el cual, además, no creo que tuviera ningún hombre]) and that they cannot form the basis for a theory about the cultural level of women in the Isabelline period (182–83). She identifies distinct groups of learned women according to their proximity to the Queen and contends that they are "progressively more learned the further away they are from the Queen's direct influence" [progresivamente más sabias según se alejan de la influencia directa de la Reina] (183).

3. Existing studies of Isabel's patterns of patronage rarely go beyond the eulogistic. Exceptions, in addition to Segura Graiño ("Sabias mujeres"), are Campo and Surtz ("Juana de Mendoza"). Although Surtz focuses on Juana de Mendoza, principal lady-in-waiting [camarera mayor] of Princess Isabel (eldest child of the Queen) and wife of Gómez Manrique, he deals subtly with gender issues generally connected to female patronage in this period.

4. Weissberger's "Deceitful Sects" discusses how Isabelline politics shapes the debate about women during the last quarter of the fifteenth century.

5. "no comencé por otra parte, que por el estudio de Salamanca, el qual, como vna fortaleza tomada por combate, no dudaua io que todos los otros pueblos de España vernian luego a se me rendir."

6. "Era mujer muy aguda y discreta... y era de tan excelente ingenio que, en común de tantos e tan arduos negocios como tenía en la gobernación de los Reynos, se dio al trabajo de aprender las letras latinas; e alcanzó en tiempo de un año saber en ellas tanto, que entendía cualquier fabla o escritura latina."

7. See Weissberger ("Confessional Politics") for a discussion of Isabel's correspondence with her confesor Hernando de Talavera as evidence that her skills in Latin were not good. Other opposing evidence for her promotion of Latin can be cited, such as her request that Nebrija edit his *Introductiones Latinae* with a Castilian translation, for the edification of nuns, which means that "these women who had to read the sacred texts written in Latin and also listen to Mass in Latin did not have a command of Latin" [no dominaban latín estas mujeres que debían leer los

textos sagrados escritos en latín y oír misa también en latín] (Segura Graiño, "Sabias mujeres," 183). On "La Latina," see Antonio de la Torre.

8. Juan never left Salamanca; shortly after his arrival, he contracted the illness that led to his death on October 4, 1497, at the age of nineteen.

9. For an overview of the important writers associated with Salamanca, starting with Alfonso Fernández de Madrigal (b. 1410?), see Deyermond, "Literatura en su contexto."

10. The best known of these nonsense poems are those by Juan de Encina, possibly written while he was himself a student at Salamanca. Lyna Ranz provides an overview of burlesque disputations in Europe.

11. See Roffé, chapter 1, for a concise discussion of the origins and characteristics of the university *disputatio* that fed the literary debate form.

12. See Cátedra, *Amor y pedagogía*, 36 n. 45 and 128 for a detailed description of the exercise and relevant documentation in the fifteenth-century papal constitutions and university charters. Consult van Liere for sample *repetitiones* delivered by the jurist Diego de Covarrubias at Salamanca in the academic year 1538–39.

13. Matulka and Ornstein view it as misogynist, Menéndez y Pelayo and Whinnom as sentimental.

14. See Cátedra's edition of the *Breviloquio* (*Del Tostado sobre el amor*, 69–127) and his extensive analysis in *Amor y pedagogía*, 22–39.

15. See chapter 5 of Cátedra's *Amor y pedagogía* for a discussion of *Sátira* as an expurgatory anti-Aristotelian polemic. Rodríguez del Padrón, whose *Siervo libre de amor* (c. 1445), is traditionally considered the initiator of the sentimental romance genre, studied at Salamanca in the first half of the fifteenth century. See Langbehn de Roland for a concise overview of the genre.

16. *De cómo al omne es necesario amar* is frequently misattributed to El Tostado; see the introduction to the edition by Cátedra (*Del Tostado sobre el amor*, x). See Langbehn de Roland for a concise overview of the genre.

17. "ese elemento natural que participa en el mundo intelectual del otoño de la edad media se trasvasa y alquitara en distintos odres y distintos ámbitos."

18. This did not prevent Ornstein, the first modern editor of the work, and Matulka from considering it a serious antifeminine treatise, a classification generally accepted—pace the demurral of Gilman—until a decade ago. I discuss later Lucena's introductory Latin verses to *Repetiçión*.

19. Besides the previously mentioned *De cómo al hombre es necesario amar* and *Sátira de felice e infelice vida*, Thompson mentions as sources El Tostado's *Sobre las diez qüestiones vulgares* (On ten common questions), *Historia de duobus amantibus* (Story of two lovers) by Enea Silvio Piccolomini, and Pedro López de Ayala's translation of Boccaccio's *De casibus virorum illustrium, Los casos e caídas de príncipes* (Fall of princes), published in 1495.

20. "salió del libro del pensamiento de Torrellas, y dizese más propiamente extravagante por no estar encorporado en el derecho." In canon law, the *extravagantes* are those decretal epistles published after the collection of decretals of Pope Clement V. They are so called because they were not digested with or incorporated into the Clementines. My thanks to Ronald Surtz for pointing out this learned joke of Lucena.

21. For the complete poem, see Pérez Priego. See Weiss ("Forming the Debate") and Weissberger ("Deceitful Sects") for a discussion of Torrellas's role in the debate about women in Isabelline Spain.

22. "delatan una burla evidente contra el auditorio, trasvistiendo en damiselas a

maestros, rector,... y estudiantes, para regodeo y mofa de todos." Cátedra goes even further, calling the address to the ladies "ideological," because nothing authorizes us to think that Lucena's work was ever actually delivered (133).

23. Gilman's description is typically vivid, if overly dependent on the fictional world of *Celestina* as a source: "The students, except in lectures and classes, carried swords and concealed daggers and very frequently wore armor under their robes. In an age of arms, the place was an armed camp.... In such circumstances, when tempers rose or when candidates of rival factions were competing for a single chair, the streets frequently were the scene of mass conflict. Private duels, nighly skirmishes with the town watch, even armed assault and robbery were as common as might be expected in such a society" (*Fernando de Rojas*, 286).

24. "Al suvir yo aquí, estas hermosísimas señoras me mandaron que la plática deste día fuese en su bulgar idioma castellano; que si vien muchas de sus señorías reconocen en sí tiempo y avilidad para saver latin, con todo esso, ay algunas de tan pocos y tiernos años que no les a dado lugar para semejante exercicio."

25. I owe this idea to Ronald Surtz.

26. Rojas claims to have found the anonymous act 1 during a university vacation (1497–98) and decided to continue it. He makes a point, however, of distinguishing the activity from his more weighty law studies (70).

27. "Es assí mesmo la muger hombre imperfecto, como dize Aristoteles, *De animalibus*, y comparasse al hombre como la sensualidad a la razón. Donde, assí como es contra natura que la sensualidad, que naturalmente obedesce a la razón, uviesse a aquélla de señorear, assí es contra natura tener ella poder de mandar." Cf. Sempronio's reproof to the lovesick Calisto: "That you submit the dignity of man to the imperfection of weak woman" [Que sometes la dignidad del hombre a la imperfección de la flaca mujer] (*Celestina*, 51).

28. Quien bien amando prosigue
Donas, a ssí mesmo destruye,
Que siguen a quién las fuye,
Y fuyen a quién las sigue;
No quieren por ser queridas,
Ni gualardonan servicios;
antes todas desconoscidas,
Por sola tema regidas,
Reparten sus beneficios.

29. "Y piensa que las mugeres fueran sufficientes para engañar a Aristóteles y Virgilio? No lo creas; antes el amor los engañó."

30. "¡O, prestante, luego excellente virtud, la qual sola es aquella que los hombres repone en estado tranquillo y seguro, y los haze señores y fuertes, ricos y libres, y les da plazeres incomutables y sempiternos, a los quales de noche y de día, en las plazas, en la soledad, en los plazeres, en los peligros acompaña...."

31. "Donde, después que la inevitable muerte ha quitado de tierra la operación virtuosa, apartando el ánima del cuerpo, la gloria y la fama renuevan en el mundo una vida libre de la contingencia y subjeción de la muerte."

32. "que no es naturalmente la andanada misógina, que, insistimos, se trae sólo como remedio teórico para que cada uno de los apasionados alcance la liberación, sino el de caracterizar en su faceta ética al individuo."

33. ¿Qué persuaden los oradores, qué pruevan los philósophos, qué demuestran los theologos sino la libertad del arbitrio, mediante la qual se estima la virtud, se celebran los consejos, se governan las ciudades?... Estando luego en nuestro poder la electión de la virtud y vicio, no deve hombre a otro que a sí mesmo accusar quando la virtud menosprecia, abrazándose con el vicio, no queriendo governarse por razón, en la qual reyna aquesta prudencia y la universal justicia, las quales son fundamento de todas las otras virtudes."

34. "Assí que, como el amor de que hablamos sea vano, áspero y amargo, y haga estar al hombre siempre enfermo, trabaja en te apartar dél, pensando siempre en el defecto de semejantes mugeres... y serás libre y señor de tí mesmo, que es el mayor bien que en este mundo puedes tener."

35. The heir to the throne died a few months after marrying Margaret of Austria. Cátedra has suggested, without explanation, an earlier dating: 1486–87, when the Catholic Monarchs wintered in the university town. Cf. Thompson for internal evidence that *Repetiçión* was written well before 1495, the date proposed by its first modern editor, Ornstein.

36. Ornstein *(Repetición); Arte de axedrez* is available in two facsimile editions, by Cossío (1953) and Pérez de Arriaga (1997).

37. "carta de presentación al príncipe Juan, heredero de la Corona, para obtener el preciado privilegio de pertenecer al selecto grupo de caballeros que eran admitidos a su servicio."

38. "a leer, escribir, tañer, cantar, / danzar y nadar, luchar, esgrimir / arcyo ballesta, llatinar y dezir, / xedrez y pelota saber bien jugar."

39. "E una mesica con su banco e una silla de espaldas e dos o tres escabelos o bancos pequeños bien pintados. Un tablero de ajedrez con sus trebejos e tablas."

40. "[escrito] por Lucena, hijo del muy sapientísimo Doctor y Reverendo Prothonotario don Johan Remírez de Lucena, Embajador y del Consejo de los Reyes Nuestros Señores, estudiando en el preclarísimo Studio de la muy noble ciudad de Salamanca."

41. "pospuestos los hechos de los romanos, y de los reyes de Egipto, los doce Césares, Troya y los asirianos."

42. In his extremely popular moralized sermon, *Ludus Scacchorum*, Jacobus de Cessolis attributed the invention of the game to Xerxes, whom he believed to be a philosopher. Xerxes supposedly intended the game as moral and mental discipline for a Chaldean king (Golombek, *History of Chess*, 65).

43. Murray (776) and other modern chess historians translate "de la dama" as "of the queen." I retain the more general *lady,* although the context no doubt made it clear which "lady" was meant.

44. See Golombek, *Encyclopedia*, chapters 7 and 8, for examples.

45. See Murphy, 555–56, for a more complete discussion of this popular chess morality.

46. Originally titled *Quaedam moralitas de Scaccario,* it is often misattributed to Pope Innocent III.

47. Eales calls *Eschés de la Dame* "the only known attempt to construct a true 'morality' around the rules of the new chess" (90).

48. In quibus aligeri flammata cupidinis arma
    Cum variis poteris nosse cupidinibus...

Cur pinnis volitans super aethera cuncta fatigat
Numina, et innumeros sauciat ille viros;
Cur nequeant Satyri, Dryades, Faunique bicornes
Effugere irati tela cruenta dei.
Hoc etiam paucis poetris cognoscere verbis,
Cur nemo ex huius vulnere sanus abit.

49. "Armatas cernes in fera bella manus; / Agmina concurrent diverso picta colore: / Calculus hinc rubeus, discolor inde ferit."

50. "¡O simple y fallace juizio, o effeminada mollicia y ceguedad del entendimiento muy escura la qual quiere antes el su defecto a otro atribuir que con la razón al sensitivo plazer repugnar, viendo que desde la primera hora la muger asimesmo llaga y destruye!"

51. The debate is exemplified in Spain by the thirteenth-century poem "Elena y María" and by some of the dramatic eclogues of Juan del Encina, Lucena's contemporary at Salamanca.

52. "quanto quiera que yo sea obligado a los letrados, aunque mi padre el prothonotario sea uno de aquéllos, no dexaré confessar la verdad, defendiendo las armas ser superiores a la scientia."

53. "entiendo escribir todos los mejores juegos que yo en Roma y por toda Italia y Francia y España he visto jugar a jugadores y yo he podido por mí mesmo alcanzar."

54. "se conoscerá la diferencia que es entre el juego que agora jugamos, que se dice de la dama, y el viejo que antes se usaba."

55. "por mandado de Yoles, su amiga, obedesciendo en esto a las fuerzas de Cupido, dexó las saetas y arco, desnudó las sus corazas... suffriendo que le pusiessen en orden como a donzella... con aquella mano con la qual asta estonze moviera la hacha darmas, movió el huso hilando."

56. "mudada su deitad, se hizo pastor del rey Admeto de Thesalia, con desseo de la hermosa donzella Alcesta.... Suffrió guardar entonces las vacas y, dexada la vihuela que a él pertenecía, llamava los thoros con albogues."

57. "Y a los que están encendidos en ellas... si quieren sanar, conviene que con diligencia agan lo que el médico los manda."

58. Cf. Toril Moi's influential analysis of the contradictions and failure of misogynistic discourse in Andreas Capellanus. Cf. Corfis for a similar approach applied to fifteenth-century Castilian "courtly love" texts. On gender and reception theory, see Flynn and Schweikart. For queens as readers, see Quilligan.

59. "Item que allegando a la barra del rey de su contrario tiene fuerza de dama, y da jaque sin trasponer, y no sólo como dama, pero si vuestras mercedes quisieren, al juego que yo uso, que por aquella vez que entra dama y el primer lance que della jugare, que prenda y dé jaque como dama y caballo, *por lo mucho que a las mujeres se les debe.*"

60. "*Repetición de amores*, sin desgajarse de su contexto universitario, nos hace pensar en el mundo cortesano y femenino del *Sermón de amores* de Diego de San Pedro."

6. The Mad Queen

1. See Weissberger, "Gendered Taxonomy," for a critique of the masculinist assumptions that attended the creation of this literary genre at the turn of the twentieth century.

2. The four are Diego de San Pedro's *Tractado de amores de Arnalte y Lucenda* (Treatise on the love of Arnalte and Lucena) (1491) and *Cárcel de Amor* (Prison of Love) (1492), and Flores's *Grisel y Mirabella* (Grisel and Mirabella) and *Grimalte y Gradisa* (Grimalte and Gradisa), both published in 1495, although probably written as much as twenty years earlier.

3. For a catalog of editions and translations, see Ivy Corfis's critical editions of *Arnalte* and *Cárcel*.

4. es yugo para los fuertes
es vida de nuestras muertes,
es luz de nuestras tinieblas
...
es tal que no auía de ser
humanidad puesta en ella,
mas quísolo Dios hazer
por darnos a conoscer
quién es El, pues hizo a ella.

5. "Verdad que en la obra presente no tengo tanto cargo, pues me puse en ella más por necessidad de obedescer, que con voluntad de escreuir, porque de vuestra merced me fue dicho que deuía hazer alguna obra del estilo de vna oración que enbié a la señora Marina Manuel, porque le parescía menos malo que el que puse en otro tractado que vido mío."

6. Additional, indirect evidence of female readership of romances exists, for example, in the many inscribed female readers in fifteenth-century romances and the frequency with which sixteenth-century moralists such as Luis Vives and Malón de Chaide decry the pernicious effects of romance reading on women's character. On the problematics of female literacy in medieval Castile as it relates to romance, see Weissberger, "Resisting Readers."

7. See Culler for an early formulation of "reading as a woman," the essays in Flynn and Schweikart that use various approaches to studying the effects of gender on literary interpretation, and the subtle analysis of the problem in Fuss's chapter "Reading like a Feminist."

8. Cf. Whetnall and Gómez Bravo for similar dialogist traces in courtly lyric of the period.

9. "en los contextos donde primero se presentan, estos temas no tienen nada de cómicos. Además está visto que los traductores francés e italiano... se estremaron en expresiones de simpatía por Arnalte y de condenación de Lucenda." For a feminist analysis of such humorous elements as Arnalte's cross-dressing in San Pedro's *Arnalte y Lucenda* and of Grimalte's ineffectiveness at completing his courtly service in Flores's *Grimalte y Gradisa*, see Weissberger, "Role-Reversal."

10. See Natalie Davis's classic analysis in *Society and Culture* of this medieval ritual and literary topos.

11. For a dating of Flores's works, see Gwara's articles; for the Tristan and Isolde letters, see Sharrer.

12. The two romances were previously thought to have been written close to their publication date of 1495.

13. Parrilla and Gwara disagree on this important point. The latter believes Flores

was of aristocratic lineage, a nephew of Pedro Alvarez Osorio, the Count of Lemos, and possibly a relative of the Duke of Alba, whom he served for a time.

14. For the biographical detective work, see Gwara's "Identity" and "Another Work," and Parrilla (*Grimalte*, viii–xvii).

15. In rethinking my earlier views, I have taken into account the thoughtful critiques of my work by von der Walde *(Amor e ilegalidad)* and Caba-Ríos.

16. It is possible that portions of the original text have been lost (Gwara, "Identity," 109).

17. On Bobadilla's active involvement in royal political and military matters, see Liss, 92, 114, 315.

18. "aunque no escatima las encomiásticas alabanzas a don Fernando... son, sin embargo, para la reina sus más cálidos elogios y panegíricos, y a ella le atribuye exclusivamente, con manifiesto error o con notoria injusticia, la iniciativa o la realización de varios negocios de importancia."

19. "El rey... creya que después de casado la reyna... le dexaría con aquel libre poder que los reyes han tenido en Castilla, sin que las reynas ayan de entender en las cosas del Reyno. Mas como ella conosçiese de sí ser más dispuesta muger que otra para la tal gouernaçión...."

20. No mention of Fernando is made after Título 53.

21. "y la reyna misma... por su persona proveya y requería a todas las necesidades, que non sé yo quál ombre tan guerrero más solícito que ella en la guerra fuese." Cf. Pulgar: "the king spent every day going from one siege to the next providing all necessary things" [el rey andaba todos los días del un cerco al otro proveyendo las cosas necesarias] (*Crónica*, 319).

22. "con mejor coraçón lo aventurara, queriendo ante tomar dubdoso peligro que çierta vergüença; porque yo, avnque muger flaca, prouara ante a la fortuna si me fuera amiga o contraria, que huyr della haziendola enemiga sin prouarla."

23. "nunca Anibal pasara los Alpes frios nin venciera la grand batalla de Canas [sic] si el coraçon tomara por mejores los flacos consejos del seso, que vnas son las reglas de la filosofía y otras las de la espada."

24. "[L]os augurios del cronista son siempre para tiempos peores, aquellos que siguieron al advenimiento al trono, justamente el asunto de la crónica: la disputa hereditaria." Gwara contends that the work as it has come down to us is more of a rough, incomplete draft than a polished final product. He believes that its disorganization, frequent deviations from chronology, avoidance of dates, errors of fact, and narrative lacunae indicate authorial haste or inexperience ("Identity," 109–11).

25. "en cada cibdad hazían justicias no acostumbradas en la vida del pasado rey; y porque quando algund corregidor embíauan el rey y reyna a cada cibdad o tierra era tan escogido, así en esforcado como en justiciero... tanto ellos eran temidos, que ningund corregidor, por principal cauallero que fuese, no avía de usar de las tiranías y codicias del tiempo [pasado]." Flores's insistence on the integrity of the *corregidores* may be defensive. The record shows that in 1477 he was charged with counterfeiting, although he was later absolved; two years later, he was accused of bribery. Nonetheless, royal confidence in him must have been great because he was given the post of investigating magistrate in Ávila to investigate charges of wrongdoing made against his closest colleagues during his tenure as *corregidor* (Parrilla, *Grimalte y Gradissa*, viii).

26. "ningund día pasaua sin grandes justiçias, tanto que los que justamente auían venido avn non osauan estar en la corte."

27. "el rey y reyna non quesieron por entonces que la execución de la justicia oviese floxura nin ningund caso criminal se perdonase avnque personas y Reynos perdiesen, auiendo por mejor de sofrir por la virtud pena, que non merecerla." For an objective account of the administration of justice in the early days of Isabel's reign, see Azcona, 450 55.

28. "Y siempre [a] las mugeres, quando en las cosas de la guerra se ponen, tienen las gentes mayor afiçión de las seruir, porque, con la verguença que han dellas se ponen con mayor gana al peligro y trabajo."

29. In "Another Work," Gwara proposes that Flores's entire corpus was written before 1485 and perhaps as early as 1475, but this last date cannot be accepted, at least for *Crónica,* which records events through December 1476. In the same essay Gwara attributes *La coronación de la señora Gracisla* (The coronation of the lady Gracisla) to Flores, partially on the basis of its many structural and stylistic similarities to *Grisel.* His date of 1475 for *Gracisla* leads to the conclusion that Flores wrote *Gracisla* after, and probably soon after, completing *Grisel.* If this assumption is correct, *Grisel* was written earlier than previously thought (Matulka placed it between 1480 and 1485), before both *Triunfo de amor* (dated 1475–76 by Gwara in "Date") and *Crónica incompleta* and more than two decades before *Grisel*'s 1495 printing. By this reasoning, the order of creation of Flores's works emerges as follows: *Grisel, Gracisla, Triunfo, Crónica, Grimalte.*

30. The following discussion of *Triunfo de amor* expands my earlier treatment in "Role-Reversal."

31. "De muchas maneras se cuenta como los amantes muertos contra el Dios de Amor se levantaron. Y lo que más se certifica es pensar como oy las cosas passan en esta vida: fazer traición los criados a los señores, de quien mayores mercedes reciben, y segunt la confusión del tiempo, toda fealdat tienen por gentileza."

32. "todo va tan roto... que ya no parece sino que mudamos el mundo de nueva condición y ley; y todos trocados tan contra razón y naturaleza."

33. "las obras de naturaleza tener un movedor y un fin que es Dios, a quien acatan; y por ser en los cielos un señor y no muchos, ser perfecta obra. Y este nuestro mundo, por aver muchos que lo señorean y mandan, se perdía o esperava del todo perescer; y agora, regidos por uno, grand remedio para los presentes males se espera."

34. "como siempre sea mayor parte de la virtud en los dioses la misericordia que la justicia, no quiero que vuestros errores en mi virtuoso costumbre muden leyes."

35. "que desde aquel día en adelante los días que estavan por venir las mugeres requiriesen a los hombres."

36. "que nuestro soberano Júpiter, criándonos a su semejança, por excellencia nos dio poder sobre todas las cosas criadas, y especialmente sobre las mugeres. Y así como su mandamiento lo quiso, así pasa en el mundo por ley: que ninguna cosa es nascida que por amor o temor no nos obedezca. Y solamente en casos de amar ellas son señoras y nosotros muy obedientes siervos."

37. "la malvada costumbre usada mucho en daño y perjuizio nuestro que la mudes y tornes a ley de razón."

38. "ellos escogen en nosotras qual más su voluntad les contenta; y sin vergüença ni temor, sin sentir pena, piden gualardón de servicios. Y nosotras, por no posponer

aquélla que nos enfrena, sufrimos mil muertes de nuestra puerta adentro; y a quien amamos, desseándole más que el bivir, damos mayores desdenes, y dízele la boca palabras que no le manda la voluntad."

39. "bien trabajosa vida sea la vuestra, teniendo los deleites míos delante, y desdeñarlos la lengua o quedandos llorando la voluntad.... Y como libertat sea el mayor bien que en este mundo entre los bienes conosco, de quien vosotras tanto carescéis ¿qué mayor merced queréis ganar conmigo? que sacaros la voluntad de tan estrecha cárcel?"

40. "Así que absueltas a culpa y a pena, como si agora naciésedes tornad; y sobre mis cuestas tomo el yerro de vuestra vergüença y la culpa de este peccado."

41. "después de averse aprovechado de las razones que a nosotros solían oír, dizían otras nuevas, que en el secreto de su saber tenían guardadas, las quales nosotros no podíamos alcançar, porque no sabíamos, como ellas, lo que se devía dezir, que más perteneciese y enamorase. Mas ellas de nuestro saber público y del suyo secreto."

42. See Weiss ("Alvaro de Luna") on the coercive nature of language in fifteenth-century amatory verse.

43. "En la sentencia a las mujeres el dios Amor rebaja la importancia del problema planteado al considerarlo una cosa coyuntural y banal: un uso, una costumbre."

44. "como brahones en tiempo que no se usan.... Pues así... las que quisieren gozar de la nueva ordenança, ternán facultad para ello; y las que en vieja condición se quisieren quedar, con aquel riebto que se pasa el que se viste ropa o hábito desusado: confórmasela con su voluntad."

45. "Así que yo no sé razón que por esto os deváis quexar, salvo alegraros, y dizir a mí por los hombres: 'Perdónalos señor, que no saben lo que se hazen.'"

46. "Mucho esta causa se alterçó et defendió por amas las partes; y aun vino en tal rompimiento, que la corte estovo munchas vezes para se perder y poner a todos en arisco de armas, con algunos cavalleros que el partido d'ellas favorescían. Mas como el Dios de Amor, viendo tan grand confusión entre sus gentes y sin remedio de los poder igualar, uvo de fuerça de contentar a los hombres, porque d'ellos gran cargo tenía, y con las mejores razones que pudo, dio contra las damas sentencia."

47. "En tan grande aprieto los tentavan, que ni les valía orar, ni rezar, rogando a Dios que los escapasse; mas ellas, como el diablo que tiene mejor cuidado de sus almas, les fazían renunciar los hábitos de religión tan estrecha."

48. Barbara Matulka was the the first scholar to treat Flores as champion of women in *Grisel* and *Grimalte*, the only works attributed to Flores before Gwara's groundbreaking research. See also Ornstein. My "Deceitful Sects" connects various debate texts to the religious and ethnic dimension of Isabelline nation formation.

49. "el que más causa o principio fuese al otro de haber amado, mereciese la muerte y el que menos, destierro."

50. "de todas virtudes amigo, y principalmente en ser justiciero; y era tanto iusto como la mesma justicia."

51. "la autoridad del Monarca no dimana ya de las virtudes militares y caballerescas del pasado, sino del culto fetichista a los ordenamientos legales, únicos asideros de su identidad."

52. The phrase "novela política" is an echo of Márquez Villanueva's important study of royal tyranny in *Cárcel de Amor*, to which the editors contrast *Grisel*. For an

analysis of the sexual politics of San Pedro's romance that is both indebted to Márquez and a feminist response to it, see Weissberger, "Politics of *Cárcel*."

53. See Grieve's discussion in "Mothers": "the author focuses on the breakdown of the family, which in turn signals a more devastating destruction of society in general" (350).

54. "Mas el Rey no pensaba sino como a la vida de Mirabella diese fin, aunque en estremo la amaba; pero la justicia era más poderosa que el amor."

55. "Pues mirad, excelente y muy illustre Reyna y nobles señoras, so cuyas leyes vivimos que quieren que muera la que es forzada y viva el forzador; y tienen razon, pues ellos son jueces y partes y abogados del mismo pleito y cierto asaz simple sería quien contra sí diese sentencia; y por esto no recebimos injuria, pues con poder absoluto nos la pueden dar."

56. "una graciosa letra... concediéndole en ella más de lo que por él le era demandado; porque con el engaño recibiese dellas la muerte."

57. "Y, mirad, que tan malicioso era que non pudo su mal secreto guardar, que... loando a sí y amenguando aquella que más cara de lo que él pensaba era de haber."

58. "cada una traía nueva invención para le dar tormentos; y tales hobo que, con tenazas ardiendo y otras con uñas y dientes, rabiosamente le despedazaron."

59. The *maestresala* served up for the ladies' delectation is the court majordomo.

60. "después que no dejaron ninguna carne en los huesos, fueron quemados; de su ceniza, guardando cada cual una bujeta por reliquias de su enemigo; y algunas hobo que por joyel en el cuello la traían, porque trayendo más a memoria su venganza, mayor placer hobiesen."

61. The best-known example of the female revenge topos in Spain is Martínez de Toledo's *Arcipreste de Talavera* or *Corbacho*. In the palinode added to the 1498 edition of the work—three years after the publication of *Grisel*—the author retracts the condemnation of women in Part II of his treatise: "On the vices and faults and bad nature of perverse women" (De los vicios e tachas e malas condiciones de las perversas mugeres). The section is an extensive catalog of women's failings: avarice, disobedience, gossip, envy, hypocrisy, fickleness, and so on (145–204). In the final retraction—"The author brings an end to this work and begs pardon if in anything he has said he has offended or misspoken" [El autor face fin a la presente obra e demanda perdón si en algo de lo que ha dicho ha enojado o no bien dicho]—Martínez de Toledo recounts a terrifying dream in which thousands of famous women "brought implements suited for torture, hitting me so hard with distaffs and slippers, fists and hanks of hair, whether it was as penance for the evils I did, and even for my sins... I ended up more dead than alive, and I dearly wanted to die rather than suffer such pain. Afflicted by torture, I woke up sweating, believing myself to have been in the power of cruel ladies" [traían esecuciones a manera de martirio, dando los golpes tales de ruecas e chapines, puños e remesones, qual sea en penitencia de los males que hize, e aun de mis pecados... quedé más muerto que vivo, que morir más amaua que tal dolor passar. Congoxado de tormento, sudando, desperté e pensé que en poder de crueles señoras me avía fallado] (305). As critics have pointed out, this famous retraction is highly ironic, because in effect it demonstrates the cruelty that the Archpriest had earlier condemned (Gerli, ed., 28). Its similarity to Torrellas's fate at the end of *Grisel* is apparent.

62. "más fuertes que otras mugeres de domar, y más retraídas y esquivas para obedescer la premia d'esta reqüesta."

63. "que por el peccado de Eva estávades las más santas enamoradas de vosotras en el infierno y limbo de la vergüença; pues alçad las manos a este Dios, que de tan grand cativerio a la libertad de los libres vos ha tornado."

64. She focuses on the anonymous *Triste deleytaçión* (1458–70), in which the character of the Madrina responds to Senyora's outrage at the double standard in the "laws of love" [leyes d'amor] in words that are reminiscent of Breçayda's indictment of legal sexism: "And now you are seeking the [protection of] the law? Don't you know that the laws are made only to protect them [men]?" [¿Y ley vas agora buscando? ¿Y tu no sabes que las leyes no son fechas sino para aquellos?] (quoted in Haywood, 19).

65. Krueger acknowledges that the identification of the dedicatee as Eleanor, although generally accepted by scholars, is inconclusive (4).

Conclusion

1. The corresponding masculine icon was, not surprisingly, a Catholic warrior, Spain's medieval epic hero, the Cid. See Lacarra, "La utilización del Cid," and Linehan's rebuttal.

2. "En la vida de la Reina Isabel de España tenéis todo un libro para estudiar. Ella conoció también de los tiempos turbulentos y materialistas. Ella se crió también abandonada entre la corrupción y el vicio. Pero supo mantener la pureza de su fe y la pureza de sus virtudes. Este es un ejemplo que tenéis que dar las mujeres españolas de hoy. Estas mujeres que en estos lugares hoscos, que más tienen de madrastras que de madres, han sabido guardar puros los sentimientos de la fe y los sentimientos de la Patria.

No acabó vuestra labor con la realizada en los frentes, con vuestro auxilio a las poblaciones liberadas, con vuestro trabajo en los ríos, en las aguas heladas, lavando la ropa de nuestros combatientes. Todavía queda más. Os queda... la reconquista del hogar. Os queda... criar ese carácter de que es ejemplo la Reina que murió tras esos muros."

Franco fulfilled the promise he made on that solemn occasion to renovate the Mota castle and house there a training school for the Sección Femenina. His biographer, Paul Preston, observes that on the occasion of the school's inauguration in 1942, Franco again indulged his fondness for regalism and compared his triumphs to Isabel's, interpreting their accomplishments in a way that aligned them with Hitler: "We received Spain in much the same way that Isabel received it... and she created a revolutionary politics, a politics that is ultimately totalitarian and fascist, because it is Catholic: a doctrine and an ideology that are extremely old, even if we rejuvenate them with the youthful spirit of our Youth Corps" [Lo mismo que nosotros recibimos a España, en forma similar la recibió Isabel de Castilla... que crea una política revolucionaria, una política totalitaria y racista al final, por ser católica; una doctrina y un ideario que se caen ya de viejos, aunque nosotros lo remocemos con el espíritu juvenil de nuestras Juventudes] (*Palabras del caudillo*, 212–13).

3. On Giménez Caballero, see Payne (51–54) and Rodríguez-Puértolas (*Literatura fascista*, passim). Giménez Caballero's conversion to fascism took place in 1928 during a visit to Rome, and he maintained close ties with Italian fascism. In 1933 he became a founding member of the Spanish fascist party and served on its first National Council. After the Nationalist uprising against the Republic in 1936, he joined Franco's entourage and began to play a leading role in the Nationalist propaganda apparatus (Labanyi, 378). Among the many important government posts he held under Franco was that of Adviser on National Education. Rodríguez-Puértolas points out (*Literatura fascista*, 1:690) that "Ge-Ce" was especially fond of his textbook. In a brilliant feminist psychoanalytic analysis of Giménez Caballero's often-reprinted *Genio de España* (1932), Jo Labanyi points out the extent to which its exaltation of fascism rests on male sexual complexes, and, specifically, the obsessive fear of women and the masses.

4. "La insignia de Falange debe verla todo el mundo, orgullosa.... Pero la medalla con España y vuestra madre nadie deberá verla; irá por dentro, pegada a vuestra carne; sintiéndola vosotros solos."

5. "Y tú, niño español, si alguien ante ti se ríe o insulta el nombre de Dios, o de España, o de tu madre, ¡no vaciles! Con tus puños, con tus dientes y tus pies, arremete contra él. Y si no lo haces, ¡cobarde! Ya no podrás llevar esa medalla de papel sobre el corazón, ni las flechas en la camisa. Y tú, niña española: si alguien ante ti se ríe o insulta el nombre de Dios, o de tu madre, o de España, ¡no te importe llorar! Llora con pena, amarga, infinita, callada."

6. "España era una princesa hija de un rey muy poderoso. Y de una reina muy bella, muy dulce y muy buena. España al heredar el trono sería también poderosa. Aunque ya era, como su madre, buena, delicada y bellísima. Todo el mundo la adoraba.... Mas un día su reina madre murió. Y el rey, al poco tiempo, volvió a casarse con una mujer muy mala y muy envidiosa.... Esta madrastra no podía soportar la belleza y el poderío de la princesa... al fin una vez, con engaños, consiguió la madrastra sus propósitos envidiosos, dándole a España una fruta embrujada que—apenas comida—la sumió en un sueño profundo, largo y como mortal: en un encantamiento. Del que sólo podía despertarla un Caudillo montado en un caballo blanco y tocándola en la frente con su espada de oro."

7. The medieval kingdom of Asturias in northern Spain was the legendary site of the initial skirmishes of the Reconquest.

8. Much important work has been done since the 1980s on the use of gender difference by the modern totalitarian regimes of Italy and Nazi Germany in order to define national and individual identities. For Germany and Italy, respectively, see Koontz and De Grazia. On Francoist Spain, consult Victoria L. Enders, especially the anthology coedited with Pamela Beth Radcliff.

9. In 2001, Goytisolo published a novel titled *Carajicomedia*, an acknowledged adaptation of the medieval poem. Timing did not permit its inclusion in my study.

10. "me sentí irritado por el empeño hagiográfico de un texto que atribuía sobrehumanas virtudes al Descubridor de América. Más tarde me topé con un increíble libro de Leon Bloy, donde el gran escritor católico solicitaba nada menos que la canonización de quien comparaba, llanamente, con Moisés y San Pedro."

11. "el aragonés [Fernando, King of Aragon] me parecía un memo, blandengue y sin carácter dominado por su mujer."

12. "jamás quise tratar de negocios con hembras, como no fuese en la cama, y era evidente que, en esta corte quien mandaba, quien montaba de verdad, era la hembra." The term *montar* may recall the "Tanto monta" of the royal motto.

13. "sólo una mujer existió para mí en el mundo que aún esperaba *por mí* para acabar de redondearse."

14. "En las noches de su intimidad, Columba... me prometía tres carabelas, diez carabelas, cincuenta carabelas, cien carabelas, todas las carabelas que quisiera: pero en cuanto amanecía, se esfumaban las carabelas, y... llegaba yo a preguntarme si mi destino no acabaría siendo el de tantos enamorados de su soberana."

15. On *Don Julián,* see the introduction to Levine's edition, which contains a useful bibliography. For overviews of Goytisolo's fiction, see Levine *(Juan Goytisolo),* and Lee Six.

16. "España es un ejemplo viviente del hecho de que reprimir el sexo equivale a reprimir la inteligencia y reprimir la inteligencia equivale a reprimir el sexo. Si no ha habido en la península una Revolución Francesa, ni gobiernos democráticos estables, tampoco ha existido un Laclos o un Baudelaire y mucho menos un Sade." The principal target of Goytisolo's criticism of Spain's repressiveness is Miguel de Unamuno and his concept of *casticismo.*

17. The term *carpetovetónico* refers to the two pre-Roman tribes, the *carpetanos* and *vetones,* that occupied Spain's central *meseta.* Goytisolo uses it frequently in his attack on *casticismo.*

18. "dueña de sí misma, animada de intensa vida espiritual, asistía a las conmociones que le deparaba la existencia con una serenidad y entereza que serían estoicas si no quedaran más exactamente definidas con decir que son hispanas." Levine explains that the description of Seneca's parents is taken from a description of Franco's parents in a biography written by Joaquín Arrarás *(Juan Goytisolo,* 184 n. 154).

19. "descubre la insólita perfección de sus piernas, suaves y bien torneadas: escuetas no, largas: abiertas en compás, rotundas, con muslos que convergen hacia el entrevisto tesoro como dos imperiosas señales de tráfico: dirección única, ley del embudo que la hispánica grey acata y sólo el traidor desdeña!"

20. "una inovidable, instructiva excursión por las honduras, recovecos y escondrijos del Bastión Teológico: por el interior del sancta sanctorum designado... como la Remota, Fantástica, jamás Explorada por Viajero Alguno Gruta Sagrada."

21. "arrojarás un panal de miel a la triple boca hambrienta y voraz de Cerbero y aprovecharás su denso y momentáneo sueño para colarte por las trompas de Falopio."

22. "Si algún impulso de solidaridad siento, no es jamás con la imagen del país que emerge a partir del reinado de los Reyes Católicos, sino con sus víctimas: judíos, musulmanes, cristianos nuevos, luteranos, enciclopedistas, liberales, anarquistas, marxistas."

23. My thanks to David Thorstad for reminding me that gay men also suffer discrimination in Muslim society.

24. I am aware that my book's focus on the male construction of femininity may be judged to participate in the erasure of women's subjectivities that was typical of late-medieval and early-modern patriarchy (cf. Breitenberg, 8). Elsewhere I have taken an initial step at studying Isabel's own discursive self-fashioning, by uncovering the sexual politics operating in an exchange of letters between the Queen and her confessor Hernando de Talavera in 1492 (Weissberger, "Confessional Politics"). As far as

we know, Isabel did not possess the literary proclivities that led Elizabeth I to compose poetry. Furthermore, as already mentioned, only a handful of the secular writers of the Isabelline period whose names are known were women. This need not discourage feminist analysis of medieval Iberian literature. The very fact that feminist Hispano-medievalists must focus their energies on male-authored texts can help avoid their marginalization, a common pitfall of feminist criticism that is centered on the recovery of women writers or "feminist" male authors (see Weissberger, "Florencia Pinar"). The paucity of named women writers in medieval Iberia compels feminist and queer critiques to use both a broader and a deeper focus on the myriad ways that patriarchy shapes and is shaped by cultural production in the foundational period of Spanish nationhood. It can only enhance our appreciation of the complexity of "the dependence of men upon women (or more accurately, their constructions of woman) for the confirmation of their own masculinity" (Breitenberg, 10) at the start of the European age of exploration.

25. Grothe analyzes the use of such rhetoric in María Pilar Morales's *La mujer: Orientación femenina*, a conduct book for women published in 1944. Its author proclaims that only woman's return to a traditional "authentic" femininity can save her and Spanish society from the dangers her freedom posed: "We believe that the great defect that is the root of all the others is women's excess of independence" [Creemos que el gran defecto que hace posibles todos los demás es el exceso de independencia en que vive la mujer] and "We want her to become more of a woman with every passing day, so that she can better fulfill her mission. Man, feeling the great attraction of sex, desires and needs femininity more than feminism" [Queremos que cada día sea más mujer, para que cumpla mejor su misión. El hombre, al sentir el gran atractivo del sexo, desea y necesita más femininidad que feminismo] (quoted in Grothe, 528–29).

26. "el carácter sacrificial del fascismo, su culto al dolor, a la abnegación y la entrega, su explotación de los sentimientos religiosos y de la maternidad enlazaban perfectamente con los rasgos del estereotipo femenino cuya vigencia perdura."

27. "Podría decirle que ... vivíamos rodeados de ignorancia y represión, hablarle de aquellos deficientes libros de texto que bloquearon nuestra enseñanza, de los amigos de mis padres que morían fusilados o se exiliaban."

28. "una chica no podía salir al extranjero sin tener cumplido el Servicio Social o, por lo menos, haber dejado suponer, a lo largo de los cursillos iniciados, que tenía madera de futura madre y esposa, digna descendiente de Isabel la Católica."

29. "La alegría era un premio al deber cumplido y se oponía, fundamentalmente, a la duda. ... Isabel jamás se dio tregua, jamás dudó. Orgullosas de su legado, cumpliríamos nuestra misión de españolas, aprenderíamos a hacer la señal de la cruz sobre la frente de nuestros hijos, a ventilar un cuarto, a aprovechar los recortes de cartulina y de carne, a quitar manchas, tejer bufandas y lavar visillos, a sonreír al marido cuando llega disgustado, a decirle que tanto monta monta tanto Isabel como Fernando, que la economía doméstica ayuda a salvar la economía nacional y que el ajo es buenísimo para los bronquios, aprenderíamos a poner un vendaje, a decorar una cocina con aire coquetón, a prevenir las grietas del cutis y a preparar con nuestras propias manos la canastilla del bebé destinado a venir al mundo para enorgullecerse de la Reina Católica, defenderla de calumnia y engendrar hijos que, a su vez, la alabaran por los siglos de los siglos."

30. "donde cada paso, viaje o decisión de la reina parecían marcados por un destino superior e inquebrantable."

31. *El Balneario* (The spa) (1954) is Martín Gaite's first novel. It begins in a fantastic mode, but ends in a realistic one.

32. —¿Sabe lo que le digo? Que sí creo en el diablo y en San Cristóbal gigante y en Santa Bárbara bendita, en todos los seres misteriosos, vamos. En Isabel la Católica, no.

—Me alegro —dice [el hombre]— está usted volviendo a perder el camino.

—¿Qué camino?

—El que creyó encontrar en la segunda parte de *El Balneario,* el camino de vuelta. ¿Se acuerda del cuento de Pulgarcito?

—Sí, claro, ¿por qué?

—Cuando dejó un reguero de migas de pan para hallar el camino de vuelta, se las comieron los pájaros. A la vez siguiente, ya resabiado, dejó piedrecitas blancas, y así no se extravió, vamos, es lo que creyó Perrault, que no se extraviaba, pero yo no estoy seguro, ¿me comprende?

Works Cited

Aguado Bleye, Pedro. "Tanto Monta: La Concordia de Segovia y la empresa de Fernando el Católico." *Estudios segovianos* 1 (1949): 381–89.
Alonso, Alvaro, ed. *Carajicomedia*. Archidona, Málaga: Ediciones Aljibe, 1995.
Alonso, Martín. *Diccionario medieval*. 2 vols. Salamanca: Universidad Pontificia de Salamanca, 1986.
Alonso Hernández, J. L. *El lenguaje de los maleantes españoles de los siglos XVI y XVII: La germanía (introducción al léxico del marginalismo)*. Salamanca: Universidad de Salamanca, 1979.
Alvarez Gato, Juan. *Obras completas*. Ed. Jenaro Artiles Rodríguez. Madrid: Nueva Biblioteca de Autores Españoles, 1928.
Alvarez Rubiano, Pablo. *La lección política de los Reyes Católicos*. Valencia: Universidad de Valencia, 1952.
Alvarez-Hesse, Gloria. *La "Crónica sarracina": Estudio de los elementos novelescos y caballerescos*. New York: Peter Lang, 1989.
Alzieu, Pierre, Robert Jammes, and Yvan Lissorgues, eds. *Floresta de poesías eróticas del Siglo de Oro*. Toulouse: Université de Toulouse-Le Mirail, 1975.
Anderson, Benedict. *Imagined Communities*. Rev. ed. London: Verso, 1991 [1983].
Aristotle. *Generation of Animals*. Trans. A. Platt. In *The Complete Works of Aristotle: The Revised Oxford Translation*, ed. Jonathan Barnes. Bollingen Series 71. 2 vols. Princeton, N.J.: Princeton University Press, 1984. 1:1111–1218.
Aronstein, Susan. "Prize or Pawn?: Homosocial Order, Marriage, and the Redefinition of Women in the *Gawain Continuation*." *Romanic Review* 82 (1991): 115–26.
Asensio, Francisco. *Floresta española*. Vol. 2 of *Floresta general*. Ed. Pablo Oyanguren. Madrid: V. Suárez, 1910–11.
Augustine. *The City of God*. Trans. Marcus Dods. New York: Random House, 1950.
Avenoza, Gemma. "Un nuevo manuscrito de las *Generaciones y semblanzas*, la *Crónica de Enrique IV* y la propaganda isabelina." *Anuario medieval* 3 (1991): 7–22.
Axton, Marie. *The Queen's Two Bodies: Drama and the Elizabethan Succession*. London: Royal Historical Society, 1977.

Ayerbe-Chaux, Reinaldo. "Las memorias de Doña Leonor López de Córdoba." *Journal of Hispanic Philology* 2.2 (1977): 11–33.

Azcona, Tarsicio de. *Isabel la Católica: Estudio crítico de su vida y su reinado*. Madrid: Editorial Católica, 1964.

Babcock, Barbara B. *The Reversible World: Symbolic Inversion in Art and Society*. Ithaca, N.Y.: Cornell University Press, 1978.

Bakhtin, Mikhail. *Rabelais and His World*. Trans. Hélène Iswolsky. Bloomington: Indiana University Press, 1984.

Ballesteros Gaibrois, Manuel. *La obra de Isabel la Católica*. Segovia: Diputación Provincial de Segovia, 1953.

Barker, Francis. *The Tremulous Private Body: Essays on Subjection*. Ann Arbor: University of Michigan Press, 1995.

Barrett, Michele. *Women's Oppression Today: Problems in Marxist Feminist Analysis*. London: Verso, 1980.

Bass, Laura. "Homosocial Bonds and Desire in the *Abencerraje*." *Revista canadiense de estudios hispánicos* 24.3 (2000): 453–71.

Bauer, Dale M., and Susan Jaret McKinstry, eds. *Feminism, Bakhtin, and the Dialogic*. Albany: State University of New York Press, 1991.

Bauman, Richard A. *Women and Politics in Ancient Rome*. London and New York: Routledge, 1992.

Beceiro Pita, Isabel, and Ricardo Córdoba de la Llave. *Parentesco, poder, y mentalidad: la nobleza castellana, siglos XII–XV*. Madrid: Centro Superior de Investigaciones Científicas, 1990.

Bedoya, Juan G. "Los obispos españoles solicitarán al Papa que canonice a Isabel la Católica." *El País*. On-line. March 2, 2002.

Belsey, Catherine. "Afterword: A Future for Materialist Feminist Criticism?" In Wayne, *Matter of Difference*, 257–70.

———. *Critical Practice*. London: Methuen, 1980.

Beltrán, Luis. "The Poet, the King and the Cardinal Virtues in Juan de Mena's *Laberinto*." *Speculum* 46 (1971): 318–32.

Benassar, Bartolomé. "El modelo sexual: La Inquisición de Aragón y la represión de los pecados 'abominables.'" In *Inquisición española: Poder político y control social*, ed. Bartolomé Benassar. Barcelona: Grijalbo, 1981.

Benson, Pamela Joseph. *The Invention of the Renaissance Woman: The Challenge of Female Independence in the Literature and Thought of Italy and England*. University Park: Pennsylvania State University Press, 1992.

Bermejo Cabrero, José Luis. "Orígenes del oficio de cronista real." *Hispania* 145 (1980): 395–409.

———. "Ideales políticos de Juan de Mena." *Revista de estudios políticos* 188 (1973): 153–75.

Bernis, Carmen. "Modas moriscas en la sociedad critiana española del siglo XV y principios del siglo XVI." *Boletín de la Real Academia de la Historia* 144 (1959): 198–210.

Berry, Philippa. *Of Chastity and Power: Elizabethan Literature and the Unmarried Queen*. London and New York: Routledge, 1989.

Biddick, Kathleen. "Genders, Bodies, Borders: Technologies of the Visible." In *Studying Medieval Women*, ed. Nancy F. Partner. Cambridge: Medieval Academy of America, 1993. 87–116.

Binotti, Lucia. "La *Epístola exhortatoria a las letras* de Juan de Lucena. Humanismo y educación en la Castilla del siglo XV." *La Corónica* 28.2 (2000): 51–80.

Blackmore, Josiah, and Gregory S. Hutcheson. *Queer Iberia: Sexualities, Cultures, and Crossings from the Middle Ages to the Renaissance.* Durham, N.C.: Duke University Press, 1999.

Blamires, Alcuin. *The Case for Women in Medieval Culture.* Oxford: Clarendon Press, 1997.

Bloch, Howard. *Medieval Misogyny and the Invention of Western Romantic Love.* Chicago: University of Chicago Press, 1991.

Boose, Lynda E. "Scolding Brides and Bridling Scolds: Taming the Woman's Unruly Member." *Shakespeare Quarterly* 42.2 (1991): 179–213.

Booth, Wayne C. "Freedom of Interpretation: Bakhtin and the Challenge of Feminist Criticism." *Critical Inquiry* 9 (1982): 45–76.

Boswell, John. *Christianity, Social Tolerance, and Homosexuality: Gay People in Western Europe from the Beginning of the Christian Era to the Fourteenth Century.* Chicago: University of Chicago Press, 1980.

Bray, Alan. *Homosexuality in Renaissance England.* London: Gay Men's Press, 1982.

Bredbeck, Gregory. *Sodomy and Interpretation: Marlowe to Milton.* Ithaca, N.Y.: Cornell University Press, 1980.

Breitenberg, Mark. *Anxious Masculinity in Early Modern England.* Cambridge: Cambridge University Press, 1996.

Bristol, Michael. *Carnival and Theatre: Plebeian Culture and the Structure of Authority in Renaissance England.* New York: Methuen, 1985.

Brocato, Linde M. "'Tened por espejo su fin': Mapping Gender and Sex in Fifteenth- and Sixteenth-Century Spain." In Blackmore and Hutcheson, *Queer Iberia*, 325–65.

Brown, Catherine. "Queer Representation in the *Arcipreste de Talavera*, or the *Maldezir de mugeres* Is a Drag." In Blackmore and Hutcheson, *Queer Iberia*, 325–65.

———. *Contrary Things: Exegesis, Dialectic, and the Poetics of Didacticism.* Stanford, Calif.: Stanford University Press, 1998.

———. "The Archpriest's Magic Word: Representational Desire and Discursive Ascesis in the *Arcipreste de Talavera*." *Revista de estudios hispánicos* 31 (1997): 377–401.

Brownlee, Marina Scordilis. *The Severed Word: Ovid's "Heroides" and the "Novela Sentimental."* Princeton, N.J.: Princeton University Press, 1990.

Bruster, Douglas. *Drama and the Market in the Age of Shakespeare.* Cambridge Studies in Renaissance Literature and Culture 1. Cambridge: Cambridge University Press, 1992.

Bugge, John. *Virginitas: An Essay in the History of a Medieval Ideal.* The Hague: Martinus Nijhoff, 1975.

Burns, E. Jane. *Bodytalk: When Women Speak in Old French Literature.* Philadelphia: University of Pennsylvania Press, 1993.

———. "The Man behind the Lady in Troubadour Lyric." *Romance Notes* 25 (1985): 254–70.

Burshatin, Israel. "Narratives of Reconquest: Rodrigo, Pelayo, and the Saints." In *Saints and Their Authors: Studies in Medieval Hispanic Hagiography in Honor of John K. Walsh.* Madison, Wis.: Hispanic Seminary of Medieval Studies, 1990. 13–26.

Burt, John R. "The Motif of the Fall of Man in the 'Romancero del Rey Rodrigo.'" *Hispania* 61 (1978): 435–42.

Burt, Richard, and John Michael Archer, eds. *Enclosure Acts: Sexuality, Property, and Culture in Early Modern England*. Ithaca, N.Y.: Cornell University Press, 1994.

Bynum, Carolyn Walker. *Fragmentation and Redemption: Essays on Gender and the Human Body in Medieval Religion*. New York: Zone Books, 1992.

Caba-Ríos, María Y. "Juan de Flores y el *Triunfo de amor* de las mujeres encima." Unpublished paper.

Campo, Victoria. "Modelos para una mujer 'modelo': los libros de Isabel la Católica." In *Actas del III Congreso de la Asociación Hispánica de Literatura Medieval*. 2 vols. Ed. Túa Blesa et al. Zaragoza: Universidad de Zaragoza, 1994. 1:85–94.

Campo, Victoria, and Víctor Infantes, eds. *"La Poncella de Francia": La historia castellana de Juana de Arco*. Vervuert: Iberoamericana, 1997.

Canales, Alfonso. "Sobre la identidad del actante (léase protagonista) de la *Carajicomedia*." *Papeles de Son Armadans* 80 (1976): 73–81.

Cancionero de obras de burlas provocantes a risa. Ed. Pablo Jauralde Pou and Juan Alfredo Bellón Cazabán. Madrid: Akal Editor, 1974.

Cancionero general recopilado por Hernando del Castillo (Valencia, 1511). Ed. Antonio Rodríguez Moñino. Madrid: Real Academia Española, 1958. *Suplemento*, 1959.

Cano Ballesta, Juan. "*Castigos y dotrinas que un sabio daua a sus hijas*: un texto del siglo XV sobre educación femenina." In *Actas del X Congreso de la Asociación Internacional de Hispanistas*, 2 vols., ed. Antonio Vilanova. Barcelona: Promociones y Publicaciones Universitarias, 1992. 139–50.

Carajicomedia. Ed. Alvaro Alonso. Málaga: Ediciones Aljibe, 1995.

Carajicomedia. Ed. Carlos Varo. Madrid: Playor, 1981.

Carpentier, Alejo. *The Harp and the Shadow: A Novel*. Trans. Thomas Christensen and Carol Christensen. San Francisco: Mercury House, 1990.

———. *El arpa y la sombra*. Mexico City: Siglo Veintiuno, 1979.

Carrasco, Rafael. *Inquisición y represión sexual en Valencia: Historia de los sodomitas (1565–1785)*. Barcelona: Laertes, 1985.

Castiglione, Baldassare. *The Book of the Courtier*. Trans. George Bull. London: Penguin Books, 1976.

———. *The Book of the Courtier*. Trans. Thomas Hoby. London: J. M. Dent, 1956.

Castigos y dotrinas que un sabio daua á sus hijas. In *Dos obras didácticas y dos leyendas*, ed. Hermann Knust. Madrid: Imprenta de M. Ginesta, 1878.

Castillo, Diego Enríquez del. *Crónica del Rey Don Enrique del Cuarto*. In *Crónicas de los reyes de Castilla*, 3:97–727.

Castro, Américo. *Aspectos del vivir hispánico*. Madrid: Alianza, 1970 [1949].

———. *La realidad histórica de España*. Rev. ed. Mexico City: Porrúa, 1966.

———. *España en su historia. Cristianos, moros y judíos*. Buenos Aires: Losada, 1948.

Cátedra, Pedro. *Amor y pedagogía en la edad media (Estudios de doctrina amorosa y práctica literaria)*. Salamanca: Universidad de Salamanca, 1989.

———. *Del Tostado sobre el amor*. Barcelona: Stelle dell'Orsa, 1986.

Cela, Camilo José. *Diccionario del erotismo*. 2 vols. Barcelona: Ediciones Grijalbo, 1976.

Cepeda Adán, José. "El providencialismo en los cronistas de los Reyes Católicos." *Arbor* 17 (1950): 177–90.

Cereceda, Miguel. *El origen de la mujer sujeto*. Madrid: Tecnos, 1996.

Cervantes, Miguel de. *Don Quijote de la Mancha*. Ed. Francisco Rico. 2 vols. Barcelona: Instituto Cervantes, 1998.

Charbonneau-Lassay, Louis. *The Bestiary of Christ*. Trans. D. M. Dooling. New York: Arkana, 1991.
Charnon-Deutsch, Lou. *Fictions of the Feminine in the Nineteenth-Century Spanish Press*. University Park: Pennsylvania State University Press, 2000.
Checa, Jorge. "*Grisel y Mirabella* de Juan de Flores: rebeldía y violencia como síntomas de crisis." *Revista Canadiense de Estudios Hispánicos* 12 (1988): 369–82.
Ciceri, Marcella. "Livelli di transgressione (dal riso all'insulti) nei Canzonieri spagnoli." In *Codici della trasgressività in area ispanica: atti del convegno di Verona, 12–14 giugnio, 1980*. Verona: Università degli Studi di Padova, 1981. 19–35.
Clarke, Dorothy Clotelle. *Juan de Mena's "Laberinto de Fortuna": Classic Epic and "Mester de Clerecía."* University, Miss.: Romance Monographs, 1973.
Clemencín, Diego de. *Elogio de la Reina Doña Isabel*. Madrid: Imprenta de I. Sancha, 1821.
Coletti, Theresa. "Purity and Danger: The Paradox of Mary's Body and the Engendering of the Infancy Narrative in the English Mystery Cycles." In *Feminist Approaches to the Body in Medieval Literature*, ed. Linda Lomperis and Sarah Stanbury. Philadelphia: University of Pennsylvania Press, 1993. 65–95.
Collins, Roger. *The Arab Conquest of Spain: 710–797*. Oxford: Basil Blackwell, 1989.
Continuación de la crónica de Pulgar. In *Crónica de los reyes de Castilla*, ed. Cayetano Rosell. Biblioteca de Autores Españoles 70. Madrid: Atlas, 1953. 3:513–31.
Coplas de la Panadera. In *Poesía crítica y satírica del siglo XV*, ed. Julio Rodríguez-Puértolas. Madrid: Castalia, 1981.
Córdoba, Martín de. *Jardín de nobles donzellas*. Ed. Harriet Goldberg. North Carolina Studies in the Romance Languages and Literatures 137. Chapel Hill: University of North Carolina Press, 1974.
Corfis, Ivy A. "Sentimental Lore and Irony in the Fifteenth-Century Romances and Celestina." In Gwara and Gerli, *Sentimental Romance*, 153–71.
Corominas, Joan. *Diccionario crítico etimológico castellano e hispánico*. 6 vols. Madrid: Editorial Gredos, 1980–91.
Corral, Pedro de. *Crónica del Rey don Rodrigo: Postrimero rey de los godos (Crónica sarracina)*. Ed. James Donald Fogelquist. 2 vols. Madrid: Castalia, 2001.
Correll, Barbara. "Malleable Material, Models of Power: Woman in Erasmus's 'Marriage Group' and *Civility in Boys*." *English Literary History* 57 (1990): 241–62.
Covarrubias, Sebastián de. *Tesoro de la lengua castellana o española*. Ed. Martín de Riquer. Barcelona: Editorial Alta Fulla, 1989.
Crónicas de los reyes de Castilla. Ed. Cayetano Rosell. 3 vols. Biblioteca de Autores Españoles 66, 68, 70. Madrid: Rivadeneyra, 1875–78.
Cruz, Anne J. "The Female Figure as Political Propaganda in the 'Pedro el Cruel' Romancero." In *Spanish Women in the Golden Age: Images and Realities*, ed. Magdalena S. Sánchez and Alain Saint-Saens. Westport, Conn.: Greenwood Press, 1996. 69–89.
———. "The Politics of Illicit Love in the 'Pedro el Cruel' Ballad Cycle." *Scandinavian Yearbook of Folklore* 48 (1992): 1–16.
Culler, Jonathan. *On Deconstruction: Theory and Criticism after Structuralism*. Ithaca, N.Y.: Cornell University Press, 1982.
Davis, Natalie Zemon. "Women on Top." In *Society and Culture in Early Modern France*. Stanford, Calif.: Stanford University Press, 1975. 124–51.

De cómo al ome es necesario amar. In *Del Tostado sobre el amor,* ed. Pedro Cátedra. Barcelona: Stelle dell'Orsa, 1986. 7–68.

De Grazia, Victoria. *How Fascism Ruled Women: Italy 1922–1945.* Berkeley: University of California Press, 1992.

Delany, Sheila. "Anatomy of the Resisting Reader: Some Implications of Resistance to Sexual Wordplay in Medieval Literature." *Exemplaria* 4.1 (1992): 7–34.

Delicado, Francisco. *The Portrait of Lozana: The Lusty Andalusian Woman.* Trans. Bruno M. Damiani. Potomac, Md.: Scripta Humanistica, 1987.

———. *La lozana andaluza.* Ed. Bruno M. Damiani. Madrid: Castalia, 1982.

Deyermond, Alan. "Women and Gómez Manrique." In *Cancionero Studies in Honour of Ian Macpherson,* ed. Alan Deyermond. London: Queen Mary and Westfield College, 1998. 69–87.

———. *Point of View in the Ballad: "The Prisoner," "The Lady and the Shepherd," and Others.* London: Queen Mary and Westfield College, Department of Hispanic Studies, 1996.

———. "Las autoras medievales a la luz de las últimas investigaciones." In *Medioevo y literatura: Actas del V Congreso de la Asociación Hispánica de Literatura Medieval,* ed. Juan Paredes. 4 vols. Granada: University of Granada, 1995. 1:31–52.

———. "La literatura en su contexto físico: Salamanca y unos momentos claves de la literatura medieval y renacentista." *Donaire* 3 (1994): 9–21.

———. "La ideología del Estado moderno en la literatura española del siglo XV." In *Realidad e imágenes del poder: España a fines del siglo XV,* ed. Adeline Rucquoi. Valladolid: Ambito Ediciones, 1988. 171–93.

———. "The Death and Rebirth of Visigothic Spain in the *Estoria de España.*" *Revista canadiense de estudios hispánicos* 9.3 (1985): 345–46.

———. "Spain's First Women Writers." In *Women in Hispanic Literature: Icons and Fallen Idols,* ed. Beth Miller. Berkeley: University of California Press, 1983. 27–53.

———. "Structure and Style as Instruments of Propaganda in Juan de Mena's *Laberinto de Fortuna.*" *Proceedings of the Patristic, Medieval, and Renaissance Conference* 5 (1980): 159–67.

———. "The Worm and the Partridge: Reflections on the Poetry of Florencia Pinar." *Mester* 7 (1978): 3–8.

———. *A Literary History of Spain: The Middle Ages.* London: Ernest Benn, 1971.

Di Camillo, Ottavio. *El humanismo castellano del siglo XV.* Valencia: Fernando Torres, 1976.

Díaz-Diocaretz, Myriam, and Iris M. Zavala, eds. *Breve historia feminista de la literatura española (en lengua castellana).* 2 vols. Madrid: Anthropos, 1993–95.

Diccionario de autoridades. Madrid: Gredos, 1990 [1732].

Diccionario de la lengua española. Madrid: Real Academia de la Lengua, 1984.

Dictionary of Christian Biography. Ed. William Smith and Henry Wace. 4 vols. London: J. Murray, 1877–87.

Díez de Games, Gutierre. *El Victorial. Crónica de Pero Niño.* Ed. Juan de Mata Carriazo. Madrid: Espasa-Calpe, 1982.

Dimler, G. Richard. "The Bee-Topos in the Jesuit Emblem Book: Themes and Contrast." In *The Emblem in Renaissance and Baroque Europe: Tradition and Variety.* Selected papers of the Glasgow International Emblem Conference, August 13–17, 1990. Ed. Alison Adams and Anthony J. Harper. Leiden: E. J. Brill, 1992. 229–46.

Domínguez, Frank. *Love and Remembrance: The Poetry of Jorge Manrique.* Lexington: University of Kentucky Press, 1988.

———, ed. *Cancionero de obras de burlas provocantes a risa.* Valencia: Albatros Hispanófila, 1978. 131–47.

Douglas, Mary. *Natural Symbols: Explorations in Cosmology.* New York: Pantheon Books, 1982.

———. *Purity and Danger: An Analysis of Concepts of Pollution and Taboo.* Harmondsworth, England: Penguin Books, 1970.

Duby, Georges. *The Knight, the Lady, and the Priest: The Making of Modern Marriage in Medieval France.* Trans. Barbara Bray. New York: Pantheon Books, 1983.

Durán, María Angeles, ed. *Nuevas perspectivas sobre la mujer: Actas de las Primeras Jornadas de Investigación Interdisciplinaria.* 2 vols. Madrid: Seminario de la Mujer de la Universidad Autónoma, 1982.

Durán, María Angeles, and M. D. Temprano. "Mujeres, misóginos y feministas en la literatura española (comentarios a/y un millar de referencias bibliográficas, a modo de epílogo)." In *Literatura y vida cotidiana,* ed. María Angles Durán y José Antonio Rey. Actas de las Cuartas Jornadas de Investigación Interdisciplinaria. Zaragoza: Universidad de Zaragoza, 1984. 413–97.

Dutton, Brian, and Jineen Krogstad. *El cancionero del siglo XV, c. 1360–1520.* 7 vols. Salamanca: Universidad de Salamanca, 1990–91.

Eales, Richard. *Chess: The History of a Game.* New York: Facts on File Publications, 1985.

Earenfight, Theresa. "María of Castile, Ruler or Figurehead? A Preliminary Study of Aragonese Queenship." *Mediterranean Studies* 4 (1994): 45–61.

Edwards, John. "Conversos, Judaism, and the Language of Monarchy in XVth-century Spain." In *Circa 1492: Proceedings of the Jerusalem Colloquium: Litterae Judaeorum in Terra Hispanica,* ed. Isaac Benabu. Jerusalem: Hebrew University of Jerusalem, 1992. 207–23.

Egido, Aurora. "*De ludo vitando.* Gallos áulicos en la Universidad de Salamanca." *El Crotalón* 1 (1984): 609–48.

Eiximenis, Francesc. Texto y concordancias del "Libro de las donas." Ed. Gracia Lozano López. Microfiche. Madison, Wis.: Hispanic Seminary of Medieval Studies, 1992.

Elliott, J. H. *Imperial Spain: 1469–1716.* New York: New American Library, 1966.

Encina, Juan del. *Obras completas.* Ed. Ana María Rambaldo. 3 vols. Madrid: Clásicos castellanos, 1978.

Enders, Victoria Lorée. "Problematic Portraits: The Ambiguous Historical Role of the Sección Femenina of the Falange." In Enders and Radcliff, *Spanish Womanhood,* 375–97.

———. "Nationalism and Feminism: The Sección Femenina of the Falange." *History of European Ideas* 15.4–6 (1992): 673–80.

Enders, Victoria Lorée, and Pamela Beth Radcliff, eds. *Constructing Spanish Womanhood: Female Identity in Modern Spain.* Albany: State University of New York Press, 1999.

Erasmus, Desiderius. *Lingua.* Ed. Johann Froben. Basel: Johann Froben, 1526.

Esperabé Arteaga, E. *Historia pragmática e interna de la Universidad de Salamanca.* 2 vols. Salamanca: Francisco Nuñez Izquierdo, 1917.

Espósito, Anthony P. "Dismemberment of Things Past: Fixing the Jarchas." *La Corónica* 24.1 (1995): 4–14.

Fantham, Elaine. "*Stuprum:* Public Attitudes and Penalties for Sexual Offences in Republican Rome." *Echos du Monde Classique/Classical Views* 35 (1991): 267–91.
Fenster, Thelma S., and Clare A. Lees. *Gender in Debate from the Early Middle Ages to the Renaissance.* New York: Palgrave, 2002.
Ferguson, Margaret W., Maureen Quilligan, and Nancy J. Vickers, eds. *Rewriting the Renaissance: The Discourses of Sexual Difference in Early Modern Europe.* Chicago: University of Chicago Press, 1987.
Fernández de Madrigal, Alfonso. *Breviloquio de amor y amiçiçia.* See Cátedra, *Del Tostado sobre el amor.*
Fernández de Oviedo y Valdés, Gonzalo. *Libro de la Cámara Real del Príncipe Don Juan.* Madrid: Viuda e Hijos de Galiano, 1870.
Ferrara, Orestes. *Un pleito sucesorio: Enrique IV, Ysabel de Castilla y la Beltraneja.* Madrid: "La Nave," 1945.
Findlen, Paula. "Humanism, Politics and Pornography in Renaissance Italy." In *The Invention of Pornography: Obscenity and the Origins of Modernity, 1500–1800,* ed. Lynn Hunt. New York: Zone Books, 1995.
Finke, Laurie. "The Rhetoric of Desire in the Courtly Lyric." In *Feminist Theory, Women's Writing.* Ithaca, N.Y., and London: Cornell University Press, 1992. 29–74.
Finucci, Valeria. "In the Name of the Brother: Male Rivalry and Social Order in Baldassare Castiglione's *Il libro del cortegiano.*" *Exemplaria* 9.1 (1997): 91–116.
———. "Jokes on Women: Triangular Pleasures in Castiglione and Freud." *Exemplaria* 4.1 (1992): 51–77.
Firpo, Arturo. "Los reyes sexuales: ensayo sobre el discurso sexual durante el reinado de Enrique de Trastámara (1454–1474)." *Mélanges de la Casa de Velázquez* 20 (1984): 212–27; 21 (1985): 145–58.
Flannigan, Clifford. "Liminality, Carnival, and Social Structure." In *Victor Turner and the Construction of Cultural Criticism: Between Literature and Anthropology,* ed. Kathleen Ashley. Bloomington: Indiana University Press, 1990. 42–63.
Flores, Juan de. *Grimalte y Gradisa.* Ed. Carmen Parrilla García. Santiago de Compostela: Universidad de Santiago de Compostela, 1988.
———. *La historia de Grisel y Mirabella.* Ed. Pablo Alcázar López and José A. González Núñez. Granada: Editorial Don Quijote, 1983.
———. *Triunfo de amor.* Ed. Antonio Gargano. Pisa: Giardini, 1981.
———. *Crónica incompleta de los Reyes Católicos.* Ed Julio Puyol. Madrid: Real Academia de la Historia, 1934.
Flynn, Elizabeth A., and Patrocinio P. Schweikart, eds. *Gender and Reading: Essays on Readers, Texts, and Contexts.* Baltimore: Johns Hopkins University Press, 1981.
Fonquerne, Yves-René, and Alfonso Esteban, eds. *La condición de la mujer en la Edad Media.* Actas del Coloquio celebrado en la Casa de Velázquez el 5–7 de noviembre de 1984. Madrid: Editorial de la Universidad Complutense, 1986.
Foster, David William. *The Early Spanish Ballad.* New York: Twayne, 1971.
Foucault, Michel. *The History of Sexuality,* vol. 1, *An Introduction.* Trans. Robert Hurley. New York: Vintage Books, 1980.
Fradenburg, Louise O. "The Love of Thy Neighbor." In Lochrie, McCracken, and Schultz, *Constructing Medieval Sexuality,* 135–57.
———. *Women and Sovereignty.* Edinburgh: Edinburgh University Press, 1992.
Frago García, Juan A. "Sobre el léxico de la prostitución en España durante el siglo XV." *Archivo de filología aragonesa* 24–25 (1979): 257–73.

Franco, Francisco. *Franco ha dicho...* Madrid: Editorial Carlos-Jaime, 1947.
———. *Palabras del caudillo, 19 abril 1937–7 diciembre 1942.* Madrid: Editorial Nacional, 1943.
Freud, Sigmund. *Beyond the Pleasure Principle.* [1920]. Ed. James Strachey. In *The Standard Edition of the Complete Psychological Works of Sigmund Freud.* 24 vols. London: Hogarth Press, 1955 18:3–64.
Freund, Scarlett, and Teófilo F. Ruiz. "Jews, Conversos, and the Inquisition in Spain, 1301–1492: The Ambiguities of History." In *Jewish-Christian Encounters over the Centuries,* ed. Marvin Perry and Frederick Schweitzer. New York: Peter Lang, 1994. 169–95.
Frye, Susan. *Elizabeth I: The Competition for Representation.* New York and Oxford: Oxford University Press, 1993.
Fuente, Vicente de la. *Historia de las universidades, colegios y demas establecimientos de enseñanza en España.* 4 vols. Madrid: Imprenta de la viuda e hija de Fuentenebro, 1884–89.
Fulks, Barbara. "The Poet Named Florencia Pinar." *La Corónica* 18.1 (1989): 33–44.
Fuss, Diana. *Essentially Speaking: Feminism, Nature, Difference.* New York: Routledge, 1989.
Galán Sánchez, Angel, and María López Beltrán. "El 'status' teórico de las prostitutas del reino de Granada en la primera mitad del siglo XVI (Las ordenanzas de 1536)." In *Las mujeres en las ciudades medievales,* ed. C. Segura Graiño. Madrid: Universidad Autónoma de Madrid, 1984. 161–70.
Galíndez de Carvajal, Lorenzo. *Anales breves de los Reyes Católicos.* In *Crónicas de los reyes de Castilla,* 3:533–67.
Gallego Méndez, María Teresa. *Mujer, falange y franquismo.* Madrid: Taurus, 1983.
García de la Concha, Víctor, ed. *Nebrija y la introducción del Renacimiento en España.* Salamanca: Universidad de Salamanca, 1983.
García Oro, José. *Cisneros y la reforma del clero español en tiempo de los Reyes Católicos.* Madrid: Consejo Superior de Investigaciones Científicas, Instituto "Jerónimo Zurita," 1971.
Gericke, Philip. "Mena's *Laberinto de Fortuna:* Apocalypse Now?" *La Corónica* 17.2 (1988–89): 1–17.
Gerli, E. Michael. "Gender Trouble in Juan de Flores' *Triunfo de Amor,* Isabel la Católica, and the Economics of Power at Court." Forthcoming.
———. "Dismembering the Body Politic: Vile Bodies and Sexual Underworlds in Celestina." In Blackmore and Hutcheson, *Queer Iberia,* 369–93.
———. "Performing Nobility: Mosén Diego de Valera and the Poetics of *Converso* Identity." *La Corónica* 25.1 (1996): 19–36.
———, ed. *Poesía cancioneril castellana.* Madrid: Ediciones Akal, 1994.
Gerli, E. Michael, and Julian Weiss, eds. *Poetry at Court in Trastamaran Spain: From the "Cancionero de Baena" to the "Cancionero General."* Tempe, Ariz.: Medieval and Renaissance Texts and Studies, 1998.
Gil, Juan. "Alejandro, el nudo gordiano y Fernando el Católico." *Habis* 16 (1985): 229–42.
Gilman, Stephen. "A Generation of *conversos.*" *Romance Philology* 33 (1979): 87–101.
———. *The Spain of Fernando de Rojas: The Intellectual and Social Landscape of La Celestina.* Princeton, N.J.: Princeton University Press, 1972.
Giménez Caballero, Ernesto. *España nuestra: El libro de las juventudes españolas.* Madrid: Ediciones de la Vicesecretaría de Educación Popular, 1943.

Gimeno Casalduero, Joaquín. "Notas sobre el *Laberinto de Fortuna.*" *Modern Language Notes* 79 (1964): 125–39.
Goldberg, Harriet. *Motif-Index of Medieval Spanish Folk Narratives.* Tempe, Ariz.: Medieval and Renaissance Texts and Studies, 1998.

———. Letter to the Editor in "Forum." *La Corónica* 24.2 (1996): 196–97.

———. "Two Parallel Medieval Commonplaces: Antifeminism and Antisemitism in Hispanic Literary Tradition." In *Aspects of Jewish Culture in the Middle Ages,* ed. Paul E. Szarmach. Albany: State University of New York Press, 1979. 85–119.

———, ed. *Jardín de nobles doncellas.* By Martín de Córdoba. Chapel Hill: University of North Carolina Press, 1974.

Goldberg, Jonathan, ed. *Queering the Renaissance.* Durham, N.C.: Duke University Press, 1994.

———. *Sodometries: Renaissance Texts, Modern Sexualities.* Stanford, Calif.: Stanford University Press, 1992.

Golombek, Harry. *Golombek's Encyclopedia of Chess.* New York: Crown Publishers, 1977.

———. *A History of Chess.* New York: G. P. Putnam's Sons, 1976.

Gómez, Jesús. "Literatura paraescolar y difusión del humanismo en el siglo XV: La *Repetición de amores* de Lucena." In *Actas del III Congreso de la Asociación Hispánica de Literatura Medieval,* 2 vols., ed. María Isabel Toro Pascua. Salamanca: Universidad de Salamanca, 1994. 1:399–405.

Gómez Bravo, Ana María. "'A huma senhora que lhe disse': Sobre la práctica social de la autoría y la noción del texto en el *Cancioneiro geral de Resende* y la lírica cancioneril ibérica." *La Corónica* (forthcoming).

Gómez Mampaso, María Valentina. "La mujer y la sucesión al trono." In *Nuevas perspectivas sobre la mujer. Actas de las primeras jornadas de investigación interdisciplinaria,* ed. Seminario de Estudios de la Mujer. 2 vols. Madrid: Universidad Autónoma de Madrid, 1982. 1:127–35.

Gómez Molleda, María Dolores. "La cultura femenina en la época de Isabel la Católica." *Revista de archivos, bibliotecas y museos* 51.1 (1995): 137–95.

Gómez Redondo, Fernando. "Lucena, *Repetición de amores*: sentido y estructura." In *Nunca fue pena mayor: Estudios de literatura española en homenaje a Brian Dutton,* ed. Ana Menéndez Collera and Victoriano Roncero López. Cuenca: Ediciones de la Universidad de Castilla–La Mancha, 1996. 293–304.

González Echevarría, Roberto. *Alejo Carpentier, el peregrino en su patria.* Mexico City: Universidad Nacional Autónoma de México, 1993.

González Iglesias, Juan-Antonio. "El humanista y los príncipes: Antonio de Nebrija, inventor de las empresas heráldicas de los Reyes Católicos." In *Antonio de Nebrija: Edad Media y Renacimiento,* ed. Carmen Codoñer and Juan Antonio González-Iglesias. Salamanca: Universidad de Salamanca, 1994. 59–76.

González-Llubera, I. See Nebrija.

Goodich, Michael. *The Unmentionable Vice: Homosexuality in the Late Medieval Period.* Santa Barbara, Calif.: ABC-Clio, 1979.

Gossy, Mary S. *The Untold Story: Women and Theory in Golden Age Texts.* Ann Arbor: University of Michigan Press, 1989.

Goytisolo, Juan. *Reivindicación del Conde don Julián.* Ed. Linda Gould Levine. Madrid: Cátedra, 1995 [1970].

———. "Supervivencias tribales en el medio intellectual español." In *Disidencias*. Barcelona: Seix Barral, 1977. 140–48.

———. *Count Julian*. Trans. Helen R. Lane. New York: Viking Press, 1974.

Gracián, Baltasar. *El político*. Ed. E. Correa Calderón. Salamanca: Ediciones Anaya, 1961.

Gravdal, Kathryn. *Ravishing Maidens: Writing Rape in Medieval French Literature and Law*. Philadelphia: University of Pennsylvania Press, 1991.

Greenblatt, Stephen J. *Learning to Curse: Essays in Early Modern Culture*. New York and London: Routledge, 1990.

———. *The Power of Forms in the English Renaissance*. Norman, Okla.: Pilgrim Books, 1982.

———. *Renaissance Self-Fashioning from More to Shakespeare*. Chicago: University of Chicago Press, 1980.

Grieve, Patricia E. *Floire and Blancheflor and the European Romance*. Studies in Medieval Literature 32. Cambridge: Cambridge University Press, 1997.

———. "Mothers and Daughters in Fifteenth-Century Spanish Sentimental Romances: Implications for Celestina." *Bulletin of Hispanic Studies* 67 (1990): 345–55.

———. *Desire and Death in the Spanish Sentimental Romance (1440–1550)*. Newark, Del.: Juan de la Cuesta, 1987.

———. "Juan de Flores' Other Work: Technique and Genre of *Triumpho de amor*." *Journal of Hispanic Philology* 5 (1980): 25–40.

Grothe, Meriwynn. "Franco's Angels: Recycling the Ideology of Domesticity." *Revista de estudios hispánicos* 33 (1999): 513–37.

Gurevich, Aron. *Medieval Popular Culture: Problems of Belief and Perception*. Trans. János M. Bak and Paul A. Hollingsworth. Cambridge, England: Cambridge University Press, 1988.

Gwara, Joseph J. "Another Work by Juan de Flores: *La coronación de la señora Gracisla*." In Gwara and Gerli, *Sentimental Romance*, 75–110.

———. "The Date of Juan de Flores's *Triunfo de amor*." *La Corónica* 16.2 (1987–88): 93–96.

———. "The Identity of Juan de Flores: The Evidence of the *Crónica incompleta de los Reyes Católicos*." *Journal of Hispanic Philology* 11 (1987) [1988]: 103–30, 205–22.

Gwara, Joseph J., and E. Michael Gerli. *Studies on the Spanish Sentimental Romance 1440–1550: Redefining a Genre*. London: Tamesis, 1997.

Hackett, Helen. *Virgin Mother, Maiden Queen: Elizabeth I and the Cult of the Virgin Mary*. New York: St. Martin's Press, 1995.

Halperin, David M. "How to Do the History of Male Homosexuality." *GLQ: A Journal of Lesbian and Gay Studies* 6.1 (2000): 87–123.

Harney, Michael. *Kinship and Marriage in Medieval Hispanic Chivalric Romance*. London: Brepols, Queen Mary and Westfield College, 2001.

———. *Kinship and Polity in the "Poema de mío Cid."* West Lafayette, Ind.: Purdue University Press, 1993.

Harris, Jonathan Gil. "This Is Not a Pipe: Water Supply, Incontinent Sources, and the Leaky Body Politic." In Burt and Archer, *Enclosure Acts*, 203–27.

Haywood, Louise M. "'Si alguna maldad hay en alguna de nosotras es por ser de varón engendradas' (Flores, *Grisel y Mirabella*): Female Voices in Spanish Sentimental Romances." Forthcoming.

Heisch, Allison. "Queen Elizabeth I: Parliamentary Rhetoric and the Exercise of Power." *Signs* 1 (1975): 31–55.

Hendricks, Margo and Patricia Parker, eds. *Women, "Race," and Writing in the Early Modern Period*. London and New York: Routledge, 1994.

Herlihy, David. *Opera Muliebria: Women and Work in Medieval Europe*. New York: McGraw-Hill, 1990.

Hermida Ruiz, Aurora. "Silent Subtexts and *Cancionero* Codes: On Garcilaso de la Vega's Revolutionary Love." In Gerli and Weiss, *Poetry at Court*, 79–92.

Hillgarth, J. N. *The Spanish Kingdoms, 1250–1516*. 2 vols. Oxford: Clarendon Press, 1976–78.

Howard, Jean. "The New Historicism in Renaissance Studies." *English Literary History* 16 (1986): 13–43.

Hull, Suzanne W. *Chaste, Silent, and Obedient: English Books for Women, 1475–1640*. San Marino: Huntington Library, 1982.

Hunt, Lynn, ed. *The Invention of Pornography: Obscenity and the Origins of Modernity, 1500–1800*. New York: Zone Books, 1993.

Hutcheson, Gregory S. "The Sodomitic Moor: Queerness in the Narratives of *Reconquista*." In *Queering the Middle Ages*, ed. Glenn Burger and Steven F. Kruger. Medieval Cultures 27. Minneapolis: University of Minnesota Press, 2001. 99–122.

———. "Desperately Seeking Sodom: Queerness in the Chronicles of Alvaro de Luna." In Blackmore and Hutcheson, *Queer Iberia*, 222–49.

———. "Cracks in the Labyrinth: Juan de Mena, Converso Experience, and the Rise of the Spanish Nation." *La Corónica* 25.1 (1996): 37–52.

Irigaray, Luce. *This Sex Which Is Not One*. Trans. Catherine Porter. Ithaca, N.Y.: Cornell University Press, 1985 [1977].

Jaén, Alonso. *Espejo del mundo. Profecía i poder al Renaixement: Texts Profètics catalans favorables a Ferran el Catòlic*. Ed. Eulàlia Duran and Joan Requesens. Valencia: Eliseu Clement, 1997. 135–297.

Jauralde Pou, Pablo, and Juan Bellón Cazabán, eds. *Cancionero de obras de burlas provocantes a risa*. Madrid: Akal, 1974.

Jed, Stephanie H. *Chaste Thinking: The Rape of Lucretia and the Birth of Humanism*. Bloomington: Indiana University Press, 1989.

Jiménez de Rada, Rodrigo. *Historia de rebus Hispaniae sive, Historia Gothica*. Turnholti: Brepols, 1987.

Johnston, Mark D. "Cultural Studies on the *Gaya Ciencia*." In Gerli and Weiss, *Poetry at Court*, 235–53.

Jones, R. O. "Isabel la Católica y el amor cortés." *Revista de Literatura* 21 (1962): 55–64.

Jordan, Constance. *Renaissance Feminism: Literary Texts and Political Models*. Ithaca, N.Y.: Cornell University Press, 1990.

———. "Woman's Rule in Sixteenth-Century British Political Thought." *Renaissance Quarterly* 40 (1987): 421–51.

———. "Feminism and the Humanists: The Case of Sir Thomas Elyot's *Defence of Good Women*." *Renaissance Quarterly* 36.2 (1983): 181–201.

Kagan, Richard L. "Clio and the Crown: Writing History in Hapsburg Spain." In *Spain, Europe, and the Atlantic World: Essays in Honour of John H. Elliott*, ed. Richard L. Kagan and Geoffrey Parker. Cambridge: Cambridge University Press, 1993. 73–99.

———. *Lawsuits and Litigants in Castile: 1500–1700*. Chapel Hill: University of North Carolina Press, 1981.

———. *Students and Society in Early Modern Spain*. Baltimore: Johns Hopkins University Press, 1974.

Kamen, Henry. "Limpieza and the Ghost of Américo Castro: Racism as a Tool of Literary Analysis." *Hispanic Review* 64 (1996): 19–29.

Kane, Eleanor S. *Refranes y frases proverbiales españolas de la Edad Media*. Madrid: Real Academia Española, 1959.

Kantorowicz, Ernst. *The King's Two Bodies: A Study in Medieval Political Theology*. Princeton, N.J.: Princeton University Press, 1957.

Kaplan, Gregory B. "Toward the Establishment of a Christian Identity: The *Conversos* and Early Castilian Humanism." *La Corónica* 25.1 (1996): 53–68.

Kappeler, Susan. *The Pornography of Representation*. Cambridge, England: Polity Press, 1986.

Karras, Ruth Mazo. "Sex, Money, and Prostitution in Medieval English Culture." In *Desire and Discipline: Sex and Sexuality in the Premodern West*, ed. Jacqueline Murray and Konrad Eisenbichler. Toronto: University of Toronto Press, 1996. 201–16.

Kaufman, Gloria. "Juan Luis Vives on the Education of Women." *Signs* 3 (1978): 891–96.

Kay, Sarah. *Subjectivity in Troubadour Poetry*. Cambridge, England, and New York: Cambridge University Press, 1990.

Kelly, Joan. *Women, History, and Theory*. Chicago and London: University of Chicago Press, 1984.

Kelso, Ruth. *Doctrine for the Lady of the Renaissance*. Urbana: University of Illinois Press, 1956.

Koontz, Claudia. *Mothers in the Fatherland: Women, the Family, and Nazi Politics*. New York: St. Martin's Press, 1987.

Kristeva, Julia. *Powers of Horror: An Essay on Abjection*. Trans. Leon S. Roudiez. New York: Columbia University Press, 1982.

Krueger, Roberta L. *Women Readers and the Ideology of Gender in Old French Verse Romance*. Cambridge: Cambridge University Press, 1993.

Kruger, Steven F. "Conversion and Medieval Sexual, Religious, and Racial Categories." In Lochrie, McCracken, and Schultz, *Sexuality*, 158–79.

———. "Racial/Religious and Sexual Queerness in the Middle Ages." *Medieval Feminist Newsletter* 16 (1993): 32–36.

Kuhn, Annette, and Ann Marie Wolpe. *Feminism and Materialism: Women and Modes of Production*. London: Routledge, 1978.

Labanyi, Jo. "Women, Asian Hordes, and the Threat to the Self in Giménez Caballero's *Genio de España*." *Bulletin of Hispanic Studies* 73 (1996): 377–87.

Lacarra, M. E. "La evolución de la prostitución en la Castilla del siglo XV y la mancebía de Salamanca en tiempos de Fernando de Rojas." In *Fernando de Rojas and Celestina: Approaching the Fifth Centenary*, ed. Ivy A. Corfis and Joseph T. Snow. Madison, Wis.: Hispanic Seminary of Medieval Studies, 1993. 33–78.

———. "Notes on Feminist Analysis of Medieval Spanish Literature and History." *La Corónica* 17.1 (1988): 14–22.

———. "La utilización del Cid de Menéndez Pidal en la ideología militar franquista." *Ideologies and Literature* 3 (1980): 95–127.

Langbehn de Rohland, Regula. *La unidad genérica de la novela sentimental de los siglos XV y XVI*. Papers of the Medieval Hispanic Research Seminar 17. London: Queen Mary and Westfield College, 1999.

———. "Un mundo al revés: La mujer en las obras de fcción de Juan de Flores." In Gwara and Gerli, *Sentimental Romance*, 173–90.

Lapesa, Rafael. "El elemento moral en el *Laberinto* de Mena: su influjo en la disposición de la obra." In *De la Edad Media a nuestros días*. Madrid: Gredos, 1959. 112–22.

Lapesa, Rafael, Diego Catalán, Alvaro Galmés, and José Caso. *Romanceros del Rey Rodrigo y de Bernardo del Carpio*. Vol. 1 of *Romancero tradicional de las lenguas hispánicas (Español-Portugués-Catalán-Sefardí)*, ed. Ramón Menéndez Pidal, María Goyri, and Diego Catalán. 12 vols. Madrid: Gredos, 1957–85.

Lawrance, Jeremy N. H. "Humanism in the Iberian Peninsula." In *The Impact of Humanism on Western Europe*, ed. Anthony Goodman and Angus MacKay. London and New York: Longman, 1990. 220–58.

———. "The Spread of Lay Literacy in Late Medieval Castile." *Bulletin of Hispanic Studies* 62 (1985): 79–94.

Layna Ranz, Francisco. "La disputa burlesca: origen y trayectoria." *Criticón* 64 (1995): 7–160.

Lee Six, Abigail. *Juan Goytisolo: The Case for Chaos*. New Haven: Yale University Press, 1990.

Le Goff, Jacques. "Head or Heart?: The Political Use of Body Metaphors in the Middle Ages." In *Fragments for a History of the Human Body*, 3 vols., ed. Michel Feher with Ramona Nadaff and Nadia Tazi. New York: Urzone, 1989. 3:12–27.

———. *The Medieval Imagination*. Trans. Arthur Godhammer. Chicago: University of Chicago Press, 1988.

Lehfeldt, Elizabeth A. "Ruling Sexuality: The Political Legitimacy of Isabel of Castile." *Renaissance Quarterly* 53.1 (2000): 31–56.

Lerner, Gerda. *The Creation of Patriarchy*. New York: Oxford University Press, 1986.

Levin, Carol. "John Foxe and the Responsibilities of Queenship." In Rose, *Women in the Middle Ages*, 113–33.

———. *"The Heart and Stomach of a King": Elizabeth I and the Politics of Sex and Power*. Philadelphia: University of Pennsylvania Press, 1994.

———. "Queens and Claimants: Political Insecurity in XVIth Century England." In *Gender, Ideology, and Action: Historical Perspectives on Women's Public Lives*, ed. Janet Sharistanian. New York: Greenwood Press, 1986. 41–66.

Levine, Linda Gould. "Introduction." In *Reivindicación del Conde don Julián*, by Juan Goytisolo. Madrid: Cátedra, 1995. 13–75.

———. *Juan Goytisolo: La destrucción creadora*. Mexico City: Joaquín Mortiz, 1976.

Lida de Malkiel, María Rosa. *Juan de Mena, poeta del prerrenacimiento español*. Mexico City: Colegio de Mexico, 1950.

———. "La hipérbole sagrada en la poesía española del siglo XV." *Revista de Filología Hispánica* 8 (1946): 121–30.

Linehan, Peter. "The Court Historiographer of Francoism?: *La leyenda negra* of Ramón Menéndez Pidal." *Bulletin of Hispanic Studies* 73 (1996): 437–50.

Liss, Peggy K. *Isabel the Queen: Life and Times*. New York and Oxford: Oxford University Press, 1992.

Logan, Marie-Rose, and Peter L. Rudnytsky, eds. *Contending Kingdoms: Historical, Psychological, and Feminist Approaches to the Literature of Sixteenth-Century England and France*. Detroit: Wayne State University Press, 1991.

López, Atanasio. "Descripción de los manuscritos franciscanos existentes en la biblioteca provincial de Toledo." *Archivo Ibero-Americano* 25 (1926): 334–82.

López Beltrán, María Teresa. *La prostitución en el reino de Granada en época de los Reyes Católicos: El caso de Málaga (1487–1516)*. Málaga: Diputación Provincial, 1985.

López de Ayala, Pedro. *Rimado de palacio*. Ed. Germán Orduna. Madrid: Castalia, 1987.

———. *Crónica del rey don Pedro*. Ed. Guillermo Díaz-Plaja. Madrid: Compañía Iberoamericana de Publicaciones, 1931.

López de Toro, José. See Palencia.

Lo-Ré, Anthony George. *La leyenda de Doña María Coronel*. Valencia: Albatros Hispanófila, 1980.

Lucena, Juan de. *Epístola exhortatoria a las letras*. In *Opúsculos literarios de los siglos XIV a XVI*, ed. Antonio Paz y Melia. Madrid: Sociedad de Bibliófilos Literarios, 1892. 209–17.

———. *Libro de vita beata*. In *Opúsculos literarios de los siglos XIV al XVI*, ed. Antonio Paz y Melia. Madrid: Sociedad de Bibliófilos Españoles, 1892. 103–206.

Lucena, Luis de. *El incunable de Lucena: Primer Arte de ajedrez moderno*. Ed. Joaquín Pérez de Arriaga. Madrid: Polifemo, 1997.

———. *Repetición de amores*. Ed. Jacob Ornstein. Studies in the Romance Languages and Literatures 23. Chapel Hill: University of North Carolina Press, 1954.

———. *Repetición de amores y Arte de axedrez*. Ed. José María de Cossío. Madrid: Joyas Bibiográficas, 1953.

Luna, Alvaro de. *Libro de las claras e virtuosas mujeres*. Ed. Manuel Castillo. 2d ed. Valencia: Prometeo, 1917.

MacKay, Angus. "Averroístas y marginadas." In *Society, Economy, and Religion in Late Medieval Castile*. London: Variorum Reprints, 1987. 247–61.

———. "Ritual and Propaganda in Fifteenth-Century Castile." *Past and Present* 107 (1985): 3–45.

Macpherson, Ian. *The "invenciones y letras" of the "Cancionero general"*. Publications of the Medieval Hispanic Research Seminar 9. London: Department of Hispanic Studies, Queen Mary and Westfield College, 1998.

———. "Celestina's Thread." In Macpherson and MacKay, *Love, Religion*, 188–95.

———. "Secret Language in the *Cancioneros*: Some Courtly Codes." *Bulletin of Hispanic Studies* 62 (1985): 51–63.

Macpherson, Ian, and Angus MacKay. "Textiles and Tournaments." In Macpherson and MacKay, *Love, Religion*, 196–204.

———, eds. *Love, Religion, and Politics in Fifteenth-Century Spain*. Leiden: Brill, 1998.

Mahu-Lot, Marianne. "Le mécénat d'Isabelle la Catholique." *Revue historique* 227.2 (1987): 289–307.

Manrique, Gómez. *Cancionero de Gómez Manrique*. 2 vols. Ed. Antonio Paz y Melia. Madrid: Imprenta A. Pérez Dubrill, 1885–86.

Maravall, José Antonio. "Los 'hombres de saber' o letrados y la formación de su conciencia estamental." In *Estudios de historia del pensamiento español*. 3d. ed. Vol. 1. Madrid: Ediciones Cultura Hispánica, 1983. 333–62.

———. *Estudios de historia del pensamiento español*. 2d ed. Madrid: Ediciones Cultura Hispánica, 1973.

———. "La idea de cuerpo místico en España antes de Erasmo." In *Estudios de Historia del pensamiento español*. 2d ed. Madrid: Ediciones Cultura Hispánica, 1973. 193–213.

———. *Estado moderno y mentalidad social (siglos XV a XVII)*. 2 vols. Madrid: Ediciones de la Revista de Occidente, 1972.

———. *El concepto de España en la Edad Media.* 2d ed. Madrid: Instituto de Estudios Políticos, 1964.

Marcuello, Pedro. *Rimado de la conquista de Granada.* 2 vols. Ed. Estrella Ruiz-Gálvez Priego and Ana Domínguez Rodríguez. Madrid: Musée Condé-Château de Chantilly-Edilán, 1995.

———. *Cancionero.* Ed. José Manuel Blecua. Zaragoza: Institución Fernando el Católico, 1987.

Marcus, Leah S. *Puzzling Shakespeare: Local Reading and Its Discontents.* Berkeley: University of California Press, 1988.

———. "Shakespeare's Comic Heroines, Elizabeth I, and the Political Uses of Androgyny." In *Women in the Middle Ages,* ed. Rose. Syracuse, N.Y.: Syracuse University Press, 1986. 135–53.

Maroto Camino, Mercedes. "'Ya no es Lucrecia, Lucrecia': Woman and *limpieza de sangre* in Rojas Zorrilla's *Lucrecia y Tarquino.*" *Revista Canadiense de Estudios Hispánicos* 221.2 (1997): 329–51.

Márquez Villanueva, Francisco. *Orígenes y sociología del tema celestinesco.* Barcelona: Anthropos, 1993.

———. "*La Celestina* as Hispano-Semitic Anthropology." *Revue de Littérature Comparée* 4 (1987): 425–53.

———. "*Cárcel de amor:* Novela política." In *Relecciones de literatura medieval.* Sevilla: Universidad de Sevilla, 1977. 75–94.

———. "Historia cultural e historia literaria: El caso de *Cárcel de amor.*" In *The Analysis of Hispanic Texts: Current Trends in Methodology.* Jamaica, N.Y.: Bilingual Press/Editorial Bilingüe, 1976. 144–57.

———. *Investigaciones sobre Juan Alvarez Gato.* Anejo del Boletín de la Real Academia Española 4. Madrid: Real Academia Española, 1960.

Martín Gaite, Carmen. *El cuarto de atrás.* Barcelona: Ediciones Destino, 1992 [1978].

———. *The Back Room.* Trans. Helen R. Lane. New York: Columbia University Press, 1983.

Martínez de Toledo, Alfonso. *Little Sermons on Sin.* Trans. Lesley Byrd Simpson. Berkeley: University of California Press, 1983.

———. *Arcipreste de Talavera o Corbacho.* Ed. E. Michael Gerli. 2d ed. Madrid: Cátedra, 1981.

———. *Arcipreste de Talavera o Corbacho.* Ed. J. González Muela. Madrid: Castalia, 1970.

Mártir, Pedro. *Epistolario.* Trans. José López de Toro. Vols. 9–12 of *Documentos inéditos para la historia de España.* Madrid: Góngora, 1953–57.

Mata Carriazo, Juan de. *Estudio preliminar. Crónica de los Reyes Católicos.* By Fernando del Pulgar. Madrid: Espasa-Calpe, 1943. 1:ix–clx.

Matter, E. Ann. *The Voice of My Beloved: The Song of Songs in Western Medieval Christianity.* Philadelphia: University of Pennsylvania Press, 1990.

Matulka, Barbara. *The Novels of Juan de Flores and Their European Diffusion.* Geneva: Slatkine, 1974 [1931].

———. "An Anti-Feminist Treatise of XVth-Century Spain: Lucena's *Repetiçión de amores.*" *Romanic Review* 22 (1931): 99–116.

McCracken, Peggy. "The Body Politic and the Queen's Adulterous Body in French Romance." In *Feminist Approaches to the Body in Medieval Literature,* ed. Linda

Lomperis and Sarah Stanbury. Philadelphia: University of Pennsylvania Press, 1994. 38–64.
McNamara, Jo Ann. "Sexual Equality and the Cult of Virginity in Early Christian Thought." *Feminist Studies* 3.3/4 (1976): 145–58.
Memorias de don Enrique IV de Castilla. Madrid: Fortanet, 1913.
Mena, Juan de. *Laberinto de Fortuna*. Ed. Maxim P. A. M. Kerkhof. Madrid: Editorial Castalia, 1995.
———. *Laberinto de Fortuna*. Ed. Louise Vasvari Fainberg. Madrid: Alhambra, 1976.
———. *Tratado de amor*. Ed. María Luz Gutiérrez Araus. Madrid: Ediciones Alcalá, 1975.
Mendoza, Iñigo de. *Cancionero*. Ed. Julio Rodríguez-Puértolas. Madrid: Espasa-Calpe, 1968.
Mendoza Negrillo, Juan. *Fortuna y Providencia en la literatura castellana del siglo XV*. Anejos del *Boletín de la Real Academia Española* 27. Madrid: Real Academia Española, 1973.
Menéndez Collera, Ana. "La poesía cancioneril de entretenimiento en la Corte de los Reyes Católicos: El 'Juego trouado' de Pinar." In *Estudios en homenaje a Enrique Ruiz-Fornells*, ed. Juan Fernández Jiménez, José Labrador Herraiz, and L. Teresa Valdivieso. Erie, Pa.: Asociación de Licenciados y Doctores Españoles en los Estados Unidos, 1990. 425–31.
Menéndez Pidal, Ramón. "Carácteres primordiales de la literatura española con referencias a las otras literaturas hispánicas, latina, portuguesa y catalana." In *Los españoles en la literatura* [1951]. Buenos Aires: Espasa-Calpe Argentina, 1960.
———. *Floresta de leyendas heroicas españolas: Rodrigo el último godo*. 3 vols. Madrid: Espasa-Calpe, 1925–27.
Menéndez Pidal de Navascues, Faustino. *Heráldica medieval española*. 2 vols. Vol. 1: *La casa real de León y Castilla*. Madrid: Hidalguía, 1982.
Menéndez y Pelayo, Marcelino. *Antología de poetas líricos castellanos desde la formación del idioma hasta nuestros días*. 10 vols. Madrid: Consejo Superior de Investigaciones Científicas, 1944–45.
Mérida, Jiménez, Rafael. *Women in Medieval Iberia: A Selected Bibliography*. Subsidia 2. Eugene, Oreg.: Society for Medieval Feminist Scholarship, 2002.
Meseguer Fernández, Juan. "Isabel la Católica en la opinión de españoles y extranjeros." *Archivo Ibero-Americano*. 2da época. 31.122–23 (1971): 1–13.
———. "Franciscanismo de Isabel la Católica." *Archivo Ibero-Americano* 19 (1959): 153–95.
Miles, Margaret R. *Carnal Knowing: Female Nakedness and Religious Meaning in the Christian West*. Boston: Beacon Press, 1989.
Miller, Nancy. "Emphasis Added: Plots and Plausibilities in Women's Fiction." In *The New Feminist Criticism*, ed. Elaine Showalter. New York: Pantheon Books, 1985. 339–60.
Mirrer, Louise. *Women, Jews, and Muslims in the Texts of Reconquest Spain*. Ann Arbor: University of Michigan Press, 1996.
———. "Men's Language, Women's Power: Female Voices in the *Romancero Viejo*." In *Oral Tradition and Hispanic Literature: Essays in Honor of Samuel G. Armistead*, ed. Michael Caspi. New York: Garland, 1995. 522–47.

———. *The Language of Evaluation: A Sociolinguistic Approach to the Story of Pedro el Cruel in Ballad and Chronicle.* Amsterdam: John Benjamins, 1986.

Mitre Fernández, Emilio. "Mujer, matrimonio y vida marital en las cortes castellano-leonesas de la baja Edad Media." In *Las mujeres medievales y su ámbito jurídico.* Actas de las II Jornadas de Investigación Interdisciplinaria. Madrid: Universidad Autónoma de Madrid, 1983. 79–86.

Moi, Toril. "Desire in Language: Andreas Capellanus and the Controversy of Courtly Love." In *Medieval Literature: Criticism Ideology, and History,* ed. David Aers. New York: St. Martin's Press, 1986. 11–33.

Moner, Michel. "Deux figures emblématiques: La femme violée et la parfaite épouse, selon le *Romancero General* compilé par Agustín Durán." In *Images de la femme en Espagne aux XVIᵉ et XVIIᵉ siècles: des traditions aux renouvellements et à l'émergence d'images nouvelles: Colloque international Sorbonne et Collège d'Espagne, 28–30 septembre 1992,* ed. Augustín Redondo. Paris: Publications de la Sorbonne, 1994. 77–90.

Montaner, Alberto. "La emblemática de los Reyes Católicos: un error de interpretación histórica." *Universidad* (University of Zaragoza) 7 (1982): 24–26.

Montañés, Luis. "La *Carajicomedia*: avatares bibliográficos de un texto maldito." *Cuadernos de bibliofilia* 9 (1982): 35–52.

Montoro, Antón de. *Poesía completa.* Ed. Marithelma Costa. Cleveland: Cleveland State University Press, 1990.

———. *Cancionero.* Ed. Francisco Cantera Burgos and Carlos Carrete Parrondo. Madrid: Editora Nacional, 1984.

Montrose, Louis Adrian. "The Elizabethan Subject and the Spenserian Text." In *Literary Theory/Renaissance Texts,* ed. Patricia Parker and David Quint. Baltimore: Johns Hopkins University Press, 1986. 303–40.

———. "Renaissance Literary Studies and the Subject of History." *English Literary Renaissance* 16 (1986): 5–12.

———. "'Shaping Fantasies': Figurations of Gender and Power in Elizabethan Culture." *Representations* 1.2 (1983): 61–94.

———. "Celebration and Insinuation: Sir Philip Sidney and the Motives of Elizabethan Courtship." *Renaissance Drama,* n.s., 8 (1977): 3–35.

Morales, María Pilar. *La mujer: Orientación femenina.* Madrid: Editora Nacional, 1944.

Morcillo Gómez, Aurora. "Shaping True Catholic Womanhood: Francoist Educational Discourse on Women." In Enders and Radcliff, *Spanish Womanhood,* 51–69.

Murray, H. J. R. *A History of Chess.* 1st ed. Oxford: Clarendon Press, 1962. 1913.

Nader, Helen. *The Mendoza Family in the Spanish Renaissance: 1350–1550.* New Brunswick, N.J.: Rutgers University Press, 1979.

Nebrija, Antonio. *Gramática de la lengua castellana.* Ed. I. González-Llubera. London: Oxford University Press, 1926.

Netanyahu, Benzion. *The Origins of the Inquisition in Fifteenth-Century Spain.* New York: Random House, 1995.

Newton, Judith. *Starting Over: Feminism and the Politics of Cultural Critique.* Ann Arbor: University of Michigan Press, 1994.

Newton, Judith, and Deborah Rosenfelt. *Feminist Criticism and Social Change: Sex, Class, and Race in Literature and Culture.* New York: Methuen, 1985.

Nieto Soria, José Manuel, ed. *Orígenes de la monarquía hispánica: propanganda y legitimación (ca. 1400–1520)*. Madrid: Dykinson, 1999.

———. *Fundamentos ideológicos del poder real en Castilla (s. XIII–XVI)*. Madrid: EUDEMA, 1988.

Niño Jesús, Carmelo del. "La dirección espiritual de Isabel la Católica." *Revista de espiritualidad* 11.43 (1952): 166–92.

Nirenberg, David. *Communities of Violence: Persecution of Minorities in the Middle Ages*. Princeton, N.J.: Princeton University Press, 1996.

O'Callaghan, Joseph F. *A History of Medieval Spain*. Ithaca, N.Y., and London: Cornell University Press, 1975.

Oñate, María del Pilar. *El feminismo en la literatura española*. Madrid: Espasa-Calpe, 1938.

Ong, Walter. *The Presence of the Word: Some Prolegomena for Cultural and Religious History*. New Haven: Yale University Press, 1967.

Ornstein, Jacob. "La misoginia y el profeminismo en la literatura castellana." *Revista de Filología Hispánica* 3 (1941): 219–32.

Ortiz, Alonso de. *Diálogo sobre la educación del Príncipe Don Juan hijo de los Reyes Católicos*. Ed. and trans. Giovanni María Bertini. Madrid: J. Porrúa Turanzas, 1983.

Ostlund, DeLys. *The Re-Creation of History in the Fernando and Isabel Plays of Lope de Vega*. New York: Peter Lang, 1997.

Otis, Leah Lydia. *Prostitution in Medieval Society*. Chicago: University of Chicago Press, 1985.

Palencia, Alfonso de. *Gesta hispaniensia ex annalibus suorum dierum collecta*. Ed. Brian Tate and Jeremy Lawrance. 2 vols. Madrid: Real Academia de la Historia, 1998.

———. *Crónica de Enrique IV*. 3 vols. Trans. Antonio Paz y Melia. Biblioteca de Autores Españoles 257, 258, 267. Madrid: Atlas, 1973–75.

———. *Cuarta Década de Alonso de Palencia*. 2 vols. Ed. and trans. José López de Toro. Archivo Documental Español 24, 25. Madrid: Real Academia de la Historia, 1970–74.

Parker, Alexander. *The Philosophy of Love in Spanish Literature: 1480–1680*. Edinburgh: Edinburgh University Press, 1985.

Parker, Patricia. "Fantasies of 'Race' and 'Gender': Africa, Othello, and Bringing to Light." In Hendricks and Parker, *Women*, 84–100.

———. "Gender Ideology, Gender Change: The Case of Marie Germain." *Critical Inquiry* 19 (1993): 337–64.

———. "On the Tongue: Cross-Gendering, Effeminacy, and the Art of Words." *Style* 23 (1989): 445–65.

———. "Coming Second: Woman's Place." In *Literary Fat Ladies: Rhetoric, Gender, Property*. New York: Methuen, 1987. 178–233.

Parrilla García, Carmen. "La *Derrota de Amor* de Juan de Flores." In Gwara and Gerli, *Sentimental Romance*, 111–24.

———. "Un cronista olvidado: Juan de Flores, autor de la *Crónica incompleta de los Reyes Católicos*." In *The Age of the Catholic Monarchs: 1474–1516. Literary Studies in Memory of Keith Whinnom*, ed. Alan Deyermond and Ian Macpherson. Special Issue of *Bulletin of Hispanic Studies*. Liverpool: Liverpool University Press, 1989. 123–33.

———. ed. *Grimalte y Gradisa*. By Juan de Flores. Santiago de Compostela: Universidad de Santiago de Compostela, 1988.

Pastor, Reyna. "Para una historia social de la mujer hispano-medieval. Problemática y puntos de vista." In Fonquerne and Esteban, *Condición de la mujer*, 187–214.
Patch, Howard R. *The Goddess Fortuna in Mediaeval Literature*. Cambridge: Harvard University Press, 1927.
Payne, Stanley. *Fascism in Spain*. Madison: University of Wisconsin Press, 1999.
Paz y Melia, Antonio. *El cronista Alonso de Palencia: su vida y sus obras*. Madrid: Hispanic Society of America, 1914.
Penna, Mario, and Fernando Rubio Alvarez, eds. *Prosistas castellanos del siglo XV*. 2 vols. Ed. Mario Penna (vol. 1) and Fernando Rubio Alvarez (vol. 2). Biblioteca de autores españoles 116 and 171. Madrid: Atlas, 1959.
Pérez, Nazario. *La Inmaculada y España*. Santander: Editorial "Sal Terrae," 1954.
Pérez de Arriaga, Joaquín, ed. *El incunable de Lucena: Primer arte de ajedrez moderno*. Madrid: Ediciones Polifemo, 1997.
Pérez de Guzmán, Fernán. *Generaciones y semblanzas*. Ed. R. B. Tate. London: Tamesis, 1965.
———. *La dotrina que dieron a Sarra*. Ed. C. B. Bourland. *Revue Hispanique* 22 (1910): 648–86.
Pérez Priego, Miguel Angel. *Poesía femenina en los cancioneros*. Madrid: Castalia, 1989.
Perry, Mary Elizabeth. *Gender and Disorder in Early Modern Seville*. Princeton, N.J.: Princeton University Press, 1990.
———. "Deviant Insiders: Legalized Prostitutes and a Consciousness of Women in Early Modern Seville." *Comparative Studies in Society and History* 27 (1985): 138–58.
Phillips, William D. *Enrique IV and the Crisis of Fifteenth-Century Castile (1425–1480)*. Cambridge: Medieval Academy of America, 1978.
Pitkin, Hannah F. *Fortune Is a Woman: Gender and Politics in the Thought of Niccolò Machiavelli*. Berkeley: University of California Press, 1984.
Pleyto del manto. In Jauralde Pou and Bellón Cazabán, *Cancionero de obras de burlas*, 46–66.
"*La Poncella de Francia*": *La historia castellana de Juana de Arco*. Ed. Victoria Campo and Víctor Infantes. Vervuert: Iberoamericana, 1997.
Portugal, Pedro de. *Sátira de felice e infelice vida*. In *Opúsculos literarios de los siglos XIV a XVI*, ed. Antonio Paz y Melia. Madrid: Imprenta de M. Tello, 1892. 47–101.
Preston, Paul. *Franco: A Biography*. New York: HarperCollins, 1994.
Primera crónica general de España que mandó componer Alfonso el Sabio y se continuaba bajo Sancho IV en 1289, Ed. Ramón Menéndez Pidal. 2 vols. Madrid: Gredos, 1955.
Pulgar, Fernando del. *Letras*. Ed. Paola Elia. Pisa: Giardini, 1982.
———. *Claros varones de Castilla*. Ed. Robert Brian Tate. Oxford: Clarendon Press, 1971.
———. *Crónica de los Reyes Católicos*. In *Crónica de los reyes de Castilla*, ed. Cayetano Rosell. 3 vols. Biblioteca de Autores Españoles 70. Madrid: Atlas, 1953. 1:223–511.
———. *Letras, Glosa a las "Coplas de Mingo Revulgo."* Ed. J. Domínguez Bordona. Clásicos Castellanos. Madrid: Espasa-Calpe, 1949.
———. *Crónica de los Reyes Católicos*. 2 vols. Ed. Juan de Mata Carriazo. Madrid: Espasa-Calpe, 1943.
Puyol Alonso, Julio. "Los cronistas de Enrique IV." *Boletín de la Real Academia de la Historia* 78 (1921): 399–415; 79 (1921): 11–28, 118–44.

Quilligan, Maureen. *Milton's Spenser: The Politics of Reading.* Ithaca, N.Y.: Cornell University Press, 1983.
Rackin, Phyllis. "Foreign Country: The Place of Women and Sexuality in Shakespeare's Historical World." In Burt and Archer, *Enclosure Acts,* 68–95.
———. "Genealogical Anxiety and Female Authority: The Return of the Repressed in Shakespeare's Histories." In *Contending Kingdoms: Historical, Psychological, and Feminist Approaches to the Literature of Sixteenth-Century England and France,* ed. Marie-Rose Logan and Peter L. Rudnytsky. Detroit: Wayne State University Press, 1991. 323–45.
Ratcliffe, Marjorie. "Adulteresses, Mistresses, and Prostitutes: Extramarital Relations in Medieval Castile." *Hispania* 67 (1984): 346–50.
Recio, Alejandro. "La Inmaculada en la predicación franciscano-española." *Archivo ibero-americano* 57–58 (1955): 105–200.
Redondo, Augustín. "Mutilations et marques corporelles d'infamie dans la Castille du XVIe siècle." In *Le Corps dans la société espagnole des XVIe et XVIIe siècles: Colloque international (Sorbonne, 5–8 octobre 1988),* ed. Augustín Redondo. Paris: Publications de la Sorbonne, 1990. 185–99.
Reinosa, Rodrigo de. *La poesía de Rodrigo de Reinosa.* Ed. José Manuel Cabrales Arteaga. Santander: Institución Cultural de Cantabria, 1980. 53–96.
Reiss, Edmund. "Symbolic Detail in Medieval Narrative: *Floris and Blancheflour.*" *Papers on Language and Literature* 7 (1971): 339–50.
Richards, Jeffrey. *Sex, Dissidence, and Damnation: Minority Groups in the Middle Ages.* London and New York: Routledge, 1991.
Rico, Francisco. *El pequeño mundo del hombre.* Ed. corregida y aumentada. Madrid: Alianza, 1986 [1970].
———. "Un penacho de penas. Sobre tres invenciones del *Cancionero general.*" *Romanistisches Jahrbuch* 17 (1966): 274–84.
Riquer, Martín de. *Heráldica española en tiempos de los Reyes Católicos.* Barcelona: Quaderns Crema, 1986.
Rivera Garretas, María Milagros. *Textos y espacios de mujeres (Europa, siglos IV–XV).* Barcelona: Icaria, 1990.
Rodríguez del Padrón, Juan. *Siervo libre de amor.* Ed. Antonio Prieto. Madrid: Castalia, 1976.
Rodríguez-Puértolas, Julio. *Literatura fascista española.* 2 vols (vol. 1, *Historia*; vol. 2, *Antología*). Madrid: Akal, 1986.
———. *Poesía crítica y satírica del siglo XV.* Madrid: Castalia, 1981.
———. "Sobre el autor de las Coplas de Mingo Revulgo." In *De la Edad Media a la edad conflictiva: estudios de literatura española.* Madrid: Gredos, 1972. 121–36.
———. ed. *Cancionero.* By Fray Iñigo de Mendoza. Madrid: Espasa-Calpe, 1968.
Rodríguez Solís, E. *Historia de la prostitución en España y América.* Madrid: Fernando Cao y Domingo de Val, 1890.
Rodríguez Valencia, Vicente. *Artículos del postulador.* Valladolid: Institución Isabel la Católica de Historia Eclesiástica, 1972.
Rodríguez Valencia, Vicente, and Luis Suárez Fernández. *Matrimonio y derecho sucesorio de Isabel la Católica.* Valladolid: Facultad de Teología, 1960.
Roffé, Mercedes. *La cuestión del género en "Grisel y Mirabella" de Juan de Flores.* Newark, Del.: Juan de la Cuesta, 1996.

Rojas, Fernando de. *La Celestina.* Ed. Dorothy S. Severin. Madrid: Alianza Editorial, 1969.
Rosalind-Jones, Ann, and Peter Stallybrass. "The Politics of 'Astrophil and Stella.'" *Studies in English Literature* 24 (1984): 53–68.
Rose, Mary Beth, ed. *Women in the Middle Ages and the Renaissance: Literary and Historical Perspectives.* Syracuse, N.Y.: Syracuse University Press, 1986.
Roth, Norman. *Conversos, Inquisition, and the Expulsion of the Jews from Spain.* Madison: University of Wisconsin Press, 1995.
Round, Nicholas. *The Greatest Man Uncrowned: A Study of the Fall of Alvaro de Luna.* London: Tamesis Books, 1986.
Rubin, Gayle. "The Traffic in Women: Notes on the 'Political Economy' of Sex." In *Towards an Anthropology of Women,* ed. Rayna Reiter. New York: Monthly Review Press, 1975. 157–210.
Rubin, Nancy. *Isabella of Castile: The First Renaissance Queen.* New York: St. Martin's Press, 1991.
Rubio Alvarez, Fernando, ed. *Jardín de nobles doncellas.* In *Prosistas castellanos del siglo XV.* Vol. 2. Biblioteca de Autores Españoles, 171. Madrid: Atlas, 1964.
Rubio Arquez, Marcial. "El 'Pleyto del manto': un caso de parodia en el *Cancionero General.*" In *Actas del IX Simposio de la Sociedad Española de Literatura General y Comparada (18–21 noviembre 1992).* 2 vols. Zaragoza: Universidad de Zaragoza, 1994. 2:237–50.
Ruether, Rosemary Radford. "Misogynism and Virginal Feminism in the Fathers of the Church." In Ruether, *Religion and Sexism,* 150–83.
———. ed. *Religion and Sexism: Images of Women in the Jewish and Christian Traditions.* New York: Simon and Schuster, 1974.
Ruiz, Juan. *Libro de buen amor.* Ed. Jacques Joset. Madrid: Clásicos Taurus, 1990.
Rushdie, Salman. "Christopher Columbus and Queen Isabella of Spain Consummate Their Relationship (Santa Fe, A.D. 1492)." In *East/West.* New York: Vintage Books, 1994. 105–19.
Russo, Mary. "Female Grotesques and Carnival Theory." In *Feminist Studies/Critical Studies,* ed. Teresa de Lauretis. Bloomington: Indiana University Press, 1986. 213–29.
Salvador Esteban, Emilia. "La precaria monarquía hispánica de los Reyes Católicos: reflexiones sobre la participación de Isabel I en el gobierno aragonés." In *Homenaje a José A. Maravall,* ed. María Carmen Iglesias, Carlos Moya, and Luis Rodríguez Zúñiga. 3 vols. Madrid: Centro de Investigaciones Sociológicas, 1985. 1:315–27.
San Pedro, Diego de. *Diego de San Pedro's Cárcel de Amor: A Critical Edition.* Ed. Ivy Corfis. London: Tamesis, 1987.
———. *Diego de San Pedro's Tractado de amores de Arnalte y Lucenda: A Critical Edition.* Ed. Ivy Corfis. London: Tamesis, 1985.
———. *Prison of Love, 1492: Together with the Continuation by Nicolás Nuñez, 1496.* Trans. Keith Whinnom. Edinburgh: Edinburgh University Press, 1979.
Sánchez-Albornoz, Claudio. *España, un enigma histórico.* Buenos Aires: Editorial Sudamericana, 1962.
Sánchez Cantón, Javier. *Libros, tapices y cuadros que coleccionó Isabel la Católica.* Madrid: Consejo Superior de Investigaciones Científicas, 1950.
———. *Los retratos de los reyes de España.* Barcelona: Ediciones Omega, 1948.

Sánchez de Arévalo, Rodrigo. *Compendiosa historia Hispanica*. Rome: Ulrich Han, 1470.
Sanchis y Rivera, José. "El Cardenal Rodrigo de Borja en Valencia." *Boletín de la Real Academia de la Historia* 84 (1924): 120–64.
Santa Cruz de Dueñas, Melchor de. *Floresta española*. Ed. María Pilar Cuartero and Maxime Chevalier. Barcelona: Crítica, 1997.
———. *Floresta española de apotegmas y sentencias, sabia y graciosamente dichas, de algunos españoles*. Sociedad de bibliófilos españoles 26. Madrid: Sociedad de bibiófilos españoles, 1953.
———. *Floresta española*. Vol. 1 of *Floresta general*. 2 vols. Ed. Pablo Oyanguren. Madrid: V. Suárez, 1910–11.
Sarasa, Esteban, ed. *Fernando II de Aragón: El Rey Católico*. Zaragoza: Institución "Fernando el Católico," 1996.
Schiesari, Juliana. "Libidinal Economies: Machiavelli and Fortune's Rape." In *Desire in the Renaissance: Psychoanalysis and Literature*. Princeton, N.J.: Princeton University Press, 1994. 169–83.
Schochet, Gordon J. *Patriarchalism and Political Thought: The Authoritarian Family and Political Speculation and Attitudes*. Oxford: Blackwell, 1975.
Scholberg, Kenneth. *Sátira e invectiva en la España medieval*. Madrid: Gredos, 1971.
Sedgwick, Eve Kosofsky. *Between Men: English Literature and Male Homosexual Desire*. New York: Columbia University Press, 1985.
Segura Graiño, Cristina. "Las sabias mujeres de la corte de Isabel la Católica." In *Las sabias mujeres: educación, saber y autoría (siglos III–XVII)*. Madrid: Asociación Cultural Al-Mudayna, 1994. 175–87.
———. *La voz del silencio*. 2 vols. Madrid: Asociación Cultural Al-Mudayna, 1992.
———. "Posibilidades jurídicas de las mujeres para acceder al trabajo." In *El trabajo de las mujeres en la Edad Media hispana*, ed. Angela Muñoz Fernández y Cristina Seguro Graiño. Madrid: Asociación Cultural Al-Mudayna, 1988. 15–26.
———. "Situación jurídica y realidad social de casadas y viudas en el medioevo hispano (Andalucía)." In Fonquerne and Esteban, *Condición de la mujer*, 121–33.
Seidenspinner-Núñez, Dayle. *The Writings of Teresa de Cartagena*. Woodbridge, England: Boydell & Brewer, 1998.
———. "Inflecting the *Converso* Voice: A Commentary on Recent Theories." *La Corónica* 25.1 (1996): 6–18.
Sharrer, Harvey L. "Letters in the Hispanic Prose Tristan Text." *Tristania* 7.1–2 (1981–82): 3–20.
Siete Partidas del rey Don Alfonso el Sabio. 3 vols. Madrid: Real Academia de la Historia, 1807.
Sigüenza, José de. *Historia de la Orden de San Gerónimo*. 2 vols. Ed. Juan Catalina García. Nueva Biblioteca de Autores Españoles. Madrid: Bailly-Baillière, 1983 [1900].
Silió Cortés, César. *Isabel la católica, fundadora de España: su vida, su tiempo, su reinado (1451–1504)*. Valladolid: Librería Santarén, 1938.
Sitges, J. B. *Enrique IV y la excelente señora llamada vulgarmente Doña Juana la Beltraneja*. Madrid: n.p., 1912.
Smith, Colin. *Spanish Ballads*. Oxford: Pergamon Press, 1964.
Smith, Paul Julian. *Representing the Other: "Race," Text, and Gender in Spanish and Spanish-American Narrative*. Oxford: Clarendon Press, 1992.

———. *Writing in the Margin: Spanish Literature of the Golden Age.* Oxford: Clarendon Press, 1988.
Smith, William, and Henry Wace, eds. *A Dictionary of Christian Biography.* 4 vols. New York: AMS Press, 1967 [1877].
Solomon, Michael. *The Literature of Misogyny in Medieval Spain: The "Arcipreste de Talavera" and the "Spill."* Cambridge Studies in Latin American and Iberian Literature 10. Cambridge: Cambridge University Press, 1997.
Solterer, Helen. Rev. of *Ravishing Maidens: Writing Rape in Medieval French Literature and Law,* by Kathryn Gravdal. *Medieval Feminist Newletter* 17 (1994): 16–18.
Soriano, Catherine. "Conveniencia política y tópico literario en el *Jardín de nobles doncellas* (1468?) de Fray Martín Alonso de Córdoba." In *Actas del VI Congreso Internacional de la Asociación Hispánica de Literatura Medieval* (Alcalá de Henares, 12–16 de septiembre de 1995). Alcalá de Henares: Universidad de Alcalá, 1997. 1457–66.
Stallybrass, Peter. "Patriarchal Territories: The Body Enclosed." In *Rewriting the Renaissance: The Discourses of Sexual Difference in Early Modern Europe,* ed. Margaret W. Ferguson, Maureen Quilligan, and Nancy J. Vickers. Chicago and London: University of Chicago Press, 1986. 123–42.
Stallybrass, Peter, and Allon White. *The Politics and Poetics of Transgression.* Ithaca, N.Y.: Cornell University Press, 1986.
Stratton, Suzanne. *The Immaculate Conception in Spanish Art.* Cambrige: Cambridge University Press, 1994.
Strong, Roy. *The Cult of Elizabeth: Elizabethan Portraiture and Pageantry.* London: Thames and Hudson, 1977.
Suárez Fernández, Luis. *Isabel, mujer y reina.* Madrid: Ediciones Rialp, 1992.
———. *Los Reyes Católicos: La conquista del trono.* Madrid: Ediciones Rialp, 1989.
———. *Los Trastámara y los Reyes Católicos.* Madrid: Gredos, 1985.
Sullivan, Constance A. "Re-reading the Hispanic Canon: The Question of Gender." *Ideologies and Literatures* 4 (1983): 93–101.
Surtz, Ronald E. "Female Patronage of Vernacular Religious Works in 15th-Century Castile: Aristocratic Women and Their Confessors." In *The Vernacular Spirit: Essays on Medieval Religious Literature,* ed. Renate Blumenfeld-Kosinski, Duncan Robertson, and Nancy B. Warren. New York: Palgrave, 2002. 263–82.
———. "Juana de Mendoza: Patron of Teresa de Cartagena and Iñigo de Mendoza." In *Power and Gender in Renaissance Spain: Eight Women of the Mendoza Family,* ed. Helen Nader. Forthcoming.
———. "Fray Juan López en travestí: sus *Historias que comprenden toda la vida de Nuestra Señora.*" V Jornadas Internacionales de Literatura Española Medieval. Universidad Católica de Argentina, Buenos Aires. August 23, 1996.
———. *Writing Women in Late Medieval and Early Modern Spain: The Mothers of Saint Teresa of Avila.* Philadelphia: University of Pennsylvania Press, 1995.
———. *The Guitar of God: Gender, Power, and Authority in the Visionary World of Mother Juana de la Cruz (1481–1534).* Philadelphia: University of Pennsylvania Press, 1990.
Tate, Robert Brian. "La historiografía del reinado de los Reyes Católicos." In *Antonio de Nebrija: Edad Media y Renacimiento,* ed. Carmen Codoñer and Juan Antonio González Iglesias. Salamanca: Universidad de Salamanca, 1994. 17–28.

———. "Políticas sexuales: de Enrique el Impotente a Isabel, maestra de engaños (magistra dissimulationum)." In *Actas del primer congreso anglo-hispano. Tomo III: Historia*, ed. R. Hitchcock and Ralph Penny. Madrid: Castalia, 1994. 165–75.

———. "Alfonso de Palencia: An Interim Biography." In *Letters and Society in Fifteenth-Century Spain: Studies Presented to P. E. Russell on his Eightieth Birthday*, ed. Alan Deyermond and Jeremy Lawrance. Llangrannoz, Wales: Dolphin Book Company, 1993. 175–91.

———. "Las Décadas de Alfonso de Palencia: un análisis historiográfico." In *Estudios dedicados a James Leslie Brooks*, ed. J. M. Ruiz Veintemille. Barcelona: Puvill, 1984. 223–41.

———. "Alfonso de Palencia y los preceptos de la historiografía." In *Nebrija y la introducción del renacimiento en España*. Actas de la III Academia Literaria Renacentista. Ed. Victor García de la Concha. Salamanca: Universidad de Salamanca, 1981. 37–51.

———. *Ensayos sobre la historiografía peninsular del siglo XV*. Trans. Jesús Díaz. Madrid: Gredos, 1970.

Thompson, B. Bussell. "Another Source for Lucena's *Repetición de Amores*." *Hispanic Review* 45 (1977): 337–45.

Torre, Antonio de la. "Unas noticias de Beatriz Galindo, 'La Latina.'" *Hispania* 17 (1957): 255–61.

Torre, Fernando de la. *Cancionero y obras en prosa*. Ed. Antonio Paz y Melia. Dresden: Max Niemeyer, 1907.

Torrellas, Pedro. *Coplas fechas por Mosén Torrellas, de las calidades de las donas*. In *Poesía cancioneril castellana*, ed. Michael Gerli. Madrid: Akal, 1994. 332–35.

Torres Fontes, Juan. "Las hazañas granadinas de Fajardo 'el Africano.'" *Hispania* 21.81–84 (1961): 3–21.

Torres Naharro, Bartolomé de. *Comedias: Soldadesca, Tinelaria, Himenea*. Ed. D. W. McPheeters. Madrid: Castalia, 1984.

Trexler, Richard. *Sex and Conquest: Gendered Violence, Political Order, and the European Conquest of the Americas*. Ithaca, N.Y.: Cornell University Press, 1995.

Val Valdivieso, María Isabel del. "Fernando de Aragón, Rey de Castilla." In *Fernando II de Aragón, el Rey Católico*, ed. Esteban Sarasa. Zaragoza: Institución "Fernando el Católico," 1996. 29–46.

Valera, Diego de. *Tratado en defenssa de virtuossas mugeres*. Ed. Mario Penna. Vol. 1, *Prosistas castellanos del siglo XV*. Biblioteca de Autores Españoles, 116. Madrid: Atlas, 1959. 55–76.

———. *Memorial de diversas hazañas*. Vol. 3 of *Crónicas de los reyes de Castilla*, ed. Cayetano Rosell. Biblioteca de Autores Españoles 70. Madrid: Atlas, 1953. 3–95.

———. *Doctrinal de príncipes*. In Penna and Rubio Alvarez, *Prosistas*, 1:173–202.

———. *Tratado de las epístolas*. In Penna and Rubio Alvarez, *Prosistas*. 1:3–46.

van Beysterveldt, Antony. "Los debates feministas del siglo XV y las novelas de Juan de Flores." *Hispania* 64 (1981): 1–13.

van Liere, Katherine Elliott. "Humanism and Scholasticism in Sixteenth-Century Academe: Five Student Orations from the University of Salamanca." *Renaissance Quarterly* 53 (2000): 57–107.

Vann, Theresa M. "The Theory and Practice of Medieval Castilian Queenship." In Vann, ed., *Queens, Regents, and Potentates*. Dallas, Texas: Academia, 1993, 125–47.

Varo, Carlos. See *Carajicomedia*.

Vasvari, Louise O. *The Heterotextual Body of the "Mora morilla."* Papers of the Medieval Hispanic Research Seminar 12. London: Department of Hispanic Studies, Queen Mary and Westfield College, 1999.

———. "The Semiotics of Phallic Aggression and Anal Penetration as Male Agonistic Ritual in the Libro de Buen Amor." In Blackmore and Hutcheson, *Queer Iberia*, 131–56.

———. "El hijo del molinero: para la polisemia popular del *Libro del Arcipreste*." In *El erotismo en las letras hispánicas*, ed. Luce López Baralt and Francisco Márquez Villanueva. Mexico City: Colegio de Mexico, 1995. 461–77.

———. "Vegetal-Genital Onomastics in the Libro de buen amor." *Romance Philology* 52.1 (1988): 1–29.

Vega y Carpio, Lope de. *Fuente Ovejuna*. Ed. Francisco López Estrada. Madrid: Castalia, 1985.

Vicens Vives, Jaime. *Historia crítica de la vida y reinado de Fernando II de Aragón*. Zaragoza: Institución "Fernando el Católico," 1962.

———, ed. *Historia social y económica de España y América*. Vol. 2, *Baja Edad Media, Reyes Católicos, Descubrimientos*. 5 vols. Barcelona: Editorial Vicens-Vives, 1982 [1957].

Vidal, José Manuel. "Isabel la Católica, ¿santa?" *El mundo: Crónica*. On-line. March 3, 2002.

Villalpando, Antonio de. *Razonamiento de las reales armas de los sereníssimos e muy exclaresçidos prínçipes e muy altos e muy poderosos reyes e señores, los señores don Fernando el quinto e doña Ysabel la segunda*. In Nieto Soria, *Orígenes*, 373–410.

Villeponteaux, Mary. "'Not as women wonted be': Spenser's Amazon Queen." In *Dissing Elizabeth: Negative Representations of Gloriana*, ed. Julia M. Walker. Durham, N.C., and London: Duke University Press, 1998. 209–25.

Vives, Juan Luis. Instrucción de la mujer cristiana. Trans. Juan Justiniano. Madrid: Fundación Universitaria, 1995.

von der Walde Moheno, Lillian. *Amor e ilegalidad: "Grisel y Mirabella," de Juan de Flores*. Mexico City: Universidad Nacional Autónoma de México, 1996.

———. "El episodio final de *Grisel y Mirabella*." *La Corónica* 20.2 (1992): 18–31.

Waley, Pamela, ed. *Grimalte y Gradissa*. By Juan de Flores. London: Tamesis, 1971.

Walker, Julia M., ed. *Dissing Elizabeth: Negative Representations of Gloriana*. Durham, N.C., and London: Duke University Press, 1998.

Walthaus, Rina. "'Gender,' Revalorización y Marginalización: La Defensa de la Mujer en el Siglo XV." In *Literatura Medieval. Actas do IV Congresso da Associação Hispânica de Literatura Medieval*, vol. 4, ed. Aires A. Nascimento and Cristina Almeida Ribeiro. Lisbon: Ediçoes Cosmos, 1993. 269–74.

Warner, Marina. *Alone of All Her Sex: The Myth and the Cult of the Virgin Mary*. New York: Random House, 1983.

Wayne, Valerie. "Some Sad Sentence: Vives' *Instruction of a Christian Woman*." In *Silent but for the Word: Tudor Women as Patrons, Translators, and Writers of Religious Works*, ed. Margaret Patterson Hannay. Kent, Ohio: Kent State University Press, 1985. 15–29.

———, ed. *The Matter of Difference: Materialist Feminist Criticism of Shakespeare*. Ithaca, N.Y.: Cornell University Press, 1991.

Weiss, Julian. "'¿Qué demandamos de las mujeres?': Forming the Debate about Women in Late Medieval Spain (with a Baroque Response)." In Fenster and Lees, *Gender in Debate*, 237–81.

———. "Political Commentary: Hernán Núñez's *Glosa a 'Las Trescientas.'*" In *Letters and Society in Fifteenth-Century Spain: Studies Presented to P. E. Russell on his Eightieth Birthday*, ed. Alan Deyermond and Jeremy Lawrance. Llangrannog, Wales: Dolphin Book Company, 1993. 205–16.

———. "Alvaro de Luna, Juan de Mena and the Power of Courtly Love." *Modern Language Notes* 106 (1991): 24–56.

———. *The Poet's Art: Literary Theory in Castile c. 1400–60*. Medium Aevum Monographs, n.s., 14. Oxford: Society for the Study of Medieval Languages and Literature, 1990.

Weissberger, Barbara F. "'Deceitful Sects': The Debate about Women in the Age of Isabel the Catholic." In Fenster and Lees, *Gender in Debate*, 237–81.

———. "The Critics and Florencia Pinar: The Problem with Assigning Feminism to a Medieval Court Poet." In *Recovering Spain's Feminist Tradition*, ed. Lisa Vollendorf. New York: Modern Language Association, 2001. 31–47.

———. "The Gendered Taxonomy of Spanish Romance." *La Corónica* 29.1 (2000): 205–29.

———. "Male Sexual Anxieties in *Carajicomedia*: A Response to Female Sovereignty." In Gerli and Weiss, *Poetry at Court*, 221–34.

———. "'Me atrevo a escribir así': Confessional Politics in the Letters of Isabel I and Hernando de Talavera." In *Women at Work in Spain: From the Middle Ages to Early Modern Times*, ed. Marilyn Stone and Carmen Benito-Vessels. New York: Peter Lang, 1998. 147–69.

———. "Resisting Readers and Writers in Sentimental Romance and the Problem of Female Literacy." In Gwara and Gerli, *Sentimental Romance*, 173–90.

———. "The Politics of *Cárcel de Amor*." *Revista de estudios hispánicos* 26 (1992): 307–26.

———. "Role-Reversal and Festivity in the Romances of Juan de Flores." *Journal of Hispanic Philology* 13.3 (1989): 197–213.

———. "Authors, Characters, and Readers in Juan de Flores's Grimalte y Gradissa." In *Creation and Re-Creation: Experiments in Literary Form in Early Modern Spain*, ed. Ronald E. Surtz and Nora Weinerth. Newark, Del.: Juan de la Cuesta Hispanic Monographs, 1983. 61–76.

Wentersdorf, Karl P. "Iconographic Elements in *Floris and Blancheflour*." *Annuale Mediaevale* 20 (1981): 79–96.

Whetnall, Jane L. "Isabel González of the Cancionero de Baena and Other Lost Voices." *La Corónica* 21.1 (1992): 59–82.

Whinnom, Keith. *The Spanish Sentimental Romance, 1440–1550: A Critical Bibliography*. London: Grant and Cutler, 1983.

———. *La poesía amatoria de la época de los Reyes Católicos*. Durham, England: Durham University Press, 1981.

———. "Hacia una interpretación y apreciación de las canciones del *Cancionero general* de 1511." *Filología* (1968–69): 361–81.

———. *Spanish Literary Historiography: Three Forms of Distortion*. Exeter: University of Exeter Press, 1967.

———, ed. *Obras completas*, vol. 1, *Tractado de amores de Arnalte y Lucenda. Sermón.* By Diego de San Pedro. Madrid: Castalia, 1973.

Woodward, Kenneth L. "'Saint Isabella'? Not So Fast." *Newsweek.* April 15, 1991. 66–67.

Yarbro-Bejarano, Yvonne. *Feminism and the Honor Plays of Lope de Vega.* West Lafayette, Ind.: Purdue University Press, 1994.

Yarza, Luaces, Joaquín. *Los Reyes Católicos: Paisaje artístico de una monarquía.* Madrid: Nerea, 1993.

Yates, Frances A. *Astraea: The Imperial Theme in the Sixteenth Century.* London: Routledge, 1975.

Zanger, Abby. *Scenes from the Marriage of Louis XIV: Nuptial Fictions and the Making of Absolutist Power.* Stanford, Calif.: Stanford University Press, 1997.

Index

Abjection, displaced, 3
absolute monarchy, 128–29, 172; fantasy of unity and purity informing Isabelline, xvii–xviii; gender-role instability and its effects on, 170–71; strengthening of, 261n.109; transformation from contractual to, 179
Acuerdo para la gobernación del reino (Concordia de Segovia), 47, 70, 166–67, 226n.60
Acuña, Alvaro de, 247n.11
Adam: Rodrigo as figure for, 110
Adam's rib as woman's prime material, 34
adultery: laws governing, 18–19
advocate: queen as, 39
Aguilar, Pedro de, 131, 132, 262n.112
Alcázar López, Pablo, 179
Alegoria de Francisco Franco (mural), 192–93
Alexander the Great, 49
Alexander VI, pope, 247n.11
Alfonso, xii, xxiii, 131; birth of, 28; death of, 29, 40
Alfonso II, 113
Alfonso V, 16, 113; contrast between Enrique IV and, 118
Alfonso X, 22, 105, 150
Alfonso XI, 18

Alfonso de Portugal, 41, 65
Allen, Cardinal William, 15
Alonso, Alvaro, 211n.14, 219n.74
Alonso Hernández, J. L., 258n.90
Alvarez Gato, Juan, 123
Alvarez Rubiano, Pablo, 62, 230n.75
amatory doctrine, Aristotelian: impact of, 140; subversion and fictionalization of, 140–48
"Amores trata Rodrigo," 107
Anacephaleosis (Cartagena), 103, 246n.3
Anales breves de los Reyes Católicos (Galíndez de Carvajal), 91
Anderson, Benedict, 96
animal husbandry motif in *Sérmon trobado*, 65–66, 236n.113
Antologia de poetas liricos castellanos (Pelayo), 238n.14
anvil, blacksmith's *(invención)*, 70
anxiety: castration, in Rodrigo ballads, 103–12, 249n.32; Freudian definition of, xv; of legitimacy, 82. *See also* masculine anxiety
Aposento en Juvera, 247n.11
Aragon: tenuousness of Isabel's sovereign rights in, 54–55
Arcipreste de Talavera o Corbacho (Martínez de Toledo), 132–33, 272n.61
Aretino, Pietro, 220n.79

aristocracy: adversarial relationship with monarchy, 5; diminution of power of, 130–31; Mendoza's advice on subduing nobles, 64–65; noblewomen in Isabel's circle, 263n.2; rescission of all rewards granted by Alfonso to, 131, 262n.110
Aristotle, 100, 259n.94, 260n.98; philosophy of love, subversion, and fictionalization of, 140–48
arms vs. letters polemic, 142, 158–59
Aronstein, Susan, 18
arrows *(flechas)* on heraldic arms, 47–49, 51–54, 229n.70
Arte de axedrez [Art of chess] (Lucena), xxv–xxvi, 135, 148–61; cultural importance of, 149; dedication to Prince Juan, 150; Lucena's pairing of *Repetiçíon* and, 156–57. *See also* chess
Artículos des postulador: Sobre la fama de santidad, vida y virtudes de la sierva de Dios, Isabel I, Reina de Castilla (Rodríguez Valencia), xi
Asamblea de Andalucía, 207n.2
Asensio, Francisco, 28, 67
Asociación Cultural Al-Mudayna of the Universidad Complutense of Madrid, 209n.15
Astorga, García de, 131–32, 260n.99, 262n.112
Athens: Varro's tale of naming of city of, 36–37, 223n.27
Augustine, Saint, 33, 223n.27, 255n.67
authority of familial/political patriarch, 39
Ave/Eva palindrome, 32–35, 116
Ávila: ritual dethronement of Enrique IV in (1465), 80–81, 101
Ávila, Francisco de, 256n.79
Azcona, Tarsicio de, xix, xxi, 32, 43, 47, 55, 67, 70, 77, 84, 101, 112, 221n.5, 226n.60, 248n.20

Bacchanalian cult: threat represented by, 217n.58
Baeza, Gonzalo de, 256n.77
Bakhtin, Mikhail, 2, 3

ballad cycle of Rodrigo, xxiv–xxv, 103–12, 249n.32
Barbosa, Arias, 138
Barrientos, Lope de, 29
Basel, Council of (1434–35), 97
beatification of Isabel I: process of, xi. *See also* messianism, Isabelline
beehive: as ideogram, 65–66
Beltrán de la Cueva, 78, 88, 215n.45, 230n.81
Benassar, Bartolomé, 74
Berenguela, 32
Bermejo Cabrero, José Luis, 165
Bernáldez, Andrés, 72
Blackmore, Josiah, 209n.17
Blanca de Navarra, 77
"blood purity": Mena's exhortation against bastardization of Castilian bloodlines, 9; preoccupation with, 74; statutes of, xiii, 99
Bloy, Leon, 195
Bobadilla, Beatriz de, 166
Boccaccio, 147
bodily enclosure: imagery of, 118–19
bodily integrity of queen, 115–16, 118. *See also* virginity
body: feminine/feminized (broken), 98, 99, 103–24, 249n.32; grotesque, 2, 3; hierarchy of upper over lower, inversion of, xxv, 7; notion of king's two bodies, 100, 246n.7
body politic: castration as traumatic originary wound of sexualized, 111; closure of Spanish, 118; linking of masculine physical body and, 80–81
Book of the Duchess (Chaucer), 154
Boose, Lynda E., 111
Borgia, Rodrigo (Pope Alexander VI), 247n.11
Bray, Alan, 73
Breçayda (Trojan heroine), 177
Bredbeck, Gregory, 71, 73
Breitenberg, Mark, xiv
Breviloquio de amor y amiçiçia (Fernández de Madrigal), 140
Brewer, Derek, 211n.7

broken (feminized) body, 98, 99; Isabel as Virgin Mary repairing Spain's, 112–24; of king in Rodrigo ballad cycle, 103–12, 249n.32
Brown, Catherine, 209n.17
Brownlee, Marina, 178
Bugge, John, 115
buggery, 24–25, 219n.75. *See also* sodomy
Bynum, Carolyn Walker, 118, 124

Calahorra, bishop of, 80
Canales, Alfonso, 12
Cancionero de obras de burlas provocantes a risa [Songbook of mirth-producing works of mockery], 3–4
Cancionero general, 3, 5, 129, 211n.5, 258n.88, 258n.89, 261n.105; *Burlas* section of, 124
cancionero poetry, 3–4; resistance to erotic paronomasia of, 4, 211n.7; "secret language" of, 4
capitulaciones matrimoniales, 29, 43–44, 56
Carajicomedia [Prick-comedy], xxii–xxiii, 5–16, 23–27, 63, 64, 188; Carajo/Fortuna parallelism in, 7, 213n.33; as classic carnivalesque text, 6, 7–11; commentary on whore Gracia, 234n.102, 236n.113; comparison to *Pleyto*, 126, 127; contemporary recasting of, 201; contradictory transgression of *Laberinto*, 23; direct and indirect references to Queen in, 13, 214n.38; exclusion from Hispano-medieval canon, as political act, 205; influence of *Celestina* on, 9, 212n.23; misogyny in, 6, 10–11; Queen as whore in, 7–16; reasons for analyzing, 1–2; staging of male impotence in, xv; terminus post quem, 212n.21, 219n.74
Cárcel de Amor (San Pedro), 142, 162, 163
Cárdenas, Gutierre de, 41, 43, 44, 225n.42
Carlos I (Carlos V), 68; *reconquista* and imperialist expansionism realized by, 105

carnival: subversion-containment debate over political significance of, 2–3. *See also Carajicomedia* [Prick-comedy]
carnivalesque works, 187–88; *Carajicomedia* as classic, 6, 7–11; transcodings characteristic of, 8–9
Carpentier, Alejo, xxvii, 194, 195–97, 199
Carrasco, Rafael, 74
Carrillo, Alfonso de, 41, 80, 221n.7, 240n.30
"carta circular" (1471), 225n.40
Cartagena, Alonso de, 59, 91, 97, 103, 233n.99
Cartagena, Pedro de, 116, 123, 246n.3
Cartagena, Teresa de, xix, 59
castidat, 18, 216n.55
Castiglione, Baldassarre, 143–44, 151
Castile: dynastic union of Aragon and, 54; Portuguese invasion of (1476), 88, 89; resistance to Isabel's royal authority in, 55
Castilian law: compendium of, 243n.62
Castillo, Enríquez del, 240n.32
Castillo, Hernán del, 3, 129–30
Castillo de la Mota (Medina del Campo): national demonstration in honor of Franco at (1939), 189–90, 273n.2
castration: as traumatic originary wound of sexualized body politic of Hispania, 111
castration anxiety in Rodrigo ballads, 103–12, 249n.32
Castro, Américo, xvii, 97, 208n.8
Catalina of Lancaster, 46, 222n.12
Cátedra, Pedro, 139, 140, 142, 146–47, 157, 161
Catherine of Aragon, 31
Cava, La, xxiv, xxv, 89, 117, 118; Arabic name given to, 108–9; containing Isabel's gender association to, 113–14; insinuation of complicity in sin, 107–8; rape by Rodrigo, 104–12, 252n.40; status as object of exchange, 252n.43
Cavallería, Alfonso de la, 226n.60

Cazzaria, La [A bunch of pricks] (Vignali), 220n.79
Cecilia, Saint, 36
Cela, Camilo José, 66
Celestina (Rojas), 9, 13–14, 145, 212n.23. See also *Comedia de Calisto y Melibea*
Cereceda, Miguel, 148
ceremonial symbolism of sword of justice, 44–47: gender inappropriateness of, 84–85
Cervantes, 52–53. See also *Don Quixote*
Cessolis, Jacobus de, 266n.42
Chacón, Gonzalo, 29, 41, 43, 72, 225n.42
Charles I of Spain (Charles V of Holy Roman Empire), xiii, xxi, 214n.35
Chartier, Alan, 183
chastity, virtue of, 160; in *Jardín*, emphasis on, 36, 40–42; in *Laberinto de Fortuna*, preoccupation with, 16–27; within marriage, 114; three descending degrees of, 37–38
Chaucer, 154, 211n.7
Checa, Jorge, 178–79
chess: clerics' use of game's rich symbolic potential, 155; history of, xxv–xxvi, 150, 266n.42; literary uses made of, 153–56; Lucena's *Arte de axedrez* on, xxv–xxvi, 135, 148–61; queen's power under new rules of, 152–53; radical alteration in rules of game, 149, 151–53
chess morality, 149, 154–61; religious morality, 155; *Repetiçión* as, 149, 156–61; secular morality, 155
Christ: assimilation of Isabel to Mary as bride of, 114–15
Christian: national self-concept as, xiii
"Christopher and Columbus and Queen Isabella of Spain Consummate Their Relationship (Santa Fe, A.D. 1492)" (Rushdie), 197–99
Chronicle of 754, 249n.27
chroniclers, royal *(cronistas)*, xxiv, 14–15, 45, 225n.42; complex gender ideology promoted by, 14; *converso* origins of many of, xxiv, 79, 91, 93, 99; creation of position of, 90;

Isabel's charge to, 71; *letrados*, political and cultural role of, 90–95. See also effeminacy in Isabelline historiography, discourse of; Flores, Juan de; Palencia, Alfonso de; Pulgar, Fernando del
Chronicon Mundi (Tuy), 97
Cicero, 217n.58
Cid, the, xxvi, 273n.1
Circle of Apollo, 19
Circle of Saturn, 21
Circle of the Moon, 16–19, 21, 22
Circle of Venus, 16, 19, 219n.73
City of God, The (Augustine), 223n.27
civil war, 69, 70, 80, 168–69; negotiations leading to, 241n.40
civil war, Spanish (1936–39), xxvi, 202
Clare, Saint, 122
Clarke, Dorothy Clotelle, 22–23
Claros varones de Castilla [Illustrious men of Castile] (Pulgar), 87, 94
Claudel, Paul, 195
claustration, monastic, 63, 120–21, 256n.74
Clavijo, battle of, 192
Clemencín, Diego, 62, 231n.84, 233n.97
clemency, shield of, 60
clerical misogyny, 209n.17
cleric and knight: debate between, 142, 158, 267n.51
cognatic succession, 32
Collins, Roger, 106, 248n.27
Colloquia (Erasmus), 92–93
Columbus, Christopher, xiii, xviii–xix, 195–99, 228n.68
Comedia de Calisto y Melibea (Rojas), 138
compassion: virtue of, 38–40, 57–58
Compendiosa Historia Hispanica (Sánchez de Arévalo), 81, 103, 246n.3
Conceptionists, order of, 121–22
conduct books for women, 62, 276n.25
consort: Fernando's relegation to role of, 45, 47; queen, xv, xxiii, 180, 210n.19
Constantinople: fall to Turks (1453), 28
Contreras, Juana de, 263n.2
converso mentality, 98

conversos, xviii, 75, 246n.6; accusations of sodomy attached to, 74; chroniclers as, xxiv, 79, 91, 93, 99; coded as feminine, xvi; messianism of writers, xvii, 208n.8; pre-bourgeois consciousness of, 214n.42; struggle for economic power and social status between "Old" and "New" Christians, 246n.8

convivencia or coexistence: deteriorating multicultural, 98

Coplas del Provincial (Songs of the provincial), 74

Coplas de Mingo Revulgo (Mendoza), 232n.92

Coplas de Vita Christi (Mendoza), 59, 116, 232n.92

Córdoba, Antonio de, 221n.6

Córdoba, Martín de, xv, xxiii, 29–44, 45, 53, 57, 66, 68, 112, 114–15, 170, 180, 221n.6, 272n.61. *See also Jardín de nobles doncellas* [Garden of noble maidens] (Córdoba)

Corfis, Ivy, 163

Corominas, Joan, 61

coronación de la señora Gracisla, La (Flores), 165, 270n.29

coronation ceremony (1474), 44, 53, 84–85

Coronel, María, 16, 17–18, 216n.52

corporeal concept of state, 38, 79–80, 100–103; amputation of diseased body parts, 102; carnivalesque parody of, 247n.11; sexing the neo-Gothic theory, 96–103; theoretical support for growing personalization of royal power, 101

corpus mysticum, xxiv, xxv, 100, 247n.17; discursive construction of Spain/Isabel as, 188; king as head of state figured as, 79; *Pleyto* and parody of, 128

Corral, Pedro del, 106, 110. *See also Crónica del Rey don Rodrigo*

corregidores, 168, 269n.25

Correll, Barbara, 92, 93, 94, 95

Cortes: of 1476, 130, 136; of 1480, 86, 130, 243n.62

Cortés, Hernán, 138

courtly love: chess's role in, 153–54; debate on meaning of, 3–4; similarity of misogyny and, 181–82

courtship: patterns, comparison to fashion, 175; reversal of traditional roles of, in *Triunfo de amor*, 172–76

Covarrubias, Sébastian de, 61, 127, 251n.38

Crónica de Alfonso III, 253n.46

Crónica de Enrique IV (Palencia), 71–95, 167; genealogy of sodomy and illegitimacy in, 81–82, 241n.46; misogyny in, 84–90; physical and psychological portrait of Enrique IV in, 75–78

Crónica de los Reyes Católicos [Chronicle of the Catholic Monarchs] (Pulgar), 46, 73, 87, 94, 137, 240n.32

Crónica del Rey Don Enrique el Cuarto (Castillo), 240n.32

Crónica del rey don Pedro (López de Ayala), 216n.52

Crónica del Rey don Rodrigo or *Crónica sarracina* (Corral), 106, 249n.32, 252n.43

Crónica incompleta de los Reyes Católicos (Flores), xxvi, 83–84, 164–71, 184; concern for strengthening royal justice, 168–69; gender-role instability and its effects on monarchic absolutism in, 170–71; glorification of women's strength and abilities in times of crisis, 166; *Triunfo de amor* as festive allegorized version of, 176–77

Crónica silense, 252n.43

cross-gendering of audience in student burlesque: use of, 141, 144

crown, dispute over, 14–15; civil/peninsular war, 69, 70, 80, 168–69, 241n.40; direct vs. collateral dynastic lines, 40–42. *See also* effeminacy in Isabelline historiography: discourse of

Cruz, Anne J., 250n.34

Cruz, Juan de la, 257n.80

cuerpo místico. *See corpus mysticum*

curial gamesmanship, 94

Curtius, Quintus, 49

d'Anghiera, Pietro Martire, 92
d'Azero, Rabo, 10
De animalibus (Aristotle), 145
death: as pernicious effect of woman, 159
De casibus illustrium virorum (Boccaccio), 147
dechado: meaning of, 61
Dechado a la muy escelente Reina Doña Isabel, nuestra soberana señora [Model for the most excellent Queen Isabel, our sovereign lady] (Mendoza), 59–62, 69, 116, 234n.99, 236n.113
De Civilitate Morum Pueriliem (Erasmus), 92–93
De clementia (Seneca), 100
De cómo al ome es necesario amar, 140
De hispanorum quirundum corruptis litterarum vocibus (Nebrija), 140
De Institutione Foeminae Christianae [The instruction of a Christian woman] (Vives), 31, 62
Delany, Sheila, 210n.2, 211n.7
Delicado, Francisco, 251n.38
De rebus Hispaniae or *Historia Gothica* (Jiménez de Rada), 97, 240n.36
De Republica Anglorum (Smith), 223n.24
De vita beata (Lucena), 101
Deyermond, Alan, 105, 218n.63
Diálogo sobre la educación del Príncipe Don Juan (Ortiz), 137
Diccionario de la Real Academia, 66
Discorsi sopra la prima Deca di Livio, 219n.78
Discourses (Machiavelli), 25–26, 219n.77
displaced abjection, 3
disputatio (repetitio), 139–40. See also *Repetiçíon de amores* [Oration on love] (Lucena)
divine right of kings, 38, 102
divinity: double-gendering of Isabel's, 123
division of labor: cultural affairs as Isabel's domain, 263n.2; male and female virtues and, 115; sexual, 62
Doctrinal de príncipes (Valera), 102, 105–6, 112–15

dominium (family rule): grounding of *imperium* (state rule) in, 18, 216n.56
Don Quixote, 229n.74
dotrina que dieron a Sarra, La (Pérez de Guzmán), 62
Duby, Georges, 18

Eales, Richard, 151, 153
Ecclesiastes: Córdoba's commentary on misogynistic passage from, 35
Edict of Expulsion, 99
education: Córdoba on prohibition of female, 36–37; fascist primary school system, 190–92; of Isabel's children, 135, 137, 149–50; Isabel's patronage of Salamanca, 135–40; in Latin, 136, 137, 138–39, 143–44, 220n.3, 263n.7; for women, Renaissance proponents of, 224n.30
Edwards, John, 100
Edward VI, 223n.24
effeminacy: defined, 237n.8; excessive passion as sign of, 109–10
effeminacy in Isabelline historiography, discourse of, xxiii–xxiv, 14–15, 69–95; cultural implications for rise of humanism, 71, 90–95; Enrique IV's impotence, 72, 77–78; genealogy of sodomy and illegitimacy, 71, 72, 73–75, 81–82, 241n.46; genealogy of weak and/or transgressive men, 89; Isabel as virago and, 82–84, 170; Palencia's *Crónica de Enrique IV*, 71–95; paradox of gender ideology upheld by Isabel, 83–84, 87; Pulgar and, 71, 72, 73, 80, 86–87, 93–95; revisions and falsifications to legitimate Isabel's assumption of crown, 79, 240n.32; role in foundational myths, 81–82; from sodomitic to misogynistic, xxiv, 84–90
Egica, King, 104, 105–6
Egido, Aurora, 139, 143
Eiximénez, Francesc, 256n.78
El arpa y la sombra [The harp and the shadow] (Carpentier), 195–97
El cuarto de atrás [The backroom] (Martín Gaite), xxvii, 202–6

Eleanor of Aquitaine, 185
Elizabeth I of England, xiv, xvi, 15, 223n.24; assimilation of integrity of body of, to integrity of state, 118–19; complex fashioning of, 208n.7; Marian representation of, 257n.86; strategies to reinforce sense of her self as male, 215n.47; use of virginity to maintain and manipulate unauthorized sovereign power, 114
Elliott, J. H., 54, 230n.78
El mejor mozo de España [The best lad in Spain] (Lope), 234n.104
Encina, Juan del, 24, 127, 138, 260n.98
enclosure, Marian imagery of, 118–19; claustration of nuns as literalization of, 120–21
Enrique II, 17, 18, 81, 82, 96, 211n.17, 250n.33
Enrique IV, xii, xxiv, 14, 16, 67, 89, 104, 188; allusions to illegitimacy of daughter Juana, 77–78; contrast between Alfonso V and, 118; dethroning effigy of (Farsa de Ávila), 80–81, 101; fascination with Islamic culture, 75–76; impotence of, 72, 77–78; Isabel's disassociation from "femininity" of, 45; Mendoza's critique of, 116–17; Palencia's *Crónica de Enrique IV* on, 71–95; propaganda campaign against, 25, 40, 41; Pulgar's *Crónica* attacking, 94; stigmatization as sodomitic, 71, 72, 73–74; Toros de Guisando pact signed by, 29, 40, 56, 77, 220n.4, 220n.5, 225n.40, 225n.41, 239n.27
Episcopal Conference of Spain, xi
Epistola exhortatoria a las letras (Lucena), 34, 83
equestrian symbol in *Dechado*, 60
Erasmus, Desiderius, 92–93, 245n.84
Eschés de la Dame, 155, 156
eschez amoureux, Les, 154
España nuestra [Our Spain] (Giménez Caballero), 190–92
Espejo del mundo (Jaén), 258n.92
Espósito, Anthony, 111
Eva/Ave opposition, 32–35, 116

Eve: identification of Isabel with, 113–14, 257n.80; Juana de Portugal compared to, by Palencia, 88–89, 244n.69; Rodrigo as figure for, 110
exclusionary policies of Isabel, 99, 238n.15

Fajardo, Alonso Yáñez, 6, 12–13, 218n.68
Fajardo, Diego, xxii, 6, 7, 8–13, 16, 23, 26, 213n.35
Fajardo family: Isabel's patronage of brothel-owning, xxii, 12–13, 214n.36
Falangist Party, xxi, 203; appropriation of Isabel as icon of "Second Reconquest" of Spain, 188–94; Sección Femenina (women's auxiliary), 189–90, 203, 204, 273n.2
familial/political patriarch: authority of, 39
fantasies of power, female, 186
Farsa de Ávila, 80–81, 101
fascism, xxvii, 188–94; living as female under, 202–6; patriarchal ideologies of, 190–92; visual propaganda of Franco, 192–94
Felipe (Philip) I, xiii, 68
female sovereignty: high and low responses to, 187–88; legitimacy of, debate about, 223n.24; mystification of anomaly of, xiv, xvii. *See also* sovereignty, fashioning Isabel's
female virtue, 37–42, 57–58, 115–18; female handiwork associated with, 62
feminine identity: Erasmian texts structuring of, 92–93
feminine or feminized bodies. *See* broken (feminized) body
Femininity: medieval construction of, 37–42, 155, 223n.30
feminist theory: primary tenets of, 7
feminization: as pernicious effect of woman, 159
Fenollar, Mossen, 154–55
Fernández, Lucas, 24, 138
Fernández de Madrigal, Alfonso ("el Tostado"), 140
Fernández de Oviedo, Gonzalo, 149

Fernando, xii–xiii; as Christ figure, 114–15; Isabel's letter of acceptance to, 42; Isabel's marriage to, xii–xiii, xxi, 29, 42–44, 49; as king consort, 45, 47; Manrique's advice in *Regimento* to, 56, 57; Mendoza's *Sermón trobado* to, 64–67; portents attending birth of, 228n.68; portrayal by Palencia, 85–86; Prince of Aragon, heraldic emblem fashioned exclusively for, 49; reaction to terms of Segovian proclamation, 226n.60; signing of *capitulaciones matrimoniales*, 29, 43–44, 56; in tournament in Valladolid, 69–70; as warrior prince, 113, 115, 254n.57; as womanizer, 229n.75

Fernando III, 32, 47, 113

Ferrara, Orestes, 78, 82

Ferrer (agent in Castilian marriage negotiations), 42

Ferrer, San Vicente, 247n.17

Findlen, Paula, 5

Finucci, Valerie, 144, 157

Firpo, Arturo, 74

flechas (arrows) on heraldic arms, 47–49, 51–54, 229n.70

Floire and Blanchefleur, 153

Flores, Juan de, xv, xxvi, 14, 69, 70, 71, 83–84, 142, 161, 164–86, 237n.3, 237n.4, 242n.57, 270n.29; biography and corpus of, 165, 268n.13; as champion of women, 177, 271n.48; *Crónica incompleta*, xxvi, 83–84, 164–71, 184; exploration of monarchic power, 176; *Grisel y Mirabella*, 142, 165, 177–86; insistence on integrity of *corregidores*, 269n.25; privileged relationship with Queen, 166–67, 179; self-conscious attempt to flatter female audience, 167–68; *Triunfo de amor*, xxvi, 165, 171–77, 182, 184, 185

Floresta española (Spanish Anthology) (Asensio), 67

florilegia, 236n.113

Fortitude, tower of, 60

Fortune, 59; Circle of Apollo, 19; Circle of Saturn, 21; Circle of the Moon, 16–19, 21, 22; Circle of Venus, 16, 19, 219n.73; classical vs. Christianized view of, 20; literary debate over nature of, 217n.62; Machiavelli's misogynist concept of, 219n.78; unpredictability of seas associated with, 20

Fortune Is a Woman: Gender and Politics in the Thought of Niccolò Machiavelli (Pitkin), 25–26

Foucault, Michel, 72, 73

foundational myths, 74; of Athens, 36–37; Iberian and Visigoth line of descent, 79; role of discourse of transgressive sexuality and gender instability in, 81–82

Fradenburg, Louise, 123

Franciscans, 256n.76; Isabel's devotion to, 121, 256n.77

Franco, Francisco, 105, 273n.2; elevation of Isabel to status of national icon, xxvi–xxvii, 189–90; growing up female during regime of, 202–6; primary school system under, 190–92; regime of, 188–94; visual propaganda of, 192–94

freedom of choice given women in *Triunfo de amor*, 175, 176

freedom of expression: connection between sexual and intellectual, 199–200

Freud, Sigmund, xv, 210n.2

fronterizo ballads, 250n.34, 252n.39

Fuenteovejuna (Vega), 169–70

Fuentes, Alonso de, 236n.113

Funes, Leonardo, 241n.44

Galíndez de Carvajal, Lorenzo, 72, 91

Galindo, Beatriz ("la Latina"), 137, 263n.2

Gallego Méndez, Maria Teresa, 203

gallo (student burlesque), 139, 143; use of vernacular and cross-gendering of audience in, 141, 144

Gargano, Antonio, 172

gender: in Age of Isabel, xi–xxvii; spirituality and, 209n.17

gender hierarchy: attack on inequities of traditional, 181; instability of

patriarchal, 180, 184–85; Isabel's inversion of medieval, 6
gender ideology: identification of woman with body in medieval, xvii; medieval, 208n.9; repressive, in *Laberinto*, 21–22
gender-role inversions, 73; by Isabel, resistance to, 83–84; Palencia's criticism of, 84–90
gender roles: hierarchical concept of monarchy equated with domestic patriarchal, 38–40
Generaciones y semblanzas (Pérez de Guzmán), 222n.12
Generation of Animals (Aristotle), 259n.94
Genesis: creation story in, 33–35; Rodrigo ballad recalling, 110
Gerli, E. Michael, 116, 123
Gil, Juan, 50
Gil, Pero, 81
Gilman, Sander, 135, 137, 138, 139, 145
Gilman, Stephen, 98
Giménez Caballero, Ernesto, 190–92, 274n.3
Girón, Pedro, 42, 240n.30
Goldberg, Harriet, 30, 221n.10, 223n.23
Goldberg, Jonathan, xviii
Gómez Molleda, María Dolores, 62
González de Mendoza, Cardinal Pedro, 101
González Echevarría, Roberto, 196–97
González Iglesias, Juan-Antonio, 51–52
González-Llubera, I., 136, 137
González Muela, J., 132
González Núñez, Jose, 179
Gordian knot: agricultural background of Alexandrian legend of, 49, 52, 65
Gothic characteristics, 96
Goytisolo, Juan, xxvii, 194, 199–202, 274n.9
Gracia Dei, Pedro de, 149–50
Granada: war against Moorish kingdom of (1482–92), xiii, 6, 99, 115, 119, 254n.57
greed as root of all sins, topos of, 131–32
Greenblatt, Stephen, xviii
Grey, Lady Jane, 223n.24

Grieve, Patricia, 178, 182
Grimalte y Gradissa (Flores), 165, 185, 242n.57
Grisel y Mirabella (Flores), xxvi, 142, 165, 177–86; contextualized by actual politics of time of composition, 178–79; dedication of, 183–84; "mad queen" of, 180–86; noblewomen's revenge in, 181–83; plot of, 177–78
grotesque body, 2, 3
Grothe, Meriwynn, 189, 276n.25
Guesclin, Bernard du, 81
Guyenne, Duke of, 41
Guzmán, Gonzalo de, 77
Gwara, Joseph, 165, 166, 167–68, 184, 269n.24, 270n.29
gynarchy: Córdoba's warning about precarious nature of, 37

Halperin, David, 237n.8
Haywood, Louise, 184
helmet crests: inventions on, 70, 237n.3
heraldic arms, xxiii, 47–55; anecdote deconstructing complex fiction of marriage and sovereignty of, 67–68; balancing act of heraldic emblem, 53; *flechas* (arrows) on, 47–49, 51–54, 229n.70; Mendoza's interpretation of yoke and yoke straps of Fernando's, 64–67; motto on, 47, 49–51; notion of force subsumed in, 52–53; proliferation of, 47–48; sense of religious evangelization in, 52, 229n.72; transposed initials on, 49, 227n.65; yoke (*yugo*) on, 47–49, 51–54, 228n.69
Hercules, 159
Hernández, Alonso, 258n.90
Hilarion, Saint (Santilario), 23–24, 127–28, 218n.70
Historia de duobus amantibus (Silvius Piccolomini), 142, 146
historia de Grisel y Mirabella, La. See *Grisel y Mirabella* (Flores)
historicism, new, xvi, 208n.5
historiographic discourse: Isabel's appreciation for propagandistic value of, 71. *See also* effeminacy in Isabelline historiography, discourse of

Holy Office of the Inquisition, xiii, 74, 99, 244n.79
homophobia: misogyny underlying, 72
homosexual: medieval definition as sodomite, 73; prehomosexual categories, 237n.8, 238n.10
homosexual rape, 259n.96
homosocial bonding in *Repetiçíon*, 143–44
honor, masculine, 18; rape as issue of, 126, 259n.96; Rodrigo's rape of Cava as crime against, 109
humanism: construction of gender in, 245n.84; Italian, introduction of, 91–92; rise of, discourse of effeminacy and, 71, 90–95
Huon of Bordeaux, 153
Hutcheson, Gregory S., 21, 81, 209n.17

Iberia: complexity of multiculturalism of, xviii
idealist literature of medieval courts of Castile, 4
"ideological dissonance," perceived double, xiv, xv–xvi
Il Cortegiano [The book of the courtier] (Castiglione), 143–44, 151
illegitimacy: Palencia's genealogy of, 81–82, 241n.46
Immaculate Conception, doctrine of, 256n.75; Isabel's interest in, 121–22
imperium (state rule): grounding of *dominium* (family rule) in, 18, 216n.56
Innocent Morality, 155
Inquisition, Holy Office of the, xiii, 99, 244n.79; attacks on "abominable sins," 74
Introductiones latinae (Nebrija), 136
invención, 70, 227n.64, 237n.3
Irigaray, Luce, 188
Isabel: anticipatory modeling as queen consort, xv; birth of, xii; campaign to discredit Enrique IV, 25, 40, 41; *Carajicomedia* as psychic response to threat of, 6, 7–16; children of, xiii (*see also* Juan, Prince; Juana, Princess [Juana la Loca]); coronation ceremony (1474), 44, 53, 84–85; death of, xiii; disputed succession to Castilian throne, 14–15, 40–42; early relationship with mother, xii; education of, 29, 220n.3; family of, xii; gender as cultural impediment to, 15; gender-political program contradiction in, xiv, xv–xvi; as icon of "Second Reconquest" of Spain, 188–94; involvement in prostitution, 13–14, 26; marriage of, xii–xiii, xxi, 29, 42–44, 49; messianic and hagiographic construction of, xvii, xix–xx (*see also* messianism, Isabelline); modern deconstruction of official story of, 194–206; as necessarily ambivalent discursive project, 98–99; official story of reign of, xxiii–xxiv, 69–95; paradox of power and gender, 118, 123–24; as paramount feminine icon of Francoist propaganda, xxvi–xxvii, 189–90; period of rule, xiv; racist concepts and exclusionary policies promoted by, 99; restoration of heteronormative and patrilineal stability as task of, 15; rhetorical masculinization of, 82–84; right to crown, consolidating, 40–44; suitors of, 41, 42, 225n.42; as usurper of Castilian crown, xii. *See also* sovereignty, fashioning Isabel's
Isabel (Isabel's daughter), 43, 47
Isabel as earthly counterpart to Virgin Mary, xxiv, xxv, 82, 112–24; to contain gender association with Eve/Cava, 113–14; Marian traits extolled, 114–16; restorative mission, 112–24
Isabella: English use of diminutive, xx
Isabel, mujer y reina [Isabel, woman and queen] (Suárez Fernández), xx–xxi
Isabel of Portugal, xii
Isabel the Queen: Life and Times (Liss), xx
Islamic culture/society: Enrique IV's fascination with, 75–76; Goytisolo's admiration of, 199–202; Muslims, attitudes toward, xiii, xvi, 108–9, 111

Italian humanism: *letrados* as conduits for introduction of, 91–92

Jaén, Alonso, 258n.92
Jardín de nobles doncellas [Garden of noble maidens] (Córdoba), xv, xxiii, 29–44, 114–15, 170, 180; defense of female sovereignty, 30, 37–44; essentializing sex-gender hierarchy of, 40; hidden ideological agenda of, 38; preoccupation with "woman's place," 34; profeminism of, analyzing, 30–37; similarity of Manrique's *Regimento* to, 57–59
Jerome, Saint, 37, 147
Jeu des eschés de la Dame, Le, 155, 156
Jews: as coded feminine, xvi; expulsion of, xiii, 74, 99. See also *conversos*
Jiménez de Rada, Rodrigo, 97, 103, 240n.36
Joan of Arc, 53, 119, 153
John Paul II, pope, xi
Juan, Prince, xiii, xxv, 43, 86, 114; birth of, 122; and chess, 149; death in Salamanca, 148, 264n.8, 266n.35; education of, 135, 137–38, 149–50; marriage to Margaret of Austria, 137–38, 148
Juana, Princess (Juana la Loca), xiii, 68
Juana de Portugal (Enrique IV's wife), xii, 14–15, 29, 30, 65; comparison to Eve in Palencia's *Crónica*, 88–89, 104, 116, 118, 243n.69; marriage of, 69
Juana I of Castile (Juana la Beltraneja) (Enrique IV's daughter), xii, 16, 65, 69, 220n.5; ascribed illegitimacy of, 15, 40, 71, 77–78, 239n.29; legitimate heir to Enrique IV, xii, xiii, 78; marriage of, 69; representing direct line of succession, 40
Juan I of Castile, 41, 46
Juan II of Aragon, 41, 42, 226n.60
Juan II of Castile, xii, xxii, 1–2, 5, 26, 40, 45, 81–82, 89, 90, 97, 113, 218n.63, 222n.12; addressed in *Laberinto de Fortuna*, 1, 18; death of, 28; Isabel's fulfillment of mission set for, 6; order of succession established in will of, 32
judge, king as, 39
Juegos de axedrez, dados y tablas, 150
"Juego trovado" (Pinar), 129–30
juglaresco, 107, 250n.35, 253n.46
Julián, Count, 104–5, 109
justice: application of, under Isabel, 168–69; balance of punishment and mercy in monarchic, gendering of, 170; compendium of Castilian law, 243n.60; female power and new kind of law, 184–85; gender bias of legal process, 181; judicial (legal) and administrative reforms, 130–31, 135–36; king's role as firm administrator of, 102, 248n.23; Mendoza's call for, 59–60; parody of judicial procedure in *Pleyto del manto*, 125–33, 258n.92
Juvenal, 147

Kantorowicz, Ernst, 100
Kappeler, Susan, 213n.27
king: divine right of, 38, 102; military role of, 5, 39, 113; two bodies of, notion of, 100, 246n.7
king bee: metaphor of, 65–66
knight and cleric: debate between, 142, 158, 267n.51
Krueger, Roberta, 160, 163–64, 185

Laberinto de Fortuna (Mena), xxii, 41, 59, 60, 188; *Carajicomedia*'s parody of, 7–16; central metaphor of, 20; classic status in late fifteenth and sixteenth centuries, 8; genre, critical disagreement over, 212n.19; influence on Isabel's moral and political formation, 22–23; Isabel's fulfillment of mission set in, 6; on king's role as warrior, 5; reasons for analyzing, 1–2; war and wifely chastity in, 16–27
labor: division of, 62, 115, 263n.2; as double-gendered, 62
Lacarra, María Eugenia, 4
Lapesa, Rafael, 217n.62

Latin: cultivation of pure, 136; Isabel's interest in learning, 137, 263n.7; study of at University of Salamanca, 138–39, 143–44, 220n.3
Laurencia in *Fuenteovejuna*: speech of, 169–70
law. *See* justice
Lawrance, Jeremy, 91–92
learning and the arts: Isabel's dedication to, 134, 262n.2; patronage of University of Salamanca, 135–40
legal code, 22; Isabelline goal of restructuring Castile's, 130–31. *See also* justice
legitimacy: anxiety of, 82
Lehfeldt, Elizabeth, 31, 63, 120, 121, 122
Lerner, Gerda, 126, 259n.96
letrados ("legists"), 244n.72, 244n.73; anxieties of effeminacy, dependence on art of words and, 245n.84; contemporary competition of, 158; *conversos* among, 91, 93, 99; dependency on monarch, 91, 92; formation of masculine identity and social status among, 144; increase in participation on Royal Council, 130; instability of position of, 93; irony of, 99; Isabel's preferment of Salamancan-trained, 136; political and cultural role of, 90–95; rise of, as premodern meritocracy, 90–91; wary cultivation of subordination, 94–95. *See also* Lucena, Luis de
letters and arms: debate between, 142, 158–59
Levin, Carole, xviii, 15
Libro de buen Amor [Book of good love], 213n.30
Licinia, 19, 217n.58
Lida de Malkiel, María Rosa, 19, 114, 217n.62
Lingua, sive de linguae usu ac abusu (Erasmus), 245n.84
Liss, Peggy, xix, xx, 31, 52, 70, 86, 122, 130, 131, 136
literary hierarchies of style and genre: cultural spheres constructed within, 2
livre de Cristophe Colomb, Le (Claudel), 195

Livy, 217n.58
"Lo hispánico y el erasmismo" (Castro), 97–98
López de Ayala, Pedro, 216n.52, 258n.92
López de Córdoba, Leonor, xix
loquacity: feminine lasciviousness linked to, 109; as gender-coded feminine, 245n.84
Lo-Ré, Anthony, 216n.52
Louis XIV of France, 54
love: courtly, 3–4, 153–54, 181–82; in *Repetiçión de amores*, 140–48; reversal of courtship roles in *Triunfo de amor*, 172–76
lozana andaluza, La (Delicado), 251n.38
Luaces, Joaquín Yarza, 47
Lucena, Juan de, 83, 99, 101, 134, 158
Lucena, Luis de, xv, xxv, 134–61; ambivalence about chosen career path, 158–59; *Arte de axedrez*, xxv–xxvi, 135, 148–61; awareness of rules of game for masculine advancement, 157; *Repetiçión de amores*, xxv–xxvi, 140–48, 149, 156–61, 186; training of, 134–35, 138
Lucretia, 17, 252n.40
Ludus Scacchorum (Cessolis), 266n.42
Luna, Alvaro de, 59, 60, 82, 89, 217n.60, 218n.63, 230n.81, 261n.109; blamed for introduction of sodomy in Castile, 74–75; as hero in *Laberinto de Fortuna*, 20, 21
lust: Mendoza's condemnation of, 116–17
Luxuria, 23

Machiavelli, Niccolò, 25–26, 219n.76, 219n.77, 219n.78
machismo, 219n.76
Macías, 127
Mackay, Angus, 63, 64
McNamara, Jo Ann, 118
Macpherson, Ian, 4, 63, 227n.64
Maldezir de mugeres [Defamation of women] (Torrellas), 141, 142, 145, 177
male bonding in *Repetiçión*, 143–44
Manrique, Gómez, xv, xxiii, 30, 56–59, 230n.80

Manrique, Rodrigo, 80
Marañón, Gregorio, 72
Maravall, José, 90, 91, 100, 129, 262n.109
Marcuello, Pedro, 50, 119, 227n.65, 255n.68
Marcus, Leah, xviii
Margaret of Austria, 138, 148
Marian metaphor, 112–24; masculinization of Isabel promoted by, 119; piety, trait of, 115; redemptive role, 114–15; virginity, trait of, 115–18
María of Aragon, xii, 16, 22
María of Castile, 16, 17
María Teresa (daughter of Felipe IV), 54, 246n.7
Mariéjol, J. H., 72
Marineo Sículo, Lucio, 137, 143, 228n.68, 231n.84, 263n.2
Marinio, Lucio, 92
Márquez Villánueva, Francisco, 13–14, 26, 214n.35, 254n.53
marriage: aristocratic, goal in Middle Ages of, 41; chastity in, 16–27, 114; Córdoba's marriage manual for Isabel, 29–44; dynastic continuity ensured by fidelity in, 40–42; functions of, 41–42; of Isabel and Fernando, xii–xiii, xxi, 29, 42–44, 49; as only viable alternative to virginity, 160; time-honored sense of equally yoked partners in, 51
"marriage contract" *(capitulaciones)*, 29, 43–44, 56
martial prowess: chess as test of, 153
Martínez de Madrigal, Alfonso, 213n.30
Martínez de Toledo, Alfonso, 132–33, 221n.8, 272n.61
Martín Gaite, Carmen, xxvii, 187, 202–6
Martire, Pietro, 137, 138, 263n.2
Mary. *See* Virgin Mary
Mary Tudor, 223n.24
masculine anxiety, xiv–xvi, xxii, 1–27, 34; in *Carajicomedia*, 6, 7–16; in discourse of *neogoticismo*, 99; in *Laberinto de Fortuna*, 16–27; in modern deconstruction of Isabel's "official story," 196–99, 201

masculine honor, 18; rape as issue of men's, 126, 259n.96; Rodrigo's rape of Cava as crime against, 109
masculine identity: Erasmian texts structuring of, 92–93; fashioning of secular. *See* effeminacy in Isabelline historiography, discourse of
masculine superiority: ideology of, 4
Mata Carriazo, Juan de, 87, 93
materialist feminism, xvi, 2, 207n.4
maternal shield: queen as, 39–40
Matheolus, 183
Matulka, Barbara, 271n.48
Memorial de diversas hazañas [Memorandum about diverse deeds] (Valera), 80
Mena, Juan de, xxii, xxiii, 1, 5, 7, 9, 41, 90, 205
Mendoza, Cardinal, 122
Mendoza, Iñigo de, xv, xxiii, 51, 59–62, 69, 121, 228n.69, 232n.88, 232n.92, 233n.99, 236n.113; *Dechado a la muy escelente Reina Doña Isabel*, 59–62, 69, 116, 234n.99, 236n.113; Marian imagery used by, 116–18
Mendoza, Juana de, 59
Mendoza, Leonor de, 214n.35
Mendoza clan, 56, 244n.76
Menéndez Collera, Ana, 129, 261n.105
Menéndez Pidal, Ramón, 110, 199, 248n.26, 251n.38, 253n.46
Menéndez Pidal de Navascues, Faustino, 228n.65
Menéndez y Pelayo, Marcilino, 22, 103, 238n.14
mercedes reform, 131, 132, 262n.110
Merriman, R. B., 72
Mesguer Fernández, Juan, 121
messianism, Isabelline, xvii, xix–xx, 15, 79, 208n.8, 240n.34; of neo-Gothic discourse, 97–98; role of Virgin Mary in, xxiv, xxv, 82, 112–24
Meun, Jean de, 183
Miller, Nancy, 186
Mirrer, Louise, 108, 209n.17, 250n.34, 252n.39
Miscelánea de anécdotas y curiosos casos (Fuentes), 236n.113

misogyny: Aristotelian, 145; of *Carajicomedia*, 6, 10–11; clerical, 209n.17; of Córdoba, in *Jardín*, 33–35; in Lucena's *Repetiçion*, 145–48, 159–60; in Palencia's discourse of effeminacy, 84–90; in "profeminist" works in medieval Castile, 31, 221n.8; Queen stereotyped as nag, 68; similarity of courtly love and, 181–82; slippage of sodomitical discourse into, xxiv, 84–90; underlying homophobia, 72
monarchy: absolute: adversarial relationship with Castilian aristocracy, 5; concepts central to medieval theories of, 100; Córdoba's theory of, in *Jardín*, 38, 39; sword of justice as symbol of, 44–47; theocratic formulation of, 39; transformation from contractual to absolutist institution, 179. *See* absolute monarchy
monastic claustration, 120–21, 256n.74
monastic reform campaign, 120–21
Moner, Michel, 252n.40
Montalvo, Alonso Díaz de, 130, 136, 243n.60, 261n.109
Montaner, Alberto, 52
montar: meaning of, 66–67
Montesino, Ambrosio, 25, 219n.74, 256n.77
Montoro, Antón de, xv
Montrose, Louis, xviii, 208n.7
Moorish invasion of 711, xxiv, 89; reason for, 104–12, 248n.27, 250n.37
Moorish kingdom of Granada: war against (1482–92), xiii, 99, 115, 119, 254n.57
Moors as enemy from without: hatred for, 111
Morcillo Gómez, Aurora, 203
mujer: Orientación femenina, La (Pilar Morales), 276n.25
multiculturalism of Iberia: complexity of, xviii; deteriorating coexistence in, 98
Münzer, Hieronymus, 78
Murray, H. J. R., 151, 152, 154, 155
Muslims: coded as feminine, xvi; Islamic culture/society, 75–76, 199–202; purging of, xiii; women, 108–9, 111
Muslim Spain: presumed "right" of Christians to, 108–9

Nader, Helen, 244n.72, 244n.76
National Catholicism ideology, xxvii, 188–94, 203
national self-concept as Christian, xiii
nation building: exclusionary ideology supporting project of, 238n.15
nation-state: medieval kingdoms of Iberia transformed into, xiv
naturalismo amoroso, 213n.30
natural philosophy, Aristotelian, 140, 145
Nebrija, Antonio de, 47, 49, 50–51, 65, 92, 134, 135, 139–40, 143, 227n.62, 241n.37, 249n.30; reformist mission of, 136–37
needlework: female labor of, 61–63; Isabel as needleworker, 62–64, 233n.97, 233n.98, 234n.104; sexual innuendo in vocabulary associated with, 63–64, 236n.113
negotiations required of female sovereign in patriarchal society, 176
neo-Gothic theory, 96–133; castration anxiety in Rodrigo ballads, 103–12; Isabel's fashioning as virginal restorer, 112–24; messianism and, 97–98; power, sex, and property in *Pleyto del manto*, 124–33; as powerful legitimizing strategy for Isabel's claim to throne, 112; revived in mid–fifteenth century, 97; sexing the, 96–103
new historicism, xvi, 208n.5
Niebla, Conde de, 11–12, 20, 23, 213n.33
Nieto Soria, José Manuel, 100, 101, 128, 261n.109
noble lineages: confusion in, 74
nobles. *See* aristocracy
Núñez, Hernán, 8, 212n.21
nuns: claustration of, 63, 120–21, 256n.74; religious reforms and, 62–63, 233n.97, 233n.98, 256n.74
"nuptial fiction," 53–54

O'Callaghan, Joseph F., 77
"official" culture, texts of Isabelline, xxiii–xxiv, 69–95, 187; modern deconstruction of, 194–206. *See also* effeminacy in Isabelline historiography, discourse of
older woman: threat of, 26
Olmedo, Battle of (1445), 218n.63
On Clemency (De clementia) (Seneca), 38
Ong, Walter, 143
oraciones del Cartujano, Las (Montesino), 256n.77
Order of Saint Clare in Barcelona: reform of, 256n.74
Ormisinda, 46
Ornstein, Jacob, 148
Ortiz, Alonso, 137

Pacheco, Juan, 41, 80, 240n.30
Palencia, Alfonso de, xv, xx, xxiv, 14, 45, 46, 97, 136, 158, 167; *converso* background of, 244n.75; *Crónica de Enrique IV*, 71–95, 167, 241n.46; influence on Spanish historiography, 71–72; as *letrado*, 244n.73; portrayal of Fernando, 85–86; variety and scope of output, 91
papal legation of 1473: billeting of members of, 247n.11
paranomasia: resistance to erotic or obscene, 4, 211n.7
parasite (mites) removal: as intimate activity, 251n.38
Parker, Alexander, 3, 4
Parker, Patricia, 33–34, 92, 125, 196, 222n.16, 237n.7
Parrilla, Carmen, 165, 168, 175
"Pártese el moro Alicante," 108
passion: condemnation of excessive, 109–10
patriarchy: authority of familial/political patriarch, 39; domestic gender roles in, hierarchical monarchy equated with, 38–40; threat of powerful, uncontrolled woman to, xxvi, 162–86
Paz y Melia, Antonio, 77, 78, 237n.7, 238n.14, 239n.27
Pedro I, 17, 18, 81, 89, 250n.33

penis: masculinist projection of desired primacy of, 10
Pérez, Nazario, 121
Pérez de Arriaga, Joaquín, 148, 149, 161
Pérez de Guzmán, Fernán, 62, 222n.12, 223n.30
Pérez Priego, Miguel Angel, 145
Philip I of Austria, xiii, 68
Phillips, William, 72
Philosophy of Love in Spanish Literature, The (Parker), 3
Phoebus, 159
piety: of Isabel, 57, 58, 231n.84; virtue of, 115
Pilar Morales, María, 276n.25
Pimentel, Leonor de, 88
Pimentel, Rodrigo, 80
Pinar, Florencia, xix, 129–30, 261n.105
Pitkin, Hannah, 25–26, 219n.76
Pius IX, pope, 195
Platonic-idealist metaphysical tradition, 210n.2
Pleyto del manto [Lawsuit over the cloak], xxv, 3, 96, 257n.88; legal terminology and authorship of, 131–32; power, sex, and property in, 124–33; threat of feminine to masculine in, 125–28
plowshare metaphor: in *Sermón trobado*, 66
poesía amatoria de la época de los Reyes Católicos, La (Whinnom), 3–4
political program: Isabel's masculinist and patriarchal, xiv, xv–xvi
Politics and Poetics of Transgression, The (Stallybrass and White), 2–3
Politics (Política) (Aristotle), 38, 100
Ponce de León, Rodrigo, 228n.68
Poncella de Francia, La [The maid of France], 53, 119
pornographic structure of representation, 213n.27
pornography: *Carajicomedia*, xxii–xxiii, 5–16, 23–27, 63, 64, 188; elements of political critique in, 5; ideological relationship between prostitution and, 10–11; *Pleyto del manto*, xxv, 3, 96, 124–33, 257n.88

power: lurking beneath surface of queenly domesticity, 234n.104; in *Pleyto del manto*, 124–33; of print, Isabel's grasp of, 136; unequal, between Isabel and Fernando, 47; visual representations of Isabelline, 44–55. *See also* absolute monarchy
prayer, image of Isabel at, 58, 231n.84
prehomosexual categories of male sex and gender deviance, 237n.8, 238n.10
Prescott, William H., 72
Preston, Paul, 273n.2
primary school system: fascist construction of womanhood in, 190–92
Primera crónica general de España, 104–5
Primogeniture *(mayorazgo)*, 18–19, 216n.48
printing press: introduction of, 136, 137
profeminism of *Jardín de nobles doncellas:* analyzing, 30–37
property: growth of private rights to, 262n.109; in *Pleyto del manto*, 124–33; rape as issue of men's, 126, 259n.96; wife as, anxieties of virility underlying patriarchal conception of, 10
prostitutes/prostitution: association of both *manta* and *manto* with, 258n.90; in *Carajicomedia*, xxii, 7–16, 23, 24–25, 26; Cava labeled as, 108–9; fear of unpredictable and uncontrollable feminine projected onto, 12; history of, in Spain, 215n.42; ideological relationship between pornography and, 10–11; Isabel's involvement in, 13–14, 26; needlework terminology referring to, 63–64, 234n.102, 234n.103; in *Pleyto del manto*, 124–33; "progressive" policy toward, 14; Queen as whore in *Carajicomedia*, 7–16; as threat to masculine identity, xvi
"protest letter" (carta-protesta) of September 1464, 78
Providencia in *Laberinto*, 21, 59
prudence: virtue of, 60
Publicia, 19, 217n.58
Pulgar, Fernando del, xv, xx, 14, 28, 45, 46, 67–68, 71, 72, 73, 80, 93–95, 97, 99, 136, 137, 149, 158, 167, 220n.3, 225n.42, 240n.32; historiographical methodology, 94–95; professional competition with Palencia, 86–87; self-exile of, 93, 244n.79
puto: use of, 74, 219n.75
Puyol Alonso, Julio, 166, 167, 240n.32

queen: Córdoba on proper role of, 39–40
queen consort: role of, xv, xxiii, 180, 210n.19
Queer Iberia: Sexualities, Cultures, and Crossings from the Middle Ages to the Renaissance (Blackmore and Hutcheson), 209n.17
queer theory, 72
Quevedo, Francisco, 236n.112

racism, 11, 99. *See also* Jews; Muslims
Rackin, Phyllis, 109, 124
Ramiro I of Asturias, King, 192, 193
rape: of Cava by Rodrigo, 104–12, 252n.40; celebration in *Pleyto* of, 126; homosexual, 259n.96; as issue of men's property and honor, 126, 259n.96; of Spain by Moors, 105; subtle mystification by feminine seductiveness, 107, 251n.37
reconquista: concept of, 105; longings of western Christendom for reconquest of Holy Land, 50, 228n.68
Reconquista (Reconquest) (1482–92), xiii, 5, 6, 10, 28, 99, 115, 118, 119, 254n.57
reform: homely approach to, 62–63, 233n.97, 233n.98; judicial and administrative, 130–31, 135–36; religious, 62–63, 120–22, 233n.97, 233n.98, 256n.74
Regimento de principes [Government of princes] (Manrique), 56–59
Reiss, Edmund, 155
Reivindicación del conde don Julián [Count Julian] (Goytisolo), 199–202
religiosity, xx–xxi
religious reform, Isabelline, 62–63, 120–22, 233n.97, 233n.98, 256n.74

Renaissance: of Castile, 244n.72; Erasmian texts structuring of feminine and masculine identity in, 92–93; sexual acts stigmatized as sodomitical in, 73
Renaissance Italy: pornography in, 5
Repetiçíon de amores [Oration on love] (Lucena), xxv–xxvi, 135, 153, 186; as chess morality, 149, 156–61; as containment strategy for power of new kind of Queen, 156–60; discursive ordering of, 141–42; festive inversions in, 141–43; love, misogyny, and male bonding in, 140–48, 159–60; Lucena's pairing of *Arte de axedrez* and, 156–57; terminus ante quem, 148
repetitio (disputatio), 139–40. *See also Repetiçíon de amores* [Oration on love] (Lucena)
Reque Meruvia, D., 193
restorative mission: Isabel's fashioning as virginal restorer, 112–24; masculinist, misogynist ideology shaping Isabel's, 99; Reconquista, xiii, 5, 6, 10, 28, 99, 115, 118, 119, 254n.57
revenge on male detractors: medieval tradition of female, 183, 272n.61
Richards, Judith, 223n.24
Rimado de la conquista de Granada (Marcuello), 119
Rimado de palacio (López de Ayala), 258n.92
Rodrigo, King, 89, 117; penance and death of, 110, 111
Rodrigo ballad cycle, xxiv–xxv, 103–12, 249n.32; inciting Christian population to avenge defeat by Moors, 111–12; rape of Cava in, 104–12, 252n.40
Rodríguez-Moñino, Antonio, 258n.89
Rodríguez-Puértolas, Julio, 190, 232n.88, 274n.3
Rodríguez Valencia, Vicente, xi, 225n.41
Rojas, Fernando de, 134, 138, 145
Rojas, Francisco de, 84
romance, sentimental, 162–64; female readers of, 163–64, 185–86, 268n.6; of San Pedro, 162–63, 268n.2
"Romance de la morilla burlada," 108

Roman de Troie (Sainte-Maure), 185
Royal Council of Castile, 243n.60; diminution of nobility's representation in, 130
royal emblem. *See* heraldic arms
royal patrimony: reclaiming of, 131, 132, 262n.110
Rubin, Gayle, 7
Rubin, Nancy, xix
Rubio Alvarez, Fernando, 30, 220n.4
Rubio Arquez, Marcial, 258n.92, 260n.98
Ruiz, Hermida, 4
Rushdie, Salman, xxvii, 194, 197–99
rustic in early Castilian theater: stock character of, 24

sacred mission of Iberian kingdoms (expulsion of Muslim conquerors), 96, 97–98; Reconquista, xiii, 5, 6, 10, 28, 99, 115, 118, 119, 254n.57
Sainte-Maure, Benoit de, 185
Salamanca, University of, 165; Aristotelian natural philosophy taught at, 140; conflictive environment at, 143, 265n.23; fiesta del Obispillo at, 139; Isabel's patronage of, 135–40; Luis de Lucena at, 134–35; student resistance to pedagogical rigors of, 138–39
Salic law, 55
Salvador Esteban, Emilia, 54–55
Sánchez Albornoz, Claudio, 199
Sánchez Cantón, Javier, 137
Sánchez de Arévalo, Rodrigo, 79, 81, 97, 100, 103, 246n.3
Sánchez de las Brozas (el Brocense), Francisco, 8, 17, 216n.55
Sancho Panza, 229n.74
San Pedro, Diego de, 161, 162–63, 268n.2
Santa Cruz, Melchor de, 236n.113
Santa Hermandad, 130
Santiago, 192, 193
Santilario, 188
Santillana, Marqués de, 59
Sardanapolis, 57
satires: carnivalesque tone of, xxii. *See also Carajicomedia* [Prick-comedy]

"Scachs d'amour" (Fenollar), 154–55
Schiesari, Julia, 219n.78
scourge-of-God theory: sexualized version of, 105
Sección Femenina (women's auxiliary), 189–90, 203, 204, 273n.2
"Second Reconquest," xxvii; Isabel as icon of fascist, 188–94
Second Republic (1931–36): reversal of women's gains in, 189, 202–3
Sedgwick, Eve, 72, 76
Segura Graiño, Cristina, 263n.2
Seminario de Estudios de la Mujer at Universidad Autónoma de Madrid, xix, 209n.15
Semiramis of Assyria, queen, 223n.24
Seneca, 38, 39, 100
Sermón de amores (San Pedro), 161
Sermón trobado que fizo Fray Iñigo de Mendoza al muy alto y muy poderoso Principe, Rey y Señor, el Rey Don Fernando, Rey de Castilla y de Aragón, sobre el yugo y coyundas que Su Alteza trahe por divisa (Mendoza), 51, 64–67, 228n.69, 236n.113
serpent: as instrument of divine punishment of Rodrigo, 110, 111
Servicio Social, 190, 203–4
sewing. *See* needlework
sexing/gendering the neo-Gothic theory, 96–103
sexual division of labor, 62
sexuality: connection of transgressive, and disturbed sociopolitical order, 71, 72–73; male sexual disfunction/deviance linked to uncontrolled female sexuality, xxii–xxiii; policing of female, 16; sexual acts stigmatized as sodomitical in Renaissance, 73
sexualized discourse of Isabelline historiography. *See* effeminacy in Isabelline historiography, discourse of
Sforza, Catherine, 153
shame: as central mechanism of social control, 173, 174; as social custom rather than inherent gender trait, 175
shield of clemency, 60

sickness: as pernicious effect of woman, 159
Siete partidas [Seven sections] (Alfonso X), 22, 32
silence: virtue of, 223n.30
Silió Cortés, César, 63, 233n.98
Silva, Beatriz de, 121–22
Silvius, Aeneas, 142
Sitges, J. B., 77
Sixth Satire (Juvenal), 147
Smith, Paul Julian, 208n.12, 238n.15
Smith, Thomas, 223n.24
sodomy, 219n.73; in *Carajicomedia*, 24–25; Enrique IV's stigmatization as sodomite, 71, 72, 73–74; introduction in Castile, Luna blamed for, 74–75; medieval view of, 73; Palencia's genealogy of, 81–82, 241n.46; as threat to masculine identity, xvi; undefined and indefinable nature of, in Judeo-Christian tradition, 76–77; use of, to attack undifferentiated vice, 73–74
soil tilling metaphor for strong governance, 66
Solomon, Michael, 209n.17
Soriano, Catherine, 31, 220n.4
sovereign power: limitations on, 262n.109
sovereignty, fashioning Isabel's, xi–xxvii, 28–68; Córdoba's marriage manual for princess, 29–44; Manrique's treatise, 55–59; Mendoza's treatise, 59–67; visual representations of Isabelline power, 44–55
"Spanish character," 103–4, 248n.26
Spanish national identity: as exclusively Christian, xiii; fashioning of Queen's gender and power and changing discourse of nationhood, xxi; role of *conversos* in creation of, xviii
Spanish reintegration [Reintegratio Hispaniae], 103–4
specula principis [mirrors of princes], xxiii, 55–68; *Dechado...* (Mendoza), 59–62, 69, 116, 234n.99, 236n.113; *Doctrinal de príncipes* (Valera), 102, 105–6, 112–15; Isabel's appreciation of, 30;

specula principis [mirrors of princes] (*continued*), *Regimento de principes* (Manrique), 56–59. *See also Jardín de nobles doncellas* [Garden of noble maidens] (Córdoba); sovereignty, fashioning Isabel's, 55–68
spirituality: gender and, 209n.17
Stallybrass, Peter, 2–3, 6, 118
Stamm, 6
state: corporeal concept of, 38, 79–80, 100–103
status loss: as pernicious effect of woman, 159
student burlesque [gallo], 139, 143; use of vernacular and cross-gendering of audience in, 141, 144
Suárez Fernández, Luis, xix, xx–xxi, 72, 231n.84
subordination: cultivating, 94–95
succession: cognatic, 32; contest for, between Isabel and Enrique IV, 14–15, 40–42; female, 32, 222n.12
Suma de la politica (Sánchez de Arévalo), 100
sumptuary laws: royal promulgation of, 13, 214n.40
Surrey, Earl of, 154
Surtz, Ronald E., 209n.17
sword of justice: ceremonial, 44–47; Mendoza's call for, 59–60

Talavera, Hernando de, 99, 122, 230n.75, 263n.7, 276n.24
Tate, Robert Brian, 79, 85, 88, 90, 93, 97, 100, 103, 239n.27, 239n.29, 241n.44, 246n.3
temperantia, Ciceronian, 216n.55
Teresa of Ávila, xi, xxvi–xxvii
threat of feminine gender and sexuality in Isabelline political culture. *See* masculine anxiety
Toledo, archbishop of, 41
Toro, battle of (1476): Isabel's harangue at, 167, 169, 170; retreat of Castilian troops from siege of, 83, 85
Toros de Guisando pact (1469), 29, 40, 56, 77, 220n.4, 220n.5, 225n.40, 225n.41, 239n.27

Torquemada, Tomás de, 257n.80
Torrellas, Pedro, 127, 141, 142, 145, 157, 177, 178, 181–83, 221n.8
Torres Naharro, Bartolomé, 24
"To the Ladie That Scorned Her Lover" (Surrey), 154
Tractado de Arnalte y Lucenda (San Pedro), 161, 162–63
Trastamaran dynasty, 211n.17; absolutist ideology, 6; ballad tradition and institution of, 249n.33; founding of, 17, 81; María Coronel as chaste martyr for, 17, 18; restoration of legitimacy of, necessity of, 114; roots of genealogical tree, 97, 103
Tratado en defensa de las virtuosas mujeres [Treatise in defense of virtuous women] (Valera), 216n.52, 224n.36
Trebizond, George, 91
trescientas, Las. *See Laberinto de Fortuna* (Mena)
Triste deleytaçión, 273n.64
Triunfo de amor (Flores), xxvi, 165, 171–77, 182, 185; courtship roles reversed in, 172–76; dedication of, 184; as festive allegorized version of *Crónica incompleta*, 176–77; inversions and reversals in plot of, 171–77; women speaking for selves in, 177
Tuy, Lucas de, 97

university: formation of masculine secular identity in privileged young men in, 143–44; queen's interest in, 135–40
Urraca, 32

vagina: fear of penis's inability to fill void of, 10; insatiability of, 12
Valdivieso, Val, 239n.27
Valera, Diego de, 44–45, 69, 71, 72, 80, 97, 100, 104, 105–6, 112–15, 216n.52, 224n.36, 247n.11, 254n.57; kingdom as *cuerpo místico* invoked by, 101–2
Valladolid: archbishop of, xi; tournament in, 69–70, 237n.3
Varo, Carlos, 6, 12, 13–14, 24, 214n.38
Varro, 36–37, 223n.27

vassalage: yoke metaphors of feudal ties of, 64–67
Vasvari, Louise O., 213n.30
Vatican Council for Christian Unity, xi
Vega, Lope de, 169–70
Venier, Antonio, 225n.40
Vergara, Isabel de, 263n.2
Vergel de principes (Sánchez de Arévalo), 100
vernacular, use of, 141, 144
Vicens Vives, Jaime, 79, 225n.40, 229n.75, 239n.27
Vignali, Antonio, 220n.79
Villalpando, Antonio de, 229n.72, 249n.30
Villena, Enrique de, 100–101
Villoslada, Bachiller, 148, 150
virago, Isabel as, 82–84, 170
virginity: metaphorical constructions of, in Middle Ages, 118–20; nuns as virginal brides of Christ, 120–22; redemptive function of, 115–18; virtue of, 160
Virgin Mary: comparison of Isabel to, in *Jardín*, 32–35; Isabel as earthly counterpart to, xxiv, xxv, 82, 112–24; as Isabel's role model, 38, 39–40; opposition between Eve and, 115, 116, 118; role in construction of Isabelline messianic myth, xxiv, xxv; as spinner and creator of thread of life, 62
virgo bellatrix, Isabel as, 119–20
virtue: female, 37–42, 57–58, 62, 115–18; female handiwork associated with, 62; Flores praise for Isabel's manly, 168–69, 170; male, 115; in *Repetiçíon*, as deeply and anxiously gendered, 157–60
Visigothic monarchy, 103; neo-Gothicism on line of descent from, 96
visual representations of Isabelline power, 44–55; ceremonial sword of justice, 44–47, 84–85; heraldic arms, xxiii, 47–55
Vives, Juan Luis, 30–31, 62
Voluntad, pleasure-seeking, 58–59
von der Walde, Lilian, 179, 183

Walthaus, Rina, 31
warrior: king's role as, 5, 39, 113
warrior prince: Fernando as, 113, 115, 254n.57; Franco as, 192–93
warrior queen: Isabel as, 119–20
warrior society of Middle Ages: abstinence as evidence of highest prowess in, 255n.67
Wayne, Valerie, 30–31, 62
Weiss, Julian, 4, 211n.9, 212n.20, 213n.33
Wendon, Thomas, 15
Whinnom, Keith, 3–4, 162, 164
White, Allon, 2–3
whore: Queen as, 7–16. *See also* prostitutes/prostitution
Witiza, king, 104, 105–6
Woman of the Apocalypse, 122
"woman on top," topos of, 164; Flores's example of, 173–75
woman reader in and of medieval romance: implied vs. inscribed readers, 185, 186; problem of, xxvi, 163–64, 185–86, 268n.6
woman/women: Augustinian conception of, 33, 34; Córdoba on purposes for creation of, 41–42; good qualities allowed, 34–35; history of, as both oppressed and oppressive, xvi; identification with body in medieval gender ideology, xvii; traits attributed to Adam's rib, 34
Women, Jews, and Muslims (Mirrer), 108
women writers in medieval Iberia, 276n.24

Xerxes, 266n.42
Ximénez de Cisneros, Francisco, 121

Y (magazine), 189, 204
Yarbro-Bejarano, Yvonne, 169
yugo (yoke) on heraldic arms, 47–49, 51–54, 228n.69; Mendoza's interpretation of Fernando's heraldic device, 64–67

Zanger, Abby, 53–54, 246n.7

Barbara F. Weissberger is associate professor in the Department of Spanish and Portuguese Studies at the University of Minnesota.